POLARIZATION AND INTERNATIONAL POLITICS

PRINCETON STUDIES IN INTERNATIONAL HISTORY AND POLITICS

Tanisha M. Fazal, G. John Ikenberry, William C. Wohlforth, and Keren Yarhi-Milo, Series Editors

For a full list of titles in the series, go to https://press.princeton.edu/series/princeton-studies-in-international-history-and-politics

Under the Nuclear Shadow: China's Information-Age Weapons in International Security, Fiona S. Cunningham

Technology and the Rise of Great Powers: How Diffusion Shapes Economic Competition, Jeffrey Ding

When the Bombs Stopped: The Legacy of War in Rural Cambodia, Erin Lin

The Insiders' Game: How Elites Make War and Peace, Elizabeth N. Saunders

A World Safe for Commerce: American Foreign Policy from the Revolution to the Rise of China, Dale C. Copeland

The Geopolitics of Shaming: When Human Rights Pressure Works—and When It Backfires, Rochelle Terman

Violent Victors: Why Bloodstained Parties Win Postwar Elections, Sarah Zukerman Daly

An Unwritten Future: Realism and Uncertainty in World Politics, Jonathan Kirshner

Undesirable Immigrants: Why Racism Persists in International Migration, Andrew S. Rosenberg

Human Rights for Pragmatists: Social Power in Modern Times, Jack Snyder

Seeking the Bomb: Strategies of Nuclear Proliferation, Vipin Narang

The Spectre of War: International Communism and the Origins of World War II, Jonathan Haslam

Strategic Instincts: The Adaptive Advantages of Cognitive Biases in International Politics, Dominic D. P. Johnson

The Post-American Liberal World Order, G. John Ikenberry

Divided Armies: Inequality and Battlefield Performance in Modern War, Jason Lyall

Active Defense: China's Military Strategy since 1949, M. Taylor Fravel

Polarization and International Politics

HOW EXTREME PARTISANSHIP
THREATENS GLOBAL STABILITY

RACHEL MYRICK

PRINCETON UNIVERSITY PRESS
PRINCETON & OXFORD

Copyright © 2025 by Princeton University Press

Princeton University Press is committed to the protection of copyright and the intellectual property our authors entrust to us. Copyright promotes the progress and integrity of knowledge created by humans. By engaging with an authorized copy of this work, you are supporting creators and the global exchange of ideas. As this work is protected by copyright, any reproduction or distribution of it in any form for any purpose requires permission; permission requests should be sent to permissions@press.princeton.edu. Ingestion of any IP for any AI purposes is strictly prohibited.

Published by Princeton University Press
41 William Street, Princeton, New Jersey 08540
99 Banbury Road, Oxford OX2 6JX

press.princeton.edu

GPSR Authorized Representative: Easy Access System Europe - Mustamäe tee 50, 10621 Tallinn, Estonia, gpsr.requests@easproject.com

All Rights Reserved

Library of Congress Cataloging-in-Publication Data

Names: Myrick, Rachel, 1991- author
Title: Polarization and international politics : how extreme partisanship threatens global stability / Rachel Myrick.
Description: Princeton : Princeton University Press, 2025. | Series: Princeton studies in international history and politics | Includes bibliographical references and index.
Identifiers: LCCN 2024051604 (print) | LCCN 2024051605 (ebook) | ISBN 9780691274614 hardback | ISBN 9780691274621 paperback | ISBN 9780691274652 ebook
Subjects: LCSH: International relations–Decision making | Polarization (Social sciences)–Political aspects | Democracy | United States–Foreign relations–Political aspects | Polarization (Social sciences)–Political aspects–United States | Democracy–United States | BISAC: POLITICAL SCIENCE / International Relations / General | POLITICAL SCIENCE / Geopolitics
Classification: LCC JZ1253 .M985 2025 (print) | LCC JZ1253 (ebook) | DDC 327.73–dc23/eng/20250328
LC record available at https://lccn.loc.gov/2024051604
LC ebook record available at https://lccn.loc.gov/2024051605

British Library Cataloging-in-Publication Data is available

Editorial: Bridget Flannery-McCoy, Dave McBride, Alena Chekanov
Production Editorial: Elizabeth Byrd
Jacket: Ben Higgins
Production: Erin Suydam
Publicity: William Pagdatoon

10 9 8 7 6 5 4 3 2 1

CONTENTS

List of Figures vii
List of Tables xi
Acknowledgments xiii
Preface xvii

1	Introduction	1
2	A Theory of Polarization and Democratic Advantage	35
3	Cross-National Trends in Polarization and Foreign Policy	81
4	Polarization and the Stability Advantage	112
5	Polarization and the Credibility Advantage	158
6	Polarization and the Reliability Advantage	210
7	Conclusion	255
8	Appendix	281

Bibliography 315
Index 349

FIGURES

1.1 Ideological polarization of legislators in the U.S. House of Representatives and Senate using DW-NOMINATE scores 17
1.2 Trends in ideological polarization among the American public using data on party and ideology from the American National Election Studies 20
1.3 Trends in affective polarization among the American public using feeling thermometer data from the American National Election Studies 22
3.1 Median level of ideological polarization between executive and opposition parties 87
3.2 Change in level of polarization in society using data from the Digital Society Project (2000–2023) 89
3.3 Affective polarization index calculated by Reiljan (2020) from recent public opinion surveys conducted by the Comparative Study of Electoral Systems 90
4.1 Partisan gap in threat perception of immigration (CCGA surveys) 122
4.2 Partisan gap in support of refugees relocating to the United States (2022 CCGA survey) 123
4.3 Partisan gap in perceptions of foreign trade (Gallup polls) 124
4.4 Partisan gap in threat perception of climate change (CCGA surveys) 126
4.5 Partisan gap in perceptions of different security threats (2022 CCGA survey) 127
4.6 Partisan gap in attitudes toward U.S. involvement in world affairs (CCGA surveys) 131

4.7	Partisan gap in attitudes toward U.S. commitment to NATO (CCGA surveys)	132
4.8	Partisan gap in attitudes toward the UN (Gallup polls)	132
4.9	Executive orders in the first 100 days of presidential administrations	150
5.1	Public attitudes toward presidential decision-making among in-party and out-party survey respondents	170
5.2	Public attitudes toward presidential policy responses among in-party and out-party survey respondents	173
5.3	Public attitudes toward obstruction of presidential foreign policy among in-party and out-party survey respondents	174
5.4	Public attitudes toward obstruction of presidential foreign policy among in-party and out-party survey respondents who display high levels of affective polarization	176
5.5	Visualizing congressional opposition on foreign policy using roll-call votes (91st to 100th Congresses)	180
5.6	Visualizing congressional opposition on foreign policy using roll-call votes (101st to 114th Congresses)	181
5.7	Relationship between international crises and polarization of congressional rhetoric	185
5.8	Speeches mentioning Iran in the *Congressional Record* (100th to 114th Congresses)	196
5.9	Partisanship of speech about Iran in the *Congressional Record* (1950–2016)	197
5.10	Partisan words in legislators' tweets about Iran (January to May 2018)	205
6.1	Attitudes toward unilateral action in entering and exiting international commitments among in-party and out-party survey respondents	216
6.2	Attitudes toward unilateral action in entering and exiting international commitments among in-party and out-party survey respondents who display high levels of affective polarization	217
6.3	Number of bilateral treaties ratified by the U.S. Senate (1949–2020)	224

6.4 Time to treaty ratification among bilateral treaties transmitted during periods of low and high polarization   228
6.5 Time in different stages of the treaty ratification process among bilateral treaties transmitted during periods of low and high polarization   230
6.6 Comparison of bilateral executive agreements and bilateral ratified treaties (1990–2016)   232
6.7 Favorability toward the US among residents of the UK (2000–2020)   242
6.8 Attitudes toward U.S. foreign policy among UK survey respondents in the control group   246

TABLES

1.1	Evidence for contemporary partisan polarization in the United States	15
2.1	Polarization and the erosion of democratic stability	56
2.2	Polarization and the erosion of democratic credibility	67
2.3	Polarization and the erosion of democratic reliability	77
3.1	Replication and extension of Mattes, Leeds, and Carroll (2015)	99
3.2	Replication and extension of Schultz (2001a)	103
3.3	Replication and extension of Leeds, Mattes, and Vogel (2009)	106
4.1	Partisan gap in country feeling thermometers during election years	120
4.2	Mexico City Policy across presidential administrations	152
4.3	Summary of findings from the Stability Hypotheses	156
5.1	Survey questionnaire for crisis scenarios	168
5.2	Survey questionnaire for negotiation scenarios	169
5.3	Competitive foreign policy roll-call votes by presidential administration	179
5.4	Summary of findings from the Credibility Hypotheses	208
6.1	Treaty ratification delay among ratified bilateral treaties	226
6.2	Legal authority of executive agreements by category	233
6.3	Effects of affective and ideological treatments on UK perceptions of United States	247
6.4	Perceptions of agreement between two major political parties	249

6.5	Summary of findings from the Reliability Hypotheses	253
8.1	Targeted and actual demographic characteristics of pooled sample	287
8.2	List of international crises triggered by foreign countries involving the United States	297
8.3	List of additional bilateral treaties involving the United States	305

ACKNOWLEDGMENTS

I AM INDEBTED to a support system of family, friends, colleagues, and mentors who made the writing and publication of this book possible. First and foremost, I owe thanks to my advisors at Stanford, where I conducted research for my PhD dissertation that became central to this book. From the project's inception, my advisors brought invaluable perspectives. Ken Schultz, whose scholarship was a big part of the reason why I wanted to pursue a PhD at Stanford, provided consistent clarity and insight on all aspects of this project. Mike Tomz's generous mentorship and expertise on survey design was integral to many empirical components in the book. In directed readings, Jeremy Weinstein encouraged me to explore the big research and policy questions that led me to the topic of polarization and foreign policy. Jonathan Rodden's feedback pushed me to think more deeply about the comparative components of the book. It was humbling as a PhD student to pitch ideas and submit memos to my committee, who are some of the smartest and most thoughtful scholars in the field.

In the early stages of this book project, I received support from a great number of colleagues and friends at Stanford. When I arrived in Palo Alto to start my PhD in 2015, it became clear that I won the lottery with an incredible, collaborative cohort. The eleven of us—Aala Abdelgadir, Ala Alrababah, Vincent Bauer, Carl Gustafson, Haemin Jee, Elisabeth van Lieshout, Hans Lueders, Will Marble, Mike Robinson, Matt Tyler, and myself—muddled through problem sets and met weekly to discuss half-baked research ideas. They shaped this book in countless ways, and I am very grateful for their feedback and friendship. In addition to my cohortmates, I was lucky to have other great intellectual communities in graduate school. Chief among those was the Security Studies Working Group at Stanford, which included excellent scholars like Feyaad Allie, Nandita Balakrishnan, Jordan Bernhardt, Jonathan Chu, Abby Fanlo, Lindsay Hundley, Soyoung Lee, Iris Malone, Katy Robinson, and

Lauren Sukin. Through ongoing and virtual conversations, many members of the International Policy Scholars Consortium and Network—including Jeb Benkowski, Kendrick Kuo, Brad Potter, Sara Plana, Will Quinn, and Rachel Tecott, among others—deepened my thinking about the implications this book's arguments have for U.S. foreign policy and grand strategy. I have Frank Gavin and Jim Steinberg to thank for creating a space like IPSCON where like-minded PhD students can find community.

I finished my first full draft of this book in anticipation of a book workshop in December 2023. At the workshop, I had the privilege of receiving feedback some of the wisest and most generous political scientists I know: Peter Feaver, Bruce Jentleson, Josh Kertzer, Ashley Leeds, Andrew Kenealy, Elizabeth Saunders, and Jessica Weeks. This group was immensely helpful in identifying the revisions I needed to make before submitting the book for review. Along the way, I also received helpful feedback on different components of the project from audiences at conferences run by the American Political Science Association, the International Studies Association, and the Peace Science Society, and seminars hosted by Duke University, Emory University, George Washington University, Georgetown University, Princeton University, University of California San Diego, University of Georgia, University of Wisconsin at Madison, and Yale University.

The political science department at Duke was a wonderful place to start my career and complete my first book. Many of my colleagues at Duke (a large number of whom were a part of the Security, Peace, and Conflict Group) provided comradery, support, and professional development advice. They shared sample book proposals, connected me with funding opportunities, and helped me figure out how to preserve time for writing during the first few years on the tenure track. Among these were Kyle Beardsley, Pablo Beramendi, Susie Colburn, Peter Feaver, Adriane Fresh, Joe Grieco, Jon Green, Ashlyn Hand, Connor Huff, Bruce Jentleson, Soyoung Lee, Shelley Liu, Simon Miles, Eric Mvukiyehe, Emerson Niou, Mara Revkin, Katy Robinson, Genevieve Rousseliere, Livia Schubiger, Dave Siegel, Shikhar Singh, Georg Vanberg, and Chen Wang. Dani Gilbert and Connor Huff were excellent "accountability buddies" who helped me hit writing goals as we navigated how to write our respective books.

Princeton University Press has been an excellent partner in the publishing process. Alena Chekanov and the editors at the Princeton International History and Politics series (Tanisha Fazal, John Ikenberry, William Wohlforth, and Keren Yarhi-Milo) saw promise in this project even before it was a completed manuscript. I received detailed feedback from extraordinarily helpful anonymous reviewers, each of whom I wish I could thank personally for their time. Erin Davis and the team at Westchester Publishing Services shepherded this book through the production process. Wes Cowley and Sally Quinn copyedited the manuscript at various stages, and Elliot Linzer compiled the index.

Writing an academic book requires a lot of institutional support. I am grateful for research support and funding from centers, institutes, and universities that made this project possible. At Stanford, I received funding from the Stanford Institute of Economic Policy Research, the Institute for Research in the Social Sciences, and the Europe Center to collect data and run surveys. At Duke, I received grants from the Josiah Charles Trent Memorial Endowment Fund and the Social Science Research Institute to host a book workshop and hire research assistants. A fellowship from the America in the World Consortium based at University of Texas at Austin was integral to completing the project. To compile datasets and literature, I worked with exceptional research assistants at Duke, including Daniel Billings, Sofia Cava, Xiaoxiao Li, and Samantha Richter.

It is an incredible privilege to be able to make a living by thinking, reading, and writing. I am indebted to mentors, advisors, and friends along the way who helped shape my career as a researcher. Undergraduate professors at the University of North Carolina at Chapel Hill like Mark Crescenzi, Niklaus Steiner, and Georg Vanberg made realize I loved political science and wanted to get a PhD. Classmates at Oxford like Miles Kellerman, Joe Riley, and Kit Dobyns made even the driest parts of international relations theory fun and engaging. Friends and housemates like Jenny Bright, Phil Yao, Chelsea Phipps, and Molly Hrudka created joy and levity during stressful, busy times. Early education teachers like Carol Reid and Sarah Wheeler developed creative, imaginative spaces where being a nerdy kid was acceptable and appreciated.

Of course, I would never have gotten started on this career path in the first place without the love and support of my family—Tom, Patty, Olivia, and Natalie—over three decades. The environment that my parents created in our home helped me develop a love of learning, reading, and teaching. As the middle sibling, I had the privilege of growing up as both a student and a teacher. Olivia shared her workbooks and let me read over her shoulder, and Natalie suffered through endless makeshift lectures when I got a small whiteboard for Christmas. From a young age, my parents impressed upon my sisters and me the importance of "staying in school as long as you can." I am not sure they expected me to take their advice quite so literally. But I know now that pursuing a doctorate was possible only because of the hard work, sacrifices, and encouragement of my parents and their parents before them.

Most importantly, I thank my partner Taylor. A professor once told me, "Your single most important career choice is your partner." This is certainly true in my case. Taylor supported my career through trans-Atlantic and cross-country moves, engaged thoughtfully with my colleagues about their research and goaded them mercilessly when their sports teams lost, cooked countless inventive dinners, and enriched my life in so many ways. He has been an incredible partner and father to our daughter Audrey, who arrived just after this book manuscript was submitted for review in March 2024. It is testament to Taylor and our broader village of family support (especially Tom, Patty, Sam, Stacy, and Ruth) that I was able to complete the final manuscript while raising a newborn. This book is dedicated to Taylor and Audrey, who brighten all my days.

PREFACE

In November 2024, one month after this book was completed, Americans elected Republican candidate and former president Donald Trump to the presidency for a second term. Within the first 100 days of his second term in the White House, it was abundantly clear that President Trump's foreign policy would represent a radical departure from that of his predecessor, Democratic President Joe Biden.

In the early weeks of his second administration, President Trump moved swiftly to undo the changes to immigration and asylum policy made during the Biden era, suspending refugee resettlement programs and pledging to crack down on undocumented immigration. Trump abandoned global commitments to reduce greenhouse gas emissions by announcing that the United States would withdraw from the Paris Agreement. He dismantled the U.S. Agency for International Development and canceled the vast majority of humanitarian aid and development programs it funded.

President Trump also took a very different approach toward many U.S. allies and adversaries. In the early days of his second term, the president escalated tensions with neighboring countries Canada and Mexico by imposing new tariffs on imported goods. He alarmed European allies by suggesting that the U.S. might abandon NATO, a longstanding security alliance. And Trump had a markedly different approach to the Russia-Ukraine War. In response to Russia's 2022 full-scale invasion of Ukraine, President Biden had offered robust support to Ukraine. By contrast, at the outset of his term, President Trump appeared more sympathetic toward Russia. He publicly criticized Ukrainian President Volodymyr Zelensky and temporarily suspended U.S. military assistance to Ukraine.

Undoubtedly, some readers will turn to this book to make sense of the current politics of U.S. foreign policy. In 2025, the United States seems to be in the midst of a realignment of partisan cleavages in foreign affairs. As the old adage goes, politics clearly no longer "stops at the water's edge." It is undeniable that the foreign policy changes of the Trump era will have consequential ripple effects on how the United States engages with the rest of the world.

However, the themes in this book are not unique to the current political moment, and the questions it raises extend far beyond a single president and country. These include questions such as: How does polarization directly and indirectly shape foreign policymaking processes? How are polarized countries viewed by their allies and adversaries? What are the broader implications of trends like polarization for global stability and international order?

Throughout history, polarization has been a recurring challenge for many democratic countries. However, some of the consequences of heightened partisanship for foreign policymaking and international politics have been underappreciated. To that end, this book aims to shed light not only on the politics of today but also on the persistent problems that polarized democracies have confronted in the past and will continue to grapple with in the future.

POLARIZATION AND
INTERNATIONAL POLITICS

1

Introduction

IN THE 1930s, France, like much of Western Europe, battled an economic depression. Growing inequality exacerbated an ideological divide between the right and the left. Far-right, proto-fascist movements in France and elsewhere in Europe perpetrated violence targeting Jews and other immigrant populations. In neighboring Germany, fascist dictator and leader of the far-right Nazi Party, Adolf Hitler, had come to power. To counter the influence of the French far right, a coalition of leftist and centrist groups formed the Popular Front, led by Léon Blum. In the 1936 French national election, the Popular Front was victorious, and Blum became both the first Jewish and the first socialist prime minister in France.

Extreme polarization deepened a sense of political crisis in France during this period. As one historian summarized, "the political polarization brought on by the fascist challenge and counterattack by the Popular Front in particular created an atmosphere of civil war."[1] During the 1936 French election, as German troops reoccupied the Rhineland demilitarized zone, which bordered France, right-wing French leaders adopted a chilling slogan: "Plutot Hitler que Blum" or "Better Hitler Than Blum."[2] The slogan exemplified the depths of partisan animus between left-wing and right-wing groups. In retrospect, the sentiment was both prescient and chilling: Nazi Germany would begin its occupation of France less than five years later.

Episodes of extreme polarization, like that of 1930s France, are uncharacteristic of healthy democracies. However, the large majority of advanced democracies have experienced at least one period of markedly high polarization in their histories. Anecdotes about these periods of intense polarization

1. Irvine 1996, 78.
2. Richards 2006.

from prior eras have resurfaced in the twenty-first century, as researchers and policymakers perceive a growing threat of political polarization in many democracies. For instance, commentators drew unsettling parallels between the partisan tribalism of France in the 1930s and the United States in the 2020s.[3]

Contemporary political polarization is "a widespread phenomenon, with common negative consequences for democracy across diverse national contexts."[4] In Israel, under the polarizing leadership of Prime Minister Benjamin Netanyahu, a 2018 poll found that Israelis increasingly cited the right–left divide as the "strongest tension in Israeli society."[5] In Venezuela, a growing ideological divide reinforced by class divisions accompanied the rise of left-wing populism under President Hugo Chávez and President Nicolás Maduro.[6] In South Korea, polarization in the South Korean National Assembly rose abruptly following the 2016 impeachment of President Park Geun-hye and continued to increase in the years that followed.[7] In the United States, as the ideological and cultural divide between Republicans and Democrats grew, polarization became the "defining characteristic of modern American politics."[8] And, in an analysis of electoral polarization across forty-seven European countries from 1848 to 2020, researchers conclude that "politics in the continent have never been so polarized."[9]

Party-based or *partisan polarization* represents an increasing divergence between major political parties or party coalitions. Polarization can be the result of substantive differences in policy positions. Preference polarization occurs when the policy preferences of parties diverge in one or more areas. A common form of preference polarization is *ideological polarization*: parties on the right become increasingly conservative and parties on the left become increasingly liberal. But divergence between parties can also be social, an artifact of negative affect and mutual dislike between political groups. The increasing tendency of people to like their political in-group but strongly dislike or even hate their political out-group is called *affective*

---

3. Applebaum 2020.
4. Carothers and O'Donohue 2019, 1.
5. Wootliff 2018.
6. Pilar, García-Guadilla, and Mallen 2019.
7. Han 2022.
8. Campbell 2016, 117.
9. Bértoa and Rama 2021.

polarization.[10] These two forms of polarization are conceptually distinct, but they often co-occur. Political environments in which ideological and affective polarization coincide are characterized by *extreme polarization*. In such contexts, both forms of polarization reinforce one another. Partisan animus rooted in identity politics can fuel disagreement over policy, and vice versa.

In the study of comparative politics, there is an exceptionally rich literature on political parties and polarization. Yet, we know surprisingly little about how polarization affects how countries relate to one another in international relations. What explains this disconnect? For one, many modern theories of international relations originated in the United States during the second half of the twentieth century. This was a unique time in American history. As Senator Arthur Vandenberg famously quipped, partisan politics was thought to "stop at the water's edge."[11] During the Cold War, there was arguably far more bipartisanship in U.S. foreign affairs than there is today. While partisan and particularistic interests at time trickled into foreign policy,[12] politicians generally united against the Soviet threat. In the 1990s, as liberal democracies triumphed over communism, a shared perception emerged that democracies had many advantages in foreign affairs relative to nondemocracies. Much research in international relations followed from this "democratic triumphalist" or "democratic advantage" tradition of thought.

In the study of American politics, much ink has been spilled on the causes and consequences of polarization.[13] However, this body of work overwhelmingly focuses on polarization's effects on domestic politics and society. Scholarship on the effects of polarization on foreign policy is much thinner. One reason for this discrepancy is the common perception that, unlike in some democracies, foreign affairs is pretty insulated from partisan politics in the United States. The executive branch—including the president, their advisors, and a set of foreign policy institutions responsible for security and defense policy—has a lot of discretion over national security.[14] The sensitivity

---

10. Druckman and Levendusky 2018; Iyengar, Sood, and Lelkes 2012; Iyengar et al. 2019; Mason 2018.

11. Vandenberg 1945.

12. For more nuanced perspectives on the Cold War consensus see, e.g., Fordham 2010; Krebs 2015; Wittkopf and McCormick 1990.

13. For overviews of polarization in American politics see, e.g., Fiorina and Abrams 2008; Lee 2015; McCarty 2019; Persily 2015.

14. Canes-Wrone, Howell, and Lewis 2008; Wildavsky 1966.

of intelligence gathering and necessity of maintaining state secrets give the executive branch far more information about foreign relations than the public or even legislators in Congress have.[15] This information gap is sustained by the technical expertise required to manage foreign relationships, which has entrenched a bipartisan foreign policy bureaucracy in Washington, D.C.[16] During times of crisis, these information asymmetries stymie polarization by suppressing criticism from the political opposition.[17] During more peaceful times, instruments of national security policy (e.g., militarization) are still less likely than other foreign policy tools (e.g., trade, immigration, foreign aid) to elicit partisan debate.[18]

Yet, increasing polarization in the United States and many peer democracies compels us to revisit how the phenomenon poses problems for democratic politics, both historically and presently. An explosion of research on extreme polarization highlights the challenges it poses for democratic governance. And today scholars of US foreign policy and international relations debate whether these deepening political and societal divisions truly "stop at the water's edge."[19] The objective of this book is to link the effects of polarization on democratic governance to theories of international relations. In doing so, the book integrates work across the fields of international relations, comparative politics, and American politics to explore how patterns of domestic polarization shape the international system.

1.1 The Argument in Brief

The primary question this book asks is: *How does extreme polarization affect the way democracies behave in international politics?* A central finding in international relations is that democratic countries have advantages in international politics when compared to nondemocratic countries. Democracies tend to keep foreign policy relatively stable across time,[20] credibly signal

15. Colaresi 2012, 2014.
16. Flynn 2014; Porter 2018.
17. Brody 1991; Brody and Shapiro 1989.
18. Milner and Tingley 2015.
19. Bryan and Tama 2022; Busby and Monten 2008; Chaudoin, Milner, and Tingley 2010; Friedman 2022; Friedrichs 2021; Friedrichs and Tama 2024; Kertzer, Brooks, and Brooks 2021; Kupchan and Trubowitz 2010; Milner and Tingley 2015; Musgrave 2019; Schultz 2018; Tama 2023.
20. See, e.g., McGillivray and Smith 2008; Mattes, Leeds, and Carroll 2015; Leeds and Mattes 2022.

information to adversaries,[21] and reliably maintain commitments to allies.[22] These advantages come from systems of constraint and accountability that check political power and provide incentives for democratic leaders to be responsive to the public and receptive to criticism.

The main argument of this book is that extreme partisan polarization reshapes the nature of these constraints on democratic leaders, which in turn erodes the advantages democracies have in foreign affairs. First, extreme polarization negatively impacts the *stability advantage*, or the ability of democracies to maintain consistent foreign policy. In highly polarized environments, politicians have incentives to undo policies of their out-party predecessors and politicize the foreign policy bureaucracy, creating volatility with leader turnover. Second, extreme polarization undermines the *credibility advantage*, or the ability of democracies to issue credible threats and promises to foreign adversaries. Polarization provides incentives for the political opposition to oppose or obstruct democratic leaders. In polarized environments, bipartisan consensus, which makes threats from democracies credible, is difficult to attain, and opposition to the executive becomes less informative to adversaries in international negotiations and crisis bargaining. Third, extreme polarization erodes the *reliability advantage*: the ability of states to make and keep international commitments to allies and partners. The combination of a polarized electorate and an obstinate political opposition makes it easier for democratic leaders to bypass institutional constraints to secure political wins. This means that international commitments in polarized democracies are more likely to be made without bipartisan support, increasing the chance democratic leaders will renege on existing agreements in the future.

The book begins by providing a cross-national perspective on polarization and the erosion of democratic advantages in foreign affairs. Using data on party platforms[23] from executive and opposition parties and coalitions in fifty-five countries, I provide preliminary evidence that democracies experiencing periods of extreme polarization likely behave differently than other democracies in international politics. On average, they tend to be more volatile in their foreign policymaking, less credible in interstate[24] disputes, and more likely to violate alliance commitments.

21. See, e.g., Fearon 1994; Schultz 2001a; Tomz 2007.
22. See, e.g., Leeds, Mattes, and Vogel 2009; Martin 2000.
23. Lehmann et al. 2018.
24. International relations scholars use the term *interstate* to describe disputes between countries, or sovereign states.

While cross-national analyses are useful in characterizing descriptive patterns of polarization and foreign policy, within-country analysis provides a better understanding of how polarization impacts policy processes. In the second half of this book, I focus on the case of contemporary U.S. foreign policy. The United States is an ideal starting point given its history of political polarization, its status as a powerful and consequential democracy, and its importance in international politics. Across three empirical chapters, I examine the pathways through which polarization erodes each of the democratic advantages in contemporary U.S. foreign policy. These empirical chapters follow a similar structure. They first focus on the public, using original survey experiments and historic public opinion polling to show how a polarized electorate reshapes the nature of democratic accountability in foreign policymaking. Then, they analyze the strategic behavior of politicians that follows from changing electoral incentives and a hyper-partisan political environment. Finally, each chapter illustrates the potential downstream implications of these behaviors for democratic advantages in foreign affairs.

Collectively, the theory and evidence provided in this book advance our understanding of the relationship between partisan polarization and international politics. I argue that polarization negatively impacts the ability of democracies to negotiate effectively and credibly signal information to adversaries. Moreover, extreme polarization in democracies can undermine democratic constraints, which in turn affects the stability of the countries' foreign policy and the reliability of their international commitments.

1.2 Democratic Advantages in Foreign Affairs

This book is grounded in a large body of research in international relations that explores how democratic countries interact with one another and with non-democracies. Most of this research focuses on what political scientists term *liberal democracies*. At a minimum, democracies must have free and fair elections to determine their political leaders. But elections alone are not enough to create a liberal democracy. Liberal democracies have institutions designed to prevent leaders from improperly exercising their power or infringing on the rights of citizens. These include, for example, institutions that facilitate checks and balances, divide power between different branches of government, and protect civil liberties. An insight that emerged from the field of international relations is that liberal democracies enjoy a number of advantages in making foreign policy when compared to countries with other regime types.[25] This book focuses on three of these democratic advantages: a stability advantage, a credibility advantage, and a reliability advantage.[26]

First, democracies have a stability advantage in that they are able to maintain relatively consistent foreign policy over time. Democracies hold routine elections that bring new leaders into power. Yet, despite frequent leader turnover, the foreign policy of democracies does not tend to abruptly shift. Leader turnover in democracies does not usually dramatically change a country's trade relations or alter the willingness of foreign investors to hold its sovereign debt.[27] In fact, leader turnover in democracies does not have large impacts on a country's foreign policy preferences in general.[28] By contrast, in nondemocracies, leader turnover can produce more volatile and unpredictable foreign policy outcomes. Political instability creates problems in foreign policy when, for example, a new autocrat comes to power through a coup or revolution.[29]

Second, democracies have a credibility advantage in that they can effectively signal information to foreign adversaries. Accountability to democratic publics and a visible political opposition restrain democratic leaders from initiating conflicts or crises they are unlikely to win,[30] and from making promises or issuing threats they do not intend to keep. This makes the threats and promises they do issue more credible.[31] The ability of democracies to credibly signal information gives them an advantage in crisis bargaining and makes them better able to resolve disputes peacefully relative to nondemocratic countries.[32] Moreover, domestic constraints on democratic leaders give them advantages in forms of bargaining that happen outside of crisis situations, such as when leaders negotiate international agreements with foreign adversaries.[33]

---

25. A country's *regime type* is its form of government. There are many ways to classify regime types, but the most basic distinction is between democracies and autocracies.
26. While the "democratic advantage" perspective is a dominant tradition of thought in contemporary international relations scholarship, not all political scientists agree with it. The main critiques of this tradition are discussed in chapter 2.
27. McGillivray and Smith 2008.
28. Leeds and Mattes 2022; Mattes, Leeds, and Carroll 2015; Smith 2016.
29. Goemans, Gleditsch, and Chiozza 2009; McGillivray and Smith 2008.
30. Reiter and Stam 1998, 2002.
31. Fearon 1994; Schultz 2001a; Tomz 2007.
32. Schultz 1998.
33. Putnam 1988.

Democratic leaders can credibly say that they will not be able to accept the terms of a negotiation if it will be unpopular back home. In short, constraints at home make democracies more credible adversaries.

Third, democracies have a reliability advantage because they are better able to commit to and comply with international agreements made with foreign partners. Democracies tend to be more cooperative than nondemocratic countries, and they are especially likely to cooperate with one another.[34] Democratic countries also typically follow through on their security commitments. They form durable military alliances with one another and maintain these alliance commitments even when a new leader comes to power.[35] Beyond security cooperation, democracies are also thought to be more cooperative in general. They are more likely to join and comply with the international trade and international monetary regimes.[36] They are better at making environmental policy commitments,[37] complying with international humanitarian law,[38] and adhering to a rules-based international order.[39] This contributes to the perception that democratic countries are reliable allies.

These three advantages are interrelated and can at times reinforce one another. They each arise from two important systems of constraint on political power within liberal democracies. *Vertical constraints*, or electoral accountability, make democratic leaders responsive to their publics. *Horizontal constraints*, or checks on executive power that arise from within government, make democratic leaders accountable to other political actors and institutions, including an active political opposition. Collectively, these constraints ensure that democratic leaders prioritize national welfare over special interests, abide by established democratic procedures when making foreign policy, and follow through on threats and promises they issue in international politics.

On the whole, democracies may have these advantages over nondemocracies. The argument of this book, however, is that we have underappreciated an important source of variation in democratic foreign policymaking: the degree to which politics and society are polarized. This book focuses on the impacts that extreme polarization has on systems of vertical and horizontal constraints

34. Leeds 1999; Martin 2000.
35. Gaubatz 1996; Leeds and Savun 2007; Leeds, Mattes, and Vogel 2009; Reed 1997.
36. Mansfield, Milner, and Rosendorff 2002; Milner and Kubota 2005; Simmons 2000.
37. Battig and Bernauer 2009; Payne 1995; Neumayer 2002; von Stein 2008.
38. Hafner-Burton and Tsutsui 2005; Hathaway 2007; Neumayer 2005.
39. Slaughter 1995.

and, in turn, the democratic advantages. I argue that as polarization becomes more extreme, its effects are largely (although not exclusively) negative for democracies in international politics.

1.3 Defining Partisan Polarization

The term polarization is invoked in many different ways by scholars, analysts, and policymakers. This book characterizes polarization with respect to three simple questions. First, who are the relevant *actors*? Political scientists tend to investigate polarization among two sets of actors: politicians and the public. These phenomena are referred to as *elite polarization* and *mass polarization*, respectively. This book discusses polarization among both sets of actors because they jointly impact systems of constraint in democratic countries. Politicians are the main actors involved in making foreign policy. Politicians leading the executive are often responsible for major foreign policy decisions, while politicians from opposition parties play a critical role in horizontally constraining these leaders. The public is also relevant for foreign policymaking because, in democracies, leaders are vertically constrained by the electorate. Public opinion can also be a useful barometer for understanding the extent to which certain issues are polarized. To explore how polarization impacts foreign policy attitudes and outcomes, this book draws on a combination of attitudinal data from the public and behavioral data from politicians.

Second, what are the relevant *groups* that these actors form? Describing a national public as polarized only makes sense if we have a shared understanding of the cleavage along which polarization occurs. This book focuses on party-based or *partisan polarization* and the relevant groups are political parties. *Political parties* are organized groups that seek political power through elections. They campaign on defined platforms that provide insight into their foreign policy positions. Parties are the main emphasis of this book because they compete for control of the executive, largely responsible for foreign policymaking.

Of course, partisan polarization is just one of many forms of political and societal polarization. In American politics throughout the nineteenth and twentieth centuries, a regional divide between the North and South, rooted in attitudes toward slavery and, later, racial segregation, has at times been much more salient than the partisan divide. At the start of the twenty-first century, some scholars argue that the root cause of polarization in Venezuelan politics was a cleavage between two different ideas of democracy. Supporters of participatory democracy (exemplified by Hugo Chávez and his supporters) believed in direct participation in government and collective rights, while supporters of representative democracy (mainly Chávez's opponents) believed in representative government and individual rights.[40] The question of the United Kingdom's status with respect to the European Union (EU) created a polarized cleavage in the 2010s between "Leavers" who advocated for withdrawing from the EU and "Remainers" who advocated against it.[41] But the advantage of studying partisan polarization rather than, for example, polarization in the UK between Remainers and Leavers, is that the former is visible across time and space while the latter reflects one historical moment. Some of the theoretical dynamics described in this book could be applied to other politically salient groups of actors. However, this book focuses on political parties because, while their composition and positions evolve over time, they remain a central organizing feature of democratic politics with important implications for foreign policy.

Third, what is the relevant *distance* between these groups? To say a political system is characterized by polarization implies distance or divergence between political groups. One form of divergence is preference based or ideological. *Preference polarization* occurs "when (a) the preferences of members become more distinctly bimodal and (b) the two modes move farther apart."[42] Polarization in advanced democracies that occurs on a right–left dimension is known as *ideological polarization*. A conservative or rightist ideology reflects economic commitments to the promotion of free markets and social commitments to traditional morals and values. By contrast, a liberal or leftist ideology reflects economic commitments to redistributing wealth and strengthening the welfare state and social commitments to protecting civil liberties.[43] While polarization on a right–left dimension has been the main focus of scholarship on political parties, there are an infinite number of issues or dimensions over which parties could diverge. Polarization in foreign policy, for example, is often measured on a hawk–dove dimension. This dimension captures the relative hawkishness of political parties, defined as their willingness to use coercive force in foreign policy.

40. Pilar, García-Guadilla, and Mallen 2019.
41. Hobolt, Leeper, and Tilley 2021.
42. Lee 2015, 263.
43. See, e.g., the categorization of right–left policy positions proposed by Laver and Budge (1992).

A different form of divergence between groups is identity based, emphasizing social distance between groups. This form of polarization, known as *affective polarization*, is a tendency to like members of one's in-party and to dislike members of one's out-party.[44] The phenomenon is driven by the fact that, in many contexts, affiliation with a political party is a social identity.[45] Attachment to one's political party shapes how individuals develop relationships, create social community, consume media, and perceive others around them.[46] In affectively polarized societies, partisan identity is a highly salient aspect of one's community. It often correlates with other social identities. Where there are higher levels of affective polarization, partisans feel stronger affinity with people who belong to the same political party. In some cases, partisans may even be hostile toward members of the opposite party. I refer to cases in which high levels of both ideological and affective polarization co-occur as cases of *extreme polarization*.[47]

1.4 Extreme Polarization and Democratic Erosion

In the early twenty-first century, with prospects for accession to the EU on the horizon, Turkey was a "beacon of success in a volatile neighborhood."[48] Straddling Europe and Asia, the predominantly Muslim nation was relatively secular and democratic. Yet, less than two decades later, Turkey was "one of the most politically and socially polarized countries in the world."[49] Polarization in Turkish politics reflected a political and social cleavage between Islamists and secularists who proposed alternative visions for Turkey's future. The major political Islamist party, the Justice and Development Party (AKP), arose in the early 2000s as an outsider party opposed to the secular establishment. As the promise of EU accession faded, the party and its polarizing leader, Recep Tayyip Erdoğan, began to take more aggressive actions. After

---

44. The tendency to dislike members of one's out-party is also called *negative partisanship* (Abramowitz and Webster 2016).

45. Berelson, Lazarsfeld, and McPhee 1954; Campbell et al. 1960; Green, Palmquist, and Schickler 2002.

46. Iyengar et al. 2019.

47. Other terms used to describe similar environments are "severe polarization" (see, e.g., Carothers and O'Donohue 2019) and "pernicious polarization" (see, e.g., McCoy and Somer 2019).

48. Kirişci and Sloat 2019.

49. Somer 2019, 42.

assuming the presidency in 2014, Erdoğan enacted antidemocratic reforms to strengthen his own political power. These included crackdowns on political dissent, censorship of media organizations, and a constitutional referendum that further expanded Erdoğan's executive power.[50] In 2018, the polarization of Turkish politics negatively impacted the health of its democracy. Freedom House's annual "Freedom in the World" index, which measures protections of civil liberties and political rights in every country, downgraded Turkey from "Partly Free" to "Not Free."[51]

The experience of Turkey serves as a cautionary tale. Even relatively strong democracies are not immune to processes of democratic backsliding. Across the world, following many decades of democratic transition and consolidation, democracy is now in decline. By 2023, Freedom House reported that "global freedom declined for the 17th consecutive year."[52] This broad trend helps us understand why so many people express concern about rising polarization. At its extremes, polarization can contribute to the erosion—or even the breakdown—of democracy.[53]

A few features distinguish environments of extreme polarization (those characterized by both high levels of ideological and affective polarization) from more moderate forms of polarization typical of a healthy liberal democracy. First, in extremely polarized countries, the stakes of winning become exceptionally high. Politics is more likely to be zero sum: gains for one party are losses for the opposite party, and vice versa. Environments characterized by high-stakes, zero-sum politics are among the most susceptible to democratic erosion.[54] This is because in extremely polarized contexts, parties and their leaders have greater incentives to "tilt the playing field"[55] to their advantage in order to see their own candidates win or their preferred policies enacted. Sometimes these changes are dramatic, but, more often, they happen incrementally.[56] In *Crises of Democracy*, for instance, political scientist Adam

---

50. Aydin-Düzgit 2019.
51. Freedom House 2018.
52. Freedom House 2023.
53. Carothers and O'Donohue 2019; Jee, Lueders, and Myrick 2022; Levitsky and Roberts 2011; Levitsky and Ziblatt 2018; Kurd 2019; Mudde 2019; Pirro 2015; Polyakova 2015; Svolik 2020; Weyland and Madrid 2019.
54. See arguments and evidence from: Arbatli and Rosenberg 2021; Clayton et al. 2021; Fossati, Muhtadi, and Warburton 2022; Goodman 2022; Kingzette et al. 2021; McCoy, Rahman, and Somer 2018; Miller 2021; Simonovits, McCoy, and Littvay 2022.
55. Graham and Svolik 2020, 407.
56. See, e.g., Bermeo 2016; Waldner and Lust 2018.

Przeworski warns of "a gradual, almost imperceptible, erosion of democratic institutions and norms, subversion of democracy by stealth."[57]

Incremental changes characteristic of democratic backsliding can be hard to identify and respond to. In their book *How Democracies Die*, political scientists Steven Levitsky and Daniel Ziblatt discuss how many democratic governments, including the U.S. government, rely on systems of "unwritten democratic norms."[58] The researchers argue that extreme polarization is especially dangerous because, in such environments, political parties are more likely to disregard such norms, which are foundational to a functioning democracy. One could imagine that this dynamic could be problematic in foreign affairs, where executives tend to already have considerable discretion over policymaking.

Second, in contexts of extreme polarization, ideological and affective polarization tend to reinforce one another. Policy disagreements can fuel affective polarization, and vice versa.[59] It becomes difficult to disentangle whether disagreements between parties are a function of sincere differences in ideological beliefs ("I am deeply committed to this policy") or a function of negative partisanship ("I dislike this policy because it's championed by the other party"). A theme of this book is that this inability to distinguish between principled and partisan disagreement can mute some of the advantages democracies have when making foreign policy.

Third, when a country is highly polarized, partisan conflict begins to spill into more policy domains. Political scientists Geoffrey Layman and Thomas Carsey term this process *conflict extension*.[60] In the United States, for example, over time, party activists extended partisan conflict from economic issues to social, cultural, and racial issues.[61] This means that extreme polarization is likely to beget more polarization. With respect to foreign affairs, this implies that even policies that are not central to a partisan cleavage ex ante can become politicized. This is especially likely to occur when such issues coincide with contentious electoral cycles or are championed by party activists or polarizing leaders.

Finally, in environments of extreme polarization, other democratic constraints—such as those from the public, media, and other government

57. Przeworski 2019, 15.
58. Levitsky and Ziblatt 2018, 8.
59. See, e.g., Algara and Zur 2023; Dias and Lelkes 2022.
60. Layman and Carsey 2002; Layman, Carsey, and Horowitz 2006; Layman et al. 2010.
61. Layman, Carsey, and Horowitz 2006.

institutions—that in theory should "check" political officials tend to be less effective. A highly polarized public is less able to hold leaders accountable because partisans are unlikely to acknowledge situations when their own team does something wrong or the other team does something right. Likewise, the political opposition is a less reliable check on executive power because it has incentives to consistently oppose or undermine the executive.

This book argues that the combination of these features of extremely polarized societies—the incentives to circumvent democratic norms, the inability to distinguish between principled and partisan disagreement, the extension of partisan conflict to new policy domains, and the erosion of constraints on executive power—collectively undermine the advantages that democracies have in foreign affairs. In developing this argument, a core contribution of this book is to connect scholarship on polarization and democratic erosion to foreign policymaking.

1.5 Partisan Polarization in the United States

In 1856, U.S. House Representative Preston Brooks, a Democrat from South Carolina, walked into the Old Senate Chamber and smashed a metal-tipped cane onto Republican Senator Charles Sumner's head, beating him unconscious. The infamous incident was prompted by a passionate speech Senator Sumner gave in favor of admitting Kansas to the Union as a free state. Sumner, an antislavery Republican, hurled a series of insults at Democrats advocating to admit Kansas as a slave state.[62] While Sumner recovered from his injuries, the physical violence that occurred inside the Senate was emblematic of the extreme polarization that gripped Congress and the rest of the nation in the years preceding the American Civil War. In his book *With Ballots and Bullets*, political scientist Nathan Kalmoe argues that partisanship tied to attitudes toward slavery plunged the United States into civil war.[63] This episode is widely cited as an example of how extreme polarization was at other points in America's history. Polarization is clearly a problem in contemporary U.S. politics. But compared to the mid-nineteenth century, the partisan antics of the present seem far less grim.

Why, then, is there growing concern about extreme polarization and democratic erosion in the United States today? To contextualize contemporary

62. Pierson 1995.
63. Kalmoe 2020.

TABLE 1.1. Evidence for contemporary partisan polarization in the United States

		RELEVANT ACTORS	
		Politicians	Public
POLARIZATION	Ideological	Strong evidence	Mixed evidence
	Affective	Mixed evidence	Strong evidence

polarization, it is useful to characterize trends related to various types of polarization in the United States over the last century. In describing partisan polarization in the United States, the relevant groups are the two major political parties: the Republican Party and the Democratic Party.[64] The Republican Party, also nicknamed the GOP ("Grand Old Party"), is considered to be more to the right and ideologically conservative, whereas the Democratic Party is considered more to the left and ideologically liberal. Table 1.1 summarizes research on polarization in American politics with respect to two dimensions: the actors (politicians or the public) and the source of the divergence between the groups (either ideological or affective polarization). This section briefly describes trends related to each of the four types of polarization in table 1.1. The main takeaway is that there is strong scholarly consensus that elite, ideological polarization and mass, affective polarization in the United States have substantially increased in recent decades. However, there is more debate and less consensus about other forms of polarization.

Beginning with elite, ideological polarization, it is well documented that ideological polarization has increased over the past few decades among politicians. Most measures of elite polarization in the United States focus on *congressional polarization*: the growing ideological divide between Republican and Democratic legislators. The main measure of congressional polarization is constructed from congressional roll-call votes that compare the (dis)similarity

---

64. On the development of the two-party system in the United States, see Aldrich 2011.

of legislators' voting records across parties.[65] A scaling procedure called DW-NOMINATE (Dynamic Weighted Nominal Three-Step Estimation) represents legislators on a common ideological space across time. The difference between the estimated ideological position of the median congressional Republican and Democrat is a measure of congressional polarization. Figure 1.1 illustrates the distribution of legislators' ideological positions in the House of Representatives and the Senate using DW-NOMINATE scores.[66]

Figure 1.1 shows that congressional polarization began gradually in the 1970s, with a sharper increase beginning in the mid-1990s as more ideologically extreme legislators enacted institutional reforms in Congress that incentivized greater party cohesion.[67] Other common measures of elite polarization—for example, measures of party unity constructed from roll-call votes,[68] ratings of legislators from special interest groups,[69] ideology scores calculated from campaign contributions,[70] and measures of partisanship of congressional rhetoric[71]—show similar trends.

Political scientists offer many explanations for the increase in congressional polarization. The most prominent explanations are multifaceted, combining discussions of changes in the electorate with insights about changing institutional rules in Congress. A major change in the electorate since the 1970s was the "Southern realignment": the movement of White Southern voters with largely conservative social values to the Republican Party.[72] Partisan realignment made the parties more distinctive and ideologically coherent, leading to new generations of more ideologically extreme legislators.[73] As these legislators assumed leadership positions in Congress, they enacted procedural reforms that gave the majority party considerable power and facilitated greater party cohesion.[74]

65. Poole and Rosenthal 1985, 1991, 1997; Lewis et al. 2019.
66. Lewis et al. 2019.
67. Cox and McCubbins 1993, 2005; Theriault 2008.
68. Bond and Fleisher 2000; Crespin, Rohde, and Wielen 2011. A party unity vote is when at least half of one party votes against at least half of the opposing party.
69. Charnock 2018.
70. Bonica 2013.
71. Gentzkow, Shapiro, and Taddy 2017.
72. Rohde 1991; Roberts and Smith 2003.
73. Campbell 2016.
74. Cox and McCubbins 1993; Rohde 1991; Sinclair 2014; Theriault 2008.

INTRODUCTION 17

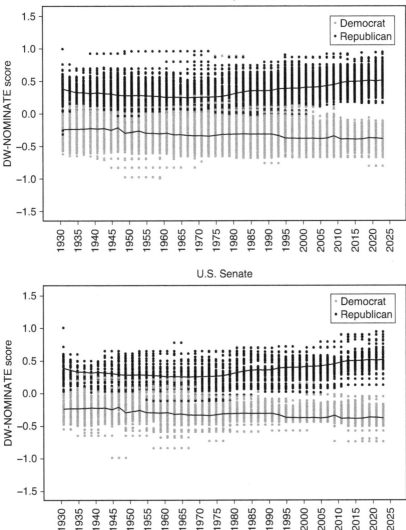

FIGURE 1.1. Ideological polarization of legislators in the U.S. House of Representatives and Senate using DW-NOMINATE scores

Some political scientists argue that elite polarization has been "asymmetric" since the 1990s. What this means, as suggested in figure 1.1, is that Republican legislators have moved further rightward than Democratic legislators have moved leftward. In their book *Asymmetric Politics*, Matt Grossman and David Hopkins argue this trend occurs because the Republican

Party has become more ideologically driven than the Democratic Party.[75] The researchers attribute this asymmetry to the rise of conservative media, the prominence of right-wing legislators and politicians, and the establishment of far-right movements like the Tea Party movement, founded in 2009. A chief concern is that more ideologically extreme politicians will be more likely to break democratic norms in order to see their preferred policies enacted or to stop legislation championed by the opposite party. Political scientists Jacob Hacker and Paul Pierson write, "In the past two decades—since asymmetric polarization has entered a new and more intense phase with the rise to power of [speaker of the House of Representatives] Newt Gingrich—the GOP has repeatedly violated established norms (without breaking legal restrictions) to gain partisan advantage."[76] Hacker and Pierson point to examples from Democratic President Barack Obama's administration (2009–2017), during which congressional Republicans used, or threatened to use, the filibuster or to shut down the government in order to stop legislation, and led efforts at the state level to restrict voting access.

Turning to mass polarization, evidence for ideological divergence among the American public is more mixed. One camp believes that ideological polarization among the mass public has not necessarily increased over time.[77] Political scientist Morris Fiorina and his collaborators, for example, argue that most Americans are relatively centrist and that politicians overestimate ideological polarization within the electorate. Similarly, in their book *The Other Divide*, Yanna Krupnikov and John Barry Ryan argue that polarization is concentrated among a minority of Americans who are very engaged in politics.[78]

However, other researchers provide compelling evidence for growing ideological polarization in the American public.[79] The fact that the average Republican is more conservative and the average Democrat is more liberal than in generations past is difficult to dispute. Figure 1.2 shows the distribution of conservative and liberal attitudes among self-identified Republicans and Democrats using data from the American National Election Studies

---

75. Grossman and Hopkins 2016.
76. Hacker and Pierson 2015, 60.
77. Fiorina and Abrams 2008; Fiorina, Abrams, and Pope 2004; Levendusky 2009.
78. Krupnikov and Ryan 2022.
79. Abramowitz 2010; Abramowitz and Saunders 2008; Campbell 2016; Hetherington 2001; Layman and Carsey 2002; Layman, Carsey, and Horowitz 2006.

(ANES).[80] Respondents rate their ideology on a seven-point scale with 1 indicating "Very Liberal" and 7 indicating "Very Conservative." Snapshots of this data in twenty-year intervals—in 1976, 1996, and 2016—reveal that, over time, there has been greater coherence between party and ideology: Republicans have become more conservative and Democrats have become more liberal. However, it is possible these patterns are a function of the electorate sorting into parties more consistent with their ideology rather than moving to the ideological extremes, per se.[81]

While the extent of ideological polarization in the public is contested, there is strong evidence that the American public exhibits higher levels of affective or social polarization relative to the past.[82] A key explanation for affective polarization in the United States is the decline in "cross-cutting" social identities.[83] Lilliana Mason's book *Uncivil Agreement* explains how other social identities are increasingly correlated with partisan identity, which can contribute to resentment and prejudice.[84] For example, gender,[85] race,[86] religion,[87] and geography[88] are strongly associated with partisanship, furthering social divisions between the parties. Other factors that could contribute to affective polarization include internet penetration and the rise of partisan news media,[89] as well as cues from ideologically polarized politicians.[90]

Affective polarization in the American public is linked to problematic political and social outcomes. Citizens who exhibit higher levels of affective polarization are unlikely to prioritize democratic principles over partisan identity and are more vulnerable to manipulation by partisan elites.[91] In

---

80. American National Election Studies 2020. The ANES is a national public opinion data collection effort around elections funded by the National Science Foundation in collaboration with social scientists at Duke University, University of Michigan, University of Texas at Austin, and Stanford University.
81. Levendusky 2009.
82. Iyengar et al. 2019.
83. Klein 2020; Mason 2015, 2018.
84. Mason 2018.
85. Box-Steffensmeier, Boef, and Lin 2004; Gillion, Ladd, and Meredith 2020.
86. Jardina 2019; White and Laird 2020; Wamble et al. 2022.
87. Campbell, Green, and Layman 2011.
88. Chen and Rodden 2013; Rodden 2010, 2019.
89. Lelkes, Sood, and Iyengar 2017.
90. Banda and Cluverius 2018; Rogowski and Sutherland 2016; Webster and Abramowitz 2017.
91. Graham and Svolik 2020; McCoy and Somer 2019; Svolik 2019.

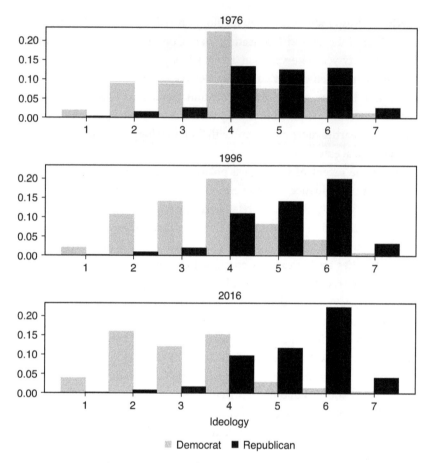

FIGURE 1.2. Trends in ideological polarization among the American public using data on party and ideology from the American National Election Studies

their book *Radical American Partisanship*, political scientists Nathan Kalmoe and Lilliana Mason warn that polarized societies can even breed intergroup hostility and partisan violence.[92] Although some researchers dispute the evidence for this overarching finding,[93] in the 2020s, Americans clearly witnessed deeply concerning episodes of escalating partisan hostility. On January 6, 2021, following Republican President Donald Trump's defeat in the 2020 presidential election, his supporters stormed the U.S. Capitol building in an attempt to overturn Democratic President-elect Joe Biden's victory. The

92. Kalmoe and Mason 2022.
93. See, e.g., Westwood et al. 2022.

resulting riots culminated in at least four deaths, emphasizing troubling links between societal polarization and extreme partisanship.[94] In the summer of 2024, Donald Trump survived two known assassination attempts while competing as the Republican presidential candidate. The Trump campaign placed blame on Democrats for using "inflammatory language" to incite partisan violence.[95]

Worryingly, public opinion surveys show that affective polarization has increased over time. The standard way to measure affective polarization in American politics is to use a feeling thermometer that captures attitudes toward one's in-party and out-party on a scale from 0 ("highly unfavorable") to 100 ("highly favorable"). Affective polarization is measured as the difference between a person's average feeling toward their in-party and out-party. Figure 1.3 shows average attitudes toward the Republican Party and the Democratic Party among self-identified Republicans (dashed lines) and self-identified Democrats (solid lines) with data from the American National Election Studies.[96] As the figure illustrates, the increase in affective polarization is driven by negative partisanship—dislike or hostility toward the out-party—rather than increasing favorability toward one's own party.

Since affective polarization has mainly been studied as a mass rather than an elite phenomenon, it is unclear whether politicians are also more affectively polarized. Growing party cohesion and "teamsmanship" dynamics are readily apparent in Congress today.[97] However, these could be attributed to political strategy or to ideological differences rather than to negative partisanship. Members of the political opposition have become more likely to oppose issues championed by an out-party president.[98] They are also more likely to grandstand in congressional hearings, particularly when they lack political power.[99] Likewise, politicians increasingly express negativity toward the opposite party on social media platforms and through political attack advertisements.[100] It is unclear, however, whether these trends reflect sincere partisan animus. The lack of consensus around affective polarization among politicians illustrates the difficulties of disentangling whether manifestations of polarization come

94. Cameron 2022.
95. Gold and Astor 2024.
96. American National Election Studies 2020.
97. Lee 2008, 2009; Theriault 2008.
98. Lee 2009.
99. Park 2021.
100. Ansolabehere and Iyengar 1996; Lau and Rovner 2009; Messing and Weisel 2017.

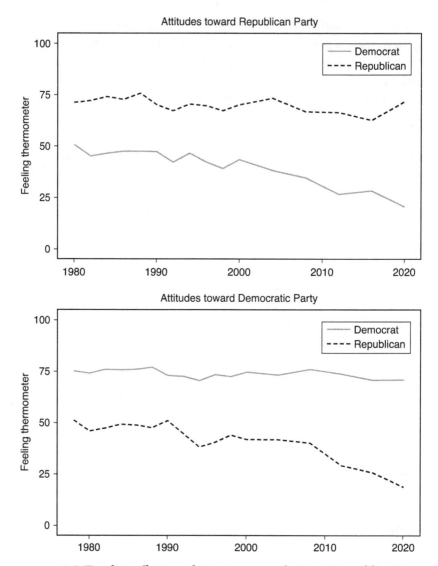

FIGURE 1.3. Trends in affective polarization among the American public using feeling thermometer data from the American National Election Studies

from ideological differences, partisan animosities, or both. Ultimately, if the observed behavior of politicians—greater party cohesion, more ideologically extreme legislators elected to Congress, increasing partisanship on roll-call votes, and heightened legislative gridlock—is the same, then understanding why these trends are occurring may not be as important as assessing their consequences.

Overall, partisan polarization has become a more salient feature of U.S. politics in the twenty-first century relative to much of twentieth-century U.S. politics. At the elite level, Republican and Democratic politicians increasingly disagree along party lines. This trend started in the late 1970s and has increased more sharply since the 1990s. Congressional voting patterns from the 1990s to the 2020s suggest the trend has been somewhat asymmetric, with Republican legislators exhibiting stronger ideological commitments relative to their Democratic counterparts. Whether politicians exhibit high levels of affective polarization is less well understood. However, teamsmanship dynamics and forms of visible hostility in Congress point to a concerning trend. With respect to mass polarization, the evidence tells us that Republicans are increasingly conservative in terms of their economic and social values and Democrats are increasingly liberal. This trend may be a function of Americans sorting into parties over time rather than changing their attitudes. Finally, growing affective polarization among the public is widely recognized as problematic. The increase in partisan hostility is related to the fact that many social identities no longer cut cleanly across party lines.

1.6 Empirical Approach of the Book

Before detailing the argument of this book, it is useful to understand its overarching empirical approach. This book asks how extreme polarization affects international politics. This is a *causal* question. Causal questions ask how an explanatory or independent variable (partisan polarization) affects an outcome or dependent variable (the stability, credibility, and reliability of a country's foreign policy). Social scientists are often interested in identifying and estimating causal effects. But, in this application, establishing causality is very difficult for two reasons.

One challenge is that the variables of interest in this book are hard to conceptualize and measure. The independent variable, polarization, itself is a fuzzy concept. As chapter 3 will explain, there is a lot of debate about how best to measure polarization across countries. Democracies have different electoral systems, various numbers of political parties, and differing beliefs about what constitutes a left-wing or right-wing party.[101] As this chapter discussed, there are also many types of polarization: polarization relating to partisanship versus

---

101. There is also a lot of scholarly debate over which countries can be classified as democracies in the first place (see, e.g., Boese 2019; Giebler, Ruth, and Tanneberg 2018; Lueders and Lust 2018).

other social identities, ideological versus affective polarization, polarization among politicians versus the public, and so forth. The dependent variables in this book, which capture various foreign policy outcomes, are equally hard to measure. Concepts like credibility of a country's threats or the reliability of a country's commitments are not purely observable. Rather, they depend on the perceptions of other countries.

Even if scholars agree on how to conceptualize and measure the key variables in this book, there is a second major challenge with identifying the "effect" of polarization. To establish causality, we would need to isolate variation created by polarization independent of other factors that influence foreign policy outcomes. The problem is that, in the real world, polarization co-occurs with many other factors that affect foreign policy. For instance, in the example of 1930s France used at the outset of this book, politics were clearly very polarized. However, France was also experiencing an economic crisis, growing economic inequality, an influx of migration, and a changing security environment—all of which plausibly influenced its foreign policy.

Scientists can estimate causal effects by conducting an experiment or randomized controlled trial. In an experiment, the unit of interest is randomly assigned to either a treatment group or a control group. Researchers recover the causal effect of the treatment (the independent variable) on an observed outcome of interest (the dependent variable) by measuring the difference in outcomes between the treated and control groups. Social scientists also conduct experiments to answer questions about politics. Some experiments in political science have asked: Does social pressure increase voter turnout?[102] Do cash transfers affect support for combatants?[103] Does foreign aid improve social cohesion in postconflict societies?[104] The researchers of these studies randomized mailers that publicized people's voting status (Michigan, USA), job training and cash transfers (Kandahar, Afghanistan), and development aid programs (Northern Liberia), respectively.

Unfortunately, many questions in international relations cannot be answered by randomized control trials. International relations scholars ask questions like: Are nuclear weapons effective tools of coercion?[105] How does

---

102. Gerber, Green, and Larimer 2008.
103. Lyall, Zhou, and Imai 2020.
104. Fearon, Humphreys, and Weinstein 2009.
105. Sechser and Fuhrmann 2017.

a country's reputation affect its behavior in international politics?[106] Do individual leaders impact war outcomes?[107] Why are some authoritarian regimes more conflict prone or better at fighting than others?[108] Nuclear weapons, reputations, leaders, and regime types are all factors that cannot be randomly assigned. Nevertheless, these questions are extremely important. Similar to other international relations books, the approach this book takes is to combine many research strategies and sources of descriptive evidence. This means that no one piece of evidence is conclusive, but, rather, when different pieces of evidence are taken collectively, they demonstrate an overarching pattern.

Before diving into the evidence, the first (and arguably most important) step is to theory build. Chapter 2 begins with a theoretical discussion of existing literature in international relations about the advantages that democracies have relative to nondemocracies. It then lays out the institutional features of democracies that confer each of those advantages. Finally, it theorizes about how extreme polarization interacts with those institutional features, and what the likely impact is on foreign policy outcomes. This leads to a set of observable implications that are explored in the empirical chapters.

The empirical analyses in chapter 3 examine descriptive patterns of polarization and foreign policy using cross-national regression analyses, or a "large-N" quantitative approach. For this book, I construct measures of extreme polarization in foreign policy and introduce them into existing analyses of democratic stability, credibility, and reliability. Although these types of regression analyses have limitations, they are an appropriate starting point because much of the evidence from the democratic advantage tradition in international relations is rooted in this approach.

The remaining empirical chapters take a deep dive into one country case: the case of contemporary U.S. foreign policy. The main justification for focusing on a single case is practical. Simply put, within-country analysis provides a more complete picture of the ways in which polarization impacts policy processes. As explored in chapter 3, the variety of electoral systems found in modern democracies make measuring cross-national polarization challenging. Many foreign policy outcomes of interest in this book are difficult to understand without examining specific cases. For example, in order to explore how polarization affects the construction of an international agreement, it

106. Crescenzi 2018.
107. Horowitz, Stam, and Ellis 2015; Saunders 2014.
108. Weeks 2012, 2014; Talmadge 2015.

is necessary to understand the domestic constraints faced by a country's negotiators and how these impact their decision-making calculus. Ultimately, while this book draws on cross-national evidence (chapter 3) to demonstrate patterns associated with polarization, within-country analyses (chapters 4 through 6) are better suited to the development of richer data sources for both explanatory and outcome variables.

Within the U.S. case, I again rely on multiple methods to illustrate how polarization has impacted democratic stability, credibility, and reliability. To investigate how polarization reshapes vertical constraints from the public, the book draws on public opinion data both from historic polls and original surveys. I use survey experiments fielded online to samples of U.S. adults to explore how partisanship conditions people's assessments of their leader's foreign policy decision-making. To understand how polarization reshapes horizontal constraints, I focus on patterns of behavior from politicians. The book relies on descriptive data from a variety of sources, including qualitative evidence (e.g., interviews with policymakers), text data (e.g., analyses of congressional speech), and other quantitative data from the executive branch and U.S. Congress (e.g., data on roll-call votes and international treaties).

Taken together, the evidence from this book suggests that the consequences of more extreme forms of polarization for foreign policymaking are largely negative. Of course, the conclusions that this book draws are probabilistic rather than deterministic. There will almost certainly be exceptions to the rule–that is, instances in which polarization benefits foreign policymaking, a possibility discussed in greater detail in chapter 7. On average, however, we should expect that as polarization becomes more extreme within a given democracy, its foreign policy will become less stable, and the country will be perceived as a less credible adversary and a less reliable ally.

1.6.1 Why Focus on Polarization in U.S. Foreign Policy?

The latter half of this book focuses on polarization and foreign policy in one primary case: the United States. Of course, polarization is neither unique to the United States nor to the current political moment, so why study its impacts on contemporary U.S. foreign policy? For one, while prior periods of extreme polarization in U.S. history are well known, the United States and the international system it belongs to today look extremely different. The most polarized period of American history was the mid-nineteenth century, when extreme internal divisions over the practice of slavery led to a deadly civil war. At this time, American economic and military power were dwarfed by the expansive British Empire. Throughout much of this era, U.S. foreign relations were characterized—at least formally—by a policy of noninterventionism. This means that the United States sought to avoid major entanglements on the European continent.

Contemporary American foreign policy looks very different. Sometimes for better and sometimes for worse, the United States is incredibly influential in international politics. The country is an economic superpower, constituting roughly a fourth of the global economy.[109] The United States invests more in research and development than any other country, making up a quarter of global R&D expenditures.[110] The American military is the most powerful in the world, and the United States makes up close to 40 percent of the global military expenditures.[111] And major decisions in American foreign policy—for example, about whether or not to intervene militarily in conflict, invest in peacekeeping or humanitarian operations, support controversial regimes, and join or withdraw from international organizations—all have consequential ripple effects.

Beyond its economic and military power, the United States wields considerable influence in the international system because it was a chief architect of the rules-based international order that arose after World War II. *International order* is a set of "governing arrangements that establish fundamental rules and principles in international politics and settle expectations among states."[112] The system that the United States and its democratic allies developed in the mid-twentieth century is commonly called the *liberal international order*, or LIO. Political scientist John Ikenberry, who writes extensively on the LIO, summarizes: "The liberal international order is not just a collection of liberal democratic states but an international mutual-aid society—a sort of global political club that provides members with tools for economic and political advancement. Participants in the order gain trading opportunities, dispute-resolution mechanisms, frameworks for collective action, regulatory agreements, allied security guarantees, and resources in times of crisis."[113]

---

109. Silver 2020.
110. Khan, Robbins, and Okrent 2020.
111. O'Hanlon 2024.
112. Lissner and Rapp-Hooper 2020, 14.
113. Ikenberry 2011, 61–62.

Bipartisan support for the principles underlying LIO—including emphasis on the rule of law, international cooperation over trade and security issues, and the promotion of liberal democratic values—has been central to contemporary American foreign policy. In the post–Cold War era, however, the widening partisan gap between the Republican and Democratic Parties spurred debates about whether the United States would continue to pursue a bipartisan, liberal internationalist agenda in the future.[114] Moving deeper into the twenty-first century, politicians on both the far right and far left have advocated for American retrenchment from foreign affairs. These partisan debates within the United States are intimately connected to other global trends. Alongside growing political polarization, many democracies are facing new challenges like growing dissatisfaction with globalization, the rise of populist movements, and a resurgence of authoritarianism globally.

Despite growing awareness of polarization, its impact on foreign policy remains contested. Some policymakers see polarization as a "national security threat,"[115] but its precise consequences are poorly understood. Scholars of American foreign policy continue to debate whether or not partisan politics is extending "beyond the water's edge."[116] On the one hand, many researchers believe there is substantial bipartisan cooperation on foreign policy issues and agreement about underlying principles of American grand strategy.[117] Scholars from this perspective see foundational elements of the LIO as intact, and some are critical of alarmist discourse about the dangers of polarization. Another group of researchers, however, express deep concern about how partisan politics encroaches on foreign affairs and the implications this may have for how the United States relates to the world.[118]

114. Hoffman 1995; Kurth 1996.

115. Rice 2020.

116. Debates about the extent to which U.S. foreign policy is polarizing tend to resurface after high-profile partisan events like the 2003 U.S. invasion of Iraq (Kupchan and Trubowitz 2007; Ikenberry 2009; Chaudoin, Milner, and Tingley 2010) and the 2016 election of Donald Trump (Chaudoin, Milner, and Tingley 2017; Friedrichs and Tama 2022, 2024; Jervis et al. 2018; Musgrave 2019; Schultz 2018).

117. See, e.g., Bryan and Tama 2022; Busby and Monten 2008; Chaudoin, Milner, and Tingley 2010, 2017, 2018; Hurst and Wroe 2016; Friedman 2024; Kertzer, Brooks, and Brooks 2021; Tama 2023.

118. See, e.g., Beinart 2008; Drezner 2021; Friedrichs 2021; Jeong and Quirk 2019; Kupchan and Trubowitz 2007, 2010; Musgrave 2019; Pillar 2023; Schultz 2018; Trubowitz and Burgoon 2023.

To adjudicate between these perspectives, this book characterizes the trajectory of polarization in U.S. foreign affairs. It argues that while foreign policy is much less polarized than domestic policy in the United States, aspects of foreign policy are becoming more partisan. This trend has worrying downstream consequences. Given the position of the United States in the international system, substantial shifts in its foreign policy that result directly or indirectly from polarization have important consequences for multilateral security, economic, environmental, and human rights regimes. Debates about the effect of polarization on U.S. foreign policy speak not only to questions in international relations theory about democratic advantages, but also to critical policy questions about the United States' role in global affairs and the future of the liberal international order.

As any observer of American politics will tell you, the United States has unique political institutions. Therefore, this book comes with the important caveat that, while many of its themes will apply elsewhere, evidence from the United States is not fully generalizable. In fact, extrapolating far beyond this context risks exacerbating a well-known American bias in international relations theory.[119] The concluding chapter, chapter 7, speaks to possibilities for the extension of this work beyond American politics. While the depth required to do so is beyond the scope of this book, comparative work on how different types of polarization are shaping foreign policy is an exciting and incredibly important area for research.

1.7 Argument and Outline of the Book

In many democracies in the 2020s, internal political divisions substantially impact foreign affairs. In India, analysts worry that societal polarization gives leaders from the Hindu nationalist Bharatiya Janata Party electoral incentives to escalate tensions with neighboring Pakistan.[120] In Taiwan, substantial divisions between the Kuomintang and the Democratic Progressive Party mean leader turnover could dramatically reshape cross-strait relations with mainland China.[121] In Israel, high levels of polarization "left Israel unprepared"[122] to anticipate and respond to terror attacks conducted by Hamas in October

---

119. Colgan 2019.
120. Mondal 2019.
121. Grossman 2023.
122. Applebaum 2023.

2023. And, in the United States, following the March 2022 Russian invasion of Ukraine, heavily partisan debates over continuing U.S. military assistance to Ukraine introduced questions about the reliability of American commitments.[123] Despite critical links between domestic and international politics, research on polarization overwhelmingly focuses on how it affects domestic politics and society. This book argues that extreme partisan polarization has important and underappreciated effects on international relations. In large part, these consequences are negative for polarized democracies.

Chapter 2 outlines a theory of partisan polarization and democratic advantage. I start by identifying three interrelated advantages democracies enjoy in foreign affairs based on existing international relations literature. Democracies maintain relatively stable foreign policies (stability advantage), make for more credible adversaries (credibility advantage), and act as more cooperative and reliable allies (reliability advantage) relative to nondemocracies. Two systems of constraint in liberal democracies confer these advantages. Vertical constraints make democratic leaders accountable to their publics, while horizontal constraints make democratic leaders accountable to other actors within government, including the political opposition. These constraints provide democratic leaders with incentives to make foreign policy choices that lead to good outcomes in international politics. In liberal democracies, democratic leaders are more likely to be responsive to the public, follow agreed upon procedures when making foreign policy, and uphold liberal principles—such as peaceful dispute resolution and commitment to the rule of law—in foreign affairs. Chapter 2 then introduces partisan polarization as an underexplored source of variation in explaining foreign policy outcomes in democracies. It traces how extreme polarization interacts with vertical and horizontal constraints in democracies to undermine each of the three advantages.

Chapter 3 provides descriptive, cross-national evidence for the relationship between polarization and foreign policy with new data on foreign policy positions of executive and opposition parties or coalitions in fifty-five democratic countries from 1945 to 2020. After characterizing contemporary patterns of polarization, this chapter incorporates measures of extreme polarization into well-known, existing models of democratic advantages in foreign affairs.[124] The analyses show that, on average, democracies appear to be

---

123. Clement, Balz, and Guskin 2023.
124. Leeds, Mattes, and Vogel 2009; Mattes, Leeds, and Carroll 2015; Schultz 2001a.

more stable, credible, and reliable than nondemocracies. However, this average effect obscures important variation among democracies that comes from domestic polarization. The chapter provides suggestive evidence that democracies experiencing extreme polarization may be more volatile in their foreign policymaking, less credible when issuing coercive threats to adversaries, and more likely to violate alliance commitments relative to other democracies. While the evidence in this chapter is far from definitive, it motivates deeper investigation of pathways through which extreme polarization might affect foreign policy outcomes.

The remaining three empirical chapters draw on evidence from contemporary U.S. foreign affairs. These chapters focus on how the United States' partisan politics could undermine the stability, credibility, and reliability of its foreign policy. Chapter 4 highlights the stability advantage: the fact that, in democracies, foreign policy tends to be less volatile than in nondemocracies.[125] The alternation of power in democracies results in a tacit "partisan truce"[126] that keeps foreign policy consistent and gives leaders incentives to invest in nonpartisan institutions to maintain continuity in foreign affairs. I argue that in highly polarized contexts, however, this partisan truce erodes. Politicians have incentives to appeal to an ideologically extreme base of core supporters rather than to a median voter in the electorate. High levels of affective polarization in the public give politicians incentives to strongly disagree with positions championed by the opposite party, extending domestic partisan conflict into areas of foreign affairs. As the stakes of partisan competition heighten and politicians become more ideologically extreme, they have fewer incentives to preserve and invest in a nonpartisan foreign policy bureaucracy.

Chapter 4 builds evidence for this argument by using public opinion polling to identify sets of issues where partisan conflict has extended to foreign affairs. These include foreign policy debates that are politicized during electoral cycles, link to aspects of social identity, involve nontraditional security threats, or reflect ideological debates about the principles of internationalism and multilateralism. In the U.S. context, these sets of issues have become increasingly susceptible to volatility with leader turnover. The chapter then describes how parties and their leaders incrementally erode a partisan truce in U.S. foreign policy. It details strategies leaders use to politicize foreign

125. Leeds and Mattes 2022; McGillivray and Smith 2008; Mattes, Leeds, and Carroll 2015; Smith 2016.
126. Alesina 1988; Gowa 1998.

policy institutions like the State Department, the military, and the intelligence community. As polarization in domestic politics increases, nonpartisan institutions involved in the creation and execution of foreign policy are more likely to be targeted by politicians. As these institutions become politicized, they are less likely to maintain continuity across successive presidential administrations.

Chapter 5 explores how polarization can erode the credibility advantage: the ability of democracies to be credible adversaries. Traditionally, in crisis bargaining, accountability to the public makes democratic leaders unlikely to issue threats they do not intend to follow through on.[127] The presence of an active political opposition can strengthen the credibility of democracies when bipartisan consensus conveys a clear signal to a foreign adversary.[128] In noncrisis situations, when negotiating with adversaries, the constraints that democracies face at home can also make them more effective negotiators relative to nondemocracies.[129] I argue that in polarized contexts, however, the nature of these constraints changes. A partisan public is less effective in checking executive power. Simultaneously, the political opposition reaps electoral rewards from opposing or undermining the executive in foreign policy. This makes the bipartisan agreement that is necessary to pursue complex international negotiations and provide credible, informative signals to adversaries less likely.

Chapter 5 uses three strategies to explore polarization and the credibility advantage. First, survey experiments illustrate how a polarized electorate both distrusts the foreign policy decision-making of an out-party leader and gives the political opposition incentives to undermine the incumbent. Analyzing congressional debates and roll-call votes, I show that responses to international crises have grown increasingly partisan, and the political opposition has steadily cohered against the president in foreign affairs. Finally, the chapter highlights a single case—the negotiation of the Joint Comprehensive Plan of Action (JCPOA), known as the Iran nuclear deal—to demonstrate how polarization coinciding with the electoral cycle affected dynamics around the negotiation and adoption of the agreement. This analysis is based on interviews of U.S. negotiators of the JCPOA and senior staff members of the Senate Foreign Relations Committee conducted in Washington, D.C. Since a highly

127. Fearon 1994; Tomz 2007.
128. Schultz 2001a.
129. Putnam 1988; Schelling 1960.

polarized environment provides incentives for domestic political opponents to represent preferences more extreme than they hold, White House officials took steps to insulate the negotiation process from partisan politics. This both reduced leverage the United States had during the negotiation and jeopardized the agreement's durability.

Chapter 6 considers how polarization negatively impacts the reliability advantage: the ability of democracies to be reliable allies. In nonpolarized contexts, vertical and horizontal constraints make it difficult for democratic leaders to renege on existing commitments.[130] I argue that in polarized settings, vertical constraints are less effective in restraining leaders from acting unilaterally in foreign policy. As polarization increases, a partisan public is more eager to see their party "win" or the preferred policy enacted. As a consequence, they are more willing to overlook other considerations, including violations of democratic norms or procedures in the foreign policymaking process. The public is also less sensitive to the reputational costs that arise when leaders renege on their international commitments. Anticipating opposition from the out-party, leaders bypass horizontal constraints to secure political wins. But when they enter into international agreements without bipartisan support, these commitments are less durable. Over time, highly polarized democracies are more likely to renege on commitments and less likely to be perceived as reliable allies.

Chapter 6 parallels the structure of chapters 4 and 5 to develop evidence for how polarization affects the reliability advantage. A survey experiment first shows a partisan public is more likely to overlook violations of democratic norms and procedures in the process of making international commitments. Partisans find it more acceptable for leaders to unilaterally enter into or exit from alliances, organizations, or major international agreements when their preferred party is in power. The chapter provides descriptive evidence that illustrates how this can manifest in a president opting to use executive agreements or nonbinding political commitments, which are less durable than international treaties, to make foreign policy. I then assess how polarization affects perceptions of U.S. reliability among its allies. Survey experiments on public and elite samples in the UK prime respondents to think about polarization in American politics and then evaluate their attitudes toward the U.S.–UK bilateral relationship. Heightening awareness of U.S. polarization negatively impacts perceptions of U.S. foreign policy and U.S.–UK relations. The survey

130. Leeds 1999; McGillivray and Smith 2000; Martin 2000.

also finds that long-term, reputational impacts of polarization for U.S. foreign policy are most concerning to allies and potentially underappreciated in American politics.

The concluding chapter, chapter 7, discusses the theoretical and practical implications of the findings outlined in the book. It considers when polarization might actually be a positive thing in foreign policy. It also describes a variety of strategies that political scientists have explored to mitigate the negative consequences of polarization in foreign affairs. Finally, the conclusion introduces potential extensions beyond the American context for future research. It explores how the effects of polarization on foreign policy might differ across various systems of government or electoral systems.

This book should not be interpreted as a dire warning for the future of democracies. Rather, it undertakes a systematic exercise to outline the impacts extreme polarization has on foreign affairs. By understanding the scope of the problem, policymakers and citizens will be better prepared to address its consequences. Much research in American politics focuses on the effects of polarization on domestic governance, but these effects extend well beyond the domestic realm. This book emphasizes that in many—but not all—cases, extreme partisan polarization has both direct and indirect negative impacts on cooperation between democracies in the international system.

2

A Theory of Polarization and Democratic Advantage

EVERY SEPTEMBER, IN a cavernous, wood-paneled room at the United Nations (UN) headquarters in New York City, delegates from member nations of the UN General Assembly (UNGA) gather to open a new session. At the outset of each the session, world leaders deliver remarks that are broadcast across the globe. At the opening of the forty-eighth session of the UNGA in September 1993, a new president of the United States took the podium. As the former governor of Arkansas, Bill Clinton had limited foreign policy experience before moving into the White House. His debut speech at the UNGA occurred at a time of both strife and optimism. In the early 1990s, political and social upheaval fueled brutal episodes of violence in Somalia and a newly independent Bosnia. But, elsewhere, new democracies were cautiously optimistic about the future. The dissolution of the Soviet Union contributed to a wave of democratization. Many democratic transitions across Eastern Europe, Latin America, Africa, and Asia had succeeded. Against this backdrop, Clinton focused his remarks on the virtues of democratic governance for international politics. In his trademark Southern drawl, Clinton announced, "Democracy is rooted in compromise, not conquest. It rewards tolerance, not hatred. Democracies rarely wage war on one another. They make more reliable partners in trade, in diplomacy, and in the stewardship of our global environment."[1]

More than a decade later, at the sixtieth session of the UNGA in September 2005, the world looked quite different. Terrorist attacks on the United States on September 11, 2001, led President George W. Bush to launch the Global War on Terrorism to combat Islamic extremism. Intense debate over U.S.-led

1. Clinton 1993.

wars in Afghanistan and Iraq shaped the atmosphere of a new UNGA session. Yet, some themes in Bush's address to the Assembly closely reflected those of his predecessor. Reiterating a similar sentiment about democracies, Bush remarked, "Democratic nations grow in strength because they reward and respect the creative gifts of their people. And democratic nations contribute to peace and stability because they seek national greatness in achievements of their citizens, not the conquest of their neighbors."[2]

The two speeches from the successive American presidents otherwise emphasized different threats and policy prescriptions. Clinton discussed dangers posed by nuclear, chemical, and biological weapons, making a strong case for nonproliferation. Bush focused on threats posed by transnational terrorism and urged other countries to unite in condemning state-sponsored terror. Clinton called upon the UN to expand peacekeeping operations. In contrast, Bush requested that the UN improve efficiency and implement cost-saving reforms.

Despite differences between the speeches, a common theme was the notion that democracies are both better at and better for international politics than nondemocracies. The idea that democracies are uniquely advantaged in foreign affairs and that a world full of democratic countries would be more just and more peaceful is shared by presidents and policymakers of both political parties in the United States. The theme recurs throughout inaugural addresses, speeches, and press releases from Republican and Democratic presidential administrations.

Such language is commonplace—and even cliché—in American foreign policy. But scholars who study international relations also refer to the concept of "democratic advantages" in the conduct of foreign affairs. This book draws on this democratic advantage tradition in international relations theory[3] to highlight three advantages democracies have in international politics. The first is a stability advantage: democracies maintain consistent policies even when the leader or party in power changes. Second, democracies have a credibility advantage: they are better able to signal information about their objectives and intentions, making them more effective negotiators and more credible adversaries. Third, democracies have a reliability advantage: they commit to and comply with international agreements, making them more reliable partners. These advantages are interrelated and not perfectly separable. At times,

2. Bush 2005.
3. This tradition of thought is also referred to as "democratic triumphalism" (Desch 2002).

they reinforce one another. All three advantages arise from two systems of constraint on democratic leaders that make them accountable to the public and to an active political opposition.

Political scientists writing about democratic advantages have an ideal democracy in mind: a liberal democracy that not only has free and fair elections, but also domestic institutions that check political power and protect civil liberties. In reality, democracies are far more complex. A natural next step is to consider how these systems of constraint and the advantages they confer in foreign affairs differ across democracies. The purpose of this exercise is not to compare democratic foreign policy to autocratic foreign policy, but rather to explore variation in foreign policymaking within and across democracies.

Of course, democracies vary in many ways that could impact foreign affairs. They differ in their system of government (e.g., presidential, semipresidential, parliamentary), which affects how easy or difficult it is for a leader to change foreign policy. They differ in terms of their electoral systems (e.g., plurality, proportional representation) and the number of parties in government, which shapes whose foreign policy interests are represented and how. Democracies also differ in terms of their geographic location, resource endowments, political culture, and a host of other things. Any given democratic country is also prone to change over time. Demography shifts, economies expand and contract, media environments change, and policy issues become more or less politically salient. In short, many domestic factors impact foreign policy outcomes.

The goal of this book is to emphasize one important and overlooked domestic source of variation in democratic foreign policymaking: partisan polarization. Chapter 1 defined partisan polarization as increasing distance between major parties or coalitions of parties. Ideological polarization refers to the increasing divergence in policy preferences between political parties along ideological dimensions. Affective polarization refers to increasing social distance: the tendency for partisans to like members of their own party and to dislike members of opposing parties.

This book focuses on extreme polarization, or contexts in which there are high levels of both ideological and affective polarization. Chapter 1 explained that environments of extreme polarization are unique because they facilitate democratic erosion. While some degree of political contestation is characteristic of liberal democracies, as polarization becomes more extreme, the stakes of winning increase. Parties and their leaders begin to disregard democratic norms in order to see their preferred policies enacted. Partisan conflict extends to other policy domains and institutions that were not previously politicized. Simultaneously, democratic constraints from the public, the media, and other actors within government are less effective in checking the power of political leaders.

Political scientists know a lot about how polarization affects democratic governance and society. However, its impact on foreign policy has been underappreciated. This chapter theorizes about those potential impacts. It begins by contextualizing the democratic advantage tradition of scholarship in international relations. It then describes systems of vertical and horizontal constraints and explains how they shape democratic foreign policymaking. Finally, it explores how extreme forms of polarization interact with these constraints to affect each of the democratic advantages. The main conclusion of this chapter is that extreme polarization can erode systems of constraint that advantage democracies in foreign affairs. On average, relative to less polarized times, during periods of high polarization, we should expect democratic foreign policymaking to be less stable and for democracies to be both less credible adversaries and less reliable allies.

2.1 The Democratic Advantage Tradition and Its Critics

In 1831, a French political philosopher named Alexis de Tocqueville arrived in the United States to conduct research on the American penitentiary system. Over nine months, Tocqueville and his travel companion visited cities and towns all over the country, collecting information for their report on prison reform for France. Yet, Tocqueville left the United States with a much broader range of observations on American politics and society. One conclusion Tocqueville drew from his study was that democracies were "decidedly inferior" in matters of diplomacy and foreign affairs.[4] He believed institutional features of democratic government were responsible for fickle and shortsighted foreign policy. Tocqueville noted: "[A] democracy finds it difficult to coordinate the details of a great undertaking and to fix on some plan and carry it through with determination in spite of obstacles. It has little capacity for combining measures in secret and waiting patiently for the result."[5]

---

4. Tocqueville 1835.
5. Tocqueville 1835, 228–230.

Tocqueville's widely cited[6] critiques of democratic foreign policy reflected the general consensus on the subject for a long time. In the United States, for example, through much of the nineteenth and twentieth centuries, policymakers and intellectuals expressed concerns about democratic accountability and the volatile nature of public opinion. George Kennan—a diplomat and architect of U.S. containment policy during the Cold War—was described as viewing democratic public opinion as "inevitably unstable, unserious, subjective, emotional, and simple-minded."[7] Intellectuals like Gabriel Almond and Walter Lippmann argued that the public was especially ill-equipped to hold leaders to account on foreign policy issues.[8]

But, in the past few decades, political scientists started to challenge this conventional thinking about democratic foreign policy. Beginning in the 1980s and 1990s, a tradition of scholarship in international relations emerged that suggested the opposite: democracies were perhaps advantaged in foreign affairs relative to their nondemocratic counterparts. Scholars in this tradition observed that institutional features of democracies that constrained political power had positive downstream consequences for foreign policymaking. It is not a coincidence that scholarship emphasizing the benefits of liberal democracy proliferated following the so-called third wave of democratization that coincided with the decline of communism and the end of the Cold War.[9] Researchers in international relations sought to investigate whether democracies were advantaged by quantifying and systematically comparing foreign policy outcomes in democracies to the same outcomes in nondemocracies.[10]

Today, the democratic advantage tradition is a cornerstone of international relations theory. The concept is most often associated with *democratic peace theory*: the tendency for democracies to resolve disputes with one another peacefully. This theory argues that democratic publics and their leaders have

---

6. Other researchers have similarly contextualized the democratic advantage tradition as a response to longstanding critiques of democracy from Tocqueville and others (see, e.g., Leeds and Mattes 2022; Kroenig 2020; Schultz and Weingast 2003).

7. Chalberg 1989, 485.

8. Almond 1950, 1956; Lippmann 1922, 1955. See, also, characterizations of the "Almond–Lippmann consensus" (e.g., Holsti 1992) about public opinion and foreign policy.

9. See, e.g., Huntington 1991; Fukuyama 1992.

10. See, e.g., Gaubatz 1996; Martin 2000; Lipson 2003; Mansfield, Milner, and Rosendorff 2002; Leeds, Mattes, and Vogel 2009; Mattes, Leeds, and Carroll 2015; Leeds and Mattes 2022; Reiter and Stam 2002; Russett 1993; Schultz 2001a.

normative commitments to peace[11] and domestic institutions that facilitate nonviolent dispute resolution.[12] Democracies that do engage in fighting are also thought to be more effective on the battlefield.[13] In their book *Democracies at War*, Dan Reiter and Allan Stam argue that democratic advantages in fighting come from both selection and performance. Because democratic leaders fear the electoral consequences of losing wars, they are more selective about the wars they fight. An emphasis on individual rights in democratic societies makes soldiers more motivated to fight for their country, further improving military performance.

Yet the advantages democracies have in foreign affairs extend beyond peace and conflict. Some researchers describe economic advantages democracies have when selling bonds or accessing credit.[14] Others refer to advantages democracies have in geopolitical competition when compared to their authoritarian rivals.[15] Still others apply the term to a general set of advantages democracies have across foreign policy domains from militarized conflict to diplomacy to economic growth.[16]

Today, the democratic advantage tradition is arguably a dominant perspective among international relations scholars. As with all traditions, however, there are critics of this body of scholarship. The first line of critique, associated with the tradition of *realism* in international relations theory, echoes earlier thinking on democratic foreign policy. The main argument is that democracies do not behave that differently from autocracies because all countries seek to maximize their power and security. Realist scholars believe that when push comes to shove, democracies will not adhere to liberal norms in international politics. Rather, they will make decisions on the basis of their national security interests. The implication of realist arguments is that we should not expect democracies to be any more cooperative or less conflict prone in international politics than their autocratic peers.[17] Democracies also should not inherently be more credible than autocracies or more reliable as alliance partners.[18]

11. Doyle 1983; Maoz and Russett 1993; Russett 1993; Tomz and Weeks 2013.
12. Bueno de Mesquita and Lalman 1992; Lipson 2003; Schultz 1998.
13. Lake 1992; Reiter and Stam 2002.
14. Beaulieu, Cox, and Saiegh 2012; DisGuiseppe and Shea 2015; Schultz and Weingast 2003.
15. Kroenig 2020.
16. Hyde and Saunders 2020.
17. See, e.g., Gartzke 2007; Gowa 1999; Mearsheimer 1990; Rosato 2003.
18. Downes and Sechser 2012; Gartzke and Gleditsch 2004.

A second line of critique of the democratic advantage thesis focuses on authoritarian advantages. Researchers in this tradition emphasize that many nondemocratic countries also have vertical and horizontal constraints on their leaders.[19] These constraints can functionally give some nondemocracies the same advantages that democracies have when making foreign policy. For example, authoritarian regimes that have higher levels of accountability to the public may be more stable and less likely to initiate conflict.[20] Some types of authoritarian regimes are also able to send signals in international politics that are just as credible as those issued by democracies.[21]

This book raises a third critique of the democratic advantage thesis. It argues that both historically and presently, democracies have faced unique internal challenges that can undermine the institutional constraints governments have on their leaders. The internal challenge this book focuses on is extreme polarization. In this vein, this book does not overturn the democratic advantage thesis but rather argues that we should expect variation among democracies in terms of their behavior in foreign policy based on their level of polarization. To understand how and why this occurs, this chapter identifies the systems of constraint that advantage democracies and explores how polarization affects them.

2.2 Democratic Constraints and Foreign Affairs

The democratic advantages that are the focus of this book come from two sets of constraints on political power found in liberal democracies.[22] The first is a system of *vertical constraints* that make democratic leaders accountable to the public. The main way that publics constrain democratic leaders is through regular elections. Elections give voters opportunities to express their satisfaction or dissatisfaction with the individual or political party in power. In anticipation of future elections, democratic leaders have incentives to make foreign policy choices that reflect the will of the public.

---

19. See, e.g., Hyde and Saunders 2020 for a discussion of how both democratic and autocratic leaders can be subject to common domestic constraints.

20. Weeks 2012, 2014.

21. Weiss 2013, 2014; Weeks 2008.

22. These democratic constraints are also referred to as systems of horizontal and vertical accountability (Lührmann, Marquardt, and Mechkova 2020). This book uses the terms "constraint" and "accountability" interchangeably.

Democratic leaders are likely to be most responsive to vertical constraints when the public is willing and able to assess the leader's policy choices. In *The Ambivalent Partisan*, Howard Lavine, Christopher Johnston, and Marco Steenbergen argue that democratic accountability is strongest when citizens can set aside their partisan commitments in evaluating politicians and their respective policies.[23] In foreign affairs, electoral accountability should dissuade leaders from making choices that lead to bad foreign policy outcomes. Politicians who mishandle international crises or lead their publics into devastating, unpopular wars are unlikely to be reelected. In extreme cases, they can face public pressure to resign. Consider the fate of Prime Minister Anthony Eden in the UK. In the 1956 Suez Crisis, Egyptian president Gamal Abdel Nassar had nationalized the Suez Canal, a critical waterway that facilitated trade between Asia and Europe. After much deliberation, Prime Minister Eden responded by launching a joint invasion of Egypt with Israel and France. The invasion was poorly executed and had disastrous political and economic consequences in Great Britain. Eden's mishandling of the crisis contributed to a wave of public disapproval that led to his resignation in 1957.[24]

By contrast, foreign policy decisions widely supported by the public boost a democratic leader's popularity and can be influential in their future electoral prospects. Ukrainian President Volodymyr Zelenskyy skyrocketed in popularity after he stood firm in response to Russian President Vladimir Putin's full-scale invasion of Ukraine in February 2022. Polling from the Kyiv International Institute of Sociology showed that, in 2022, 84 percent of Ukrainians trusted President Zelenskyy. The following year, after a largely unsuccessful counteroffensive campaign against Russia, the majority of Ukrainians still supported Zelenskyy but trust in the president had declined to 62 percent.[25]

Even leaders who are not facing reelection may still be responsive to public opinion on key foreign policy issues. Democratic leaders pay attention to public sentiments because they care about their image or how they are portrayed in the press and popular culture. They take public opinion into consideration out of concern for their legacy or the future of their political party. Surveys show that democratic politicians care what the public thinks about foreign policy, even when it comes to "high stakes" national security issues. For example, in a survey experiment in Israel, political scientists Michael Tomz, Jessica

23. Lavine, Johnston, and Steenbergen 2012.
24. James 1987.
25. Hrushetskyi 2023.

Weeks, and Keren Yarhi-Milo found that providing members of the Israeli Knesset information about public attitudes toward military strikes on terrorist bases influences those ministers' opinions about using military force.[26] A similar study of UK members of Parliament showed that the politicians were responsive to public opinion on the question of whether or not the UK should maintain military presence in the South China Sea.[27]

The second set of constraints on democratic leaders is a system of *horizontal constraints*. These intragovernmental constraints ensure that democratic leaders are accountable to other actors and institutions within government. In foreign affairs, horizontal constraints operate in many forms. They can arise through a separate legislature like the U.S. Congress or an independent judiciary that checks executive power.[28] Horizontal constraints can also arise from within the executive. Democratic leaders can be constrained by other elites, advisors, and bureaucrats in their own administrations who shape foreign policy decision-making.[29]

Because this book focuses on partisan polarization, the main horizontal constraint I emphasize is the political opposition. In democracies, the *political opposition* is the major political party, or coalition of parties, that opposes the incumbent party and intends to challenge it for power in future elections.[30] Opposition parties use many tools to constrain leaders. At the extremes are tools that can remove leaders or their parties from office. These include no-confidence votes or impeachment proceedings that take place in national legislatures. Opposition parties played critical roles in ousting Paraguayan President Fernando Lugo in 2012, Brazilian President Dilma Rousseff in 2016, and South Korean President Park Geun-hye in 2017.[31]

Foreign policy disasters can prompt an opposition party to remove or attempt to remove an incumbent leader. Interestingly, one of the earliest no-confidence votes was rooted in a poor foreign policy outcome. During an expensive and protracted war across the Atlantic in America's thirteen colonies, American revolutionary forces defeated the British, who surrendered

26. Tomz, Weeks, and Yarhi-Milo 2020.
27. Chu and Recchia 2022.
28. Howell and Pevehouse 2005, 2007; Kriner and Shickler 2016; Staton and Moore 2011.
29. Halperin and Clapp 2007; Jost 2024; Saunders 2015, 2022, 2024.
30. My focus on opposition parties does not mean that other actors within government are not important to foreign policy. Historically, for example, independent courts have played a critical role in constraining the power of democratic leaders.
31. Ginsburg, Huq, and Landau 2021.

in Yorktown, Virginia. The British defeat propelled anti-war sentiment in the House of Commons and led to a vote of no confidence in Prime Minister Lord North and his cabinet, who subsequently resigned.[32]

Beyond removing or threatening to remove democratic leaders, the opposition party has other ways to influence foreign policy. In many democracies, the political opposition plays a formal role in making foreign policy decisions through the legislative process. Entering into international treaties or issuing declarations of war often necessitates some input from a legislative body. In Denmark, the power to deploy military troops lies with the Danish parliament, the Folketing. In Uruguay, the legislative branch—the Asamblea General—authorizes the president's declaration of war. In Japan, the Diet must grant the prime minister approval to deploy troops within three weeks of the deployment.[33] These arrangements make it unlikely that consequential foreign policy decisions will be enacted purely along partisan lines.

The political opposition also constrains democratic leaders informally. Opposition parties hold hearings, conduct inquiries, shape media coverage, or influence public opinion.[34] One of the most powerful things that the opposition can do is to subject leaders to scrutiny. During U.S. President Ronald Reagan's second term in office (1985–1989), a scandal known as the Iran-Contra Affair prompted the U.S. Congress to investigate the Republican administration. White House officials covertly sold arms to the Iranian government and used the revenue to fund the Contras, a Nicaraguan rebel group. Democratic legislators chaired the investigative committees in both the House of Representatives and the Senate, releasing a damning report about White House involvement in the scandal. In theory, anticipation of this type of blowback spearheaded by an opposition party should give democratic leaders incentives to avoid foreign policy decisions that will lead to bad outcomes.

Systems of vertical and horizontal constraint are common to liberal democracies, irrespective of their system of government or electoral system. These democratic constraints consist of formal institutions, such as elections or impeachment processes, that check executive power. But they also include informal institutions that constrain democratic leaders indirectly. Informal institutions and norms play an especially important role in foreign affairs,

---

32. Whiteley 1996.
33. Wagner, Peters, and Glahn 2010.
34. Baum and Potter 2015; Howell and Pevehouse 2005, 2007; Kriner and Shickler 2016.

where executives tend to have more discretion than in domestic policy. These systems of constraint give rise to three advantages democracies have in foreign affairs relative to nondemocracies: a stability advantage, a credibility advantage, and a reliability advantage.

2.3 The Stability Advantage

Between 1930 and 1976, six military coups interrupted brief periods of democratic rule in Argentina. Throughout this era, political instability created volatile economic conditions. In the final coup d'état in 1976, a right-wing military dictatorship overthrew Isabel Perón, who presided over Argentina after the death of her husband Juan Perón. The Peróns were left-wing populists whose support was concentrated in Argentina's lower and middle classes. After ousting Perón, the military dictatorship began a systematic campaign of state-sponsored terror. This dark period of Argentinian politics, known as La Guerra Suecia or the Dirty War, resulted in the death and disappearance of tens of thousands of political dissidents who opposed the Argentine dictatorship.[35]

The right-wing military juntas that ruled Argentina from 1976 to 1983 differed on many dimensions from the left-wing Peronistas, including in their foreign policy. Unlike their predecessors, they supported other right-wing dictatorships in Latin America and maintained close relations with the U.S. government, which endorsed the 1976 coup d'état.[36] Reflecting conservative, neoliberal economic principles, the junta pursued free market economic policies that increased Argentina's foreign debt.[37] And, in 1982, the junta embarked on a misguided land grab, invading the British-owned Falklands Island off the Argentine coast. Many researchers characterize the Falklands War as a diversionary conflict, intended to distract from economic and political problems in Argentina.[38]

After the UK defeated Argentina in the Falklands War, mounting social and economic unrest, coupled with international scrutiny of the dictatorship's human rights violations, put increasing pressure on the military junta, which lost power in 1983. Since then, three political parties in Argentina have held

---

35. Brennan 2018.
36. Osorio 2021.
37. Munck 1985.
38. Oakes 2012. Although, see Fravel 2010.

the presidency.[39] These parties differ in terms of their economic and foreign policy preferences. However, democratic transition in Argentina brought considerable stability to the country's foreign policy relative to the previous era. The contrast between these periods in Argentina's history illustrates a stability advantage that democracies have relative to nondemocracies.

The first advantage democracies have in foreign affairs is that they maintain relatively stable foreign policies. By relatively stable, I mean that foreign policy in democracies does not tend to abruptly shift. We understand this pattern based on studies that analyze the relationship between regime type and foreign policy positioning over time.[40] Although leadership turnover in democracies is more frequent than in autocracies, leadership changes are regularized.[41] Democratic leaders are less likely to be removed through irregular means such as a military coup, assassination, or exile.[42] This is important because leaders who anticipate an unpleasant fate upon removal from power engage in more volatile policymaking. Desperate autocrats may attempt to stave off domestic challengers by continuing a conflict abroad or initiating new conflicts.[43] But, in healthy democracies with contested elections, leadership turnover is inevitable. Democracies expect future turnover and can work to minimize the uncertainty that accompanies leadership transitions.

The stability advantage arises in part because, in democracies, the foreign policy preferences of major parties tend to be quite similar. Why? Both vertical and horizontal constraints in democracies work to keep foreign policy consistent. Vertical constraints shape the foreign policy preferences of political parties and their respective candidates in two key ways. First, in many democracies, electoral accountability tends to make parties pursue policies consistent with the "median voter" in the electorate. In his famous article, "An Economic Theory of Political Action in Democracy," Anthony Downs builds on theories of group decision-making to develop a spatial theory of voting.[44] In this conception, we can think about ideological positions of political parties arrayed on a single dimension, such as a right–left or conservative–liberal spectrum. Each voter has their own position on the ideological spectrum,

---

39. At the time of writing, these three parties were Unión Civica Radical, Partido Justicialista, and Propuesta Republicana.
40. Leeds and Mattes 2022; Mattes, Leeds, and Carroll 2015; Smith 2016.
41. Riker 1982; Gaubatz 1996.
42. Goemans, Gleditsch, and Chiozza 2009.
43. Chiozza and Goemans 2011; Goemans 2000.
44. Downs 1957. See also Black 1948; Hotelling 1929.

referred to as their ideal point. Voters select the party whose positions are closest (i.e., most similar) to their ideal point. If parties are competing for a majority of votes, under certain assumptions, they tend to converge toward the ideal point of the median voter in the electorate. This insight, referred to as the median voter theorem or the median voter model, applies most directly to two-party, winner-take-all democratic systems.

Although much research in political science introduces complications to the median voter model, the central implication is straightforward. In democracies with competitive elections, candidates vying for nationwide office have few incentives to run on a platform that reflects extreme views that are dissimilar from those of the median voter. If foreign policy is salient for electoral politics, successive democratic leaders in the same country over time are unlikely to adopt radically different foreign policy preferences.

Second, and closely related, vertical constraints make democratic leaders more likely to pursue foreign policies that provide public goods. In their book *The Logic of Political Survival*, a group of four political scientists—Bruce Bueno de Mesquita, Alastair Smith, Randolph Siverson, and James Morrow—introduce the concept of *selectorate theory* to explain how electoral accountability results in better foreign policy outcomes in democracies relative to autocracies.[45] Selectorate theory starts with the premise that leaders or parties from all regime types wish to remain in power. However, regime types differ in the size of their selectorate (the total population involved in selecting a leader) and the size of their winning coalition (the subset of the selectorate needed for a leader to maintain power). In autocracies, leaders must appease a small group of supporters to maintain political control. For example, an autocrat may need to co-opt other political elites in order to dissuade them from staging a coup. But, in democracies, leaders need to secure the support of a majority or plurality of the electorate. To do so, they pursue policies that benefit a large portion of the selectorate. Bueno de Mesquita and coauthors explain that because democratic leaders are accountable to a large group of people rather than a small group of elites, they are better at providing public goods.

The logic of selectorate theory explains why democratic leaders are less beholden to special interests relative to autocrats when they make foreign policy.[46] When making trade policy, for example, democracies tend to pursue economic openness and international cooperation because reducing barriers

45. Bueno de Mesquita et al. 2002.
46. McGillivray and Smith 2008; Bobick and Smith 2013.

to trade improves national welfare overall.[47] If leaders only needed to appease a small winning coalition to stay in power, they might enact protectionist policies that advantage their core supporters. When a new autocrat comes to power with different core supporters, foreign policy will shift dramatically. In their book *Punishing the Prince*, Fiona McGillivray and Alastair Smith draw on selectorate theory to explain how foreign policy remains consistent in democracies despite leadership turnover.[48] The researchers demonstrate across many issues—including crisis bargaining, trade, and sovereign debt— that leadership turnover in democracies tends to have little impact on foreign relations.

Beyond vertical constraints, horizontal constraints also reinforce stability in democratic foreign policy. Recall that a key horizontal constraint in democracies is the presence of an active political opposition. In healthy democracies, politicians know that their political party will not remain in power in perpetuity. How parties behave when they are in power will have implications for how they are treated by political opponents who assume leadership positions in the future.

Political economist Alberto Alesina formalizes this logic.[49] His model begins with a political system in which two parties compete for the median voter. Without the expectation of future elections, political parties have an incentive to campaign on a moderate policy platform but, once elected, "defect" by implementing their preferred, more extreme policy. In this scenario, parties are unable to credibly commit to a more moderate policy. However, Alesina argues that the expectation of future elections can induce parties to cooperate by creating a "partisan truce" in which both parties commit to, and implement, the moderate policy that benefits society as a whole. One example Alesina uses is monetary policy. Since parties expect future electoral cycles, they tend to avoid manipulating monetary policy to spur economic growth in advance of an upcoming election. Instead, they create nonpartisan institutions, like independent central banks, to govern monetary policy. This tacit cooperation prevents economic volatility and benefits the public.

Other researchers, like political scientist Joanne Gowa, point out that a similar partisan truce exists in national security.[50] If there were no future

---

47. Mansfield, Milner, and Rosendorff 2002.
48. McGillivray and Smith 2008.
49. Alesina 1987, 1988.
50. Gowa 1998.

elections, parties might try to increase public support by initiating international disputes. Disputes could create a "rally round the flag" effect, boosting an incumbent's popularity during a security crisis.[51] But, using data from the United States, Gowa finds no correlation between presidential election years and entrance into international disputes. She concludes that these results are "consistent with the existence of a tacit partisan truce, a self-enforcing agreement between the parties to abstain from using force abroad to prosecute political battles at home."[52] In other words, the inevitability of future leadership constrains the actions of the leader in power and the opposition party.

Tacit partisan cooperation can be uniquely beneficial in foreign affairs. For one, good foreign policymaking requires long time horizons. Since international politics does not stop when leaders exit office, politicians must prepare for foreign policies to extend beyond their term. Successful foreign policymaking also requires substantial technical expertise. To make strategic decisions, leaders rely on experts who are deeply knowledgeable about other countries and maintain relationships with foreign leaders.

Recognizing the necessity of insulating foreign policy from domestic partisan pressures, politicians invest in nonpartisan institutions that create continuity in foreign policy. These include ministries and agencies that manage diplomatic relations with other countries and are substantially staffed by career civil servants.[53] They also include defense agencies and professional militaries whose day-to-day operations are unaffected by leader turnover. And they include intelligence agencies like the Central Intelligence Agency in the United States, the Australian Secret Intelligence Service, and the Bundesnachrichtendienst in Germany, which collect and analyze information about national security issues. Well-designed national security bureaucracies facilitate better foreign policy decision-making.[54] In liberal democracies, many of these institutions act as another horizontal constraint on executive power and are considered above the fray of traditional partisan politicking.

51. Mueller 1970, 20.
52. Gowa 1998, 307.
53. Some foreign ministries, like the UK's Foreign, Commonwealth & Development Office and the Japanese Ministry of Foreign Affairs, for instance, are managed by career civil servants. Others, like the U.S. State Department and the French Ministry for Europe and Foreign Affairs, are run by political appointees, but career civil servants make up a significant portion of the daily functioning of the agencies.
54. Jost 2024.

Together, both vertical and horizontal constraints contribute to a stability advantage by keeping the foreign policies of democracies consistent over time. Vertical constraints contribute to foreign policy stability by inducing responsiveness to a median voter, deterring democratic politicians from taking extreme foreign policy positions. Vertical constraints also keep democratic leaders accountable to the electorate as a whole rather than to particular interest groups. Horizontal constraints contribute to the stability advantage by giving the executive and opposition parties incentives to uphold a tacit partisan truce in foreign policy. The inevitable alternation of power in democracies keeps foreign policy positions of the parties consistent and provides incentives for politicians to invest in nonpartisan institutions integral to foreign policymaking. The lack of similar constraints in autocracies means that irregular leader turnover in these countries in theory produces more volatile foreign policy.

2.3.1 Polarization and the Erosion of Democratic Stability

How, then, does extreme polarization affect the stability advantage? I argue that, as polarization becomes more extreme, it interacts with both sets of democratic constraints to create different dynamics that, on average, lead to more volatility in foreign policy when the party controlling the executive switches.

Consider first how polarization interacts with vertical constraints. In theory, electoral accountability should induce politicians to compete over a median voter and provide public goods that maximize national welfare. But, in highly polarized contexts, vertical constraints may not necessarily give politicians these same incentives. For one, extreme polarization can make politicians more likely to appeal to an ideologically extreme base of core supporters rather than to a median voter in the electorate. To understand this logic, consider the distinction between two strategies that political parties use when campaigning. On the one hand, a party can opt to mobilize its base by targeting members of the electorate who are already likely to support that party with the goal of increasing turnout among its supporters. On the other hand, a party can canvas broadly with the goal of persuading potential voters who do not already support the party to vote for its candidate.

In heavily polarized democratic systems, a strategy focused on mobilization becomes more appealing to candidates than a strategy focused on persuasion. Cross-national analyses of polarization and election campaigns show that parties in more polarized democracies have fewer incentives to canvas broadly.[55] In these contexts, persuading voters to abandon their ideological commitments to vote for a different party becomes difficult. Parties instead focus on messaging that energizes their core supporters or special interests associated with their party rather than on messages crafted to appeal to a median voter.

Shifting messaging strategies in contemporary U.S. presidential campaigns reflect this dynamic. In the United States, partisan sorting within the electorate resulted in greater coherence between ideology and partisan identity.[56] For national elections, it is now increasingly difficult to persuade voters to vote for candidates from the opposing party. Experimental research on election outcomes shows that it is very challenging for political campaigns to convince voters to change their minds.[57] At times, persuasive campaigning can even backfire.[58]

In lieu of tailoring policies toward a median voter, candidates may opt for messaging that energizes and mobilizes their political base. In foreign policy, this messaging sometimes includes controversial or divisive statements. In the 2016 U.S. presidential election, for example, Republican candidate Donald Trump made fiery rhetoric about China a centerpiece of his campaign. While campaigning in Indiana, he exclaimed, "We can't continue to allow China to rape our country, and that's what we're doing. It's the greatest theft in the history of the world."[59] Trump used similar inflammatory language during national debates and election rallies to paint China as a major foreign threat and criticize their trade practices. Other Republican candidates followed suit.

Second, high levels of affective polarization in the public can fuel polarization on salient foreign policy issues, especially when these issues coincide with electoral cycles. This process could be considered a form of *conflict extension*, which occurs when party activists and ideologues extend partisan conflict into policy areas that were not previously politicized.[60] This can happen in affectively polarized settings, where politicians have electoral incentives to

55. Karp 2012. This is most likely in systems where voting is not compulsory and voter turnout is relatively low. See, e.g., Karp and Banducci 2007.
56. Levendusky 2009.
57. Kalla and Broockman 2018.
58. Bailey, Hopkins, and Rodgers 2016.
59. BBC News 2016.
60. Layman and Carsey 2002; Layman et al. 2010.

strongly disagree with (or even to mock or deride) positions championed by the opposite party. It could be especially tempting for politicians to manipulate public opinion in foreign policy, where the electorate tends to have less information relative to domestic policy.[61]

Of course, some foreign policy issues are more prone to politicization than others. Areas of foreign policy linked to both social and partisan identities are among those most vulnerable to polarization. Consider, for example, the politicization of foreign policy that followed the rise of the Bharatiya Janata Party (BJP), a right-wing Hindu party, in Indian politics. After the 1947 partition of India and Pakistan, the relatively centrist Indian National Congress (known as the Congress Party) dominated Indian politics for decades. In the 1980s, the BJP emerged as a Hindu nationalist party against a backdrop of growing sectarian violence between Hindus and Muslims. The BJP won a majority of the Lok Sabha, the lower house of the Indian Parliament, in the 2014 national elections, and the leader of the campaign, Narendra Modi, became prime minister.

Prime Minister Modi's ascent is associated with increased social and political polarization in India.[62] As polarization grew, national security policy also became more politicized. Hindu nationalism shaped the BJP's counterterrorism policies and more hawkish stance toward its neighbor Pakistan, a Muslim-majority country. A report published by the Carnegie Endowment for International Peace warned about politicization of security issues in India, which are "discussed in hyper-nationalistic rhetorical terms. For instance, the BJP and the Congress Party respectively wield terms like 'jihadi terror' and 'Hindu terror' to try to cast their opponents in the worst light possible."[63]

Such examples illustrate how vertical constraints are unlikely to moderate political leaders in a highly polarized democracy. Instead, responsiveness to a partisan public may make politicians more likely to take extreme positions and to instrumentalize negative partisanship in foreign affairs. Even if foreign policy is not central to a country's main political cleavage, foreign policy issues that become salient in a polarized context can be politicized when championed by a partisan figure or group. These attitudes should in theory be reflected in public opinion polling. As chapter 4 will explore, some issues in foreign affairs are more susceptible to politicization than others. But, overall,

61. Zaller 1992; Guisinger and Saunders 2017.
62. Masih and Slater 2019.
63. Sahoo 2020, 17.

we should expect greater foreign policy divergence to follow from extreme polarization as partisan conflict extends to foreign affairs.

Stability Hypothesis 1: *As polarization becomes more extreme, domestic partisan conflict is more likely to extend into foreign affairs.*

Extreme polarization also impacts the horizontal constraints that contribute to the stability advantage. In nonpolarized contexts, the inevitability of party turnover can induce a partisan truce between the opposition and executive parties in foreign affairs.[64] Given the importance of long time horizons in foreign policymaking, parties have incentives both to not implement extreme policies and to invest in institutions that keep foreign policy relatively nonpartisan. As polarization becomes more extreme, however, short-term political incentives outweigh long-term considerations. Two processes in particular contribute to the erosion of the partisan truce in foreign affairs.

For one, politicians that hold more ideologically extreme positions have more reasons to defect from a partisan truce by campaigning on and enacting extreme foreign policies. These incentives could come from increases in affective polarization and negative partisanship, which make politicians eager to differentiate themselves from the opposite party. They could also come from deeply held ideological commitments, which manifest to varying degrees in aspects of foreign affairs. In Hungary, popular discontent with the leadership of the left-wing Hungarian Socialist Party led to the rise of right-wing Fidesz under Viktor Orbán in 2010. Prime Minister Orbán's conservative values and populist tendencies are reflected in his foreign policy positions: he held more anti-immigrant and Euroskeptical views relative to his predecessors. Once in office, Orbán acted on these policy positions, reshaping the nature of Hungary's foreign relations by strengthening relations with China and Russia relative to the EU.

Another way politicians could erode the partisan truce in foreign affairs is by politicizing foreign policy institutions. In extremely polarized societies, attacks on nonpartisan government institutions, including foreign policy institutions like defense agencies and intelligence agencies, become more common.[65] If an incumbent leader perceives an ostensibly nonpartisan institution to be aligned with the opposition party, they may relentlessly criticize the

---

64. See, e.g., Alesina 1987, 1988; Gowa 1998.

65. While not the focus of this book, a similar argument can be made about the politicization of nonstate institutions that constrain executive power, such as the media and civil society.

institution or use it as a scapegoat for foreign policy failures. If instead the institution is aligned with the executive party, it may be politicized in the process of helping a leader entrench their power.

One example of this is growing concern about the politicization of defense agencies and militaries in highly polarized societies. In an ideal liberal democracy, professionalized militaries are nonpartisan; they are not solely aligned with one leader or political party. It is no coincidence, however, that many polarized countries have fraught civil–military relations. Consider the case of Venezuela under left-wing Presidents Hugo Chávez and Nicolás Maduro of the United Socialist Party of Venezuela. During their respective presidential administrations, Venezuelan politics was sharply polarized along socioeconomic lines, reflecting support for, or opposition to, Chávez's socialist policies.[66] Chávez took a number of steps that politicized the military. In reorganizing Venezuela's armed forces, the distinction between the military and other domestic state security institutions was blurred. Chávez displayed favoritism by promoting officers who expressed loyalty to his administration.[67] He also increased the visibility of military officers holding prestigious political positions, including positions in the president's cabinet.[68]

While Venezuela poses an extreme case, researchers are concerned that polarization could undermine civil–military relations in democracies. In the United States, for example, politicization of the military and the defense establishment may undermine its credibility as a nonpartisan institution.[69] In *Thanks for Your Service*, political scientist Peter Feaver explains that the combination of high public confidence in the U.S. military and a polarized public makes it tempting for political leaders to politicize the military for partisan gain.[70] These examples suggest that in a polarized climate, as the stakes of winning increase, parties have fewer incentives to maintain a tacit partisan truce in foreign policy. Short-term incentives for political gain outweigh longer-term considerations about the stability of foreign policy. Politicians enact more ideologically extreme policies that energize their core supporters

66. Pilar, García-Guadilla, and Mallen 2019.
67. Trinkunas 2022.
68. Perera 2019.
69. See, e.g., concerns raised by scholars of civil–military relations: Beliakova 2021; Brooks 2020; Feaver 2023b; Golby 2021; Krebs, Ralston, and Rapport 2023; Lee 2022; Robinson 2022.
70. Feaver 2023b.

and may resort to politicization of nonpartisan foreign policy institutions to their political advantage.

Stability Hypothesis 2: *As polarization becomes more extreme, politicians are more likely to politicize the foreign policy bureaucracy.*

In extremely polarized societies, changing preferences of both the public and politicians undermine the stability advantage. By definition, as ideological polarization increases, political parties are more inclined to disagree on policy. Yet, even when there are sharp disagreements on domestic policy, foreign affairs may still be insulated from the partisan divide. What differs about environments of extreme polarization is that the effects of affective and ideological polarization compound and reinforce one another. In such contexts, partisan conflict is more likely to extend to foreign policy.

Affective polarization further gives politicians incentives to campaign on reversing policies of the opposite party to mobilize their core supporters. In some instances, they may activate social identities that link to foreign affairs. The BJP's linking of Hindu nationalism to counterterrorism policies and heightened tensions with Pakistan is one such example of this. In the United States, issues like trade, aid, and immigration for which attitudes are correlated both with partisan identity and other forms of social identity are more likely to be susceptible to this dynamic.

In theory, nonpartisan institutions should help to stabilize foreign policy, in much the same way that independent central banks stabilize macroeconomic policy in democracies. These institutions should operate outside the realm of party politics, fostering continuity in policy across successive administrations. In environments of extreme polarization, however, these nonpartisan institutions are not immune to politicization. In fact, they may be especially attractive targets for enterprising politicians.

The weakening of vertical and horizontal constraints on executive power means that, in the long run, we should observe greater divergence in foreign policy preferences in extremely polarized democracies. These patterns should contribute to more changes in foreign affairs across successive executives. To be clear, policy change is itself not a bad thing. However, the volatility in foreign policymaking that originates from partisan politics can be problematic in multiple respects. In *Volatile States in International Politics*, political scientist Eleonora Mattiacci explains how volatility—the combination of change and inconsistency—is shaped by various domestic groups competing for

TABLE 2.1. Polarization and the erosion of democratic stability

	Ideal-type democracy	**Highly polarized democracy**
Vertical constraints	The public is more likely to reward politicians for taking foreign policy positions consistent with the median voter and enacting policies that provide public goods. Domestic partisan conflict is less likely to extend into foreign affairs.	The public is more likely to reward co-partisan politicians for taking ideologically extreme positions and reversing policies of an opposing party. Domestic partisan conflict is more likely to extend into foreign affairs.
Horizontal constraints	Politicians are more likely to maintain a tacit "partisan truce" in foreign policy. They are more likely to cooperate with opposing parties, pursue moderate foreign policies, and invest in institutions that maintain continuity in foreign affairs.	Politicians are less likely to maintain a tacit "partisan truce" in foreign policy. They are more likely to take extreme positions on foreign policy issues and to politicize the foreign policy bureaucracy for partisan gain.
Implication for democratic advantage	Democracies are more likely to display stability in their foreign policymaking over time.	Democracies are less likely to display stability in their foreign policymaking over time.

influence in foreign affairs.[71] Mattiacci argues that volatility contributes to fear and crisis escalation in international politics. Volatility also undermines trust between allies and creates a broader sense of uncertainty about the direction of a country's foreign policy.

Table 2.1 outlines how polarization erodes the ability of democracies to maintain relatively stable foreign policies, which is explored in chapter 4. The

71. Mattiacci 2023.

first column of the table explains how systems of constraint, and the corresponding democratic advantages, function in an ideal-type liberal democracy with low to moderate levels of polarization, which is the relevant counterfactual or point of comparison for this study. The second column shows what happens in an extremely polarized country, with high levels of both affective and ideological polarization.

Stability Hypothesis 3: *As polarization becomes more extreme, democracies are less likely to display stability in their foreign policymaking over time.*

2.4 The Credibility Advantage

In 1898, British troops marched up the Nile River toward an Egyptian village called Fashoda. Their aim was to build a railway through the African continent. When the British arrived, however, they encountered quite a surprise: a French military force beat them to Fashoda. The small village became the unexpected site of an international diplomatic crisis. The French force demanded concessions in order to leave the area, while the British refused to concede.

Back in England, the prime minister Lord Salisbury emphasized the hard line the British would take in negotiations with the French. He released details about the incident to the public, stressing Britain's resolute position. In doing so, Lord Salisbury effectively tied his hands: he could not order British troops to back down without risking public outrage. After details of the incident were released, the main opposition party in the British Parliament, the Liberal Party, came out in support of the prime minister's position on the Fashoda Crisis. Since the Liberal Party had no incentive to collude with the prime minister, its support of Lord Salisbury's position was credible. It became clear to the French that the British did not intend to compromise. Not willing to risk a full-fledged war, the French army withdrew its troops from Fashoda, effectively ending the crisis.[72]

Political scientist Kenneth Schultz drew attention to the Fashoda Crisis as a crucial example of how effective democracies can be in communicating their resolve in international politics.[73] Schultz's research emphasizes a second advantage democracies have relative to nondemocracies: a credibility

---

72. Schultz 2001b.
73. Schultz 2001b.

advantage in signaling information to their adversaries in international relations. In general, when countries negotiate over issues in international politics, they have incentives to misrepresent their position in order to gain a more favorable deal.[74] Leaders may bluff by saying they are unwilling to compromise on their stance when in fact compromise is possible. These incentives make it challenging to credibly communicate information to foreign counterparts. Democracies, however, have institutional features that make it hard for democratic leaders to bluff, which makes their word more credible relative to autocrats.[75]

There are many uses of the term "credibility" in international relations. Here, I am interested in credibility of signals sent to other actors—especially foreign adversaries—in international politics. These signals come in the form of threats or promises directed at other countries. There are also a lot of implications of the credibility advantage.[76] This book focuses on two implications. First, democracies are better able to issue credible threats and signal their resolve to their adversaries in the context of an international crisis. Second, democracies are better able to credibly express their positions in international negotiations, giving them greater leverage in the negotiation process.

A first implication of the credibility advantage is that democracies are better able to issue credible threats because systems of vertical and horizontal constraints make them accountable to domestic actors. Vertical constraints make leaders accountable to the public. The logic of *audience costs* assumes that leaders are punished by their publics for not following through on their word.[77] When a democratic leader escalates a dispute and then backs down, we anticipate they will be penalized electorally.[78] The anticipation of audience costs prevents democratic leaders from bluffing, or issuing threats that they do not intend to follow through. As a result, the threats that are issued by democracies should in theory be more credible.

74. Fearon 1995.
75. Fearon 1994; Schultz 2001a.
76. For example, an implication of the credibility advantage that is not a focus of this book is that it allows democracies to resolve disputes peacefully with one another. Institutional features that make democracies more transparent and credible can mitigate information problems that contribute to the onset of war. See, e.g., Schultz 1999, 2001a.
77. Fearon 1994; Smith 1998.
78. Kertzer and Brutger 2016; Levendusky and Horowitz 2012; Levy et al. 2015; Tomz 2007.

But democratic leaders have additional tools to enhance the credibility of their threats. One thing they can do is to leverage the agreement of domestic actors like the public and the political opposition. Because democratic leaders are vertically constrained, foreign observers know that leaders care about public opinion on important foreign policy decisions. During times of crisis, strong public rallies around decision-makers are visible to foreign adversaries. Leaders can wield public displays of support to deter potential challengers or signal resolve.

Democratic leaders can also leverage horizontal constraints to increase the credibility of their threats. A key insight from Kenneth Schultz is that the political opposition gives democracies an informational advantage relative to autocracies in crisis bargaining.[79] In *Democracy and Coercive Diplomacy*, Schultz argues that domestic political opponents prevent democratic leaders from issuing threats they do not plan to carry out. Leaders fear that empty threats will have political repercussions.[80] As a result, democracies are more selective about the threats they make, which increases the credibility of the threats we observe. Schultz emphasizes that, when the political opposition agrees with a leader's crisis decision-making, this is a particularly credible signal. In Schultz's analysis of the Fashoda Crisis, the British appeared resolved to the French because the opposition party (the Liberal Party) supported Lord Salisbury's position.[81] This example suggests that democratic leaders can leverage agreement between the executive and the opposition to enhance the credibility of their threats in a crisis.

Interestingly, in other contexts, democratic leaders may also be able to leverage *disagreement* between domestic actors to improve policy outcomes. This relates to a second implication of the credibility advantage: domestic constraints can improve the negotiating position of democracies when they bargain with other countries. Economist Thomas Schelling articulates this intuition, referred to as the "Schelling conjecture,"[82] with application to U.S foreign policy in his book *The Strategy of Conflict*: "If the executive branch is free to negotiate the best arrangement it can, it may be unable to make any position stick and may end by conceding controversial points. . . . But, if the executive branch negotiates under legislative authority, with its position

---

79. Schultz 1998, 1999, 2001a.
80. Schultz 2001a.
81. Schultz 2001b.
82. Milner 1997.

constrained by the law ... then the executive branch has a firm position that is visible to its negotiating partners."[83]

Political scientist Robert Putnam formalized this logic by describing an international negotiation as a "two-level game."[84] At the first level, negotiators from different countries bargain with one another to construct an agreement. At the second level, domestic actors within each country choose whether or not to adopt the agreement. Putnam argues that the size of a country's domestic *win-set*—the set of international agreements that would be ratified by domestic actors—depends on its political institutions. Since democracies have more domestic constraints, they have a smaller win-set than autocracies. When negotiating with a foreign counterpart, a democratic leader can point to the visible position of the public or the political opposition in order to obtain an international agreement closer to their preferred outcome. Since their hands are tied by domestic politics, democratic leaders can credibly say, "This deal would be unacceptable to the public" or "The opposition won't agree to ratify this treaty." Given that autocrats do not face similar constraints, they have less leverage than their democratic counterparts. Much subsequent work explores the conditions under which democracies negotiate more or less effectively based on the policy preferences of parties, legislatures, and other domestic actors.[85]

To illustrate how this leverage works in practice, political scientists Howard Lehman and Jennifer McCoy detail negotiations of a 1988 agreement between the Brazilian government and its international creditors to restructure Brazil's debt.[86] During the negotiations, Brazil was in the midst of a democratic transition. The combination of crippling debt and fledgling democratic institutions created huge challenges for Brazilian President José Sarney. As inflation skyrocketed, domestic pressure on President Sarney prompted him to declare a moratorium on interest payments to creditors. International banks retaliated with sanctions to pressure Brazil into restarting payments. But, over time, the Brazilian government was able to lift the moratorium and achieve an agreement that was relatively favorable to Brazil. How? Commercial banks recognized that it would not be politically feasible for President Sarney to accept

83. Schelling 1960, 28.
84. Putnam 1988.
85. Friedrichs 2022; Mayer 1992; Mo 1995; Milner and Rosendorff 1996, 1997; Milner 1999; Tarar 2001.
86. Lehman and McCoy 1992.

harsh austerity measures. In fact, Brazil's leverage came from the fact that the Sarney administration was so constrained domestically. Lehman and McCoy argue that, in this instance, Brazilian negotiators were able to "manipulat[e] the perception of domestic weakness and turmoil to their advantage in negotiations with creditors, especially in the context of a transition to democratic politics."[87] Had Brazil remained an autocracy, the researchers posit that the final agreement would have been much less favorable to Brazil.

These examples show that the constraints democratic leaders face at home can make the information they reveal in international politics more credible. Accountability to the public and the political opposition deters leaders from bluffing in international politics. Leaders are also able to leverage both support and dissent from domestic actors when they bargain with foreign adversaries. During international crises, when domestic actors set aside partisan politics and support the leader's decision-making, this provides a clear signal of resolve to adversaries. Democratic leaders can also leverage more moderate forms of domestic disagreement; they credibly indicate that their hands are tied by domestic politics when negotiating international agreements. In theory, the credibility advantage makes it easier for democracies to negotiate effectively and ensures the threats they issue will be taken seriously, making them more formidable adversaries overall.

2.4.1 Polarization and the Erosion of Democratic Credibility

Extreme polarization diminishes the credibility advantage by making it more difficult for democracies to signal information to adversaries. In highly polarized environments, a democratic leaders's credibility may be undermined because major internal disagreements within their country are also visible to foreign rivals. To understand how polarization jeopardizes democratic credibility, first consider how polarization interacts with vertical constraints. In a nonpolarized context, vertical constraints provide leaders with incentives to make decisions in foreign policy that appeal to broad sections of the electorate. Polarization itself does not necessarily weaken this electoral accountability. In fact, some degree of party cohesion is essential so that voters can hold parties accountable for policy outcomes. But, as polarization becomes more extreme, the nature of vertical constraints changes in important ways.

---

87. Lehman and McCoy 1992, 640.

For one, partisans in a highly polarized society become increasingly distrustful of an out-party leader and, by extension, their foreign policy decision-making. Successful foreign policy hinges on the assumption that a democratic leader acts in the best interest of the general public to maximize national welfare. A strong degree of trust in the executive is uniquely important in foreign affairs. Relative to domestic policy, in foreign policy, leaders have much more of an information advantage and more autonomy to execute decisions. For democratic leaders to be able to effectively leverage public support in an international crisis, the public must trust their leader's decision-making. But, in societies characterized both by ideological and affective polarization, a partisan public will be skeptical of the values and policies of a leader from an opposing party. Strong partisans will be especially likely to be biased in their evaluations of a leader's policy response, engaging in what is widely known as politically motivated reasoning.[88] This means that a more polarized public will be less likely to rally behind the leader and support their policy response in a time of crisis. As a consequence, leaders will struggle to leverage support from their domestic publics to signal resolve.

Since 2010, Israel has faced sharply increasing levels of political polarization, including on national security issues. One of the hallmarks of Israeli prime minister Benjamin Netanyahu's foreign policy is his hawkish stance toward Iran. While supporters of Netanyahu's conservative Likud Party tend to agree with the prime minister's characterization of the Iranian threat, some supporters of other parties question whether Netanyahu exaggerates the threat for political gain.[89] In 2022, Bloomberg News published an op-ed entitled, "Some Israelis Are More Scared of Netanyahu Than Iran," highlighting skepticism of Netanyahu's foreign policy among Israeli voters on the left.[90] If a new crisis were to arise between Iran and Israel, partisans who distrust Netanyahu's judgment may be unlikely to support his policy response.

In extremely polarized societies, the nature of electoral accountability also changes by more closely tying individual assessments of politicians to the

---

88. On politically motivated reasoning see, e.g., Guay and Johnston 2022; Kraft, Lodge, and Taber 2015; Leeper and Slothuus 2014; Lodge and Taber 2013. For examples of motivated reasoning in public opinion on foreign policy see, e.g., Gaines et al. 2007; Kertzer, Rathbun, and Rathbun 2020.

89. Leslie 2022.

90. Chafets 2022.

performance of their party. Politicians are rewarded for their party's wins and benefit from the other party's failures. This dynamic can be driven both by ideological and affective polarization. Where the public is more ideologically polarized on certain foreign policy issues, they are more committed to their preferred policies. As a consequence, they will be more favorable toward co-partisan politicians who try to prevent leaders from the opposite party from enacting their own policies. Likewise, where the public is more affectively polarized, they will be more likely to see losses for the opposing party as "wins" for their own party. As both ideological and affective polarization grow, the public will both be more likely to distrust leaders from the opposite party and reward members of their own party for obstructing those leaders.

> Credibility Hypothesis 1A: *As polarization becomes more extreme, the public is less likely to trust the foreign policy decision-making of leaders from an opposing party.*

> Credibility Hypothesis 1B: *As polarization becomes more extreme, the public is more likely to reward co-partisan politicians for obstructing leaders from an opposing party.*

These incentives have implications for horizontal constraints, or how the opposition party or coalition constrains the executive. In a highly polarized society, partisan competition increasingly becomes zero sum. Political wins become not only policy successes of one's own party, but also failures of the out-party. In foreign policy, this means that an executive's opponents reap benefits from strongly criticizing or obstructing the executive. A more polarized public gives the opposition party incentives to ensure that the executive is less successful in enacting its foreign policy agenda.

In the United States, this phenomenon is well documented by congressional scholars, who detail the institutional changes that have increased congressional polarization since the 1990s.[91] In *Beyond Ideology*, for example, political scientist Frances Lee provides evidence for teamsmanship dynamics in the Senate, including in foreign affairs.[92] She shows that contemporary patterns of Senate polarization cannot merely be explained by growing ideological differences between Republicans and Democrats. In an analysis of congressional roll-call votes, Lee distinguishes between votes with ideological

---

91. Cox and McCubbins 1993, 2005; Lee 2009; Theriault 2008.
92. Lee 2009.

content and procedural votes with nonideological content. She demonstrates that while votes related to ideological issues have become more polarized, there has also been remarkable party cohesion on nonideological issues. This teamsmanship dynamic is reinforced by institutions within Congress and by an affectively polarized public.[93]

Affective polarization and teamsmanship dynamics are neither specific to the United States nor to the current historical moment. Chapter 1, for instance, discussed one of the more extreme historical cases of polarization in 1930s France. During the 1936 election, which resulted in the election of the first socialist prime minister, Léon Blum, a slogan adopted by right-wing French leaders—"Better Hitler Than Blum"—implied that foreign occupation by Nazi Germany might be preferable to left-wing leadership in France.[94] As foreign policy polarizes, political parties may have fundamentally different relationships with foreign adversaries. In the most extreme cases, like in 1930s France, a deeply polarized society could lead politicians to be more favorable toward a foreign adversary than a domestic political opponent. In practice, of course, such cases are very rare. Instead, we might expect that a polarized environment leads politicians to focus on preventing "wins" from the other side. This could include attempts to obstruct the other side through grandstanding and criticizing how a leader handles a crisis or a negotiation with a foreign adversary.

Credibility Hypothesis 2A: *As polarization becomes more extreme, politicians are less likely to defer to a leader from an opposing party in times of crisis.*

Credibility Hypothesis 2B: *As polarization becomes more extreme, politicians are more likely to consistently oppose or actively undermine leaders from an opposing party in foreign policy.*

How does polarization affect the credibility advantage? In brief, it reshapes the strategic incentives of the political opposition in crisis bargaining and international negotiations. In ideal liberal democracies with more moderate levels of polarization, during a security crisis the position of the domestic opposition can be informative in democracies. A threat issued by the executive and backed by the opposition is highly credible.[95] During times of crisis, we

---

93. Abramowitz 2010; Abramowitz and Webster 2016; Iyengar, Sood, and Lelkes 2012; Mason 2015; Rogowski and Sutherland 2016; Iyengar et al. 2019.
94. Richards 2006.
95. Schultz 2001a.

expect opposition parties to recognize the gravity of the issue at stake and set partisan politics aside. This is why, traditionally, the opposition party supports or defers to the executive during national security crises.[96]

However, in extremely polarized contexts, the opposition virtually always has incentives to disagree with the executive. In extreme cases, national security crises are not immune from this problem. The credibility advantage that comes from presenting a unified front to a foreign adversary is diminished. In practice, it becomes difficult for both the executive and the adversary to interpret disagreement by the opposition party. Does criticism from the opposition reflect sincere preferences or is it political posturing?[97] Is distrust of how an out-party executive is handling a crisis warranted or not? In a highly partisan environment, signals from the opposition that may be informative to an adversary in a nonpolarized context may be uninformative at best and could sow even greater confusion at worst.

Analysts are concerned, for example, about how political polarization in South Korea could impact its ability to be viewed as a credible adversary by North Korea. In the 2022 presidential election, the two primary parties in South Korea—the right-wing People Power Party and the left-wing Democratic Party—espoused very different positions on North Korea policy. The People Power Party favored a much more hawkish stance toward North Korea. In the election, the People Power Party's candidate, Yoon Suk Yeol, narrowly defeated the presidential candidate from the incumbent Democratic Party. Commentators worried that, if a crisis were to arise on the Korean peninsula, leadership from the two parties would be unable to agree on an appropriate response. Heightened polarization could also diminish presidential accountability by eroding audience costs. Dong Joon Park argued, for example, that if President Yoon's supporters were unlikely to hold him accountable for issuing empty threats, the threats he issued would be viewed as less credible by North Korean leader Kim Jong Un.[98] Park explained that such dynamics could exacerbate tensions on the Korean peninsula by increasing the likelihood that North Korean leadership would provoke South Korea to test the president's resolve.

---

96. Brody 1991.

97. This logic parallels the insight from Kreps, Saunders, and Schultz (2018) that polarization can make it difficult to distinguish between partisan bias and hawkishness among legislators when ratifying arms control agreements.

98. Park 2022.

Extreme polarization also poses problems for international negotiations.[99] In principle, the fact that democratic leaders are constrained in international negotiations should work to their advantage: they can credibly say that an agreement will not be ratified without buy-in from the political opposition. This implies that, at low to moderate levels of polarization, democracies are advantaged when negotiating with nondemocratic adversaries. Yet, in highly polarized settings, the probability of any zone of agreement between the executive and the opposition becomes significantly less likely in the first place. Once again, this divergence may arise from ideological disagreements over the foreign policy issue at stake. But it can also arise from teamsmanship dynamics or from electoral incentives rooted in an affectively polarized public.

Irrespective of how partisan divergence arises, at its extremes there are multiple possible implications for international negotiations. For one, if negotiations are ongoing, extreme polarization can increase the likelihood that they will collapse or that an agreement will fail to be ratified. A high degree of polarization can also prevent negotiations from occurring at all. Anticipating dissent from the political opposition, leaders may believe they do not have the political capital required to initiate a complex negotiation with a foreign adversary. In the United States, Republican President Donald Trump withdrew the United States from the Joint Comprehensive Plan of Action (JCPOA), an agreement addressing Iran's nuclear program, in 2018. Democratic presidential candidate Joe Biden pledged during his 2020 presidential campaign to rejoin the agreement. Once President Biden took office in 2021, however, renewed attempts to negotiate quickly faltered. The combination of shifting politics in Iran and the politicization of U.S.–Iranian relations in Washington complicated diplomatic negotiations. By July 2021, the *New York Times* reported that "whatever deal [the Biden administration] strikes will be a political problem in Washington."[100] The following year, a White House spokesperson confirmed the deal had been all but abandoned, noting, "The JCPOA is not our focus right now. It's not on the agenda."[101]

This discussion highlights how extreme polarization can make it more difficult to respond to an adversary in a unified manner during a security crisis.

---

99. Although this book focuses on how polarization affects democracy's credibility while negotiating with an adversary, other researchers have identified additional ways that polarization impacts international negotiations (see, e.g., Friedrichs 2022).

100. Sanger, Jakes, and Fassihi 2021.

101. Ravid and Nichols 2022.

TABLE 2.2. Polarization and the erosion of democratic credibility

	Ideal-type liberal democracy	Extremely polarized democracy
Vertical constraint	The public is more likely to trust the foreign policy decision-making of their elected leaders. They are more likely to reward politicians for making decisions that lead to good foreign policy outcomes.	The public is less likely to trust the foreign policy decision-making of leaders from an opposing party. They are more likely to reward co-partisan politicians for obstructing leaders from an opposing party.
Horizontal constraint	Politicians are more likely to rally behind a leader during times of crisis. They are likely to oppose leaders only when there is principled disagreement over foreign policy.	Politicians are less likely to defer to a leader from an opposing party during times of crisis. They are more likely to consistently oppose or actively undermine leaders from an opposing party in foreign policy.
Implication for democratic advantage	Democracies are more likely to send credible signals to adversaries in international negotiations and crisis bargaining.	Democracies are less likely to send credible signals to adversaries in international negotiations and crisis bargaining.

It can also make it challenging to effectively leverage partisan disagreement during a complex negotiation with a foreign adversary. As table 2.2 shows, these processes can erode the credibility advantage democracies have in foreign affairs. The second column of table 2.2 summarizes the hypotheses that will be tested in chapter 5.

Credibility Hypothesis 3: *As polarization becomes more extreme, democracies are less likely to send credible signals to adversaries in international negotiations and crisis bargaining.*

2.5 The Reliability Advantage

On February 7, 1992, in the Dutch city of Maastricht, representatives from twelve European countries signed an agreement that laid the foundation for the EU. The Maastricht Treaty spurred the integration of economic and security policy in Europe, paving the way for a shared currency and free movement of European citizens across national borders. There was much fanfare on the signing day. As one media outlet reported, "There were hussars and a band to welcome the dignitaries, glorious spring flowers everywhere, the Limburg Symphony Orchestra playing Mozart and, of course, a champagne reception and banquet."[102]

Despite the celebratory mood, the signatures themselves did not fully commit the countries to an agreement. Each country would need to ratify the agreement through a separate process. Some countries, like Ireland, France, and Denmark, chose to put the treaty to a public vote through a national referendum. Other countries, like Italy, Greece, and the Netherlands, opted for a ratification process that required the support of a large majority of legislators in their respective parliaments. After a lengthy ratification process spanning twelve countries, the treaty entered into force on November 1, 1993, nearly twenty-one months after the signing date.[103]

Throughout the 1990s, there were persistent fears that countries would renege on the agreement. But, successive rounds of enlargement through the mid-2000s strengthened the EU. One explanation for the resilience of the agreement was the arduous process for entering it. These ratification processes required some degree of buy-in from the public, an opposition party, or both. Precisely because many domestic stakeholders were involved in the ratification process, the agreement was more firmly entrenched.

Ratification of the Maastricht Treaty and similar major international agreements reflect a third advantage democracies have in international affairs: a reliability advantage. Relative to nondemocracies, democracies are better able to commit to, and comply with, international agreements. This makes democracies more cooperative in international politics.[104] Democracies tend

---

102. Wolf 1992.

103. Abbey and Bromfield 1994.

104. International cooperation occurs when "actors adjust their behavior to the actual or anticipated preferences of others, through a process of policy coordination" (Keohane 1984, 51–52).

to be more reliable partners because they sacrifice short-term interests for long-term policy successes.[105]

Like the other two advantages, the reliability advantage is shaped by vertical and horizontal constraints. Vertical constraints make it more likely that leaders follow agreed-upon procedures and adhere to standards of acceptable behavior, or *norms*, when entering into and exiting from international agreements. Two sets of preferences internalized by liberal publics in theory reinforce the reliability advantage.

The first expectation is that, all else equal, democratic publics will prefer that their leaders follow established policymaking procedures domestically when they enter into, or exit from, international agreements. Democratic governments share an understanding with the public about the process by which their country can make commitments to foreign nations. Some aspects of this process may be formalized. International agreements may be subject to public referenda or ratification by a legislature. Other aspects of this process could include informal norms or unwritten rules. Leaders could be expected, for example, to educate the public or consult with members of the opposition before entering into a major international agreement.

If democratic publics internalize these norms, they should be averse to their leaders acting unilaterally or on their own without the support of the public or opposition parties. Observational and experimental work shows that democratic publics in fact care about some of these process concerns. For example, the public responds negatively when leaders act unilaterally without the consent of the public,[106] are not transparent in the process of negotiating international agreements,[107] or deliberately lie or mislead the public about foreign affairs.[108] Effective vertical constraints should provide incentives for leaders to follow norms of acceptable behavior in the foreign policymaking process.

The second expectation is that democratic publics prefer that their leaders do not renege on existing commitments made to allies. There are multiple reasons why publics could hold these preferences. One potential reason is

---

105. Note that the reliability advantage is related to the stability advantage in that they both imply consistency across time. However, reliability also implies sustained partnership, cooperation, or adherence to international law across time.
106. Reeves and Rogowski 2018.
107. Myrick 2024.
108. Maxey 2021; Yarhi-Milo and Ribar 2023.

normative: democratic publics may internalize liberal norms of cooperation, peaceful dispute resolution, and adherence to the rule of law.[109] For these citizens, abandoning international commitments is not appropriate behavior for a democratic ally. Another potential reason is self-interest: democratic publics dislike it when leaders violate international commitments because these violations damage their country's reputation in foreign affairs.[110] For these citizens, the concern is that abandoning commitments has reputational costs. Public opinion research supports these arguments by showing that, in general, democratic citizens tend to be averse to their leaders reneging on existing international commitments, especially security commitments made to allies and partners.[111]

While vertical constraints give democratic leaders incentives to not violate their commitments, horizontal constraints contribute to the reliability advantage by making it challenging to do so in practice. Often, entry into, or withdrawal from, an international agreement requires some degree of support from other domestic political stakeholders. In *Democratic Commitments*, political scientist Lisa Martin argues that intragovernmental constraints on the executive from legislatures create durable forms of international cooperation.[112] When legislatures anticipate conflict with the executive over foreign policy, they find ways to institutionalize their participation in international agreements. In the long run, institutionalized legislative participation in foreign affairs makes democracies more reliable. The involvement of national European parliaments in the creation of the EU's internal market was, according to Martin, critical for a more durable form of regional integration.

In the case of the Maastricht Treaty and the related agreements that followed, both vertical and horizontal constraints reinforced commitments to the EU. If a leader of one of its member countries opted to unilaterally withdraw from the EU, it is likely they would face domestic backlash. Countries that choose to exit the EU do so only with the explicit consent of domestic stakeholders. In the 2015 Brexit vote, for example, the majority of voters in a national referendum voted for the UK to leave the EU.

The reliability advantage is evident across multiple foreign policy domains. International relations scholars primarily emphasize the reliability of security

---

109. Katzenstein 1996; Risse-Kappen 1997; Adler and Barnett 1998.
110. Leeds 1999; McGillivray and Smith 2000.
111. Tomz 2008; Tomz and Weeks 2021.
112. Martin 2000.

commitments, often in the form of military alliances. *Alliances* are formal international agreements related to security cooperation. Alliance partners, for example, may pledge to come to each other's aid in the event that their security is threatened. Democracies are perceived as more reliable because they are less likely to renege on their alliance commitments. Political scientists demonstrate that alliances between democracies are less likely to fail relative to alliances that include nondemocratic countries.[113] Democratic alliances are durable even in the face of leadership turnover. Political scientists Ashley Leeds, Michaela Mattes, and Jeremy Vogel show that, while there is no correlation between leadership turnover and alliance violations, a change in the leader's supporting societal coalition increases the likelihood of a violation. However, this effect is driven by autocratic rather than democratic countries. The researchers conclude that democratic institutions provide stability even when there are major changes in a country's leadership.[114]

Beyond alliances and security cooperation, the reliability advantage impacts international economic outcomes and adherence to international law. A substantial literature illustrates that democratic countries better attract foreign direct investment from multinational corporations than do autocracies.[115] Constraints on democratic leaders make the expropriation of foreign investment less likely and reduce the amount of political risk foreign firms face when investing abroad.[116] Democratic countries are also advantaged with superior access to international credit and higher sovereign bond ratings given that they are seen as less likely to renege on their commitments by defaulting.[117]

Strong domestic commitment to the rule of law is a central reason why democracies tend to also adhere to international law.[118] Democratic countries are more likely to follow rules constructed by the international monetary system,[119] engage in trade cooperation,[120] resolve trade disputes within existing

---

113. Gaubatz 1996; Reed 1997; Leeds and Savun 2007.
114. Leeds, Mattes, and Vogel 2009.
115. Jensen 2003, 2008; Li 2009; Pandya 2014.
116. Jensen 2003, 2008.
117. Beaulieu, Cox, and Saiegh 2012; Schultz and Weingast 2003.
118. As Simmons (2000, 822) summarizes, "Governments that have invested in and rest on a stable legal framework at home are unlikely to jeopardize this reputation by lightly flouting international legal obligations."
119. Simmons 2000.
120. Mansfield, Milner, and Rosendorff 2002.

legal frameworks,[121] and comply with human rights treaties they ratify.[122] While democracies may be more selective about the agreements they enter, they are less likely than nondemocracies to renege on their commitments made to other countries. Likewise, democracies tend to cooperate with other states, pursue multilateral solutions, and comply with international agreements, making them more reliable partners.

2.5.1 Polarization and the Erosion of Democratic Reliability

How does polarization impact the reliability advantage? In nonpolarized environments, vertical constraints reinforce the reliability of democratic commitments. We assume that democratic leaders will be held accountable by the public for entering into international agreements unilaterally or for reneging on those commitments once they are made. These vertical constraints could arise from internalized commitments to democratic governance and rule of law. But they could also arise from self-interested publics who are simply concerned about the reputational costs of abandoning existing agreements.

I argue that, in an extremely polarized environment, the nature of this electoral accountability changes. As a function of diverging ideological preferences or increasing affective polarization, a partisan public cares more about their party's ability to implement its policies. As a consequence, they are less likely to object when co-partisan leaders violate democratic procedures or renege on existing agreements. This impacts both entry into, and withdrawal from, international agreements, in turn affecting the reliability of democratic commitments.

In terms of entering international agreements, in a polarized environment vertical constraints are insufficient to ensure that democratic leaders abide by norms of the foreign policymaking process. A partisan public highly values a co-partisan incumbent enacting their preferred policy. This gives leaders more incentives to act unilaterally in foreign affairs to secure political wins and accomplish policy objectives favored by their supporters.

In 2016, for example, Democratic President Barack Obama entered the United States into the Paris Agreement on climate, a multilateral agreement negotiated at the 2015 UN Climate Change Conference. The Paris Agreement aimed to mitigate global temperature increases by reducing greenhouse

---

121. Davis and Bermeo 2009; Kim 2008.
122. Hathaway 2007.

gas emissions. Unlike the Kyoto Protocol, a climate agreement that President Bill Clinton signed in 1998 but was never ratified by the U.S. Senate, the Obama administration adopted the Paris Agreement as a nonbinding political commitment. This was widely seen as an effort to bypass the Senate ratification process given high levels of congressional polarization and the difficulty of passing international treaties.[123] U.S. entry into the agreement was overwhelmingly supported by Democratic voters; public opinion polls estimate that 86 percent of self-identified Democrats supported the Paris Agreement.[124] Congressional Republicans raised objections to what they described as executive overreach, emphasizing that major international agreements like the Paris Agreement should be subject to Senate ratification. Republican Senator Jim Inhofe from Oklahoma released a statement condemning the climate agreement and noting that "Americans do not support it when their president sidesteps Congress."[125] However, because of the popularity of the Paris Agreement among Obama's core supporters and the perceived impossibility of generating the bipartisan support necessary to ratify the agreement, the Obama administration had incentives to make the international commitment unilaterally.

In terms of exiting international agreements, in highly polarized environments vertical constraints also become less likely to reinforce cooperation between countries if domestic interests conflict with international agreements. As polarization increases, voters put more weight on seeing their own team win or their preferred policy enacted relative both to normative commitments to multilateral cooperation and to concerns about the reputational costs associated with reneging on existing commitments. This intuition is consistent with public opinion research on international commitments. Political scientist Stephen Chaudoin, for example, shows that members of the public who have strong prior opinions about trade are less likely to punish leaders for reneging on their promises by breaking an international trade agreement.[126] Chaudoin's findings suggest that individuals who have strong policy preferences are more willing to overlook violations of international commitments,

---

123. As one scholar of international law wrote, "Obama joined the United States to the Paris Agreement without seeking specific legislative approval ... precisely because such approval would not have been forthcoming" (Galbraith 2017, 1681).
124. Marlon, Fine, and Leiserowitz 2016.
125. Inhofe 2016.
126. Chaudoin 2014.

especially when those violations result in outcomes consistent with their own preferences. Setting aside policy preferences, in extremely polarized settings, strong partisans may even be willing to overlook more blatant violations of international law simply because they result in a "win" for their own party.

Returning to the example of the Paris Agreement, in 2017, when Republican President Donald Trump announced that he would withdraw the United States from the agreement, Democratic legislators raised many objections. One objection was that reneging on this commitment would undermine U.S. credibility and global standing. However, Trump believed that his core supporters, who were skeptical both of multilateralism and of environmental movements, would reward him for reneging on the deal. The *New York Times* ran an article entitled "In Rejecting Popular Paris Accord, Trump Bets on His Base" that explained, "[I]n Mr. Trump's calculation, withdrawing from the accord will be a political winner."[127] From the perspective of the Trump administration, these considerations outweighed the reputational costs the United States might incur by reneging on the agreement. Such examples illustrate that, in polarized societies, where ideological beliefs, partisan loyalties, or both drive divergence in policy preferences, a partisan public is less likely to constrain a leader's actions when they undermine existing international commitments.

> Reliability Hypothesis 1: *As polarization becomes more extreme, the public is less likely to punish co-partisan leaders who act unilaterally when making foreign policy or who renege on international commitments.*

The reliability advantage is also undermined by how extreme polarization interacts with systems of horizontal constraint. In a polarized environment, it is difficult to reach the cross-party consensus needed to pass major foreign policy legislation. In the UK, a polarizing Brexit debate meant that Conservative prime minister Theresa May was unable to garner enough cross-party support for a "soft" Brexit agreement in 2017, which would have left the UK more tightly tied to the EU. Failure to compromise, coupled with the strength and ideological commitments of the Eurosceptic wing of the Conservative Party, led to the election of Boris Johnson in July 2019 and the subsequent passage of a "hard" Brexit agreement that severed UK–EU ties.[128]

---

127. Baker 2017.
128. Quinn, Allen, and Bartle 2024.

In presidential systems like the United States, an increase in polarization creates legislative gridlock that makes governing challenging. As political scientist Sarah Binder summarizes, "When ideological and electoral incentives propel the parties to the wings, abandoning the political center, lawmakers struggle to find broadly palatable solutions to the range of problems they face."[129] Gridlock creates incentives for the president to bypass the legislature entirely when making foreign policy. These incentives exist in other areas of policymaking. However, they are especially pronounced in foreign affairs, where the president has an informational advantage over the legislature.[130] If the president takes this approach, legislators will find it difficult to check presidential power. Checks on executive power are most effective when they come from a bipartisan group of legislators. Yet, in a polarized environment, in-party legislators have little incentive to stop the president from enacting their preferred policy. Electoral accountability will also be unlikely to prevent the executive from acting unilaterally since high levels of polarization make the public less able to effectively constrain the executive.

One observable implication of this logic in American politics is that polarization makes the passage of international treaties—which must be ratified by a two-thirds vote in the U.S. Senate—especially difficult.[131] In a gridlocked U.S. Senate, this level of bipartisan consensus is hard to attain. During polarized times, we should expect to see the executive using alternative ways to enter into international agreements. This includes more expansive use of executive agreements and nonbinding political commitments, neither of which require Senate ratification. U.S. entry into the Paris Agreement is one such example. While these types of international commitments are easier to make, they are also easier for subsequent leaders to exit, making them less durable than international agreements ratified by a legislature.

Reliability Hypothesis 2: *As polarization becomes more extreme, politicians are more likely to bypass horizontal constraints in committing to international agreements, leading to less durable commitments.*

If polarized democracies are less likely to enter into durable commitments, this has important, second-order reputational effects. Allies may be worried that polarized democracies will renege on promises made by

---

129. Binder 2014, 14.
130. Wildavsky 1966; Canes-Wrone, Howell, and Lewis 2008.
131. Schultz 2018; Peake 2017, 2022.

previous administrations. Countries may also be reluctant to initiate new agreements with highly polarized democracies, given doubts about the credibility of their commitments and uncertainty over the future of their foreign policy.

Global responses to the foreign policy of Brazilian President Jair Bolsonaro, who served in office from 2019 to 2022, illustrate this point. Throughout his 2018 campaign and subsequent presidential administration, Bolsonaro championed socially and fiscally conservative policies. But Bolsonaro's presidency also extended ideological and partisan conflict into foreign affairs. The president espoused strong anti-globalist and anti-communist sentiments, reimagining Brazil's partnerships with other nations. While in office, Bolsonaro strengthened Brazil's relationship with Israel under Prime Minister Benjamin Netanyahu and the United States under President Donald Trump while taking a more hostile approach to relations with Venezuela and China. Rejecting principles of multilateralism, Bolsonaro threatened to withdraw from intergovernmental organizations like the UN and international agreements like the Paris Agreement.[132]

While Bolsonaro ultimately did not follow through on his more extreme campaign promises in foreign affairs, his foreign policy positions created a great deal of uncertainty for the future. In a series of interviews with foreign policy experts, Brazilian scholar and journalist David Buarque recounts one expert as remarking that "people are confused about what to expect from the new leadership, and whether Brazil is a country that still can be considered a potential partner."[133] Worries about the long-term relationship between Brazil and its allies in the face of leader turnover reflect concerns about how highly polarized democracies face more uncertainty in the future and therefore are likely to be perceived as less reliable allies.

Table 2.3 outlines the relationship between polarization and the reliability advantage. Again, these hypotheses contrast how we expect vertical and horizontal constraints to function in an ideal-type liberal democracy versus in an extremely polarized democracy. The hypotheses in this table, and their implications for the reliability advantage, are explored in chapter 6.

> Reliability Hypothesis 3: *As polarization becomes more extreme, democracies are more likely to renege on international commitments and less likely to be perceived as reliable allies.*

132. Buarque 2022.
133. Buarque 2022, 2458.

TABLE 2.3. Polarization and the erosion of democratic reliability

	Ideal-type liberal democracy	Extremely polarized democracy
Vertical constraint	The public reinforces democratic norms and procedures around entering into, and exiting from, international agreements. They are more likely to punish leaders who act unilaterally when making foreign policy or who are uncooperative in international politics.	The public is less likely to reinforce democratic norms and procedures around entering into, and exiting from, international agreements. They are less likely to punish co-partisan leaders who act unilaterally when making foreign policy or who renege on international commitments.
Horizontal constraint	Politicians seek cross-party support for major foreign policy legislation. Leaders secure buy-in from the political opposition to commit to international agreements, increasing the durability of these agreements.	Politicians struggle to build cross-party support for legislation. Leaders are more likely to bypass horizontal constraints in committing to international agreements, leading to less durable agreements.
Implication for democratic advantage	Democracies are less likely to renege on international commitments and more likely to be perceived as reliable allies.	Democracies are more likely to renege on international commitments and less likely to be perceived as reliable allies.

2.6 Interrelation of the Democratic Advantages

It is important to emphasize that the three democratic advantages discussed in this chapter are interrelated. As will be evident throughout this book, there are many cases in which growing polarization in foreign policy negatively impacts more than one of the three advantages. Moreover, if extreme polarization erodes one democratic advantage, this could affect the others. If a highly polarized democracy frequently changes its foreign policy when a new party comes to power (affecting the stability advantage), its allies are likely to express doubts about the country's ability to maintain its commitments in the future (affecting the reliability advantage). While the stability and reliability advantage share some similarities, they are conceptually distinct. It is possible for a country to frequently change its policy positions without reneging on its international commitments. For example, under the two successive presidential administrations of Republican President Donald Trump (2017–2021) and Democratic President Joe Biden (2021–2025), the United States experienced dramatic swings in immigration and refugee policy that reflected the politicization of these issues. However, these policy changes did not impact the ability of the United States to maintain its security commitments to its foreign allies.

Likewise, credibility and reliability are also related. Both involve understanding how a country is perceived by other actors in the international system. For the purposes of this book, two distinctions between credibility and reliability are worth reemphasizing. The first relates to the relevant counterpart. In the examples used in this book, I refer to the credibility of signals in the context of bargaining with a foreign adversary. Such bargaining could occur during a crisis scenario or in a noncrisis scenario, such as while negotiating an international agreement. By contrast, I refer to the reliability of commitments made to foreign allies and partners. Chapters 5 and 6 will speak to how extreme polarization affects the ability of a democratic country to be a credible adversary and a reliable ally, respectively. The second distinction between credibility and reliability relates to time horizons. In the applications used in this book, credibility typically involves a judgment at a given moment in time (e.g., "Is the threat this country issued today credible?"), whereas reliability involves perceptions of a country's behavior at a future point in time (e.g., "Will the commitment that this country made be upheld in the future?"). Again, while these two judgments are related in practice, they are distinct in theory.

2.7 Conclusion

This chapter outlined three advantages democracies have in international politics relative to non-democracies. These advantages arise from systems of vertical constraint (accountability to an electorate) and horizontal constraint (accountability to other institutions within government). It then explained how extreme polarization could undermine each advantage by eroding these systems of constraint and their ability to effectively check political power.

A first, overarching advantage democracies have in foreign affairs is a stability advantage. Despite regular leadership turnover, accountability to a large electorate and the median voter within it moderates foreign policy and prevents dramatic swings when a new leader comes to power. Parties have incentives to invest in nonpartisan institutions that maintain continuity in foreign policy across administrations. However, extreme polarization can make politicians less responsive to a median voter. As the public polarizes, officials may cater their policies toward ideologically extreme core supporters, and work to undo policies of the opposite party. And as the stakes of winning heighten in a polarized atmosphere, parties have fewer incentives to maintain a tacit partisan truce in foreign affairs. As a consequence, highly polarized democracies are likely to be associated with more foreign policy volatility.

The second democratic advantage is a credibility advantage. Democracies are better able to credibly signal information than autocracies can. Democratic leaders can use domestic constraints in various ways to their advantage when bargaining with foreign adversaries. Leaders can leverage agreement between domestic actors to credibly signal resolve in an international crisis. They can also leverage moderate disagreement between domestic actors to extract concessions during an international negotiation. However, growing affective polarization in the public and teamsmanship dynamics give the political opposition incentives to obstruct leaders from the opposing party. As a result, it is difficult for polarized democracies to capitalize on the signaling advantages that arise from either bipartisan agreement or more moderate forms of partisan disagreement. The net effect is that highly polarized countries are less likely to send credible signals to their foreign adversaries.

The third democratic advantage is a reliability advantage. Democracies are more reliable because they are better able to commit to, and comply with, agreements made with international partners than are nondemocracies. However, polarization jeopardizes this advantage by giving democratic leaders incentives to bypass horizontal constraints when making agreements, which are easier to undo when a new party comes to power. A polarized public will be less able to hold their leader accountable for reneging on commitments made to allies and partners.

The next four chapters develop evidence for the argument that extreme polarization can undermine democratic advantages in foreign policy. Chapter

3 draws on cross-national data to show associations between extreme polarization and troubling foreign policy outcomes. The remaining empirical chapters (chapters 4, 5, and 6) test the hypotheses in the contemporary American political context, demonstrating how polarization could negatively impact the ability of the United States to maintain stable foreign policy, and to be both a credible adversary and a reliable ally.

3

Cross-National Trends in Polarization and Foreign Policy

IN JANUARY 2016, Tsai Ing-wen secured the presidency of Taiwan in a victory for the Democratic Progressive Party (DPP). Tsai's election was significant for multiple reasons. She was the first female president of Taiwan, and only the second from the DPP, which had not held the presidency since 2008. Tsai's victory sparked debate about how the new president would reshape Taiwan's foreign policy and its relations with mainland China.[1] Tsai and other DPP leaders openly rejected the "one country, two systems" approach pursued by Chinese President Xi Jinping, marking a shift in cross-strait relations between China and Taiwan.[2]

During Tsai's administration, Taiwan faced increasing levels of domestic polarization. Polarization in Taiwanese politics is somewhat puzzling.[3] Taiwan has a majoritarian system dominated by two major parties: the Kuomintang (KMT, or the "blues") and the DPP (or the "greens"). In such systems, political scientists expect policy preferences to converge as the major parties compete for the median voter in the electorate. However, throughout the 2010s and into the 2020s, Taiwan grappled with heightened polarization, characterized both by divergence between the parties as well as factionalism within each party.

The DPP and the KMT grew especially far apart on issues related to national identity and questions about Taiwanese relations with the United States and China. Partisan debates around the possibility of unification with mainland China intensified. Voters who identified with the DPP were far less supportive

1. Wu 2016.
2. Lee 2019.
3. Clark and Tan 2012.

of unification than those who identified with the KMT.[4] The rhetoric and policies of Tsai Ing-wen's administration reflected this difference. President Tsai also reformed other aspects of Taiwan's foreign and defense policies. She established closer ties with the United States and the EU and presided over large increases in military spending in an effort to secure Taiwan's defense.[5] During the 2024 Taiwanese election, major questions about Taiwanese foreign policy and relations with Beijing were again at the heart of the presidential race. DPP candidate Lai Ching-te—labeled "Beijing's least favorite candidate"[6]— emerged victorious from the three-way contest with over 40 percent of the vote. The election left little doubt that electoral outcomes in Taiwan continue to be highly consequential for China–Taiwan relations.

Partisan politics in Taiwan appears to complicate its foreign policy. Were a crisis with mainland China to arise, domestic divisions in Taiwan could hamper a unified response. Polarization could also make it hard for Taiwan to establish a coherent and consistent China policy. As Richard Bush of the Brookings Institution writes, "Meeting the China challenge is made all the more difficult because decisions must be processed through Taiwan's democratic system.... Yet divisions between and within camps constrain any effort to forge a coherent policy."[7] In the future, we may also expect foreign and defense policies to differ substantially under DPP versus KMT presidential administrations.

The Taiwan case demonstrates that polarization creates challenges for democratic foreign policymaking. Chapter 2 argued that democracies tend to have advantages in making foreign policy relative to nondemocracies. However, as polarization becomes more extreme, democratic advantages are steadily eroded. In highly polarized times, a democracy is much less likely to be a credible adversary and a reliable ally. A polarized democracy's policies will be more likely to fluctuate with leader and party turnover, creating volatility in foreign affairs.

To begin exploring these patterns, this chapter draws on descriptive evidence about trends in cross-national polarization and foreign policy using new data on ideological positions of executive and opposition parties and coalitions in democracies. I identify contexts that display extreme levels

---

4. Wang 2019.
5. Shepherd and Chen 2022.
6. Atlantic Council 2024.
7. Bush 2021.

of ideological polarization on a right–left spectrum and extreme levels of polarization in foreign affairs on a hawk–dove spectrum. I then incorporate these measures of polarization into existing, well-known models of democratic advantages in international relations. First, analyses of the stability advantage consider how extreme polarization correlates with changes in foreign policy positions based on roll-call voting at UNGA. Second, analyses of the credibility advantage look at the relationship between extreme polarization and the credibility of threats issued in interstate disputes. Third, analyses of the reliability advantage probe the association between extreme polarization and the ability of democracies to maintain alliance commitments.

Collectively, these analyses show support for the overarching democratic advantages: relative to nondemocracies, democracies appear to be more stable, credible, and reliable in foreign affairs. However, the findings also suggest considerable variation among democracies that arises from different levels of polarization. Democracies experiencing extreme polarization on either a right–left spectrum or a hawk–dove spectrum appear to be less advantaged in foreign affairs relative to democracies with low to moderate levels of polarization. These analyses suggest that, to the extent there may be consequences of extreme polarization for foreign policy outcomes, these consequences are likely to be negative.

There are limitations to these analyses. The main limitation relates to measurement and data availability. As chapter 1 emphasized, cross-national polarization is hard to measure. Public opinion data on affective polarization is especially limited in geographic and temporal scope. But it is also challenging to measure the foreign policy outcomes of interest in this book. Outcomes for which we have reliable cross-national data tend to be major international events, like starting a war or joining a military alliance. Other important changes in foreign policy, like the shift in cross-strait relations under Taiwanese President Tsai Ing-wen, are not easily identifiable in these types of datasets. Moreover, concepts like credibility and reliability are perceptual outcomes. These outcomes hinge on the perspectives of foreign adversaries and allies rather than behaviors that are easily observed. Such perceptual variables are hard to capture in what international relations scholars term "large-N" cross-national studies.

A second limitation relates to the inferences we can draw from this type of analysis. As discussed in chapter 1, polarization is a structural, multicausal phenomenon. It is not randomly assigned across countries but rather intimately connected with economic, social, and political change. These shifts also impact a country's foreign policy. This makes it challenging (if not impossible) to isolate the causal effect of polarization on foreign policy outcomes. This is why the analyses in this chapter are not intended to test the theory in chapter 2. Rather, they serve as a sort of "plausibility probe"[8] for further investigation about whether polarization erodes democratic advantages. Because foundational scholarship from the democratic advantage tradition in international relations largely relies on evidence from cross-national analyses, this is an appropriate starting point. However, the limitations of analyses in this chapter motivate the focus on the relationship between polarization and foreign policymaking in a single country (the United States) in the latter half of this book.

3.1 Cross-National Trends in Polarization

What do we know about trends in partisan polarization globally? To characterize this variation, we need comparable measures of polarization across time and space. A key issue is that scholars disagree about what measures to use. For one, the terms "left" and "right" or "liberal" and "conservative" do not mean the same thing in different political contexts. A political party that the Swedish public considers "center right" may be perceived by the American public to be on the "left." A right–left divide may also not be the only—or even the most—salient political cleavage in a democracy. The disjuncture, for example, between secularists and Islamists in Turkish politics does not neatly map to the right–left spectrum that characterizes politics in neighboring Greece. And in other countries, different dimensions of ideological conflict may be more relevant than the right–left divide. For instance, political scientists Liesbet Hooghe, Gary Marks, and their co-authors characterize parties in many European democracies on the "GAL–TAN" spectrum, which distinguishes between parties that are "green, alternative, and liberal" and those that are "traditional, authoritarian, and nationalist."[9]

Measures of partisan polarization are complicated by the fact that countries have different electoral systems, legislative processes, and policy agendas. When measuring polarization within a country, researchers commonly use legislative roll-call votes to identify the policy positions of political officials or

---

8. According to Levy (2008, 6), "A plausibility probe is comparable to a pilot study in experimental or survey research. It allows the researcher to sharpen a hypothesis or theory."

9. Hooghe, Marks, and Wilson 2002; Hooghe, Marks, and Kamphorst 2025.

their parties. A similar cross-national approach is difficult because countries have very different policy agendas at any given time.[10]

Despite these challenges, researchers offer some ways to measure ideological polarization and affective polarization among politicians (elite polarization) and the public (mass polarization). To measure ideological polarization on a right–left spectrum among politicians, one approach relies on expert surveys to categorize ideological positions of political parties. The Varieties of Democracy project based at the University of Gothenburg draws on expert surveys to code positions of parties on many issue dimensions.[11] Expert surveys have strengths and limitations. They are easy to directly interpret, but the assessments of human experts can be subjective and prone to bias.[12] Expert surveys are also limited to specific countries, parties, or years. The Chapel Hill Expert Survey, based at the University of North Carolina at Chapel Hill, for instance, has been conducted every four years since 1999 and focuses on political parties in Europe.[13]

Another approach is to compare parties based on the policy positions they describe in their party platform or manifesto. Party leaders release platforms in advance of upcoming elections to communicate to voters what their party stands for. The Manifesto Project (MARPOR), based at the WZB Berlin Social Science Center, collects these platforms from political parties worldwide and codes policy positions based on statements from each platform.[14] Political scientists then devise ways to measure a party's ideological position based on these coded statements.[15] For example, statements that support capitalism and free-market economics are coded as "right wing," while those supporting labor and the welfare state are coded as "left wing."

---

10. An exception is efforts to compare policy positions of countries in international institutions where votes occur at the country level. For example, political scientists use roll-call votes in UNGA (Bailey, Strezhnev, and Voeten 2017) to estimate a country's policy preferences. However, since these approaches are focused on foreign policy votes, they do not map neatly onto a right–left spectrum.

11. Lührmann et al. 2020.

12. Bollen and Paxton 2000.

13. Bakker et al. 2020. An expansion of the dataset in 2020 focuses on Latin American parties (Martínez-Gallardo et al. 2023).

14. Lehmann et al. 2018.

15. For example, Laver and Budge (1992) use factor analysis to identify which issues should be considered right wing or left wing and then construct an additive right–left index based on this coding.

In democracies with more than two major parties or multiple salient ideological cleavages, using a right–left index to measure polarization becomes complex. To simplify the comparison between two-party and multiparty systems, I create a dataset that identifies the party (or coalition) of the executive and the party (or coalition) of the primary opposition group. In this dataset, described in more detail later in this chapter, I match democratic leaders identified by the Archigos dataset of political leaders[16] to their respective party platforms in the MARPOR data[17] and then manually identify the party of the primary opposition.[18] I calculate the measure of ideological polarization as the absolute distance between the right–left index of the party or coalition of the executive and that of the opposition for every executive term.

Figure 3.1 shows the median level of ideological distance between the executive and opposition party (or parties) in each country, averaging across all executive terms for each country in the MARPOR database from 1921 to 2022. According to this measure, for much of the twentieth century, the most ideologically polarized countries are Switzerland, France, Denmark, Sweden, and Greece. The United States, highlighted, falls in the middle of this set of countries. While ideological polarization in the United States increased substantially in the twenty-first century, figure 3.1 emphasizes that the average ideological distance between the Democratic and Republican Parties during the full time period is not as large as that between left-wing and right-wing parties in many democracies. Lots of other countries experience similar or even higher levels of ideological polarization.

This figure shows only one of many approaches to measure ideological polarization among political elites cross-nationally. Measuring polarization among the public, or mass polarization, can be even more complex. Some researchers draw inferences about mass polarization from public opinion surveys. The World Values Survey, fielded since 1981 in a large cross-section of countries, asks respondents questions about their partisan affiliation and political ideology. Researchers use these answers to approximate the position of political parties or to create measures of ideological polarization among the public.[19] This can be a tricky process. Even when researchers agree on which

---

16. Goemans, Gleditsch, and Chiozza 2009.

17. Lehmann et al. 2018.

18. The primary opposition is coded as the party or coalition with the most votes that is not part of the governing coalition (see appendix).

19. See, e.g., Inglehart et al. 2014.

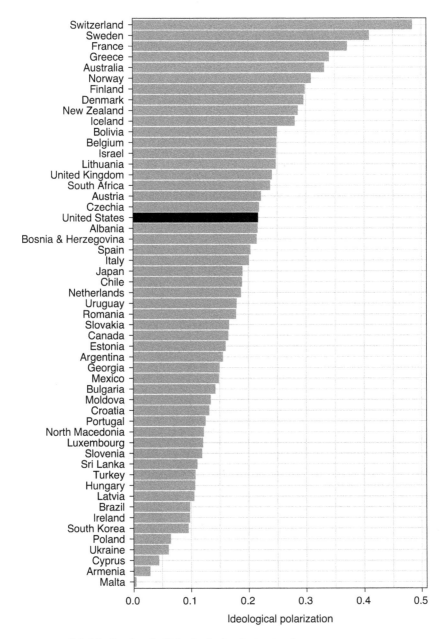

FIGURE 3.1. Median level of ideological polarization between executive and opposition parties

data source to use, questions arise when translating that data source into a measure of polarization. For instance, with data from MARPOR on party platforms, how should the categories of right and left be measured? Should we separate the right–left spectrum into a social and an economic dimension? To calculate polarization, should we incorporate all parties in the measure or just the party of the executive and the opposition? If the former, should we weight the measure by the strength of parties? If weighting, should we weight by total votes or by seats in the legislature? These questions illustrate why political scientists use many different measures of polarization.

Another way to measure mass polarization is to rely on expert judgments. The Digital Society Project, started in 2018, produces a "polarization of society" measure that asks country experts: "How would you characterize the differences of opinions on major political issues in this society?"[20] The answer options are coded as: serious polarization, moderate polarization, medium polarization, limited polarization, and no polarization. The geographic coverage of this measure is better than most comparable measures, since experts conceptualize polarization in both autocracies and democracies. According to the data, roughly 27 percent of country-years between 2000 and 2023 were considered by experts to be "seriously polarized."

Figure 3.2 shows how this measure of mass polarization has changed since 2000. Countries where polarization has increased (decreased) according to this measure are in black (gray). Countries that saw no changes in this period, or for which data is missing, are in white. The figure shows that the level of mass polarization has increased in many countries since the beginning of the twenty-first century. It is notable that sharp increases have occurred in many advanced democracies. Countries with the largest increases in polarization are concentrated in Europe, the Americas, and South Asia. By contrast, levels of mass polarization in sub-Saharan Africa and East Asia have remained relatively stable. In only a handful of countries has polarization decreased since 2000.

Research on cross-national affective polarization—the tendency of people to like their in-party and dislike their out-party—is thin but rapidly growing. The primary approach to measuring affective polarization is to draw on data from the Comparative Study of Electoral Systems (CSES), a public opinion survey conducted since 1996 in twenty democracies. The CSES asks participants to rate each political party on a scale from 0 (strongly dislike) to 10 (strongly like). Researchers then calculate measures of affective

---

20. Mechkova et al. 2024.

FIGURE 3.2. Change in level of polarization in society using data from the Digital Society Project (2000–2023)

polarization based on how survey respondents rate their in-party versus their out-party. In *American Affective Polarization in Comparative Perspective*, political scientists Noam Gidron, James Adams, and Will Horne compare ratings from supporters of the largest left-wing party and the largest right-wing party in each country.[21] A larger gap in ratings signifies a higher level of affective polarization. By their calculations, between 1996 and 2017, the three countries in the sample with the highest level of affective polarization were Spain, Greece, and Portugal. The three countries with the lowest levels of affective polarization were the Netherlands, Finland, and Iceland. The United States is not an extreme outlier but rather falls in the middle, ranking as having the eighth highest level of affective polarization of the twenty countries in their study.[22]

Political scientist Andres Reiljan and his coauthors take a similar approach in constructing an index of affective polarization based on CSES survey data, but they weight the evaluations of parties based on their size.[23] Figure 3.3 shows the level of affective polarization in 2020 calculated from the last CSES survey conducted in each country.[24] Because the CSES surveys began in the 1990s and are not fielded annually in each country, researchers are limited in

21. Gidron, Adams, and Horne 2020.
22. Gidron, Adams, and Horne 2020, 23.
23. Reiljan 2020; Reiljan et al. 2023.
24. Data from Reiljan 2020.

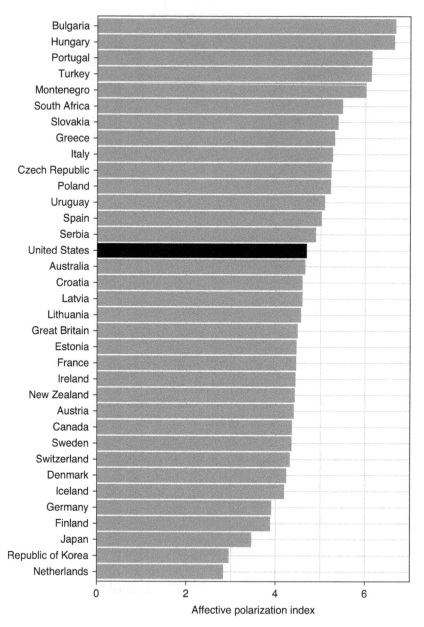

FIGURE 3.3. Affective polarization index calculated by Reiljan (2020) from recent public opinion surveys conducted by the Comparative Study of Electoral Systems

their ability to generate more fine-grained cross-national measures of affective polarization. This data also suggests that the United States falls at middling levels of polarization. In this figure, the United States ranks as the fifteenth most affectively polarized democracies out of thirty-five democracies in the sample. According to Reiljan's measure, affective polarization in the United States has grown very sharply over the past two decades. In the 1990s, the United States was not nearly as affectively polarized as it is in the 2020s.

Although there are many ways to conceptualize and measure ideological and affective polarization cross-nationally, a few trends are worth emphasizing. For one, most research suggests that mass polarization has increased in the twenty-first century and has been particularly problematic since the mid-2010s. The growth in polarization is not limited to new democracies but rather affects a wide range of countries. Those in Europe and the Americas have struggled in particular. In addition, while the United States is clearly polarized, other democracies experience similar problems with growing ideological polarization, affective polarization, or both. This means that the United States is not an outlier when it comes to polarized politics. Since the mid-2010s, however, the United States has experienced very high levels of both affective and ideological polarization that are unique in the country's recent history. According to many of these measures, it would be reasonable to characterize American politics in the 2020s as "extremely polarized."

3.1.1 Measuring Polarization for Cross-National Analyses

The objective of this book is to explore the relationship between extreme polarization and foreign policy outcomes. To characterize this relationship, I look for a cross-national measure of polarization that does three things. First, the measure needs to focus on the executive, such as a prime minister, president, chancellor, or the equivalent position. Many cross-national measures of polarization capture polarization within legislatures. Yet, in presidential systems where the president is responsible for making foreign policy, measures of legislative polarization are less useful than measures of ideological distance between the president and the opposition party.

Second, the measure must have good spatial and temporal coverage. This is needed to trace how polarization correlates with foreign policy outcomes within a given country over time. Many interesting survey-based measures of polarization, including measures of cross-national affective polarization, rely on data from public opinion surveys. As previously discussed, these surveys are limited in the sample of countries and years that they cover, making them less useful in characterizing long-term change within countries.

Third, ideally the measure of polarization could also characterize partisan divergence on aspects of foreign affairs. Most cross-national measures of ideological polarization focus on economic and/or social issues arrayed on a conservative–liberal or right–left spectrum. However, ideological preferences on a right–left scale are distinct from (although may be correlated with) foreign policy preferences that capture the relative hawkishness of political parties and their leaders.

I construct a new dataset that develops multiple measures of polarization to meet these conditions. This dataset begins with a crosswalk of two well-known existing resources. The first is the Archigos dataset on political leaders, collected by researchers at the University of Essex, the University of Rochester, and Vanderbilt University.[25] The second is the MARPOR dataset on party platforms, based at WZB Berlin.[26] Since my focus is on executives, I use the Archigos data to determine the leader of each democracy in a given country-year. I reorganize the Archigos data into executive terms because party platforms are released in conjunction with elections.[27] For example, the observation ID for U.S. President George W. Bush, who served two consecutive four-year terms, in the Archigos dataset is USA-2001. In the new dataset, President Bush would receive two entries, USA-2001 and USA-2005, one for each term in office.

After separating the data by executive terms, I manually match each leader listed in the Archigos leaders dataset with their political party in the MARPOR, locating the most recent party platform that corresponds to their election. MARPOR collects and codes political party platforms in fifty-five democracies for which platforms are publicly available.[28] Platforms or manifestos are statements released in advance of elections that describe the goals and values of a political party or candidate running for office. The advantage of looking at party platforms is that they provide clear policy positions before a party is in office. Rather than inferring a party's policy positions from political behavior, one can assess how well the party's stated positions align with

25. Goemans, Gleditsch, and Chiozza 2009.
26. Lehmann et al. 2018.
27. I code the first year of the executive term as year t if the election occurs between January and May of year t, or as year $t + 1$ if the election occurs June through December.
28. Lehmann et al. 2018.

policy outcomes. Another advantage of the MARPOR data is that it provides insights into policy preferences on many dimensions, including foreign policy preferences.[29]

The MARPOR data records the percent of votes each party receives and the percent of total seats the party obtains in the legislature. But, in some instances, the executive—typically a president or prime minister—is not from the majority party in legislature. This may be the case, for example, in presidential systems where legislators and executives are elected independently. It could also be the case in parliamentary systems ruled by a coalition in which the prime minister comes from a minority party.[30] This motivates the crosswalk between Archigos and MARPOR to identify the political party of the executive rather than the majority party in the legislature. In addition to identifying the party or coalition to which the executive belongs, I also record the party or coalition of the primary opposition group. To simplify the comparison between two-party and multiparty systems, the opposition party is defined as the party or coalition with the most votes that is not part of the governing coalition. Using the MARPOR data, I identify positions of the executive and opposition parties on both a right–left dimension and a hawk–dove dimension as a basis for constructing measures of polarization and extreme polarization.

3.1.2 Right–Left and Hawk–Dove Polarization

A right–left dimension captures whether a party is a conservative or liberal. Economically, parties on the right tend to support the free market and oppose government intervention in the economy; parties on the left tend to support government regulation of the economy and expansion of the welfare state. Socially, parties on the right support traditional sources of authority and morals, while parties on the left support social change. A *hawk–dove* dimension captures positions on foreign policy. The relative hawkishness of a party reflects how willing they are to use military force to address international problems. Intuitively, whether polarization will impact foreign policy depends in part on the dimension on which party preferences diverge. It is possible for

---

29. Alternative potential data sources, like the Database of Political Institutions from the World Bank (Scartascini, Cruz, and Keefer 2021), include indicators for a right–left dimension but not for other policy dimensions.

30. See appendix for coding rules.

political parties to differ on domestic issues but agree on foreign affairs, or vice versa.

To calculate the right–left position of the executive and opposition party, I follow a coding scheme from the MARPOR project that identifies right-wing and left-wing ideas in policy platforms.[31] I use the total number of "right" statements and "left" statements in each platform in the MARPOR dataset. I then measure the right–left position of a given political party based on a measure proposed by Kenneth Schultz.[32] This measure ranges from approximately 0 (all statements are left leaning) to 1 (all statements are right leaning). To reduce noise, the approach developed by Schultz biases the measure toward 0.5 for platforms in which there is relatively little information. I construct this measure cumulatively, such that successive platforms generate more information about the party.

$$\text{Right–Left Position} = \frac{right + 1}{right + left + 2}$$

To measure polarization over foreign policy, I repeat the same process, using MARPOR codes of positive or negative statements about militarism in each of the party platforms. The hawk–dove position measures the relative hawkishness of the parties, with higher values indicating more favorability toward militarization and the use of military force.

$$\text{Hawk–Dove Position} = \frac{milpos + 1}{milpos + milneg + 2}$$

These dimensions are measured separately because although the right–left and hawk–dove dimension are positively correlated, the correlation is weak ($\rho \approx 0.13$). There are many political systems in which parties on the right are not necessarily more hawkish than parties on the left. The conventional expectation is that hawkish parties tend to be more ideologically conservative (e.g., Likud Party in Israel) and dovish parties tend to be more ideologically liberal (e.g., French Socialist Party). However, we also see instances of dovish parties on the right, like the Croatian Democratic Union, which is economically conservative but has an anti-interventionist foreign policy. We also observe hawkish parties on the left, like the Norwegian Labour party, which,

31. Laver and Budge 1992.
32. Schultz 1995.

while economically liberal, has historically been anti-communist and a strong supporter of NATO.

From these two dimensions, I create measures of both right–left and hawk–dove polarization for a given executive term. After matching the corresponding opposition party with their party platform data in MARPOR, I calculate the distance in ideological position between the executive party/coalition (indexed by e_i) and the opposition party/coalition (indexed by o_i) in a given country (i) at any one point and time (t). I measure polarization on both a right–left and hawk–dove dimension for all executive terms in the dataset. right–left and hawk–dove measures of polarization are also positively correlated, although again the correlation is weak ($\rho \approx 0.18$).

$$\text{Right–Left Polarization}_{it} = \left| \frac{right_{e_it} + 1}{right_{e_it} + left_{e_it} + 2} - \frac{right_{o_it} + 1}{right_{o_it} + left_{o_it} + 2} \right|$$

$$\text{Hawk–Dove Polarization}_{it} = \left| \frac{milpos_{e_it} + 1}{milpos_{e_it} + milneg_{e_it} + 2} - \frac{milpos_{o_it} + 1}{milpos_{o_it} + milneg_{o_it} + 2} \right|$$

3.1.3 Extreme Polarization

The theory in chapter 2 focused on how extreme polarization, in which countries experience high levels of both ideological and affective polarization simultaneously, has negative consequences for foreign policymaking. One of the main ideas in this book is that, while more moderate levels of polarization help to confer some of the advantages that democracies have in foreign affairs, extreme forms of polarization can undermine these advantages.

As previously discussed in this chapter, however, cross-national data on affective polarization is very limited. Therefore, in the analyses that follow, I focus on extreme levels of ideological polarization. I code polarization as *extreme* on either a right–left or a hawk–dove dimension in a given executive term if it is at the ninetieth percentile or above across the full sample of executive terms in the dataset for the respective dimension.

Many contemporary examples of societies experiencing extreme right–left polarization are well known. For instance, the polarization measure classifies two recent executive terms in the United States (President Donald Trump's first term from 2017 to 2021 and President Joe Biden's term from 2021 to 2025) as extreme on a right–left dimension. Since the mid-twentieth century, American politics has shifted from relatively low levels of right–left and hawk–dove polarization in the mid-twentieth century to relatively high levels of right–left polarization in the twenty-first century. Today, the Republican and Democratic Parties tend to be farther apart on social and economic issues, but they do not differ substantially on foreign policy issues. Other countries experience high levels of hawk–dove polarization but low to middling levels of right–left polarization. For example, in some Eastern European countries, parties strongly disagree about their orientation with respect to relations with the EU, NATO (North Atlantic Treaty Organization), and Russia, exhibiting greater partisan divergence on a hawk–dove dimension.

Instances of extreme polarization are not concentrated within a small group of countries. According to the measure constructed for this chapter, roughly half of countries in the dataset (twenty-seven out of fifty-five countries) experienced extreme polarization on either the right–left or hawk–dove spectrum at some point in the MARPOR dataset. And 80 percent of countries experienced high levels of polarization on either dimension, falling at the seventy-fifth percentile or above. This suggests that polarization is an important feature—sometimes occasionally, and sometimes in a more sustained way—of democratic politics.

The approach that the rest of this chapter takes is to incorporate these measures of extreme polarization into well-known, existing analyses of the three democratic advantages: the stability, credibility, and reliability advantages. We should think of the analyses that follow not as a test of different hypotheses, but rather as a descriptive first cut to investigate the association between polarization and democratic foreign policy.

3.2 Polarization and Foreign Policy Stability

The dominant view among international relations scholars is that democracies have a stability advantage in foreign affairs.[33] Despite the fact that democracies experience more frequent leader turnover on average, they tend to maintain consistent foreign policies relative to non-democracies. As described in chapter 2, this stability advantage arises from two systems of constraint on

---

33. See, e.g., Leeds, Mattes, and Vogel 2009; McGillivray and Smith 2008; Mattes, Leeds, and Carroll 2015; Smith 2016.

political power. Vertical constraints make democratic leaders accountable to the public through regular elections. Politicians campaigning for nationwide office have incentives to appeal to a median voter in the electorate and pursue foreign policies that provide public goods and maximize national welfare. Horizontal constraints, such as the presence of an active political opposition and the existence of a nonpartisan foreign policy bureaucracy, check democratic leaders and make them less inclined to pursue ideologically extreme policies.

There is considerable empirical support for the stability advantage. To demonstrate the stability of democratic foreign policy, a common approach is to look at the association between regime type (i.e., whether a country is a democracy or not) and changes in foreign policy positions over time. For instance, scholars examine patterns of roll-call votes at UNGA to show that foreign policy remains consistent in democracies. UNGA roll-call votes are used to generate ideal point estimates of the foreign policy positions of countries in a given year.[34] This measure is advantageous because it lends itself to cross-national comparisons; all countries vote on the same set of issues at the same time. UNGA roll-call votes are also useful because they include votes on many topics related to foreign affairs rather than a single issue area like trade policy. Because the votes in UNGA are nonbinding, they are thought to reflect sincerely expressed foreign policy positions.[35]

UNGA voting patterns emphasize that democratic foreign policy is not particularly volatile. Political scientist Alastair Smith, for example, shows that leader turnover in autocracies is associated with large changes in UN ideal point estimates, but turnover in democracies is not.[36] Political scientists Ashley Leeds, Michaela Mattes, and their coauthors analyze the impacts of both leader and party turnover on foreign policy stability.[37] Their analyses corroborate Smith's finding that leader turnover does not significantly impact patterns of UN voting in democracies. However, they go an additional step further to show that a change in the societal supporting coalition of a leader—for example, a change in the party of the executive—does not affect foreign policy in democracies but does affect autocratic foreign policy.

---

34. Voeten, Strezhnev, and Bailey 2009; Bailey, Strezhnev, and Voeten 2017; Voeten 2021.
35. Bailey, Strezhnev, and Voeten 2017.
36. Smith 2016.
37. Mattes, Leeds, and Carroll 2015; Mattes, Leeds, and Matsumura 2016; Leeds and Mattes 2022.

In *Domestic Interests, Democracy, and Foreign Policy Change,* Ashley Leeds and Michaela Mattes show that this pattern holds across other domains of foreign policy.[38]

This book does not dispute the overarching logic behind the stability advantage. However, it emphasizes that there is variation among democracies that comes from different levels of polarization. Periods of extreme polarization within democracies should be associated with more volatility in foreign policy. This should especially be the case in areas of foreign affairs where executives exercise substantial discretion. Many foreign policy decisions do not require formal domestic approval processes like popular referenda or legislative votes. As a plausibility probe for the relationship between polarization and foreign policy stability, I replicate and extend existing research by Mattes, Leeds, and Carroll who study patterns of regime type and UNGA voting.[39]

In table 3.1, the unit of analysis is the country-year, and the sample extends from 1946 to 2008. The dependent variable *"change in UN voting"* captures the magnitude of the annual change in a country's foreign policy position. This variable is calculated as the absolute difference in the country's estimated ideal point (constructed from UNGA roll-call votes) relative to the previous year.[40] Larger values of the dependent variable indicate larger changes in foreign policy preferences, and therefore less foreign policy stability. The model includes control variables from Mattes, Leeds, and Carroll's original analysis that contribute to volatility in foreign policy: indicators for whether or not the country had a defense pact with the United States (*"U.S. ally"*) or the Soviet Union (*"USSR ally"*), indicators for the period from 1989 to 1991 that spans the end of the Cold War when many countries experienced major domestic and foreign policy changes (*"Cold War end"*), and an indicator for whether a country experienced a regime change (*"regime transition"*).[41] Each model also includes country fixed-effects with standard errors clustered by country. This means that comparisons are made within the same country over time.

38. Leeds and Mattes 2022.
39. Mattes, Leeds, and Carroll 2015.
40. See Bailey, Strezhnev, and Voeten 2017 for data on UNGA roll-call votes. Following the original analyses, this variable is log-transformed to better approximate a normal distribution.
41. The authors code regime transitions as country-years in which a country transitioned from a democracy to a nondemocracy or vice versa, based on the value of the country's polity score (Marshall and Gurr 2018). They code countries scoring a six or above democracies.

TABLE 3.1. Replication and extension of Mattes, Leeds, and Carroll (2015)

	Change in UN voting			
	Full sample	Democracies only		
	(1)	(2)	(3)	(4)
Extreme right–left polarization			0.130 (0.106)	
Extreme hawk–dove polarization				0.675*** (0.173)
SOLS change	0.178*** (0.053)	0.055 (0.070)	0.143 (0.092)	0.150 (0.092)
Other leader transition	0.072 (0.059)	0.044 (0.088)	0.086 (0.108)	0.076 (0.107)
Democracy	−0.360*** (0.051)			
Cold War end	0.058 (0.062) (0.107)	0.097 (0.103)	0.003 (0.141)	−0.026 (0.140)
U.S. ally	−0.143 (0.092)	−0.300** (0.124)	−0.269* (0.143)	−0.277* (0.142)
USSR ally	0.078 (0.124)	0.487** (0.221)	0.545** (0.233)	0.602*** (0.232)
Country FEs	✓	✓	✓	✓
Observations	7,049	2,731	1,383	1,383

Note: *p < 0.1; **p < 0.05; ***p < 0.01

Model 1 in the table replicates Mattes, Leeds, and Carroll's original model, which includes data from both democratic and nondemocratic countries. The first thing to note in this model is that the coefficient on "*democracy*" is negative and statistically significant. This emphasizes the existence of a democratic stability advantage: on average, democracies tend to experience less volatility in their foreign policy positions relative to nondemocracies. The researchers also look at the relationship between leader turnover and foreign policy stability. They draw a distinction between a change in the societal coalition supporting a leader (what they term a "*SOLS change*") and other forms of leadership turnover that do not involve a major transition of power ("*other leader transition*"). Importantly, the coefficient on "*SOLS change*" is positive and statistically significant, whereas the coefficient on "*other leader transition*" is not. Only leader transitions that involve a change in the societal coalition supporting a leader (for example, a change in the party controlling the executive in a democracy), are associated with major foreign policy changes.

Models 2 through 4 extend the analysis by focusing only on the subset of democratic countries in the sample. Model 2 is the baseline model that includes the control variables from model 1.[42] Here, we see that among democracies, the coefficient on *"SOLS change"* is positive but no longer statistically significant at conventional levels. As Mattes, Leeds, and Carroll (2015) explain, this suggests that the relationship observed in model 1 is mainly driven by instability within non-democracies. In democracies, party changes are not correlated with foreign policy volatility, on average. Models 3 and 4 extend the analyses by adding in new measures of *"extreme right–left polarization"* (model 3) and *"extreme hawk–dove polarization"* (model 4) in democracies. Both measures are positively associated with changes in UN voting patterns, indicating more instability in foreign policy. However, only the coefficient on *"extreme hawk–dove polarization"* (model 4) is statistically significant. The magnitude of this coefficient is also quite sizeable; it corresponds to roughly 0.5 standard deviations of the dependent variable.

The models in table 3.1 emphasize a few takeaways. The first is that democracies, on average, tend to have more stable foreign policies than nondemocracies. Even leader turnover and party turnover in democracies is not associated with major fluctuations in democratic foreign policy. This reaffirms the democratic stability advantage identified by many international relations scholars. However, the table also suggests that some democracies behave differently than other democracies. In particular, democracies experiencing periods of extreme polarization may display less foreign policy stability. Countries experiencing higher degrees of hawk–dove polarization may be especially volatile in their foreign policy positions.

3.3 Polarization and Democratic Credibility

Beyond the stability advantage, chapter 2 described additional advantages that democracies have relative to nondemocracies when making foreign policy.

---

42. *Democracy* and *regime transition* are not included in these models because all country-years in this subset are democracies, none of which experiences regime changes.

For one, responsiveness to the public and accountability to the political opposition makes democratic leaders unlikely to issue threats or promises that they cannot keep. As a result, the threats and promises they do make should be taken seriously by foreign adversaries, giving democracies a credibility advantage. Credibility is hard to evaluate because it is a perceptual outcome. We can observe changes in foreign policy that indicate stability or instability, but whether or not a country's threats and promises are credible hinges on the perceptions of other countries.

Fortunately, existing research on democratic credibility identifies some observable implications of the credibility advantage in international relations. A well-known implication comes from Kenneth Schultz's *Democracy and Coercive Diplomacy*.[43] Schultz's insight is that, because coercive threats made by democracies are, on average, perceived as more credible, their adversaries are less likely to respond to democratic challengers with militarized action. To test his theory, Schultz focuses on the relationship between a country that starts a dispute (initiator), often by issuing a coercive demand, and the intended recipient of the demand (target) in the context of a militarized interstate dispute, or MID. MIDs are conflicts between countries that fall short of major war. Data on these disputes is collected by the Correlates of War Project, which started at University of Michigan in the 1960s.[44] Schultz's theory predicts that disputes initiated by democracies are less likely to be reciprocated relative to disputes initiated by nondemocracies. A MID is considered reciprocated when a target takes a militarized action (like mobilizing troops or using force) in response to a coercive demand.

The theory in chapter 2 of this book does not dispute the argument that democracies may be, on average, more credible relative to nondemocracies. Rather, it suggests there should be variation among democracies in terms of their perceived credibility. Democracies experiencing extreme polarization should be less credible in issuing threats. Chapter 2 explained that, in highly polarized times, partisans place more value on scoring political wins or seeing their preferred policy enacted rather than other considerations in the policymaking process. Politicians from the opposing party have incentives to actively oppose the executive's foreign policy agenda. The erosion of vertical

43. Schultz 2001a.
44. Palmer et al. 2020.

and horizontal constraints undermines the credibility of signals sent to foreign adversaries.

To probe the relationship between extreme polarization and credibility, I replicate and extend Schultz's canonical models of democratic credibility in table 3.2.[45] All models in this table are logistic regression models in which the dependent variable (*"MID reciprocation"*) is an indicator for whether the dispute was reciprocated by the target country. Model 1 replicates the pooled Schultz model, which includes disputes initiated both by democracies and nondemocracies. The key independent variable in model 1 is an indicator for whether the dispute was started by a democracy (*"democratic initiator"*). The coefficient on *"democratic initiator"* is negative and statistically significant, showing that MIDs started by democracies are less likely to be reciprocated relative to those initiated by nondemocracies. Schultz takes the main implication of this finding to be that democracies have a credibility advantage in interstate disputes.

Models 2 through 4 extend Schultz's model. The sample in these models is composed only of disputes initiated by democracies. Model 2 is the baseline model, which includes a set of other factors that Schultz identifies as potentially impacting the likelihood that a MID is reciprocated. These control variables are: indicators for power asymmetries between the countries in dispute (whether the initiator and/or the target of the dispute was a major power or a minor power), the initiator's share of capabilities, whether the countries in dispute are contiguous (i.e., whether they share a geographic border), foreign policy similarity (measured by the similarity of alliance portfolios), and the type of issue in dispute (i.e., whether the dispute was over territory, policy, etc.).[46]

Models 3 and 4 add indicators of *"extreme right–left polarization"* (model 3) and *"extreme hawk–dove polarization"* (model 4) to the baseline model. The theory in chapter 2 suggests that democracies experiencing extreme polarization are perceived as less credible than democracies that are not experiencing extreme polarization. This means that disputes initiated by extremely polarized democracies should be *more* likely to be reciprocated. In model 3, the coefficient on *"extreme right–left polarization"* is in the expected direction (positive) but is substantively small and not statistically significant at

---

45. This replication uses data from Downes and Sechser (2012), who reconstruct analyses from Schultz 2001a.

46. See Schultz 2001a for a discussion of these control variables.

TABLE 3.2. Replication and extension of Schultz (2001a)

| | MID reciprocation ||||
| | Full sample || Democracies only ||
	(1)	(2)	(3)	(4)
Democratic initiator	−0.468** (0.188)			
Democratic target	0.005 (0.166)			
Both democratic	0.500 (0.363)			
Extreme right–left polarization			0.034 (0.648)	
Extreme hawk–dove polarization				2.672** (1.272)
Major initiator–major target	−0.508** (0.247)	−0.591 (0.595)	0.249 (1.047)	0.367 (1.059)
Major initiator–minor target	−0.359* (0.186)	0.484 (0.467)	0.315 (0.981)	0.145 (1.001)
Minor initiator–major target	0.174 (0.248)	0.739 (0.539)	3.255** (1.273)	3.378** (1.322)
Initiator's share of capabilities	0.111 (0.247)	−0.095 (0.526)	2.492* (1.373)	2.730* (1.413)
Contiguous	0.594*** (0.158)	0.388 (0.335)	−0.735 (0.537)	−0.638 (0.552)
Alliance portfolio similarity	−0.113 (0.202)	0.119 (0.487)	−0.302 (1.108)	−0.134 (1.150)
Status quo evaluation of initiator	0.181 (0.188)	−0.118 (0.424)	−1.889** (0.944)	−2.038** (0.966)
Status quo evaluation of target	−0.476** (0.193)	−0.177 (0.428)	0.011 (0.855)	−0.072 (0.886)
Territory	0.298* (0.173)	0.302 (0.373)		
Government	0.311 (0.386)	−0.412 (0.758)	−2.242 (1.466)	−3.211** (1.638)
Policy	−1.203*** (0.158)	−1.600*** (0.338)	−1.839*** (0.509)	−1.979*** (0.531)
Other	−0.491 (0.593)	−0.843 (1.276)		
Constant	0.214 (0.243)	0.075 (0.501)	−0.099 (0.852)	−0.222 (0.868)
Observations	1,153	286	117	117

Note: *p < 0.1; **p < 0.05; ***p < 0.01

conventional levels. In model 4, however, the coefficient on *"extreme hawk–dove polarization"* is positive and statistically significant. Countries targeted in a dispute initiated by a democracy experiencing extreme polarization in foreign policy appear more likely to respond with militarized action, on average. To be more concrete, a substantive interpretation of the baseline model (model 1) predicts that MIDs initiated by nondemocracies are reciprocated in roughly 40 percent of cases, but MIDs initiated by democracies are reciprocated less frequently in roughly 30 percent of cases.[47] Model 4 suggests that, on average, MIDs initiated by extremely polarized democracies are reciprocated in upwards of 75 percent of cases.

Again, this type of analysis is suggestive but not definitive. Some other scholars have taken issue with Schultz's approach to measuring democratic credibility by using a country's behavior during an interstate dispute.[48] This analysis is also limited to relatively few observations because only 117 disputes initiated by democracies appear both in Schultz's data and in MARPOR data. This means that the results are driven only by a few cases of countries experiencing extreme polarization. As a result, it difficult to discern systematic or persistent patterns. However, table 3.2 implies that democracies seem to be more credible than nondemocracies (model 1), but that democracies experiencing extreme polarization on foreign policy issues may be *less* credible relative to other democracies (model 4).

3.4 Polarization and Reliability of Commitments

The final advantage introduced in chapter 2 was the reliability advantage. International relations scholars find that democracies tend to be better at making and keeping international commitments. Domestic constraints provide incentives for leaders to pursue cooperative policies and avoid reneging on international commitments. As a result, democracies should be more reliable partners relative to nondemocracies.

Like credibility, reliability is perceptual. What matters is the perspective of current or potential allies and partners, which is hard to measure. Nevertheless, there are some indicators of a country's tendency to follow through on its commitments. Perhaps the most common approach to assess

47. This interpretation uses a "typical" case of an interstate crisis between a democracy and a nondemocracy that are minor powers, are geographically contiguous, and have a conflict over policy. All continuous variables are held at their medians.

48. See, e.g., Downes and Sechser 2012.

how likely a country is to make or break international commitments is to look at patterns of alliance violation.[49] The Alliance Treaty Obligations and Provisions (ATOP) project, housed at Rice University, collects data on *military alliances*, which ATOP defines as, "formal agreement[s] among independent states to cooperate militarily in the face of potential or realized military conflict."[50] Because alliances are among the most important international commitments, violations of these agreements should create major concerns about a country's reliability.

One consistent finding in the literature on alliance politics is that democratic alliances tend to be more durable.[51] Democracies are less likely to violate alliance agreements than their non-democratic peers.[52] Chapter 2, however, argued that democracies vary in terms of the reliability of their commitments. In extremely polarized democracies, institutional constraints on democratic governance are eroded. Highly partisan voters that want their party or policy to win are unlikely to demand that leaders uphold democratic norms and procedures when entering into or exiting from international commitments. They are also less likely to be concerned about the reputational costs of reneging on an agreement, weakening the vertical constraints that reinforce democratic commitments. At the same time, leaders in polarized contexts have more incentives to circumvent the opposition when making international agreements, weakening horizontal constraints. This should make heavily polarized democracies more likely to renege on commitments and less likely to be perceived as reliable allies.

To explore the relationship between extreme polarization and democratic reliability, table 3.3 replicates and extends canonical work by political scientists Ashley Leeds, Michaela Mattes, and Jeremy Vogel, who theorize about how a country's interests and political institutions shape decisions to violate alliance agreements.[53] The sample in these models includes military alliances from 1919 to 1989 in the Alliance Treaty Obligations and Provisions dataset, and the unit of analysis is the alliance member-year. Following Leeds, Mattes, and Vogel, all models in table 3.3 are logistic regression models with controls for temporal dependence[54] and standard errors clustered by alliance.

49. See, e.g., Leeds 2003; Leeds, Mattes, and Vogel 2009; Leeds and Savun 2007; LeVeck and Narang 2017; Mattes 2012.
50. Leeds et al. 2002.
51. Gaubatz 1996.
52. Leeds and Savun 2007; Leeds, Mattes, and Vogel 2009.
53. Leeds, Mattes, and Vogel 2009.
54. Carter and Signorino 2010.

TABLE 3.3. Replication and extension of Leeds, Mattes, and Vogel (2009)

	Alliance violation					
	Full sample			Democracies only		
	(1)	(2)	(3)	(4)	(5)	(6)
Leader change	0.446 (0.315)					
SOLS change		0.889** (0.436)				
			0.910 (0.568)			
				0.213 (0.778)		
Extreme right–left polarization					3.329*** (0.716)	
Extreme hawk–dove polarization						0.976 (2.027)
Change in international power	0.817** (0.327)	0.803** (0.331)	0.062 (1.096)	0.020 (1.067)	17.602*** (1.825)	17.663*** (0.589)
Change in political institutions	0.150 (0.306)	0.131 (0.308)	−0.852 (1.092)	−0.866 (1.115)	−2.630* (1.544)	−1.434 (1.171)
Decrease in threat for this state or increase in threat for ally	0.424 (0.273)	0.421 (0.271)	−1.049 (0.648)	−0.992 (0.646)	−0.910 (1.644)	−0.691 (1.373)
New outside alliance	1.091*** (0.254)	1.070*** (0.254)	0.649 (0.582)	0.698 (0.589)	−17.291*** (0.725)	−17.561*** (0.932)
Democratic state	−1.217*** (0.360)	−1.322*** (0.393)				

One major + one minor power	−0.417	−0.408	0.474	0.483	16.205***	16.597***
	(0.258)	(0.259)	(0.939)	(0.919)	(1.441)	(1.303)
Nonmilitary cooperation	−0.744***	−0.746***	−0.715	−0.706	0.419	0.313
	(0.259)	(0.258)	(0.820)	(0.853)	(1.359)	(1.364)
Treaty requiring ratification	−0.091	−0.083	−0.412	−0.275	−1.631*	−1.492*
	(0.358)	(0.355)	(0.812)	(0.828)	(0.924)	(0.894)
Peacetime military coordination	0.557***	0.557***	−0.369	−0.401	0.200	0.070
	(0.180)	(0.180)	(0.311)	(0.330)	(0.939)	(1.133)
Time	−0.090	−0.086	−0.181	−0.143	0.305	−0.074
	(0.078)	(0.077)	(0.170)	(0.181)	(0.399)	(0.546)
Time squared	0.001	0.001	0.023	0.020	0.005	0.020
	(0.004)	(0.004)	(0.014)	(0.015)	(0.036)	(0.041)
Time cubed	0.00001	0.00002	−0.001*	−0.0005	−0.0003	−0.001
	(0.0001)	(0.0001)	(0.0003)	(0.0003)	(0.001)	(0.001)
Constant	−4.465***	−4.448***	−4.813***	−4.649***	−42.599***	−39.734***
	(0.437)	(0.441)	(1.457)	(1.381)	(1.935)	(1.769)
Observations	6,612	6,612	1,865	1,865	1,101	1,101

Note: *p < 0.1; **p < 0.05; ***p < 0.01

Across all models, the dependent variable ("*alliance violation*") is an indicator for whether the alliance was violated by an alliance member in a given year. Models 1 and 2 include the full sample of countries used by Leeds, Mattes, and Vogel (2009), which pool together alliance members that are democracies and nondemocracies.[55] The models also include control variables that could explain a country's decision to violate existing alliance commitments: shifts in international power, changes in the country's domestic political institutions, changes in the threat environment, the formation of a new outside alliance, the level of democracy within the state, power asymmetries within the alliance, and key features of the alliance agreement (for example, whether the agreement requires domestic ratification and/or includes nonmilitary cooperation or peacetime military coordination).

Using the full sample of alliance members, models 1 and 2 show key takeaways identified by Leeds, Mattes, and Vogel. In model 1, the coefficient on "*leader change*" is not statistically significant at conventional levels, which suggests no systematic association between a change in leadership within a given alliance member and a corresponding alliance violation. However, as seen in model 2, when pooling together the sample of democracies and nondemocracies, a "*SOLS change*" (a change in the societal coalition supporting a leader, such as a turnover of the executive party in a democracy) is associated with an increased likelihood of alliance violation. Finally, in both models 1 and 2, the coefficient on "*democratic state*" is negative and statistically significant, emphasizing that, on average, democracies are less likely than nondemocracies to violate alliance commitments.

Models 3 through 6 extend the analysis from Leeds, Mattes, and Vogel by focusing only on the subsample of democratic alliance members. Within democracies, "*leader change*" (model 3) and "*SOLS change*" (model 4) do not appear to be correlated with alliance violations. Importantly, model 4 shows that turnover of the executive party does not result in substantial shifts in alliance behavior. This finding emphasizes that the results in model 2 are largely driven by foreign policy instability in nondemocracies, consistent with findings from Leeds, Mattes, and Vogel.

Models 5 and 6 introduce indicators for "*extreme right–left polarization*" (model 5) and "*extreme hawk–dove polarization*" (model 6). Both of the coefficients are in the expected direction (positive), but only the coefficient on

---

55. Model 2 in table 3.3 replicates model 1 in table 1 in Leeds, Mattes, and Vogel 2009.

"*extreme right–left polarization*" is statistically significant at conventional levels. Model 5 suggests that countries with very high levels of right–left polarization are, on average, more likely to violate their alliance commitments relative to democracies that do not face similar levels of domestic polarization.

In interpreting these models, it is important to emphasize that alliance violations are pretty rare. Across the full sample, violations occur in only 1.1 percent of alliance member-years. A substantive interpretation of model 5 suggests that, holding all other variables at their median values, extremely polarized democracies violate alliances in 2.9 percent of alliance member-years.[56] In other words, while the baseline rate of alliance violation is relatively low, extremely polarized democracies appear to be two to three times more likely to violate alliances on average.

The results of models 5 and 6 are inconclusive, largely because they hinge on just a few alliance violations within democracies.[57] Nevertheless, they demonstrate the plausibility of hypotheses outlined in chapter 2. The primary takeaway from this set of analyses is that, while there is considerable evidence for the democratic advantages, variation in the behavior of democracies likely arises from different degrees of polarization. In the models presented in this chapter, not all coefficients on indicators of extreme polarization were significantly associated with the respective foreign policy outcomes. However, the results collectively suggest that, to the extent extreme polarization plays a role in shaping foreign policy, the effects are more likely to be negative than positive. This dynamic warrants a closer look, particularly given concerns about rising polarization in many advanced democracies around the world.

3.5 Conclusion

This chapter drew on an original dataset tracking the political party and ideological positions of the executive and the opposition parties in fifty-five democracies from 1945 to 2020. The dataset was developed with a crosswalk of the Archigos leader project and MARPOR on party platforms. I used the data to develop measures of extreme polarization on both a right–left

---

56. This interpretation uses a "typical" case of an alliance partnership involving one major and one minor power, which consists of a treaty that requires domestic ratification.

57. In models 5 and 6, factors like the change in international power, the presence of a new outside alliance, and the asymmetry of power between alliance partners appear highly correlated with alliance violations. This is driven by the fact that there are relatively few alliance violations in this smaller sample of democracies.

and a hawk–dove spectrum that reflected partisan divergence on liberal–conservative ideology and relative hawkishness in foreign affairs, respectively. I then incorporated these measures into foundational models of the democratic advantage in international relations. This exercise serves as a plausibility probe to motivate investigating the relationship between extreme polarization and the democratic advantages.

The first set of analyses focused on the stability advantage: the fact that democracies tend to maintain consistent foreign policy despite leader turnover. Using measures of country-level foreign policy positions constructed from roll-call votes in UNGA, I first replicated results from Mattes, Leeds, and Carroll that supported the stability advantage, showing that democracies tend to have more stable foreign policies than nondemocracies.[58] Then, introducing new measures of extreme polarization, I demonstrated that democracies experiencing high levels of hawk–dove polarization appeared to have greater instability in foreign policy relative to other democracies.

The second set of analyses focused on the credibility advantage: the ability of democracies to issue credible coercive threats to their foreign adversaries. I replicated and extended findings from Kenneth Schultz's classic models of reciprocation in militarized interstate disputes.[59] Schultz shows that because threats issued by democracies tend to be perceived as credible, the targets in a dispute are less likely to take military actions in response to coercive demands made by democracies. An extension of Schultz's analyses showed that when democracies experiencing extreme hawk–dove polarization initiated disputes, their targets were more likely to respond with threats or displays of force. This finding suggests that extremely polarized democracies could be perceived as less credible.

The final set of analyses investigated the reliability advantage: the ability of democracies to maintain their international commitments and be perceived as reliable partners. For these analyses, I extended research by Leeds, Mattes, and Vogel on alliance violations.[60] Replicating results from these researchers, I showed that democracies tend to be less likely to violate alliance commitments than nondemocracies. However, democracies experiencing extreme right–left polarization may be more likely to violate alliance commitments relative to their less polarized democratic peers.

58. Mattes, Leeds, and Carroll 2015.
59. Schultz 2001a.
60. Leeds, Mattes, and Vogel 2009.

There are limitations to these analyses. Most importantly, the measures used in cross-national analyses of polarization are imperfect. It is difficult to construct reliable and valid measures of polarization that enable comparisons across different contexts and political systems. We also lack reliable longitudinal data on affective polarization that could help us evaluate the behavior of extremely polarized democracies (i.e., democracies that experience high levels of ideological and affective polarization concurrently). Moreover, the outcome variables that we can observe cross-nationally, such as military actions taken during interstate disputes or violations of alliance agreements, focus on large changes in foreign policy behavior. Other important changes in foreign policy are not captured by these measures. Given the limitations of the data, many of the key results in these analyses are driven by only a few cases.

The evidence presented in this chapter is not definitive. Rather, this chapter serves as a plausibility probe to examine the relationship between extreme polarization and democratic advantages. Since polarization is a multicausal and structural phenomenon, descriptive analyses cannot isolate the causal effect of polarization on a given foreign policy outcome. However, since foundational scholarship in the democratic advantage tradition relies on cross-national analyses of regime type and foreign policy outcomes, this approach is a useful starting point. It further motivates careful within-case analysis of the relationship between polarization and foreign policy. The three remaining empirical chapters focus on the case of contemporary U.S. foreign policy, illustrating the logic behind each of the three democratic advantages and describing how these advantages are eroded by extreme forms of polarization in practice.

4

Polarization and the Stability Advantage

IN 1984, AT the International Conference on Population in Mexico City, Republican President Ronald Reagan introduced a policy that restricted the U.S. government from funding nonprofit organizations that "perform or actively promote abortion as a method of family planning."[1] The policy, nicknamed the Mexico City Policy given the location of its introduction, would become a highly partisan issue.[2] When Democratic President Bill Clinton arrived in office in 1993, he issued an executive order that repealed the policy. Across subsequent presidential administrations, following party turnover at the White House, Democratic presidents rescinded the Mexico City Policy while Republicans reinstated it.

Volatility across presidential administrations poses challenges for international organizations that depend on the United States for foreign aid. According to researchers, dramatic shifts in development aid that are conditional on which party occupies the White House can have far-reaching consequences for global health.[3] Surprising U.S. electoral results make it difficult for global health organizations to engage in long-term planning. For instance, since the vast majority of pollsters failed to predict Republican candidate Donald Trump's victory over Democratic candidate Hillary Clinton in the 2016 presidential election, foreign partners had not anticipated a reinstatement of the Mexico City Policy. In 2017, however, a newly inaugurated President

---

1. White House Office of Policy Development 1984.
2. Critics of the Mexico City Policy also refer to it as the "Global Gag Rule."
3. See, e.g., Hunter 2023; Lane, Ayeb-Karlsson, and Shahvisi 2021; Mavodza, Goldman, and Cooper 2019.

Trump not only reinstated but also expanded the policy, renamed Protecting Life in Global Health Assistance. The expanded policy applied to a broader range of foreign programs and partners, creating "a wave of uncertainty in aid-dependent countries."[4]

Abortion and related social issues tend to be domestic policy issues. Yet, as the Mexico City Policy illustrates, there are times when debates about social policy impact foreign affairs. Political scientists Geoffrey Layman and Thomas Carsey coined the term *conflict extension* to describe the process by which partisan conflict extends from one policy domain to another. The researchers use this term to characterize how party activists in the United States extended partisan conflict from economic issues to social, racial, and cultural issues in the 1970s and 1980s.[5] This process fostered greater coherence between ideology and partisanship, fueling polarization.

The phenomenon of conflict extension could also be applied to the extension of partisan conflict from domestic policy to foreign affairs. Some foreign policy issues are more susceptible to these forms of politicization. One way this occurs is when politicians or party activists link issues related to social identity to foreign and defense policy. For instance, partisan debates around race, gender, and sexuality are gradually extended to areas of foreign affairs. Discussions about immigration and refugee policy are interwoven with ethnic and racial identity. And, as illustrated by the Mexico City Policy, questions of gender, religion, and other social identities can inform foreign aid and development policies.

In some sense, growing partisan divisions in foreign and defense policy in the United States are surprising. Chapter 2 discussed how democratic leaders are kept accountable by two systems of constraint. They are constrained by the public (vertical constraints) and by other actors within government (horizontal constraints), including the political opposition and the bureaucracy. In theory, these constraints should moderate foreign policy by keeping policies of major parties consistent, giving democracies a stability advantage in foreign affairs. This is one reason why, in American politics, foreign affairs tend to be much less polarized than domestic affairs are.[6]

This chapter considers how polarization affects foreign policy stability, drawing on examples from contemporary U.S. foreign policy. It first explores

---

4. Bearak and Morello 2018.
5. Layman and Carsey 2002; Layman et al. 2010.
6. Bryan and Tama 2022; Kertzer, Brooks, and Brooks 2021; Tama 2023.

vertical constraints and the role of the public. In a healthy liberal democracy, leaders have incentives to provide public goods and act in the national interest. However, in environments of extreme polarization, politicians may be less likely to target messaging at the median voter and instead work to mobilize their political base. Growing affective polarization in the public encourages politicians to instrumentalize aspects of social and partisan identity in a way that links to foreign policy. I use longitudinal public opinion data to identify areas where partisan conflict has extended into foreign affairs. I first establish that the politicization of foreign policy often happens in conjunction with electoral cycles. I then argue that three areas of U.S. foreign policy have been especially vulnerable to this dynamic over the past two decades: issues in foreign affairs that either activate social identity, involve nontraditional security threats, or reflect ideological debates about multilateralism and internationalism.

Even if foreign policy preferences increasingly diverge along partisan lines, horizontal constraints should in theory still prevent democratic leaders from implementing extreme policies. One such constraint in the United States is a relatively nonpartisan foreign policy bureaucracy that maintains continuity in foreign affairs across presidential administrations. However, I argue that, as polarization becomes more extreme, politicians have greater incentives to politicize foreign policy institutions like the U.S. State Department, the U.S. Department of Defense, and the Central Intelligence Agency. Polarization increases the intensity and frequency of episodes of politicization. Over time, politicization could erode the credibility of nonpartisan foreign policy institutions, preventing them from effectively checking presidential power.

Together, the incremental erosion of vertical and horizontal constraints due to polarization can undermine the stability advantage. Diverging attitudes among both the public and politicians coupled with affective polarization encourage leaders to undo aspects of the other party's foreign policy. Ultimately, as polarization becomes more extreme, democratic foreign policymaking is likely to become more volatile over time. Although policy change is not inherently a bad thing, growing unpredictability could be troubling in foreign affairs, where successful policymaking often requires long time horizons.

4.1 Vertical Constraints and the Stability Advantage

A system of vertical constraints—or electoral accountability—helps democratic leaders remain responsive to the public through regular, contested elections. Electoral accountability aligns foreign policy with the median voter in the electorate and encourages leaders to pursue policies that provide public goods rather than policies that serve special interests.[7] By contrast, in many autocracies, leaders have fewer incentives to provide public goods. Autocrats instead respond to whichever group helps them maintain power. This may be a small group of core supporters, wealthy oligarchs, or ruling party members.

Chapter 2 explained that accountability to a highly polarized public introduces different incentives for democratic leaders. As polarization becomes more extreme, politicians look toward electoral strategies of mobilization rather than strategies of persuasion. To mobilize their base, political leaders could adopt more ideologically extreme policies that align with the values of core supporters. When there are high levels of affective polarization, politicians are also eager to campaign on undoing policies of the opposite party. This means that, in extremely polarized environments, electoral accountability may not have a moderating effect on foreign policy. Instead, electoral dynamics could pull foreign policy issues into the partisan divide. Growing partisanship in foreign affairs should be both reflected in, and reinforced by, public attitudes.

Stability Hypothesis 1: *As polarization becomes more extreme, domestic partisan conflict is more likely to extend into foreign affairs.*

To understand whether polarization is weakening vertical constraints through conflict extension in the United States, I investigate the extent to which public attitudes toward foreign policy issues have become more partisan following overarching trends of polarization in domestic politics. The conventional wisdom is that, despite high levels of polarization in contemporary American politics, key debates in foreign policy tend to be fairly bipartisan.[8] Republicans and Democrats are aligned on core principles of maintaining U.S. alliance commitments, actively engaging in global affairs, and countering security threats posed by adversaries like China and Russia. Yet, since the early 2000s, we have seen troubling signs that foreign policy is becoming increasingly partisan. There are many theories as to why this is the case. Some researchers attribute partisan divergence to a critical juncture around

---

7. Bueno de Mesquita et al. 2002; McGillivray and Smith 2008.
8. Bryan and Tama 2022; Chaudoin, Milner, and Tingley 2010; Friedman 2024; Kertzer, Brooks, and Brooks 2021; Tama 2023.

the Iraq War in 2003, which became heavily politicized.[9] Others believe that this trend reflects the decline of moderates in Congress who sustained a bipartisan consensus on foreign affairs through the 1990s.[10] Still others believe that contemporary polarization on foreign policy is attributable to the collapse of a common enemy, the Soviet Union, that oriented American grand strategy for decades.[11]

This chapter argues that, on the whole, while foreign policy remains less polarized than does domestic policy, issues related to foreign affairs are steadily being pulled into partisan politics. However, some foreign policy issues are more vulnerable to partisan conflict extension than others. To identify these sets of issues, I draw on longitudinal public opinion data. The primary data source is a set of public opinion surveys fielded by the Chicago Council on Global Affairs (hereafter, CCGA).[12] The CCGA has administered surveys to large, nationally representative samples of U.S. adults since 1974. Unlike other major national surveys about American politics, such as the American National Election Studies or the Cooperative Election Study, the CCGA surveys emphasize foreign policy, providing a valuable perspective on issues that have become more or less polarized. I focus on CCGA data from the past twenty-five years (1998–2022 surveys).[13] Since there is not a publicly available longitudinal data file that connects CCGA surveys at the time of this writing, I construct a longitudinal file and variable codebook, linking together common questions based on the variable descriptions across survey waves (see appendix for details). The resulting data includes fifteen survey waves with over 32,000 total respondents. A total of 139 substantive questions related to foreign policy appear in at least one survey wave, and fifty-six questions appear in at least three different surveys. In addition to the CCGA surveys, I also draw on public opinion data collected by the Pew Research Center and Gallup News.

Drawing on this survey data, I first establish that electoral cycles tend to correlate with more partisan attitudes toward foreign policy. Intuitively,

9. Jeong and Quirk 2019.
10. Kupchan and Trubowitz 2007.
11. Bafumi and Parent 2012; Desch 1998; Kurth 1996.
12. Smeltz et al. 2023.
13. The 1998 survey is the first survey for which variable descriptions are available in the CCGA public datasets and codebooks, making it possible to link common variables across different survey waves.

issues championed by polarizing figures or groups, particularly in the context of a major election, are more likely to be politicized. I next highlight three additional factors that make a foreign policy issue more susceptible to partisan polarization in the United States. The first is whether an issue represents a nontraditional (nonmilitarized) security threat rather than a traditional (militarized) threat. The second is whether an issue can be easily connected to other aspects of social identity that are correlated with partisan identity. The third is whether an issue involves an ideological debate around multilateralism.

4.1.1 Electoral Cycles

Prior to the 2004 presidential election between incumbent Republican President George W. Bush and Democratic Senator John Kerry, the Democratic primary debates featured more foreign policy questions than any set of presidential debates in recent memory. Unsurprisingly, an overwhelming proportion of these questions focused on the Iraq War. By early 2004, the Bush administration conceded that it had failed to find evidence of Iraqi weapons of mass destruction (WMDs). Concerns about WMDs had precipitated the March 2003 U.S.-led invasion of Iraq. Across seven debates, moderators asked a total of thirty-one questions about the Iraq War, averaging over four questions per debate. Yet, despite the fact that the United States was engaged in two major wars in the Middle East, public opinion polls during the 2004 election cycle showed that the two issues American voters cared most about were domestic: the economy and healthcare policy.[14]

Foreign policy is one of the most important aspects of a president's job. However, it tends to play a minor role in presidential elections. Analyses of presidential campaign discourse since the 1960s show a sharp decline in the amount of attention that Republican and Democratic candidates give to national security issues during campaigns.[15] Beyond the 2004 election, only a handful of presidential elections—such as the 1968 and 1972 elections during the Vietnam War era—could be considered "foreign policy elections," where foreign affairs played a central role in campaigns, debates, and election coverage.[16]

---

14. Hickey and Gandhi 2019. Although, see debates about the impact of the Iraq War on the 2004 presidential election: Gelpi, Reifler, and Feaver 2007; Karol and Miguel 2007; McAllister 2006.
15. Sigelman and Buell 2004.
16. Aldrich 1977.

In most presidential elections, however, the American public does not base their vote choice on foreign policy. Early studies of public opinion on foreign policy suggested that this was because Americans did not hold coherent or ideologically consistent views on foreign policy. Instead, the public simply followed elite and party cues.[17] Subsequent generations of researchers writing about public opinion and foreign policy, however, challenged this argument.[18] The current consensus is that Americans do have opinions on major foreign policy events, especially with respect to use-of-force questions.[19] They tend to be fairly prudent in their assessments of U.S. foreign policy and attuned to the country's successes and failures abroad.[20] They view foreign policy competence as an important trait for the presidency.[21] The public also has largely coherent foreign policy orientations that, while shaped in part by elite and party cues, are also influenced by social networks and moral values.[22] However, it still is rare for foreign policy issues to be a decisive factor in presidential vote choice, or for Americans to view foreign policy issues as more pressing than domestic social and economic issues. This pattern holds outside of regular electoral cycles. On average, between 1939 and 2015, less than a quarter of Americans viewed an issue related to foreign relations as "the most important problem" faced by the United States.[23]

Nevertheless, as polarization in American politics has increased, foreign policy issues have also grown more partisan. While the Iraq War may not have played a pivotal role in the results of the 2004 election, the electoral cycle amplified partisan divisions in public attitudes toward the war.[24] During election campaigns, increases in attack advertisements and negative campaigning make political rhetoric more divisive.[25] These trends dovetail with the rise of online and social media. Politicians have incentives to "go negative" in their

17. Almond 1950; Campbell et al. 1960; Converse 1964; Lippmann 1955.
18. See, e.g., Aldrich et al. 2006; Aldrich, Sullivan, and Borgida 1989; Holsti 1992; Kertzer 2023.
19. Mueller 1973; Page and Shapiro 1992.
20. Jentleson 1992; Jentleson and Britton 1998; Nincic 1992.
21. Friedman 2023.
22. On elite cues, see Guisinger and Saunders 2017; Zaller 1992. On social networks, see Kertzer and Zeitzoff 2017. On moral values, see Holsti 1996; Hurwitz and Peffley 1987; Kertzer et al. 2014; Wittkopf 1990.
23. Heffington, Park, and Williams 2019.
24. Berinsky 2009.
25. Geer 2006.

online presence because posts on social media that criticize and mock the other party generate more engagement.[26] Unsurprisingly, more ideologically extreme politicians are more likely to display hostility toward the opposite party on social media.[27]

It is difficult to systematically show that public opinion on foreign policy issues is more partisan during election years relative to nonelection years because public opinion polls tend to focus on different sets of foreign policy issues during each election. To address this problem, I draw on the longitudinal CCGA surveys to analyze a comparable set of foreign policy issues asked across many survey waves: attitudes toward other countries. The CCGA asks a series of feeling thermometer questions in which survey respondents rate their attitudes toward other countries from 0 ("a very cold, unfavorable feeling") to 100 ("a very warm, favorable feeling"). I consider whether there are larger partisan gaps in Americans' attitudes toward U.S. allies and adversaries during election years relative to nonelection years. Table 4.1 shows a correlation between the timing of presidential elections and the partisan gap in how Democrats and Republicans report feeling about other countries. Models 1 and 2 pool across countries, while model 3 includes country fixed effects, comparing assessments of the same country over time. In all models, the estimated coefficient on Election Year is positive and statistically significant, indicating that there are larger partisan differences in perceptions of other countries in surveys run during election years. These effects are modest: the magnitude of the estimated coefficient on Election Year in model 1 corresponds to 0.5 standard deviations of the dependent variable. However, they suggest that, on average, public opinion on foreign policy issues might be more partisan during election years relative to nonelection years in the twenty-first century.

What happens when foreign policy issues get caught up in the electoral cycle? In the long run, these trends could have implications for the stability advantage democracies have in foreign affairs. In highly polarized environments, politicians have incentives to differentiate themselves from the opposition on the campaign trail. They may engage in negative campaigning, attacking the foreign policy of the opposite party. High levels of affective polarization among the electorate give incentives for politicians to campaign on promises to undo the foreign policy of the opposite party. The next sections detail which areas of foreign policy are most vulnerable to this dynamic.

---

26. Ansolabehere and Iyengar 1996; Rathje, Van Bavel, and van der Linden 2021.
27. Yu, Wojcieszak, and Casas 2024.

TABLE 4.1. Partisan gap in country feeling thermometers during election years

	Dependent variable		
	Partisan gap		
	(1)	(2)	(3)
Election year	1.947**	1.954**	1.523**
	(0.940)	(0.945)	(0.661)
U.S. ally		0.307	
		(0.863)	
France			3.029**
			(1.460)
Great Britain			−1.055
			(1.460)
Germany			−4.197***
			(1.411)
Iran			0.707
			(1.411)
Israel			5.255***
			(1.370)
Japan			−4.199***
			(1.411)
North Korea			−2.260
			(1.370)
South Korea			−3.226**
			(1.409)
Russia			−2.425
			(1.528)
Saudi Arabia			−4.151***
			(1.460)
Taiwan			−4.550**
			(1.924)
Turkey			−4.469***
			(1.611)
Constant	4.517***	4.334***	5.992***
	(0.497)	(0.717)	(1.027)
Observations	93	93	93
R^2	0.045	0.046	0.602
Adjusted R^2	0.035	0.025	0.537

Note: *$p < 0.1$; **$p < 0.05$; ***$p < 0.01$

4.1.2 Activation of Social Identity

In April 2019, during a roundtable on immigration and borders in Calexico, California, President Donald Trump remarked, "The system is full. . . . Whether it's asylum, whether it's anything you want, it's illegal immigration. We can't take you anymore. We can't take you. Our country is full."[28] Throughout his first term, President Trump introduced many policies that reflected these sentiments. The Trump White House increased immigration enforcement and deportations, imposed new restrictions on asylum seekers, and enacted an infamous travel ban that affected entrants from many Muslim-majority countries.[29]

Immigration and refugee policy are examples of foreign policy issues that are tied to social identity. Given the increasing correlation between social identities and partisan identity in the United States, foreign policies that activate social identity are especially susceptible to politicization. Immigration debates, for instance, are interwoven with racial, ethnic, and regional identities. Majority White areas and Southern, rural communities express greater concern about border security and more hostility toward immigrants, especially immigrants who are undocumented.[30] In contemporary politics, a large majority of documented and undocumented immigrants to the United States are of Hispanic origin. According to anthropologist Leo Chavez, politicians amplify what he terms the "Latino threat" narrative, cultivating fear and anxiety among White Americans that their communities will be jeopardized by an influx of outsiders.[31]

Polling from CCGA demonstrates a growing partisan divide on attitudes toward immigration. Figure 4.1 plots the percentage of self-reported Republicans (in black) and Democrats (in gray) who perceive "large numbers of immigrants and refugees coming into the U.S." to be a "Critical Threat" to the United States.[32] The figure shows that Democrats have become much less likely to perceive immigrants and refugees as a threat over time, while Republicans have become more concerned about the issue.

Like immigration policy, refugee policy is linked to social and partisan identity. In the United States and many other Western democracies, refugee

---

28. Trump 2019.
29. Pierce, Bolter, and Selee 2018.
30. Fennelly and Federico 2008; Jardina 2019.
31. Chavez 2001.
32. Smeltz et al. 2023.

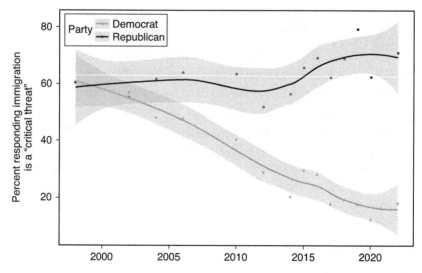

FIGURE 4.1. Partisan gap in threat perception of immigration (CCGA surveys)

resettlement has become an ethnic and racial issue. CCGA surveys show large gaps between the percentages of Republicans (in black) and Democrats (in gray) who approve of policies that relocate refugees to the United States. Figure 4.2 uses data from the 2022 CCGA survey, which asked whether survey respondents would support or oppose policies that accepted refugees from Afghanistan, Taiwan,[33] and Ukraine. Across all three countries, Democrats are consistently more likely to support the relocation of refugees. The largest partisan gap is for Afghanistan: 74 percent of Democrats but only 36 percent of Republicans favor accepting Afghan refugees.

Other social identities, such as class and socioeconomic identity, can also become salient to foreign affairs. Debates around international trade, for instance, often reflect regional, occupational, and socioeconomic differences. In contemporary politics, a broad cleavage exists between groups who favor reducing barriers to trade and tend to support U.S. entry into new trade agreements, versus those who advocate for more protectionist policies. Through the latter half of the twentieth century, U.S. trade policy was fairly bipartisan, with strong support in both parties for free trade policies. However, since the 1990s, and especially following the passage of the North American Free Trade

---

33. The survey question on Taiwan was framed as a hypothetical: "If China were to invade Taiwan, would you support or oppose the United States: Accepting Taiwanese refugees into the United States?"

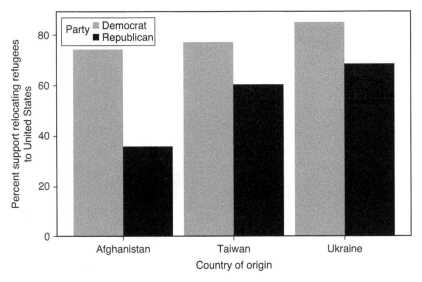

FIGURE 4.2. Partisan gap in support of refugees relocating to the United States (2022 CCGA survey)

Agreement between the United States, Canada, and Mexico, robust bipartisan support for free trade began to erode.

Initial partisan divergence over trade policy was rooted in regional and socioeconomic differences. In the 1990s, many politicians in the Democratic Party who associated with labor and the working class became critical of free trade policies and advocated for greater protections for labor. The Republican Party aligned with "free traders" who favored reducing barriers to trade to improve national welfare. Regional disparities also shaped attitudes toward proposed trade agreements. Beginning in 2001, after China acceded to the World Trade Organization, rising exports from China contributed to the decline of manufacturing in the United States. Regions that were strongholds of manufacturing, such as Midwestern states that formed the Rust Belt, were disproportionately negatively impacted by free trade policies.[34]

The precise impact of the "China shock" is a subject of much debate.[35] Yet, perceptions and realities of economic dislocation amplified economic grievances in working-class communities, particularly in the Midwest and

34. Autor, Dorn, and Hanson 2021.
35. Kennedy and Mazzocco 2022.

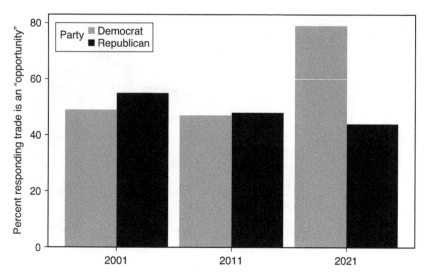

FIGURE 4.3. Partisan gap in perceptions of foreign trade (Gallup polls)

South, as industrial centers hollowed out. In the 2016 U.S. presidential election, areas of the Rust Belt that were formerly aligned with the Democratic Party realigned with Republican then-candidate Donald Trump, who criticized trade agreements like the Trans-Pacific Partnership and trade practices of U.S. competitors like China.[36]

Figure 4.3 illustrates the partisan reversal in attitudes toward international trade using data across three decades from Gallup.[37] The data is based on polls conducted in 2001, 2011, and 2021, which ask, "What do you think foreign trade means for America? Do you see foreign trade more as an opportunity for economic growth through increased US exports or a threat to the economy from foreign imports?" The figure shows the percentage of self-identified Republicans (in black) and Democrats (in gray) who view foreign trade as an economic opportunity. In 2001, Republicans were slightly more likely (55%) than Democrats (49%) to view trade as an opportunity for the United States. By 2021, these attitudes shifted, with 79 percent of Democrats and only 44 percent of Republicans viewing foreign trade as an opportunity.

The political cleavages in the contemporary trade debate are complex. While there remains a good deal of interparty polarization on trade, there

36. Autor et al. 2016.
37. Younis 2021.

is also a surprising amount of intraparty polarization on the issue.[38] Substantial minorities in both parties express skepticism toward proposed trade agreements. In their book *Sailing the Water's Edge*, political scientists Helen Milner and Dustin Tingley explain that areas like trade policy are more likely to realign along partisan cleavages because they have distributive consequences.[39] Politicians instrumentalize narratives around "winners" and "losers" from trade policies to serve their political ends.

In other areas of foreign policy, links to social identity are not self-evident. Yet, as polarization in American politics grows more extreme, we could see social issues bleed into debates in some of these areas. One interesting example is U.S.–China relations. In the 2020s, the "China threat" has become a rare topic of bipartisan consensus among Democrats and Republicans, who increasingly view China as an adversary that threatens U.S. interests.[40] However, if aspects of China policy become more explicitly connected to social issues, this bipartisan agreement may not hold. Some commentators express concerns, for instance, that politicians are racializing the China threat.[41] Heightened threat perceptions of China coincided with a disturbing number of reports of anti-Asian racism and hate crimes targeting Asian American and Pacific Islander communities in the United States.[42] While many aspects of U.S. policy toward China are likely to remain bipartisan in the short run, other areas that link to social identity could be instrumentalized by opportunistic politicians. The interconnections of social identity and foreign policy are likely to affect the (in)stability of policies across presidential administrations. When a different party controls the presidency, policies could dramatically shift depending on who is in office.

4.1.3 Nontraditional Security Threats

In the first debate of the 2024 Republican presidential primary, hosted in Milwaukee, Wisconsin, the moderator asked, "Do you believe human behavior is causing climate change? Raise your hand if you do." None of the eight Republican presidential candidates on stage raised their hand. The response from Republican politicians contrasted sharply with messaging from Democratic

---

38. Friedrichs 2022; Mutz 2021.
39. Milner and Tingley 2015.
40. Myrick, Eng, and Weinberg 2022.
41. Zhou 2021.
42. Jeung 2023; Kim 2022.

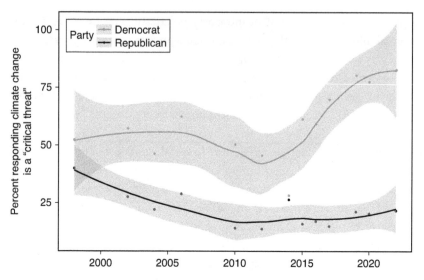

FIGURE 4.4. Partisan gap in threat perception of climate change (CCGA surveys)

politicians in the White House. In 2021, the first year of Democratic President Joe Biden's administration, the White House Press Office had released a statement emphasizing that, "From Day One, the Biden–Harris Administration has prioritized addressing the climate crisis both at home and as a core element of our national security and foreign policy."[43]

Partisan divergence in attitudes toward climate change and other aspects of environmental security continues to grow in the United States. As figure 4.4 shows, over time, Democrats have become increasingly worried about the threat posed by climate change, while Republicans have grown increasingly skeptical. In the 2022 CCGA survey, over three-fourths of Democrats but only one-fourth of Republicans said that climate change was a "Critical Threat." Large partisan gaps also persist in attitudes toward climate agreements and other areas of environmental policy.[44]

Debates around climate policy highlight a distinction between attitudes toward traditional (militarized) and nontraditional (nonmilitarized) security threats. While there is a fair amount of agreement across the parties about defense commitments, nuclear policy, and threats posed by adversaries like

43. White House Press Office 2021a.
44. Dunlap, McCright, and Yarosh 2016.

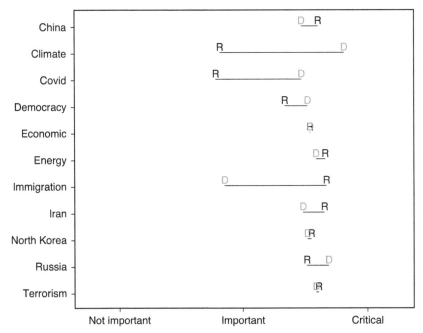

FIGURE 4.5. Partisan gap in perceptions of different security threats (2022 CCGA survey)

Russia and China, there is substantial disagreement about nontraditional security threats, such as those related to climate change, immigration, and global health security. Using data from Republican and Democratic party platforms in the twenty-first century, political scientist Jeffrey Friedman finds that both parties remain committed to the core principles of U.S. grand strategy, but these bipartisan commitments do not persist in other areas of foreign policy.[45] Friedman explains that perceptions that the bipartisan consensus in foreign affairs is eroding have less to do with disagreement over core principles and more to do with an expanding set of foreign policy issues.

An implication of Friedman's analysis is that debates around nontraditional security threats are more polarized than those around traditional ones. Data from the 2022 CCGA survey supports this observation. Figure 4.5 shows the average threat perception of Republicans and Democrats across eleven issue areas: China, climate change, the COVID-19 pandemic, democracy, the economy, energy, immigration, Iran, North Korea, Russia, and terrorism. The

45. Friedman 2024.

average Republican response is represented by an "R" (in black) and the average Democratic response is represented by a "D" (in gray). The line segment connecting the two averages illustrates the partisan gap in threat perception. As the figure shows, the largest gaps in threat perception are around what we might term nontraditional security threats, including threats posed by climate change, immigration, and the COVID-19 pandemic.

What causes partisan divergence around perceptions of nontraditional threats? One possibility is the timing in which these threats have arisen. Concerns about climate change and border security emerged in an era of heightened partisan polarization, and responses to security threats often reflect the degree of polarization in the existing political environment.[46] Another possibility is that it is easier for politicians to manipulate perceptions of nontraditional threats. In their book *Anxious Politics*, political scientists Bethany Albertson and Shana Gadarian draw a distinction between "unframed threats" that are inherently frightening to the public and "framed threats," which induce fear primarily through political messaging.[47] Concerns about border security in the United States, for example, may not inherently frighten the American public, but these fears can be cultivated by politicians and political media.

In the wake of the COVID-19 pandemic, another nontraditional security threat that has received much attention is global health security. Throughout 2020, Republican President Donald Trump downplayed the virus, proclaiming that "It's going to disappear" (February 27, 2020) and "It affects virtually nobody" (September 21, 2020).[48] During the 2020 Democratic presidential primary, then-candidate Joe Biden took the opposite tack, criticizing President Trump for being "dismissive" of COVID-19.[49] In part due to elite and party cues, Democrats and Republicans had different beliefs about and attitudes toward the COVID-19 pandemic and the subsequent vaccination campaign.[50] Public assessments of the response of the World Health Organization and the role that the United States should play in distribution of COVID-19 vaccines globally were also highly partisan.[51]

46. Myrick 2021.
47. Albertson and Gadarian 2015.
48. Summers 2020.
49. Swasey 2020.
50. Gadarian, Goodman, and Pepinsky 2022.
51. Moncus and Connaughton 2020; Sparks et al. 2021.

One could also envision future scenarios where Democratic administrations largely focus U.S. grand strategy on nontraditional threats like climate change and global health security, whereas Republican administrations focus on an entirely different set of priorities.[52] Even if the parties do not reorient grand strategy, partisan divergence in nontraditional areas of security suggests that policies in these areas will be more volatile with leader turnover.

4.1.4 Debates around Multilateralism and Internationalism

Partisan debates around multilateralism (the principle of working together with countries to resolve political problems) and internationalism (the extent to which a country engages in international politics) are not new. In *U.S. Global Leadership Role and Domestic Polarization*, Gordon Friedrichs emphasizes that these debates reflect different ideological values and beliefs about the role that the United States should play in the world.[53] Political scientists Benjamin Fordham and Michael Flynn characterize a deep undercurrent of skepticism in the Republican Party toward internationalism and multilateralism in particular.[54] These attitudes manifest in different ways throughout U.S. history. Most famously, in the 1920s, congressional Republicans like Henry Cabot Lodge strongly opposed Democratic President Woodrow Wilson's internationalist policies and collective security arrangements like the League of Nations.[55] In the 1920 Republican Party Platform, Republicans proclaimed that the Versailles Treaty signed at the end of World War I "threatened the very existence of the United States as an independent power."[56] Throughout the latter half of the twentieth century, conservative Republicans continued to oppose international courts and international institutions like the UN.[57]

Following World War II, America's orientation toward multilateralism reflects two sets of commitments associated with a grand strategy of "deep engagement."[58] The first set is security guarantees made to allies that the United States will come to their aid in the event that their security is threatened. These commitments are reinforced by a network of military alliances

---

52. See, e.g., Busby 2021; Colgan 2021; Jentleson 2020.
53. Friedrichs 2021.
54. Fordham and Flynn 2023.
55. Kupchan 2020; Rose 2021.
56. Republican Convention 1920, 551.
57. Fordham and Flynn 2023.
58. Brooks and Wohlforth 2016.

and the presence of over 200,000 active-duty U.S. military personnel overseas. In Europe, U.S. membership in the North Atlantic Treaty Organization (NATO) fosters security cooperation and economic ties between the United States and its European allies. In Asia, the presence of American military personnel reinforces U.S. security commitments to South Korea and Japan and balances against Chinese influence. In the Middle East, U.S. military bases in the Persian Gulf facilitate access to oil and natural gas, cooperation on counterterrorism, and deterrence against Iranian aggression.

The second set of commitments is to international institutions that promote cooperation among states. These include institutions like the UN, the World Trade Organization, the International Monetary Fund, and the World Bank, which facilitate cooperation around security and human rights, trade, monetary policy, and economic development, respectively. These commitments also encompass the network of multilateral agreements that span different domains of foreign policy, promoting adherence to a rules-based international order.

Public opinion surveys explore whether attitudes toward multilateralism and internationalism have diverged along partisan lines in the eyes of the American public. One question asked across many waves of the CCGA surveys captures an internationalist orientation, asking respondents, "Do you believe the US should play an active role in world affairs or stay out?" In their 2020 report, the CCGA emphasized that a strong majority of Americans continue to support the United States playing an active role in the world.[59] This observation is often used to characterize a persistent bipartisan consensus in foreign policy.[60] Figure 4.6 shows that while a majority of both parties still support the United States taking an active role in foreign affairs, the gap between Republicans and Democrats has slightly increased in the last few years, with Republicans becoming more isolationist.

Of course, the phrase "active in world affairs" is somewhat ambiguous. Some respondents might have in mind the United States playing a more active role in overseas wars and military interventions. Others may be thinking about the United States playing an active role in international institutions, trade, and development programs. Public opinion data on perceptions of international organizations like NATO and the UN can provide a clearer picture of the partisan gap in attitudes toward multilateralism. The CCGA asks respondents:

---

59. Smeltz et al. 2020.
60. See, e.g., Chaudoin, Milner, and Tingley 2010.

POLARIZATION AND THE STABILITY ADVANTAGE 131

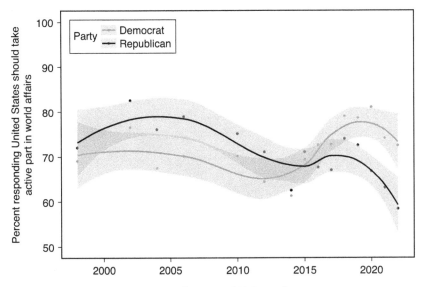

FIGURE 4.6. Partisan gap in attitudes toward U.S. involvement in world affairs (CCGA surveys)

"Do you feel we should increase our commitment to NATO, keep our commitment what it is now, decrease our commitment to NATO, or withdraw from NATO entirely?" Figure 4.7 plots the percentage of respondents who believe either that the United States should decrease its commitment or withdraw from NATO entirely. Over the past two decades, Republicans have expressed more skepticism toward NATO than have Democrats. However, attitudes among partisans were not significantly different until about 2014. During the first Trump administration, attitudes toward NATO diverged further along partisan lines. The figure shows that in 2020, for example, close to 40 percent of self-identified Republicans advocated for the United States decreasing its commitment or withdrawing entirely, while only 10 percent of Democrats expressed a similar view. Following the full-scale Russian invasion of Ukraine in February 2022, Republicans became more favorable toward the alliance. In the 2022 CCGA survey, only one-quarter of Republicans believed that the United States should decrease its commitment to NATO or withdraw from the institution.

Polling from Gallup News shows a similar partisan gap in attitudes toward the UN. Figure 4.8 shows the results of surveys conducted by Gallup in 2000, 2010, and 2020.[61] The plot displays the percentage of respondents

---

61. Brenan 2020.

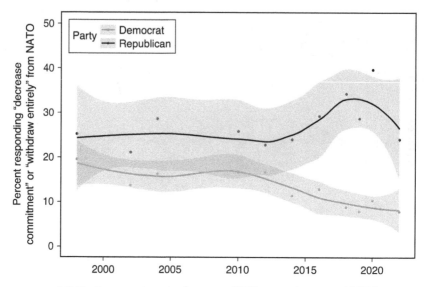

FIGURE 4.7. Partisan gap in attitudes toward U.S. commitment to NATO (CCGA surveys)

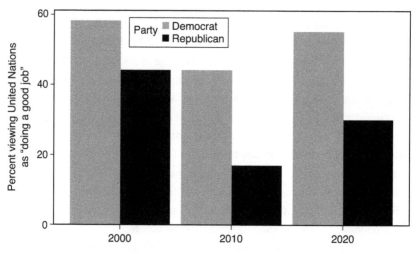

FIGURE 4.8. Partisan gap in attitudes toward the UN (Gallup polls)

who think that "the United Nations is doing a good job ... in trying to solve problems it has had to face." Republicans have been persistently more skeptical of the UN than have Democrats. In the 2020 Gallup survey, 55 percent of Democrats but only 30 percent of Republicans felt that the UN was effectively tackling international problems. The persistent trend in Republican skepticism of multilateralism is likely to continue into the future. Given the current configuration of partisan preferences, we should anticipate on average that Republican presidents will be more likely to criticize or threaten to withdraw from international institutions, creating the potential for inconsistency with leader turnover.

4.2 Horizontal Constraints and the Stability Advantage

Drawing on public opinion data, this chapter provided evidence that some foreign policy issues have grown increasingly partisan since the early 2000s. However, even if foreign policy preferences diverge along party lines, other features of democracies should still help to uphold the stability advantage in international politics. One such feature is a system of horizontal constraints, or intra-governmental checks on executive power. Some horizontal constraints arise from an active political opposition, which carefully monitors the incumbent leader. As discussed in chapter 2, a unique aspect of foreign policymaking is the importance of long time horizons. International commitments stretch beyond the leader who made them, and democratic leaders anticipate that they will not remain in power in perpetuity. This expectation of future turnover gives incentives for parties and their leaders to maintain what researchers refer to as a "tacit partisan truce" in foreign affairs.[62] To preserve a partisan truce in foreign policy, leaders invest in nonpartisan institutions that create continuity in foreign affairs across different administrations. Bureaucrats at these institutions provide necessary expertise and maintain stability in these policy areas. A large majority of members of these institutions are nonpartisan professionals or "careerists" who implement government policies across successive presidential administrations.

Chapter 2 argued that as polarization becomes more extreme, politicians have fewer incentives to maintain this partisan truce. They may, for example, seek to appeal to their political base by campaigning on and enacting more ideologically extreme policies. In addition, they may attempt to score political points or policy wins by politicizing nonpartisan foreign policy institutions. While such actions might lead to short-term political gains, in the long run they erode the credibility of nonpartisan institutions and make them less effective in checking executive power. Coupled with the partisan divergence in foreign policy preferences, the weakening of horizontal constraints

62. Alesina 1987, 1988; Gowa 1998.

on executive power can lead to larger charges in foreign policy with leader turnover.

Stability Hypothesis 2: *As polarization becomes more extreme, politicians are more likely to politicize the foreign policy bureaucracy.*

This chapter explores how environments of extreme polarization contribute to the politicization of foreign policy institutions and the erosion of horizontal constraints on executive power. To do so, it develops a typology of strategies of politicization and examines trends across three major sets of institutions associated with foreign and defense policy in the United States: the State Department, the Department of Defense, and the Central Intelligence Agency. I argue that parties and their leaders erode a partisan truce by politicizing foreign policy bureaucracies using four main strategies.[63] First, through a process of *bandwagoning*, politicians associate themselves with well-regarded institutions in order to gain support or legitimacy in the relevant foreign policy domain. If a highly polarizing figure or group is associated with—or perceived to be associated with—a nonpartisan institution, this increases the perception that the institution has a partisan agenda. For example, a polarizing politician might try to associate with the U.S. military, given persistently high levels of confidence in the military among the American public.

Other strategies of politicization are more likely when there is a misalignment of ideology or interests between the president and the respective foreign policy institution. Three strategies are common in these cases. The first is a strategy of *pressuring*, where politicians lean heavily on nonpartisan institutions to support their own agenda. This is most likely to occur when institutions have high credibility that politicians seek to leverage for their advantage. Concerns about this strategy of politicization arise, for example, when leaders pressure the intelligence community to reach conclusions that align with the leaders' own views.

Next, in processes of *sidelining*, leaders circumvent an institution and centralize policymaking functions elsewhere. Leaders are most likely to do this

---

63. Beyond these four strategies, there are other ways that institutions become politicized. For example, in processes of "active politicization" (Robinson 2022), professionals within an institution align themselves with polarizing political figures. However, since this discussion focuses on the erosion of horizontal constraints, I emphasize the efforts of parties and their leaders to politicize bureaucracies rather than the actions of individuals within these bureaucracies.

when they are not ideologically aligned with the institution. For example, the increase in the use of special envoys, special representatives, and advisory committees to conduct U.S. foreign relations is viewed by some as a way of *sidelining* career diplomats in favor of political appointees at the State Department.

Finally, through the process of *transformation*, leaders attempt to purge political opponents or appoint loyalists to the bureaucracy. This strategy is likely when a department or agency is ideologically dissimilar from the president.[64] In American politics, the conventional understanding is that since the administration of President Richard Nixon (1969–1974), presidents have increasingly sought to centralize their power by nominating political appointees to the federal bureaucracy who share their ideological values.[65] In the foreign policy bureaucracy, presidents are less likely to make bipartisan appointments as congressional polarization increases.[66]

The rest of this section describes the three sets of foreign policy institutions, highlighting trends in politicization. A few overarching trends are notable. First, politicization happens in many ways. When there is misalignment between the ideological preferences of a leader and the foreign policy institution, it is more likely that the leader will attempt to sideline or transform an institution. By contrast, when the institution is well regarded and aligned with the leader, leaders attempt to bandwagon, associating themselves with the institution to increase their credibility.

Second, instances of blatant politicization are somewhat rare. Most processes of politicization are what political scientist Joshua Rovner refers to as "soft politicization."[67] This comes in many forms. For example, individuals working with the bureaucracy may feel constrained by the political environment. Partisan figures may associate with nonpartisan institutions, eroding their perceived credibility. Leaders may gradually shift power away from nonpartisan actors and institutions to more partisan ones.

Third, politicization is not new, and polarization is not the only factor that contributes to the politicization of the foreign policy bureaucracy. However, polarization appears to increase the intensity and frequency of instances of politicization. Polarization also increases the likelihood that the opposing

64. Lewis 2009.
65. Helco 1977; Moe 1985; Nathan 1983; Rudalevige 2005.
66. Flynn 2014.
67. Rovner 2013.

party will accuse the executive of politicizing the bureaucracy, whether or not such accusations are merited. While the strategies of politicization discussed in this chapter are not exhaustive, they provide a starting point to identify ways in which the partisan truce can be eroded.

4.2.1 The Department of State

The U.S. Department of State, headed by the secretary of state, is the locus of U.S. foreign relations and diplomacy. The State Department performs many functions, from maintaining embassies and consulates abroad, to negotiating treaties with foreign partners, to overseeing the distribution of U.S. aid. The department is divided into regional and functional bureaus. Regional bureaus deal with U.S. foreign relations with geographic areas (e.g., Bureau of East Asian and Pacific Affairs) while functional bureaus deal with foreign policy issue areas (e.g., Bureau for Democracy, Human Rights, and Labor).

The State Department consists of multiple sets of employees. At the core of the department are Foreign Service Officers (FSOs), who spend considerable time overseas representing the diplomatic interests of the United States. Employees of the civil service support these missions from Washington, D.C., and elsewhere in the United States. In 2023, the State Department contained "13,000 members of the Foreign Service, 11,000 Civil Service employees, and 45,000 locally employed staff at more than 270 diplomatic missions worldwide."[68] Many leadership positions at State are occupied by political appointees who are appointed by the president. Appointees make up a relatively small proportion of the total employees but tend to hold important leadership positions. The majority are high-level appointees (i.e., at the assistant secretary level or higher) that must be confirmed by the U.S. Senate. Another group of political appointees at State are "Schedule C" appointees, who do not require confirmation and often serve as assistant or policy advisors.

Early studies of the politicization of bureaucratic politics emphasized that departments like the State Department, which requires specialization and expertise on foreign affairs, tended to have a higher number of political appointees that were—at least officially—unaffiliated with a political party. For example, a study conducted in the 1980s examined party affiliation among Senate-confirmed political appointees from 1961 to 1980.[69] The study

---

68. As quoted in U.S. Department of State (2024).
69. Brown 1982.

found that a higher proportion of top-ranking appointees working in foreign and defense policy at the State Department and the Department of Defense self-identified as Independents. It should therefore be unsurprising that the history of U.S. foreign relations is full of prominent examples of diplomatic figures who served in both Republican and Democratic administrations. A more recent expert survey of the ideology of executive agencies published in 2008 suggested that the State Department is perceived to be ideologically moderate (albeit slightly left of center) on a liberal–conservative spectrum.[70]

While the State Department—and particularly careerists within the department—remains relatively nonpartisan, a few trends suggest incremental processes of politicization. The first and most noteworthy is the process of sidelining that occurs as the locus of decision-making in foreign affairs increasingly moves away from the State Department into the White House. The influence of the State Department has always waxed and waned across time under different presidents.[71] However, the overarching trend has been toward a centralization of presidential power. Historian Arthur Schlesinger coined the term "imperial presidency" in 1973 to describe the expansion of presidential power under President Richard Nixon. One aspect of the imperial presidency that Schlesinger focused on was Nixon's unchecked authority in foreign affairs.[72] Researchers have since applied the concept to characterize expansive foreign policy decisions under both Democratic and Republican presidents, including the Clinton administration's (1993–2001) involvement in Bosnia,[73] the George W. Bush administration's (2001–2009) Global War on Terrorism, and the Obama administration's (2009–2017) drone program in the Middle East.[74]

In foreign affairs, the sidelining of the State Department has in part been a consequence of presidents centralizing power through the National Security Council (NSC). The NSC is a forum of senior officials in the White House that advises the president on national security matters. Over time, the size of the NSC has ballooned, from dozens of professionals in the

70. Clinton and Lewis 2008.
71. Dudley 2023, for example, creates a measure of "civil–diplomatic relations" across presidential administrations to characterize the relative proximity of the president and State Department leaders.
72. Schlesinger 1973.
73. Banks and Straussman 1999.
74. Hendrickson 2015.

mid-twentieth century to a staff of hundreds.[75] The growth of the NSC is partly explained by the large number of national security threats that presidents contend with in contemporary politics. However, the polarization of domestic politics also strengthens the NSC relative to the State Department. A report by the Brookings Institution explained that polarization "pulls the national security adviser closer to the political side of the White House. And it pushes the secretary of state, normally less attuned to partisan matters, farther away from the mix of factors the president will weigh in making decisions."[76]

In addition to the sidelining of the State Department, commentators have pointed to processes of transformation that the State Department has undergone in recent decades as presidents privilege noncareer political appointees over career Foreign Service Officers. In a 2013 op-ed published by the *Washington Post*, a group of current and former career diplomats said, "The professional career service that is intended to be the backbone of that diplomacy no longer claims a lead role at the State Department or in the formulation or implementation of foreign policy."[77]

A 2015 report released by the American Academy of Diplomacy expanded on these trends, emphasizing "the politicization of and reduction in the role of the professional Foreign Service in diplomacy."[78] Three trends described in the report are suggestive of the politicization of U.S. diplomacy, although their potential consequences are not well understood. The first trend, consistent with processes of transformation, is that senior leadership positions at State are increasingly occupied by noncareer political appointees rather than career Foreign Service Officers.[79] The report showed that, in 1975, 37 percent of senior leadership positions were held by noncareer political appointees. By 2014, that percentage had swelled to 51 percent.

A related trend is the surge of vacancies or "acting" political officials who hold senior leadership positions. Acting officials are typically political appointees who have not yet been confirmed by the Senate. Vacancies or acting officials were 0 percent of the senior leadership positions in 1975 but

75. In 2021, at the outset of the Biden administration, the NSC staff consisted of more than 350 people (Lippman, Toosi, and Forgey 2021).
76. Destler and Daalder 2000.
77. Johnson, Neumann, and Pickering 2013.
78. American Academy of Diplomacy 2015, 9.
79. The authors of the report define senior leadership as holding a position as assistant secretary or above.

12 percent in 2014.[80] This is consistent with a growing trend of vacancies observed across executive agencies.[81] In part, vacancies are a byproduct of congressional polarization and anticipated opposition during the Senate confirmation process for high-level political appointees. However, presidents may also choose to delay nominations strategically to exert more control over the bureaucracy.[82]

The third trend described by the American Academy of Diplomacy report, also consistent with processes of sidelining, is the growth in the use of special envoys, special representatives, or advisory committees that operate outside of the routine State Department structure. Special envoys are appointed by the president and tasked with duties related to foreign affairs. Often, special envoys fill a particular function that is not well addressed by the State Department. The report highlighted that close to two-thirds of these positions were held by noncareer appointments, while only 23 percent were held by either active or retired Foreign Service Officers.[83] Under the Obama administration, the number of special envoys expanded considerably. President Barack Obama appointed prominent political figures and diplomats either to oversee various geographic regions or address functional issue areas. The increase in special envoys and representatives also parallels the growth in advisory committees; ad hoc committees that tend to be more ideologically aligned with the president.[84]

While some of these trends are recent, there are many historical examples of partisan attacks on the State Department. In the 1950s, in a particularly disturbing episode of transformation, President Dwight Eisenhower attempted to rid the State Department both of suspected communists and of personnel who identified as LGBTQ+ (lesbian, gay, bisexual, transgender, queer/questioning, plus).[85] Arguably no president in recent memory, however, has done more to politicize the State Department than President Trump. A 2020 report prepared for the Senate Committee on Foreign Relations examined the first Trump administration's relationship with the foreign policy bureaucracy.[86] The report noted that Trump repeatedly attacked the nonpartisan character of the State Department and attempted to reduce its funding. In

80. American Academy of Diplomacy 2015.
81. O'Connell 2009.
82. Piper 2022.
83. American Academy of Diplomacy 2015.
84. Feinstein and Hemel 2020.
85. Flynn 2014; Johnson 2004.
86. Democratic Staff 2020.

an official statement, the Trump White House characterized the department as full of "radical unelected bureaucrats."[87] Political scientist Dan Drezner wrote that Trump's relentless attacks on the department "eroded the influence of career professionals and triggered an exodus of senior personnel."[88] Such attacks indicate a worrying trend that may continue if future presidents perceive that careerists at State do not support their political agenda.

There are important caveats to this discussion. One is that both processes of sidelining and transformation visible in the U.S. State Department are not solely attributable to polarization. There are multiple factors that impact the hollowing of the foreign service or the appointment of special envoys. Another caveat is that these processes do not necessarily mean that we should expect "worse" foreign policy outcomes. Some may argue that if senior leadership is more ideologically aligned with the president, the president will be more receptive to policy input.

Research on the effectiveness of careerists versus noncareerists at the State Department is limited. A handful of studies analyze the performance of diplomatic ambassadors and show that, on average, career ambassadors outperform noncareer ambassadors. For example, Ryan Scoville finds that career ambassadors are more qualified for their positions than are noncareer ambassadors.[89] Evan Haglund uses data from embassy inspections conducted by the State Department to show that political appointees receive lower scores on ambassadorial performance relative to career diplomats.[90] And Matt Malis shows that turnover of career ambassadors has a greater effect on foreign policy outcomes than does turnover of political appointees.[91] However, findings from these studies do not necessarily generalize to other high-level political appointees at the State Department.

It is difficult to know what to conclude from processes of sidelining and transformation at the State Department. But, in an increasingly polarized Washington, D.C., we should expect more instances of politicization, as well as the sort of direct criticism and partisan attacks levied by politicians like President Trump. If presidents engage in transformation by increasingly appointing like-minded officials to major leadership positions, we should anticipate more

---

87. As quoted in Benen 2019.
88. Drezner 2020, 396.
89. Scoville 2019.
90. Haglund 2015.
91. Malis 2021.

dramatic swings in foreign policy with leader turnover. And if presidents sideline State Department officials altogether, we should also expect less stability in foreign policy as the party controlling the presidency changes over time.

4.2.2 The Intelligence Community

The U.S. intelligence community is made up of eighteen different organizations. The two most well known of these are independent agencies: the Office of the Director of National Intelligence and the Central Intelligence Agency (CIA). The Office of the Director of National Intelligence oversees the intelligence community and coordinates across different departments and agencies. The CIA is responsible for U.S. national security intelligence. The rest of the intelligence community consists of entities within other departments across the executive branch, such as the Department of Defense (e.g., the Defense Intelligence Agency), the State Department (Bureau of Intelligence and Research), and the Department of Homeland Security (Office of Intelligence and Analysis).[92]

Most discussion of politicization focuses on the CIA, the intelligence agency most salient for foreign affairs. Headquartered in Langley, Virginia, the CIA gathers and analyzes intelligence, and conducts covert operations abroad. Like the rest of the intelligence community, the CIA has historically been considered to be apolitical and nonpartisan. The agency was established under President Harry Truman in 1947. Despite President Truman's reservations about the creation of the agency, the CIA enjoyed wide public support across party lines in its early years.[93]

Throughout the Cold War, however, the CIA became viewed with increasing skepticism as it expanded its role in covert activities.[94] In the 1950s, the Eisenhower administration set a precedent for aggressive use of covert action in response to the growing threat of communism.[95] While many of these activities only involved propaganda or political action, the most well-known

---

92. Portions of this section are reprinted from Myrick 2020.

93. Jeffreys-Jones 2022.

94. Covert action is "an activity or activities of the United States Government to influence political, economic, or military conditions abroad, where it is intended that the role of the United States Government will not be apparent or acknowledged publicly (*U.S. Code*, Title 50, Chapter 44, Section 3093(e)).

95. Daugherty 2006.

cases—including covert actions in Iran (1953), Guatemala (1954), Congo (1961), Cuba (1961), Indonesia (1965), Chile (1973), Angola (1975), and Nicaragua (1980)—consisted of paramilitary operations or extensive military assistance to insurgent groups.

By the late 1980s, scandals related to covert activities during the Reagan administration—most notably the Iran-Contra affair—led to increasing congressional oversight. The CIA's reputation was damaged given its involvement in the Iran-Contra affair.[96] Distrust of covert operations, coupled with the fall of the Soviet Union and the dwindling threat of communism, led to the declining use of covert action as a foreign policy tool throughout the 1990s.[97]

While the intelligence community is no stranger to political controversy, it has remained insulated from partisan politics given the importance of careerists who gather and analyze intelligence. Most concerns about partisanship are reactions to political appointees that hold important positions in the intelligence community. Like in many areas of the bureaucracy, presidents are increasingly likely to appoint political allies to lead agencies in the intelligence community, sometimes in an attempt to transform institutions. In the 1980s, for example, President Ronald Reagan faced criticism for nominating his former presidential campaign manager, William Casey, to be the director of the CIA. Then-Democratic Senator Joe Biden strongly campaigned against the nomination, but Casey ultimately received strong bipartisan support in his Senate confirmation process.[98]

Beyond appointing ideological allies to lead intelligence agencies, another concerning process of politicization relates to partisan pressuring of the intelligence community. Allegations of pressuring are hard to evaluate, especially in the intelligence community, which is shrouded with secrecy. Because of the CIA's role in intelligence gathering and analysis, its reputation hinges on its reliability as a credible, nonpartisan source of information. Allegations of blatant pressuring are fairly rare. A more common form of pressuring is soft politicization: when intelligence leaders feel pressured to "tone down their conclusions on major issues, or withhold estimates on minor ones, in order to avoid offending policymakers."[99]

96. Woodward 2005.
97. Johnson 1989.
98. Scahill 2021.
99. Rovner 2013, 56.

A case commonly associated with the politicization of intelligence is the U.S.-led invasion of Iraq.[100] The George W. Bush administration launched the initial invasion in March 2003 on the pretense that Iraqi dictator Saddam Hussein was harboring weapons of mass destruction.[101] Ultimately, no such weapons were found. The case, considered a major intelligence failure, drew questions about whether the intelligence community was subject to undue political influence from the Bush administration. Commissions established after the invasion found that faulty intelligence assessments were not the result of direct pressuring, but, rather, forms of soft politicization.[102] Members of the intelligence community, for example, were repeatedly asked by the White House to scrutinize the relationship between Iraqi dictator Saddam Hussein and the al-Qaeda terrorist network, despite no evidence of clear links between the two.[103] Allegations of Iraqi weapons of mass destruction were not caveated with appropriate assessments of uncertainty. Some of these dynamics could have arisen because intelligence analysts "wanted to avoid the unpleasantness of laying unwelcome analysis on a policymaker's desk."[104] As political scientist Robert Jervis wrote of the Iraq intelligence failures, "The crudest form of politicization is easy to dismiss. … Less direct forms are harder to judge, especially the subtle form of politicization in which the desire to avoid the painful value trade-off between pleasing policymakers and following professional standards."[105]

Beyond the Iraq case, there have been other allegations of pressuring and politicization in the intelligence community. In 1976, President Gerald Ford attempted to sideline the CIA by creating a "Team B" that produced alternative assessments of Soviet capabilities.[106] During the Obama administration's negotiation of the Joint Comprehensive Plan of Action in the 2010s, the White House faced allegations that CIA involvement in Obama's Iran policy biased their intelligence assessments of the nuclear threat.[107]

During the first Trump administration, former senior leaders of the intelligence community raised alarms about President Trump's alleged tendency

---

100. Coletta 2018.
101. Bush 2002.
102. Rovner 2013.
103. Pillar 2006.
104. Pfiffner and Phythian 2008, 238.
105. Jervis 2010b, 133.
106. Freedman 2008; Rovner 2011.
107. Gentry 2019.

to pressure the intelligence community to support his policies.[108] A report from the intelligence community analytic ombudsman in January 2021 cited a number of instances of suspected politicization of intelligence assessments, most notably with respect to allegations of Russian interference in U.S. elections.[109] In submitting the report to the Senate Select Committee on Intelligence, the ombudsman emphasized how extreme partisanship contributed to processes of politicization. He wrote, "The polarized atmosphere has threatened to undermine the foundations of our Republic, penetrating even into the Intelligence Community. Though, as intelligence professionals, we have the ethical responsibility to remain unbiased and objective in our work, we are human beings and can still feel the pressures from society and our political leaders."[110]

Of course, not all forms of pressuring connect to polarized politics. However, growing polarization can affect the intensity or frequency of these incidents. As the stakes of winning become higher, leaders face greater temptation to lean on nonpartisan institutions to help them enact a political agenda or retain office. Simultaneously, members of the opposition party have more cause to allege that the other side is engaging in pressuring. Even if these allegations do not reflect reality, perceptions that an agency is under pressure from political leaders may undermine its credibility or legitimacy.

The implications of pressuring for the stability advantage are more subtle than processes of transforming or sidelining. They could consist, for example, of shifts in the assessment of security threats across presidential administrations. More concerning impacts of pressuring happen further downstream. If a traditionally nonpartisan institution is thought to be politicized, it will be perceived as less credible. In the future, it will be less able to effectively check political leaders, eroding horizontal constraints on executive power.

4.2.3 The Department of Defense

The U.S. Department of Defense (DoD) is one of the country's largest employers, with "a military workforce of about 2.1 million service members and a civilian workforce of about 770,000 employees."[111] The DoD is headed

---

108. Morell, Haines, and Cohen 2020.
109. Barnes, Savage, and Goldman 2021.
110. Letter accessed in Zulauf 2021.
111. Field and Perkins 2023, 2.

by the secretary of defense, who oversees the military departments and multiple intelligence agencies. The objective of the DoD, headquartered in the Pentagon just outside of Washington, D.C., is to defend and preserve the national security interests of the United States.

On average, the DoD is perceived as more ideologically conservative than other executive agencies.[112] Despite the ideological leanings of its members, the defense establishment is considered a very nonpartisan institution. Top leaders at the Pentagon have served in both Republican and Democratic administrations. Multiple secretaries of defense—including William Cohen, Robert Lovett, Robert McNamara, Robert Gates, and Chuck Hagel—were Republicans who served under Democratic presidents.

The nonpartisan character of the DoD is related to perceptions of an apolitical military force. This ideal is rooted in a tradition of scholarship on civil–military relations. In his classic text *The Soldier and the State*, political scientist Samuel Huntington writes of the importance of separating civilian and military spheres in democratic societies.[113] In the conventional view, a professionalized military should not make policy decisions. Rather, the military and its leadership should remain far removed from partisan politics. This became the dominant paradigm of thinking about civil–military relations in the United States and many other advanced democracies. However, in the twenty-first century, scholars questioned whether Huntington's concept of military professionalism applied to the contemporary political landscape.[114]

Much has been written about the politicization of the U.S. military. This is partly due to the fact that the military is a large and visible institution in politics and popular culture. The DoD operating budget dwarfs the budget of other institutions like the State Department and the CIA.[115] Historically, the Department of Defense and the U.S. military have been on occasion caught in the crossfires of intense political debates about American involvement in foreign conflicts like the Vietnam War and the Iraq War. The DoD periodically grapples with important social topics and debates about the armed forces that became highly politicized. Such debates include the Truman administration's

---

112. Clinton and Lewis 2008.
113. Huntington 1957.
114. Brooks 2020; Beehner, Brooks, and Maurer 2020; Feaver 2003.
115. In fiscal year 2024, for example, DoD requested more than $800 billion in funds from Congress (CBPP 2023).

ban of racial segregation in the armed forces in 1948, the Clinton administration's "Don't Ask, Don't Tell" policy concerning military service of LGBTQ+ service members in 1998, and the Obama administration's removal of the ban on women serving in combat roles in 2013.

Many researchers argue, however, that polarization in American politics increases the frequency and intensity of politicization of the defense establishment.[116] A common way that civilian leaders politicize the military is through bandwagoning, associating themselves or their policies with the institution. The U.S. military is an attractive target for partisan bandwagoning because there are persistently high levels of confidence in the institution. A 2022 Gallup Poll shows that 65 percent of respondents reported having either a great deal or a lot of confidence in the military, much higher than comparable governmental institutions like the presidency, the Supreme Court, or Congress. By comparison, similar polls suggest that, in 2022, public confidence in Congress dropped to its lowest point, at 7 percent.[117] While overall confidence in the military remains high, public attitudes have become more partisan. Republicans are much more likely to express high confidence in the U.S. military than Democrats, and this gap is widening.[118]

High public confidence in the military gives politicians an opportunity to improve their image by associating with the institution. During his 2016 presidential campaign, Republican then-candidate Donald Trump often invoked active-duty officers and military veterans. President Trump later attributed part of his electoral success to "getting the vote of the military."[119] Once in office, Trump bandwagoned with military leaders, blurring the traditional civilian–military divide. He tied himself closely to the defense establishment, referring to "my generals"[120] and including both active-duty and retired military officers in policymaking. These actions contributed to what political scientist Polina Beliakova terms "erosion by deference," or excessive involvement of the military in policymaking spaces that may undermine norms of civilian control.[121]

---

116. Banerjee and Webeck 2024; Beliakova 2021; Brooks 2020; Brooks, Golby, and Urben 2021; Feaver 2023b; Feaver and Kohn 2021; Golby 2021; Robinson 2022.
117. Jones 2022.
118. Burbach 2019; Feaver 2023b.
119. Haas 2017.
120. Glasser and Baker 2022.
121. Beliakova 2021.

Perhaps of greatest concern, Trump threatened to deploy the military within the United States expressly for political ends. In 2018, the Trump administration sent active-duty officers to the Mexican border in what was described as a "striking political stunt."[122] During the summer of 2020, President Trump threatened to deploy military troops to U.S. cities to subdue Black Lives Matter protests.[123] And on January 6, 2021, as supporters of President Trump stormed the U.S. Capitol building, the president allegedly asked if National Guard troops could be deployed to protect them.[124]

Not all recent presidents have bandwagoned with the military. At the outset of President Barack Obama's administration in 2009, a deeply unpopular war in Iraq had shifted American sentiments toward the defense establishment. In the first year of President Obama's term, a series of blunders and heated debates led to an environment of mutual mistrust between the White House and the Pentagon. Tense debates about the number of U.S. troops in Afghanistan fueled tensions between the administration and senior military leaders. And, in 2013, following the infamous "red line" crisis, during which President Obama threatened military action were Syrian President Bashar al-Assad found to have used chemical weapons, senior military leaders contradicted Obama's statements. Reports followed that President Obama had effectively been sidelining the generals throughout his administration, "preferr[ing] the military to be seen but not heard."[125]

One concern is that if public confidence in the military becomes increasingly partisan, with Republicans more favorable to the military than are Democrats, the institution will be seen as more politicized. Republican presidents will have increasing incentives to bandwagon with the defense establishment, whereas Democratic presidents will have more incentives to sideline military leaders or attempt to transform the institution.

Politicizing the military to advance one's own partisan agenda could have broader negative consequences. One likely consequence is that associating the military with partisan figures or polarizing policies could erode confidence in the institution. In *Thanks for Your Service*, political scientist Peter Feaver shows that copartisans respond asymmetrically to partisan behavior by the U.S. military. Feaver finds that when the public believes the military is aligned

122. Haas and Schake 2020.
123. Filkins 2020.
124. Wolfe 2021.
125. Brooks 2013.

with their own party, they do not think politicization is a problem.[126] By contrast, when the public is told that the military is aligned with the opposite party, their confidence in the military declines precipitously. In his book *Dangerous Instrument*, political scientist Michael Robinson also emphasizes that polarization has multiple negative effects.[127] Beyond undermining the credibility of the military, it poses problems for the military's ability to recruit and function effectively on the battlefield, and it complicates civil–military relations by weakening democratic governance.

Most relevant for this book, there are also potential consequences to the stability of foreign policy. If the defense establishment becomes more politicized, the priorities of the DoD could change under successive presidential administrations, leading to less continuity in defense policy. At these extremes, we might observe substantive changes in U.S. defense commitments as new leaders assume office. The country saw a glimpse of this potential future following the 2022 Russian invasion of Ukraine. Democratic President Joe Biden's initial response, which consisted of a Western-led sanctions regime and substantial U.S. investment in arming Ukraine, had strong support from both parties. However, bipartisanship began to erode as the conflict progressed. Soon, a vocal minority of congressional Republicans expressed doubts about sustained U.S. commitments to Ukraine,[128] which was reflected in public opinion polling. By the following year, attitudes had more strongly polarized. An August 2023 poll conducted by CNN showed that 61 percent of Democrats but only 30 percent of Republicans supported the U.S. government providing weapons to Ukraine.[129] If these types of debates become more partisan in the future, party turnover could jeopardize the ability of the U.S. government to maintain its security commitments, a topic I revisit in chapter 6.

4.3 Application: Foreign Policy Volatility across Presidential Administrations

This chapter argued that extreme forms of polarization weaken both vertical and horizontal constraints on democratic leaders. In doing so, polarization

126. Feaver 2023b.
127. Robinson 2022.
128. Demirjian 2023.
129. Agiesta 2023.

can increase the likelihood of volatility in foreign policymaking. As chapter 2 explained, in highly polarized environments, politicians seek to mobilize their base by appealing to core supporters. Responding to both ideological and affective polarization within the public, politicians have incentives to campaign on enacting more partisan policies and reversing policies of the opposing party.

Once in office, politicians are more likely to politicize nonpartisan foreign policy institutions, unraveling a tacit partisan truce in foreign affairs. Because politicized bureaucratic institutions are less willing and less able to check executive power, it becomes easier for leaders to implement extreme policies. Over time, this could erode the stability advantage that democracies tend to have in foreign affairs.

Stability Hypothesis 3: *As polarization becomes more extreme, democracies are less likely to display stability in their foreign policymaking over time.*

There are early indicators that the United States may, on average, experience more volatility in foreign policy as polarization continues to increase. For one, the weakening of vertical constraints in foreign policy means that we should observe presidential candidates from the opposition party explicitly campaigning to undo aspects of the incumbent's foreign policy. While it is typical for a presidential challenger to define their platform in opposition to an incumbent, these distinctions are amplified in recent years. For example, a primary theme of Barack Obama's 2008 foreign policy platform was opposition to the Bush administration's "dumb war" in Iraq.[130] In foreign affairs, Obama portrayed himself as the "anti-Bush,"[131] rejecting the unilateralist approach of his predecessor. During the 2016 presidential campaign, then-candidate Donald Trump took negative partisanship one step further. Efforts to explicitly undo Obama-era policies were arguably the central, unifying theme of Trump's foreign policy.[132] Commentators characterized much of Trump's 2016 platform and subsequent actions in the White House as an "all-out assault on the Obama legacy."[133]

In extremely polarized environments, we should also observe presidents trying to undo policies of their out-party predecessors once in the White

130. Obama 2002.
131. Patrick 2009.
132. Sokolsky and Miller 2019.
133. Smith 2018.

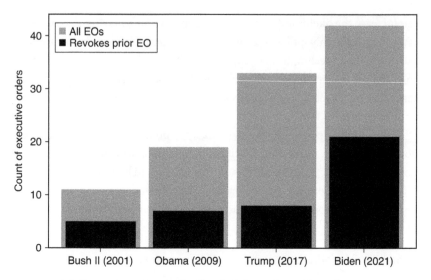

FIGURE 4.9. Executive orders in the first 100 days of presidential administrations

House. One example of this pattern is the use of executive orders, especially in the first 100 days of a presidential administration, to revoke orders from previous presidents.[134] Figure 4.9 shows the number of executive orders issued by recent presidents in their first 100 days in office.[135] The black-shaded regions on the figure illustrate the proportion of executive orders that explicitly revoke actions taken by the previous administration. When Democratic presidential candidate Joe Biden campaigned for the presidency prior to the 2020 election, he promised a variety of actions on "Day One" that would undo Republican President Donald Trump's policies. These included rejoining the Paris Agreement on climate change, ceasing U.S. withdrawal from the World Health Organization, and revoking travel and immigration restrictions implemented by the first Trump administration.[136] Likewise, following his re-election to the presidency in 2024, Donald Trump was largely expected to use his first 100 days to "unwind Biden's policies and resume where he left off after his first term in office."[137]

---

134. Chapter 6 discusses the broader trend in the use of executive orders in foreign policy-making.
135. Data from Woolley and Peters 2021.
136. White House Press Office 2021b.
137. Ordoñez 2024.

POLARIZATION AND THE STABILITY ADVANTAGE 153

defense establishment in the first place due to "the woke partisan agenda of political appointees"[143] in the Biden administration. Ultimately, the Senate bill sidestepped partisan debates related to abortion and healthcare for transgender service members, and the final version was passed with substantial bipartisan support. However, the episode illustrates how issues related to social identity will be more likely to trickle into foreign and defense policy as polarization grows.

The second domain in which partisan conflict has extended into foreign policy relates to nontraditional security issues like climate security and global health security. Reversals of U.S. engagement with major climate agreements illustrate this dynamic. In 1997, Democratic President Bill Clinton signed the Kyoto Protocol that aimed to reduce global emissions of greenhouse gases contributing to climate change. The protocol was never ratified by the U.S. Senate, and the next Republican administration, under President George W. Bush, withdrew the United States from the agreement in 2001. In 2015, Democratic President Barack Obama entered the United States into another multilateral climate agreement, the Paris Agreement, in which countries committed to taking steps to reduce their emissions. In 2017, Republican President Donald Trump announced U.S. withdrawal from the agreement, an action subsequently reversed by Democratic President Joe Biden in 2021. Entering and exiting international agreements leads other countries to question U.S. commitments to address climate change.

A final domain where partisan conflict extends to foreign policy concerns questions of multilateralism and internationalism in American foreign policy. This chapter described an undercurrent of Republican skepticism of these principles reflected in both historic and contemporary public opinion polling. These attitudes manifest in foreign policy decisions across presidential administrations. During the George W. Bush administration (2001–2009), an aversion to multilateralism was on display in decisions to conduct military strikes in Afghanistan and Iraq, withdraw the United States from the Anti-Ballistic Missile Treaty, and reject the 1997 Kyoto Protocol.[144] The next Republican administration under Donald Trump (2017–2021) largely rejected both internationalist and multilateral principles. Trump's "America First" platform emphasized that the United States would not be beholden to other international interests. During his first term, for example, President

---

143. As quoted in Mitchell 2023.
144. Howell and Kriner 2007.

Trump withdrew the United States from a series of institutions or agreements, including the Trans-Pacific Partnership, the UN Educational, Scientific, and Cultural Organization, and the UN Human Rights Council, underscoring a rejection of internationalist principles. The extent to which President Trump permanently eroded America's liberal internationalist orientation in foreign affairs remains a subject of much debate,[145] but it is clear that the Republican and Democratic Parties continue to grow farther apart on this issue. Trump's reelection to the presidency in 2024 in many ways reaffirmed Republican commitments to an "America First" foreign policy.

Why should we care about stability in foreign policy? Political contestation is a normal part of democratic politics and an important aspect of foreign policymaking. Foreign policy changes across presidential administrations are not always bad.[146] In fact, a criticism levied at the political parties in the United States is that they tend to display excessive bipartisanship, particularly on national security issues. Too much partisan agreement could result in politicians adopting or maintaining status quo policies uncritically, leading to suboptimal outcomes.

However, foreign policy volatility that originates from domestic politics, especially when it is a function of hyperpartisanship rather than principled policy disagreement, can have multiple negative consequences. Foreign affairs is unique from many aspects of domestic policy because it requires long time horizons. International politics consists of repeated interactions between countries. For international cooperation to be maintained, countries must believe their counterparts will uphold commitments irrespective of partisan politics.

Many researchers also argue that foreign policy instability increases the likelihood of bad outcomes in international politics. In *Volatile States in International Politics*, political scientist Eleonora Mattiacci argues that volatility that arises from domestic politics contributes to an environment of fear and uncertainty that makes security crises more likely to escalate.[147] In addition, instability creates uncertainty about the direction of a country's foreign policy in the future, dissuading other countries from pursuing partnerships with a highly polarized country. Finally, instability can further contribute to the

---

145. Busby and Monten 2018; Chaudoin, Milner, and Tingley 2018; Rathbun 2018.
146. Chapter 7 discusses in greater detail when partisan divergence in foreign policy might actually be a positive phenomenon.
147. Mattiacci 2023.

erosion of two additional democratic advantages—the credibility advantage and the reliability advantage—which are discussed in the next two chapters.

4.4 Conclusion

A shared view among international relations scholars is that democracies have a stability advantage in foreign affairs.[148] Despite frequent leader turnover, democracies maintain consistent foreign policy over time relative to nondemocracies. This chapter used different empirical strategies, summarized in Table 4.3 to explore how more extreme forms of polarization might undermine the stability advantage that democracies have when making foreign policy.

In healthy liberal democracies, vertical constraints, or accountability to the public, contribute to the stability advantage by moderating politicians in foreign affairs. Democratic leaders who are responsive to a median voter in the electorate have incentives to provide public goods. Environments of extreme polarization, however, make politicians less likely to target messaging at the median voter and more inclined to mobilize their political base. This process can gradually extend partisan conflict to salient foreign policy issues. This chapter drew on longitudinal data on public opinion in the United States to demonstrate that certain areas of foreign policy are susceptible to this dynamic. These include issues in foreign affairs that relate to nontraditional security threats, tie to social identity, reflect debates about multilateralism, or coincide with electoral cycles.

Horizontal constraints, or accountability to political institutions within government, also contribute to the stability advantage. Recognizing the unique importance of long time horizons in making foreign policy, political parties that expect competitive elections in the future often reach a tacit partisan truce in foreign affairs. One aspect of this truce is the expectation that leaders will invest in nonpartisan institutions that create continuity in foreign policy across successive administrations.

However, when politicians operate in extremely polarized environments, they favor short-term wins over long-term concerns about foreign policy stability. This chapter described how the politicization of foreign policy institutions in the United States like the State Department, the DoD, and

---

148. See, e.g., Leeds, Mattes, and Vogel 2009; McGillivray and Smith 2008; Mattes, Leeds, and Carroll 2015; Leeds and Mattes 2022; Smith 2016.

TABLE 4.3. Summary of findings from the Stability Hypotheses

	As polarization becomes more extremes . . .	Empirical strategy	Summary of findings
Vertical constraints	Domestic partisan conflict is more likely to extend into foreign affairs.	Use longitudinal public opinion data to investigate whether public attitudes toward U.S. foreign policy have increasingly polarized, following trends of polarization in domestic politics.	Public opinion polls show that, over time, partisan conflict has extended to issues in foreign affairs that represent nontraditional security threats, connect to aspects of social identity, or involve ideological debates about multilateralism.
Horizontal constraints	Politicians are more likely to politicize the foreign policy bureaucracy.	Explore whether, as polarization in domestic politics increases, politicians have become more likely to politicize U.S. foreign policy institutions like the State Department, the intelligence community, and the Department of Defense.	Although politicization of the foreign policy bureaucracy is not new, polarization increases its intensity and frequency, reducing the ability of the bureaucracy to effectively constrain the president.
Implication for democratic advantage	Democracies are less likely to display stability in their foreign policymaking over time.	Observe whether, as polarization increases, there has been more volatility in foreign policy with executive party turnover.	Leaders increasingly undo foreign policy accomplishments of the opposite party, especially in areas where partisan conflict has extended to foreign affairs and the president exercises discretion in policymaking.

the intelligence community takes many forms. Leaders politicize nonpartisan institutions by transforming their composition, sidelining them in the policy-making process, pressuring them to follow the party line, or bandwagoning with institutions that are highly regarded by the public. While many such examples of politicization exist in the history of U.S. foreign policy, growing domestic polarization increases the frequency and intensity of these episodes.

The extension of partisan conflict and the gradual erosion of a partisan truce in foreign policy undermine the stability advantage in the long run. Conflict extension contributes to diverging preferences in foreign affairs and provides incentives for politicians to undo policies enacted by the opposing party. Nonpartisan foreign policy institutions that are politicized by the incumbent are less able to effectively constrain democratic leaders. The result is that democracies experiencing extreme polarization are likely to be characterized by greater uncertainty and more volatility in foreign policymaking with leader turnover. These effects have not yet been fully realized in the United States. However, increasing partisanship in foreign affairs and more frequent episodes of politicization of bureaucratic institutions provide early indications that U.S. foreign policy is likely to become less stable over time.

5

Polarization and the Credibility Advantage

IN MARCH 2015, Senator Tom Cotton, a Republican junior senator from Arkansas, published an open letter to the Iranian government that was cosigned with forty-six other Republicans. Senator Cotton released the letter a few months before Democratic President Barack Obama announced the Joint Comprehensive Plan of Action (JCPOA), a multilateral agreement designed to restrict Iran's nuclear ambitions. The "Cotton letter" warned Iranian leadership that any nuclear agreement signed by President Obama would quickly be undone: "It has come to our attention while observing your nuclear negotiations with our government that you may not fully understand our constitutional system. . . . [W]e will consider any agreement regarding your nuclear-weapons program that is not approved by the Congress as nothing more than an executive agreement between President Obama and Ayatollah Khamenei. The next president could revoke such an executive agreement with the stroke of a pen and future Congresses could modify the terms of the agreement at any time."[1]

The Cotton letter was provocative and somewhat unprecedented. Some commentators viewed it as a partisan power play designed to catapult Senator Cotton's career by undercutting the Obama administration, which was widely unpopular with the junior senator's constituency.[2] Critics called the

---

1. Cotton 2015.
2. A 2015 poll in Arkansas fielded just before the letter was released had Senator Tom Cotton's net approval rating at +20 and President Barack Obama's at -44 among Arkansas residents (Brock 2015).

letter "mutinous" and a "gross breach of discipline."[3] The editor of *Foreign Policy* magazine, David Rothkopf, remarked on Twitter that it signified that Republicans were "blazing new trails of politicization of foreign policy."[4]

Others thought the Cotton letter revealed sincere disagreements that had not been adequately addressed by the White House. These commentators characterized the letter as taking a "valid position" and noted it was "fair play to oppose the Iran deal on those grounds."[5] Senator Cotton's actions reflected a deep distrust of Iran, which he would later describe as being governed by a regime whose "religious fanaticism is rivaled only by their duplicity."[6] The senator's views on Iran were likely unchangeable. It was doubtful that there was *any* plausible nuclear agreement the White House could enter into with the Iranian regime that he would find acceptable. But what about the views of the forty-six other Republican senators? Would they refuse any deal with the Iranian regime, or were there some who could be persuaded to lend their support to a final agreement?

Shortly after the letter was released, the U.S. delegation would travel to Lausanne in Switzerland to resume the JCPOA negotiations. The Iranian delegation would no doubt perceive the U.S. negotiators as being undermined by their own domestic political opposition. Should the American negotiators take seriously congressional efforts to derail the negotiation process, or simply roll their eyes? Was there a way to effectively leverage domestic opposition to negotiate a better deal with the Iranian regime? Or should they ignore partisan politics at home and focus on the content of the agreement?

The reaction to the Cotton letter illustrates how a polarized environment can easily create an atmosphere of mutual distrust between the executive and the political opposition. In this context, it became hard for the Obama administration to distinguish between pure spoilers—Republican legislators who wished to undermine the negotiation process—and legislators who simply wanted a better deal. Some Republicans who signed the letter, for example, insisted that they wanted a nuclear deal between the United States and Iran but believed that signaling strong congressional disapproval of the negotiation would make the agreement's final terms more favorable to the United States. Republican Senator Rob Portman of Ohio, one of the other forty-six

3. Capehart 2015.
4. Rothkopf 2015.
5. Fisher 2015.
6. Cotton 2017.

signatories, remarked, "I signed [the letter] for a very simple reason, which is I want a good agreement with Iran, and I think it helps to get a good agreement."[7]

Senator Portman's statement reflects the intuition behind the "Schelling conjecture" in international politics. In *The Strategy of Conflict*, economist Thomas Schelling explains that domestic constraints in democracies enhance a negotiator's credibility.[8] Credibility in international relations refers to the perception that countries will follow through on the threats and promises that they make.[9] Since democratic leaders can credibly say that they are accountable to their publics and constrained by a political opposition, Schelling explains that this gives democracies more leverage in an international negotiation.

The credibility advantage that democracies have is reinforced by two sets of constraints on democratic leaders: vertical constraints make leaders accountable to the public and horizontal constraints make them accountable to other actors within government, such as the political opposition. The advantage has many implications for international politics. Two of these, which both relate to bargaining with foreign adversaries, are highlighted in this chapter. First, during an international crisis[10] between countries, democracies can leverage agreement between domestic actors to signal their resolve—or their willingness to fight—to adversaries abroad. When the public and/or the political opposition rallies to support their leader in a crisis, the leader's threats will be seen as more credible. This matters because countries perceived as more resolved to follow through on their threats are better able to get what they want in international politics.[11] Second, during international negotiations, democracies can leverage moderate forms of disagreement between

---

7. As quoted in Dennis and Chacko (2015).

8. Schelling 1960.

9. Chapter 2 explained that credibility has many meanings in international relations. This chapter focuses on the credibility of signals sent in the context of international negotiations and crisis bargaining, which generally involves the judgments of a foreign adversary at a given moment in time. The next chapter will explore the reliability of commitments, which generally involves the perceptions of a foreign ally or partner at a future point in time.

10. In international relations, an *international crisis* is defined as an event in which decision-makers identify three conditions: "(a) a threat to basic values, with simultaneous or subsequent (b) high probability of involvement in military hostilities, and the awareness of (c) finite time for response to the external value threat" (Brecher 1979).

11. On the importance of signaling resolve in crisis bargaining see, e.g., Kertzer 2016; McManus 2017; Yarhi-Milo 2018.

domestic actors to extract concessions from adversaries. Leaders can credibly say that their hands are tied by the public and/or the political opposition in order to make the terms of international agreements more favorable to them.

This chapter examines how partisan politics undermines the credibility advantage. The chapter proceeds in three sections. It first evaluates the relationship between polarization and vertical constraints, exploring how a highly partisan public can erode electoral accountability. In a survey experiment fielded in advance of the 2024 U.S. presidential election, I randomly assign respondents to read about hypothetical outcomes of the election in which either Kamala Harris (Democratic candidate) or Donald Trump (Republican candidate) wins the presidency. Respondents then assess that president's actions in foreign policy scenarios that involve either an international crisis or a negotiation with an adversarial country. The results show that a polarized public is much more likely to distrust the foreign policy decision-making of a president from the opposite party. Survey respondents are also more likely to disapprove of the exact same foreign policy decisions if they are introduced by an out-party leader. Moreover, they are more likely to approve of co-partisan legislators obstructing the president and preventing them from carrying out those decisions. Such dynamics could be increasingly problematic if polarization continues to increase in the United States.

The chapter next explores the relationship between polarization and horizontal constraints, focusing on the behavior of politicians from the opposition party. Patterns of congressional voting in foreign affairs and defense policy show that, as polarization in domestic politics has increased, legislators from the opposition party have been more likely to cohere against the White House. Using data from congressional speeches, I also show that, as polarization has increased, the political opposition has become less likely to defer to leaders in times of crisis. Congressional rhetoric about foreign adversaries has become increasingly partisan. These findings suggest that, as polarization becomes more extreme, politicians will be less likely to present a unified front, undermining democratic advantages in signaling information to other countries and jeopardizing their ability to initiate complex negotiations.

Finally, the chapter uses a contemporary case to illustrate how, together, these processes could limit the ability of the U.S. government to credibly signal information to its adversaries. I focus on the U.S.–Iranian relationship and the negotiation of the 2015 JCPOA during the Obama administration. Congressional Republicans were rewarded by co-partisans for active opposition to the

JCPOA, and electoral dynamics preceding the 2016 Republican presidential primary fueled the politicization of the agreement. The Schelling conjecture[12] and theories of two-level games[13] would anticipate that Republican opposition during the negotiation process—including more dramatic actions like Senator Cotton's open letter—were credible signals of disapproval that could provide greater leverage for U.S. negotiators. However, I show that, in practice, these actions had little influence on the substantive content of the agreement. Instead, they reinforced an environment of mutual distrust between the White House and congressional Republicans. Drawing on interviews conducted in Washington, D.C., with senior congressional and White House officials, I explain that the Obama administration began to view all Republican legislators as potential spoilers. As a result, they took further steps to insulate the JCPOA negotiation from domestic partisan politics. This culminated in little bipartisan support of the nuclear agreement, which jeopardized its durability in the long run. The case emphasizes that, while low to moderate levels of polarization often benefit democracies during international negotiations, more extreme forms of polarization can lead to suboptimal outcomes.

5.1 Vertical Constraints and Democratic Credibility

Vertical constraints contribute to the credibility advantage democracies have in foreign affairs by making democratic leaders accountable to their publics. One finding in international relations is that democratic leaders anticipate *audience costs*: they expect to be punished by their publics for not following through on their threats and promises in international politics.[14] As a result, the threats and promises that democratic leaders do issue should, on average, be more credible relative to those issued by nondemocratic leaders.

In a healthy democracy, leaders making decisions in foreign affairs are at least somewhat constrained by public opinion. Effectively leveraging this public constraint can help democratic leaders signal information when they bargain with adversaries abroad. For one, public support for important foreign policy decisions, such as declarations of war, can be a highly credible signal of resolve during an international crisis. When democratic publics judge

---

12. Schelling 1960.
13. Putnam 1988.
14. See, e.g., Baum 2004; Fearon 1994; Kertzer and Brutger 2016; Schultz 2001a; Smith 1998; Tarar and Leventoglu 2009; Tomz 2007; Trager and Vavreck 2011.

their leader to be a competent decision-maker, they are likely to rally behind them during times of crisis. This reflects a "rally round the flag" phenomenon, in which popular support for a leader increases during times of conflict or crisis.[15] These domestic shows of public support are visible to other governments, who may in turn be more likely to back down when confronted by a highly resolved democracy. They are part of the reason why democracies are considered to be formidable adversaries in international conflicts.[16]

Democratic leaders also leverage public constraints to their advantage when negotiating international agreements. During international negotiations, some degree of domestic disagreement, debate, or polarization is usually a good thing. Leaders can credibly point to public opinion about an ongoing negotiation and say, "My people will not accept an agreement under these terms. You must make the terms more favorable." This strategy allows democratic leaders to wield public opinion to extract concessions from their foreign counterparts.

Chapter 2 argued, however, that extreme polarization reshapes vertical constraints on leaders, lessening the ability of polarized democracies to be credible adversaries. One reason this occurs is because in highly polarized environments, the public is more likely to distrust the foreign policy decision-making of a leader from the opposite party. Partisans may be skeptical that politicians from the other party have their best interests in mind. Some of this skepticism comes from fundamental disagreements about policies. But, strong partisans might even begin to question the character and intentions of leaders from the other party.

Consider how this mistrust could impact how a democratic government responds to an international crisis. As polarization becomes more extreme, rather than rallying around a leader, a partisan public might suspect that leaders from an opposing party are stoking crises for political gain. The public may begin to discount information the leader provides about security threats or, in extreme cases, start to express support for a foreign adversary rather than their own government. The opening chapter of this book, for example, discussed how right-wing French politicians in the 1930s adopted the slogan, "Better Hitler Than Blum," to express their distaste for left-wing candidate Léon Blum.

15. Baum 2002; Brody 1991; Brody and Shapiro 1989; Colaresi 2007; Jentleson 1992; Mueller 1970, 1973; Oneal and Bryan 1995.

16. Lake 1992; Reiter and Stam 1998, 2002.

Public distrust of leaders could be amplified by politicians from the opposition who, in polarized times, are also unlikely to rally behind the executive. Although citizens hold coherent beliefs about major foreign policy issues,[17] an asymmetry of information between politicians and the public can make the impact of cues from politicians especially strong in foreign affairs.[18] For example, during the 2003 Iraq War, political scientist Adam Berinsky demonstrates that partisan conflict among politicians fueled a corresponding divergence along party lines in popular attitudes toward the war.[19] This divergence was exacerbated by the combination of cues from politicians as well as heavily partisan media about the war.[20]

A partisan public also reshapes the nature of vertical constraints in a way that can impact other aspects of foreign affairs beyond international crises. In societies characterized by extreme polarization, political competition between parties becomes zero sum. When affective polarization is high, a loss for the party of the president becomes a win for the opposition party. A partisan public will be more likely to reward co-partisan politicians for preventing the other side from enacting their policies or derailing their anticipated achievements in foreign policy. This logic is reflected in the hypotheses outlined in chapter 2:

> Credibility Hypothesis 1A: *As polarization becomes more extreme, the public is less likely to trust the foreign policy decision-making of leaders from an opposing party.*

> Credibility Hypothesis 1B: *As polarization becomes more extreme, the public is more likely to reward co-partisan politicians for obstructing leaders from an opposing party.*

Since these hypotheses focus on how the public vertically constrains democratic leaders, a natural starting point is public opinion. The ideal way to test these hypotheses would be to conduct a public opinion survey about foreign policy across two time periods: an earlier, less polarized era and a contemporary, more polarized era. Of course, without a time machine to return to a less polarized era, this type of research design is not feasible. Although we cannot vary the overall atmosphere of polarization, we can still think about how partisanship shapes public attitudes toward foreign policy decisions. This can

---

17. Aldrich, Sullivan, and Borgida 1989; Aldrich et al. 2006.
18. Guisinger and Saunders 2017; Zaller 1992.
19. Berinsky 2007, 2009.
20. Baum and Groeling 2009a,b.

help us anticipate what might happen as polarization becomes more extreme. As the electorate becomes more polarized, more members of the public will identify with a political party, and partisan identity will grow stronger. This would amplify any partisan biases we observe today.

To test these hypotheses, I conducted a survey experiment in advance of the 2024 U.S presidential election between the incumbent Vice President Kamala Harris (Democrat) and the former President Donald Trump (Republican). Survey respondents were randomly assigned to think about hypothetical scenarios in which one of the two candidates won the election. The idea behind the survey experiment was to hold fixed different foreign policy decisions, varying the party of the president who made them see how partisanship shapes public attitudes toward foreign affairs.

I embedded the experiment in an online public opinion survey fielded to a sample of 4,330 adults living in the United States on August 6–8, 2024, directly after Kamala Harris secured the Democratic nomination for president.[21] The timing of the survey increases the realism of this thought experiment. Rather than describing hypothetical Republican or Democratic candidates, the survey describes real presidential candidates and instructs participants to envision alternative outcomes to the 2024 election. Given that the theory in chapter 2 focuses on contexts in which polarization is relatively extreme, it is appropriate to evaluate this hypothesis at a moment when politics and partisan identity were salient in the United States. When the survey was fielded, Americans were deeply polarized in advance of the election.[22]

Survey respondents were first asked about their demographic information.[23] Then, each respondent was randomly assigned to read one of two situations describing a possible election outcome. Half of the respondents were asked to think about a scenario in which Kamala Harris won the 2024

---

21. This survey was reviewed by the Duke University Campus Institutional Review Board (protocol no. 2024-0536). See appendix for survey details.

22. This survey was fielded twice. The first survey was fielded to a sample of 4,269 adults on June 25–27, 2024, directly before the first presidential debate of the 2024 election. The incumbent president and Democratic nominee, Joe Biden, performed poorly at the debate and ultimately dropped out of the race and endorsed his Vice President Kamala Harris for the Democratic nomination. The second survey was run on August 6–8, 2024, after Harris's official nomination as the Democratic candidate for president. The main takeaways from both surveys are very similar.

23. These questions included whether or not they identified with a political party, whether or not they approved of the current president, and whether they intended to vote in the 2024 U.S. presidential election.

election, while the other half thought about a scenario in which Donald Trump won. In practice, this means that respondents were assigned to either an out-party or an in-party treatment condition depending on whether they shared a partisan identity with the hypothetical victor of the 2024 election or not. Respondents who identified as Republicans (Democrats) and received the Trump (Harris) scenario were considered to be in the in-party condition, whereas respondents who identified as Republicans (Democrats) and received the Harris (Trump) scenario were considered to be in the out-party condition.[24] Respondents reflected on this hypothetical outcome in an open-ended response to reinforce its realism. The survey text was accompanied by a visual cue: a picture of either Donald Trump or Kamala Harris on the campaign trail. The survey text read:

> As you may know, the 2024 US presidential election is happening in November. Republican candidate and former president Donald Trump is running for president against Democratic candidate and current Vice President Kamala Harris. We want to understand what Americans expect will happen in foreign policy if [T1: Donald Trump / T2: Kamala Harris] wins the election.
>
> In a few sentences, tell us what kinds of things you would expect President [T1: Donald Trump / T2: Kamala Harris] to do in foreign policy over the next few years if [he/she] wins the election.

Respondents next reacted to two foreign policy scenarios that featured the same president they read about earlier. Because the focus of this chapter is on the ability of democracies to issue credible threats and promises to their adversaries, these scenarios focused on international crises and international negotiations. The first scenario described the president responding to a crisis initiated by another country: either a Russian invasion of Estonia or a Chinese invasion of Taiwan.[25] The second scenario described the president engaging

---

24. Following research in American political behavior, the analysis includes partisan "leaners": respondents who initially answered that they are "Independent" but, in a follow-up question, say that they lean toward either the Republican or Democratic Party. Keith et al. (1986, 155) conclude that, "most professed Independents are not neutral between the parties, but are nearly as partisan as avowed Democrats and Republicans."

25. See, e.g., U.S. concerns about a Chinese invasion of Taiwan (Stewart and Ali 2024) or, after the 2022 Russian invasion of Ukraine, concerns about a Russian invasion of Estonia or another Baltic country (Reeves 2024).

in negotiations with an adversarial country: either negotiating a new nuclear agreement with Iran or restarting talks with North Korea about its nuclear program.[26] The countries featured in the scenarios were selected for their salience in the news and the realism of the situations during the time the survey was fielded. The countries also represented different types of adversaries with varying degrees of hostility toward the United States.

Each respondent read both a crisis and a negotiation scenario. After each scenario, participants were asked three questions. First, they evaluated the president's judgment and foreign policy decision-making. Next, they reacted to the president's policy decision, which was either to send in U.S. troops (in the crisis scenario) or to initiate negotiations with an adversarial country (in the negotiation scenario). Finally, they identified how they thought that legislators from the opposition party (congressional Democrats if the treatment was about Donald Trump or congressional Republicans if the treatment was about Kamala Harris) should respond to the president's policy. Table 5.1 and table 5.2 show the text of the survey questionnaire.

Credibility Hypothesis 1A anticipates that, in polarized environments, the public will be skeptical of the foreign policy decision-making of a president from the opposite party. To evaluate this hypothesis, I asked respondents to assess the president's decision-making in the context of the crisis or the negotiation. For the Russia–Estonia and China–Taiwan crises, respondents were asked: "How likely or unlikely do you think it is that President [T1: Donald Trump / T2: Kamala Harris] would show good judgment in responding to this crisis?" For the Iran or North Korea negotiations, respondents were asked: "How likely or unlikely do you think it is that President [T1: Donald Trump / T2: Kamala Harris] would negotiate an agreement with Iran that is good for the United States?" For both questions, the answer options were displayed on a five-point scale: "Very unlikely" (1) / "Somewhat unlikely" (2) / "Neither likely nor unlikely" (3) / "Somewhat likely" (4) / "Very likely" (5).[27] A larger difference in the public's evaluations of an in-party versus an out-party president's decision-making would support the first hypothesis.

The top panel of figure 5.1 shows the proportion of respondents from each party who said that the president was either "Somewhat likely" or "Very

---

26. See, e.g., discussions about the possibility of new U.S. negotiations with Iran (Shahla 2024) or North Korea (Tankersley 2021) about their respective nuclear programs.

27. To simplify the presentation of figures in this chapter, this variable is coded as a 1 if the respondent answered "Somewhat likely" or "Very likely" and a 0 otherwise.

TABLE 5.1. Survey questionnaire for crisis scenarios

	Russia–Estonia crisis	China–Taiwan crisis
Background text	Since Russia's invasion of Ukraine in 2022, the United States has been concerned that Russia may try to invade another country in Eastern Europe.	Over the last several years, the United States has grown increasingly concerned that China may invade Taiwan.
	Consider the following hypothetical scenario: [T1: Donald Trump / T2: Kamala Harris] is re-elected President in 2024. During the administration, Russia launches a military attack on Estonia, a NATO member country in Eastern Europe.	Consider the following hypothetical scenario: [T1: Donald Trump / T2: Kamala Harris] is re-elected President in 2024. During the administration, China launches a military attack against Taiwan in an attempt to reunify it with mainland China.
Evaluation of presidential judgment	How likely or unlikely do you think it is that President [T1: Donald Trump / T2: Kamala Harris] would show good judgment in responding to this crisis? Very unlikely / Somewhat unlikely / Neither likely nor unlikely / Somewhat likely / Very likely	How likely or unlikely do you think it is that President [T1: Donald Trump / T2: Kamala Harris] would show good judgment in responding to this crisis? Very unlikely / Somewhat unlikely / Neither likely nor unlikely / Somewhat likely / Very likely
Evaluation of policy response	In response, President [T1: Donald Trump / T2: Kamala Harris] decides to send more US military troops to help Estonia.	In response, President [T1: Donald Trump / T2: Kamala Harris] decides to send more US military troops to help Taiwan.
	In this scenario, would you approve or disapprove of President [T1: Trump / T2: Harris] sending US military troops to Estonia? Disapprove strongly / Disapprove somewhat / Neither approve nor disapprove / Approve somewhat / Approve strongly	In this scenario, would you approve or disapprove of President [T1: Trump / T2: Harris] sending US military troops to Taiwan? Disapprove strongly / Disapprove somewhat / Neither approve nor disapprove / Approve somewhat / Approve strongly
Endorsement of obstruction	Which of the following do you think [T1: Democrats / T2: Republicans] in Congress should do in response to [T1: Trump's / T2: Harris's] actions? Do nothing / Express disapproval / Express approval (but not / and also) take actions to (prevent / support) the president	Which of the following do you think [T1: Democrats / T2: Republicans] in Congress should do in response to [T1: Trump's / T2: Harris's] actions? Do nothing / Express disapproval / Express approval (but not / and also) take actions to (prevent / support) the president

TABLE 5.2. Survey questionnaire for negotiation scenarios

	Iran negotiation	North Korea negotiation
Background text	Over the last several years, the United States has considered negotiating with Iran over their nuclear weapons program. In 2015, the US signed a nuclear agreement with Iran but later withdrew from the agreement in 2018.	Over the last several years, the United States has considered negotiating with North Korea about their nuclear weapons program. The most recent round of negotiations between the US and North Korea occurred in 2019, but an agreement was not reached.
	Consider the following hypothetical scenario: [T1: Donald Trump / T2: Kamala Harris] is re-elected President in 2024. Their administration attempts to negotiate a new nuclear agreement with Iran.	Consider the following hypothetical scenario: [T1: Donald Trump / T2: Kamala Harris] is re-elected President in 2024. Their administration attempts to negotiate an agreement with North Korea about nuclear weapons.
Evaluation of presidential judgment	How likely or unlikely do you think it is that President [T1: Donald Trump / T2: Kamala Harris] would negotiate an agreement with Iran that is good for the United States? Very unlikely / Somewhat unlikely / Neither likely nor unlikely / Somewhat likely / Very likely	How likely or unlikely do you think it is that President [T1: Donald Trump / T2: Kamala Harris] would negotiate an agreement with North Korea that is good for the United States? Very unlikely / Somewhat unlikely / Neither likely nor unlikely / Somewhat likely / Very likely
Evaluation of policy response	In this scenario, would you approve or disapprove of President [T1: Donald Trump / T2: Kamala Harris] negotiating a new nuclear agreement with Iran? Disapprove strongly / Disapprove somewhat / Neither approve nor disapprove / Approve somewhat / Approve strongly	In this scenario, would you approve or disapprove of President [T1: Donald Trump / T2: Kamala Harris] restarting talks with North Korea about their nuclear weapons program? Disapprove strongly / Disapprove somewhat / Neither approve nor disapprove / Approve somewhat / Approve strongly
Endorsement of obstruction	Which of the following do you think [T1: Democrats / T2: Republicans] in Congress should do in response to [T1: Trump's / T2: Harris's] actions? Do nothing / Express disapproval / Express approval (but not / and also) take actions to (prevent / support) the president	Which of the following do you think [T1: Democrats / T2: Republicans] in Congress should do in response to [T1: Trump's / T2: Harris's] actions? Do nothing / Express disapproval / Express approval (but not / and also) take actions to (prevent / support) the president

170 CHAPTER 5

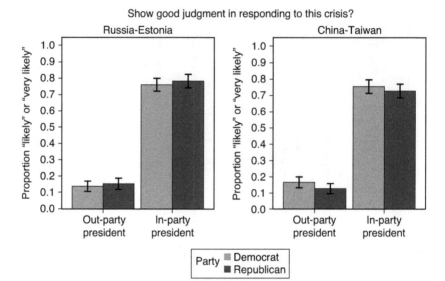

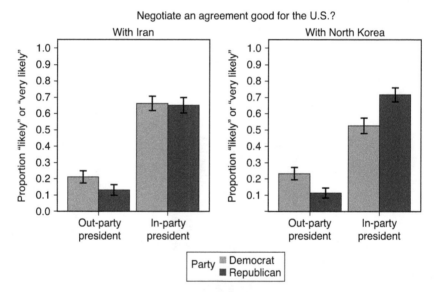

FIGURE 5.1. Public attitudes toward presidential decision-making among in-party and out-party survey respondents

likely" to show good judgment in responding to a Russia–Estonia crisis (left panel) or a China–Taiwan crisis (right panel). Within each plot, the first set of bars shows the average response from survey respondents who were in the out-party treatment condition. These respondents either identified as Republicans but read about Kamala Harris or identified as Democrats but read about Donald Trump. The second set of bars in each plot shows the results from respondents in the in-party treatment condition who share the same party as the president in the scenario. In both the Russia–Estonia and China–Taiwan crisis scenarios, the findings were very similar. A large majority of respondents in the survey (between 72 and 78 percent) thought that the president who shared their partisan affiliation would be likely to show good judgment during the crisis. By contrast, a small minority of respondents (between 13 and 16 percent) expressed confidence in the crisis decision-making of the out-party president. Overall, the results for Democrats (in light gray) parallel the results for Republicans (in dark gray). While it may be unsurprising that survey respondents displayed a clear partisan bias, the very large discrepancy between evaluations of in-party and out-party presidential candidates in the crisis scenarios is striking.

The bottom panel of figure 5.1 displays the results from the negotiation scenarios, where respondents evaluate whether the president would negotiate an agreement with either Iran (left panel) or North Korea (right panel) that was good for the United States. Again, we see large differences in average responses among respondents in the out-party treatment condition (left) and the in-party condition (right). In negotiations with North Korea, however, there is a larger gap between respondents in the in-party and out-party treatment conditions among Republicans. For example, roughly 71 percent of Republicans in the sample think that Donald Trump would negotiate an agreement with North Korea that is good for the United States, while only 11 percent think that Kamala Harris would do the same.

These findings are consistent with Credibility Hypothesis 1A: a partisan public tends to distrust the foreign policy decision-making of presidents from the opposite party. As polarization becomes more extreme and the electorate grows more partisan, we would expect distrust of an out-party president's decision-making to grow. An even harder test of this hypothesis, however, would examine whether partisans approve of a policy response endorsed by their in-party president but disapprove of the same response endorsed by their out-party president. To explore this in the survey, I hold the policy response constant across the different presidents and scenarios. In the crisis scenarios, I tell respondents that the president decided to send U.S. troops to defend Estonia or Taiwan. In the negotiation scenarios, I tell respondents that the president decided to negotiate a new nuclear agreement with Iran or restart talks with North Korea. Respondents are then asked how much they approve or disapprove of the president's actions.[28]

Figure 5.2 plots the proportion of respondents who report that they "Approve somewhat" or "Approve strongly" of the president's decision to send in troops in the crisis scenarios. On average, respondents are more likely to approve of the policy when they share the party of the president. However, Democrats are more mixed in their assessments of the policy response, and the difference among Democrats in the in-party versus out-party groups is not as large as the difference among Republicans. For instance, a majority of Republicans approve of sending troops to defend Estonia (54 percent approve) and Taiwan (55 percent approve) under a Trump administration, but are less likely to approve of sending troops to Estonia (32 percent approve) and Taiwan (29 percent approve) under a Harris administration.

In the negotiation scenarios, we see large differences across the in-party and out-party treatment conditions for both Republicans and Democrats. A large majority of the sample approves of their co-partisan president negotiating an agreement with Iran (62–63 percent approve) or North Korea (63–74 percent approve) but overwhelmingly disapproves of the president from the opposite party negotiating the agreement. Like in the crisis scenarios, there are greater differences between the in-party and out-party treatment conditions among Republicans than Democrats. Republicans are much more likely to approve of Trump negotiating with Iran or North Korea but disapprove of Harris negotiating. These findings are broadly consistent with Credibility Hypothesis 1A, illustrating the phenomenon of partisan distrust in foreign policy decision-making of leaders from the opposite party.

The second hypothesis, Credibility Hypothesis 1B, anticipates that a partisan public not only disapproves of the actions taken by presidents of the opposite party, but also advocates for co-partisan legislators to obstruct the president. To test this hypothesis, after both sets of scenarios, I ask survey respondents: "Which of the following do you think [T1: Democrats / T2: Republicans] in Congress should do in response to [T1: Trump's / T2: Harris's] actions?" Respondents select whether legislators from the opposition party should express approval, disapproval, or do nothing, and also whether

---

28. Survey responses are recorded on a five-point scale from Disapprove strongly (1) to Approve strongly (5). To simplify the presentation of results, the figures plot the proportion of respondents in each group "Approve somewhat" or "Approve strongly."

POLARIZATION AND THE CREDIBILITY ADVANTAGE 173

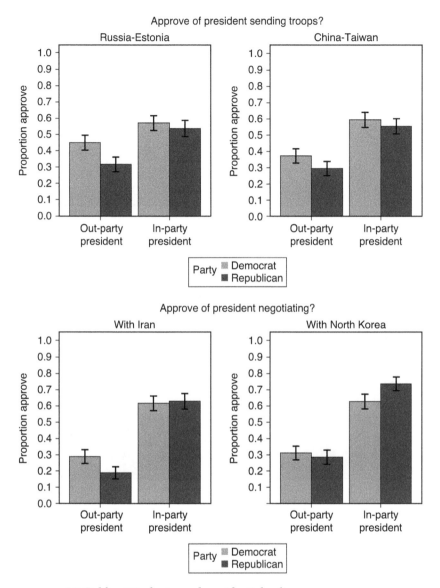

FIGURE 5.2. Public attitudes toward presidential policy responses among in-party and out-party survey respondents

or not they should take additional actions to support or oppose the president's policy. I code respondents endorsing obstruction as those who both express disapproval and also advocate for legislators to take additional actions to prevent the president from either sending troops (in the crisis scenario) or from negotiating with an adversary (in the negotiation scenario).

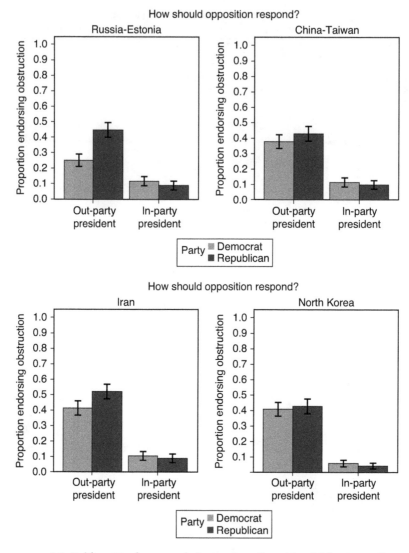

FIGURE 5.3. Public attitudes toward obstruction of presidential foreign policy among in-party and out-party survey respondents

Figure 5.3 plots the proportion of respondents in each of the four scenarios who endorse the opposition party taking actions to obstruct the president. Consistent with what we would expect from Credibility Hypothesis 1B, we see a higher percentage of respondents (between 25 and 52 percent, depending on the scenario) endorsing obstruction when they are in the out-party treatment relative to when they are in the in-party condition (between 4 and

12 percent), holding fixed the policy response. In most cases, the majority of respondents do not endorse obstruction. However, given these patterns, we would expect that, as the electorate grows more polarized, a partisan public will increasingly reward co-partisan politicians for preventing a president from the opposing party from enacting their policies.

Another additional implication of Credibility Hypothesis 1B is that more affectively polarized members of the public should be even more likely to endorse obstruction in foreign policymaking. Figure 5.4 shows results of the obstruction questions among a subset of respondents who displayed high levels of affective polarization. In the survey, affective polarization was measured before the experiment took place as the difference between a respondent's feelings toward their in-party and out-party. The question read: "We'd also like to get your feelings about some groups in American society. Rate the following groups between 0 and 100. Ratings from 50–100 degrees mean that you feel favorably toward the group; ratings from 0–50 degrees mean that you don't feel favorably toward the group and that you don't care too much for that group: Democrats, Republicans."[29] Respondents were coded as displaying high levels of affective polarization if they scored in the seventy-fifth percentile or above. Figure 5.4 indicates that respondents displaying high levels of affective polarization are even more willing to endorse obstruction, especially in the negotiation scenario. For example, the bottom panel of the figure shows that a majority of both Democrats and Republicans in this subset of respondents think that the congressional opposition should both express their disapproval of the president's policy and try to take additional actions to stop the president from negotiating with an adversary.

What are the implications for the credibility advantage? The findings in this survey suggest that attitudes toward foreign policy decision-making are already quite partisan. As I have argued elsewhere, it appears that international crises and high-stakes international negotiations are not immune to polarization.[30] As a democracy becomes increasingly polarized, it is likely that members of the public will more strongly adhere to their partisan identity. It could be harder to galvanize the bipartisan support from the public and political officials needed to send a strong signal of resolve or to initiate a complex negotiation with a foreign adversary. This could diminish the ability of

---

29. The wording of this question comes from the American National Election Studies.
30. Myrick 2021.

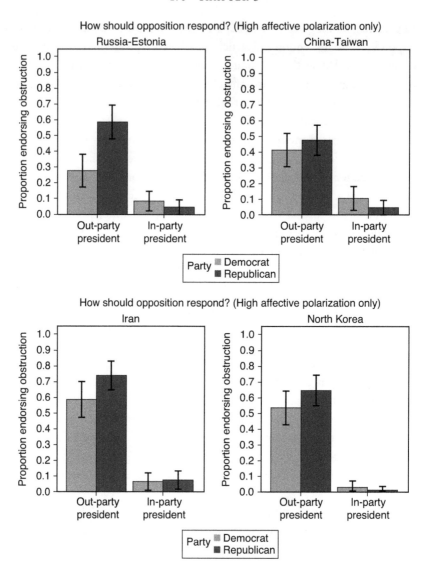

FIGURE 5.4. Public attitudes toward obstruction of presidential foreign policy among in-party and out-party survey respondents who display high levels of affective polarization

highly polarized democracies to issue credible threats and promises to other countries. Many of these effects have not yet been fully realized in American politics, but the overarching trends should be concerning. The next section investigates whether these public attitudes are also reflected in the behavior of politicians from the opposition party.

5.2 Horizontal Constraints and Democratic Credibility

So far, this chapter focused on how polarization affects public attitudes, reshaping vertical constraints on democratic leaders that confer signaling advantages in international politics. But an additional reason why democracies have a credibility advantage is because their leaders are constrained not only by the public but also by other actors within government. Recall that an important horizontal constraint in democracies is the presence of an active political opposition. When a democratic leader makes poor choices in foreign affairs, their political opponents will be quick to criticize bad policy decisions. These horizontal constraints ensure some degree of bipartisan support for major foreign policy actions.

To understand how polarization could impact horizontal constraints in the U.S. context, I analyze patterns in the political opposition's behavior in foreign affairs over time. Using data from congressional roll-call votes, I show that, since the 1970s, the opposition party has increasingly cohered against the president in foreign affairs, paralleling other trends in domestic politics. I then look at how legislators have responded to international crises initiated by adversaries of the United States. I show that legislators' responses to security threats tend to reflect the partisanship of the domestic political environment in which new crises are introduced. As a result, crisis responses have generally become more partisan over time.[31]

5.2.1 Politicians and Obstruction in Foreign Affairs

Some threshold of partisan disagreement is undoubtedly good for foreign policymaking. An independent political opposition is essential for democratic accountability in foreign affairs.[32] When leaders' decisions are subject to scrutiny, they make better choices in international politics. Diverse perspectives and spirited disagreement contribute to a "marketplace of ideas" that improves foreign policy outcomes.[33]

In chapter 2, however, I argued that, as polarization becomes more extreme, it creates a toxic political environment that limits the ability of the political opposition to effectively check executive power. When there are high levels of affective polarization among the public, members of the opposition party

---
31. Portions of this section are reprinted from Myrick (2021).
32. Baum and Potter 2015.
33. Snyder 1991; Reiter and Stam 1998, 2002.

benefit from actively opposing presidential authority in foreign affairs. These incentives make it difficult to distinguish between principled and partisan disagreement from the political opposition. Principled disagreement arises from ideological differences between the parties that create a divergence in policy preferences. Partisan disagreement arises from political and electoral incentives that reinforce a "teamsmanship"[34] dynamic in Congress. Situations in which the opposition persistently undermines or obstructs the executive will lead them to suspect that the opposition's motives are partisan rather than principled. This contributes to an environment of mutual distrust that has important second-order consequences for foreign policymaking, which I explore later in this chapter.

Credibility Hypothesis 2A: *As polarization becomes more extreme, politicians are more likely to consistently oppose or actively undermine leaders from an opposing party in foreign policy.*

To investigate this hypothesis, I look descriptively at whether, as domestic polarization has increased in the United States, the political opposition has become increasingly likely to oppose the president in foreign affairs. To do so, I first draw on data from congressional roll-call votes, which is the most common approach to infer political preferences of legislators or parties in American politics.[35] Data on roll-call votes comes from the VoteView project, which maintains a comprehensive database of congressional votes.[36] I identify votes related to "foreign affairs and defense policy"[37] for eight recent presidential administrations. Table 5.3 shows the number of foreign policy roll-call votes included for each administration.[38] I then estimate the positions (referred to by political scientists as "ideal points") of each congressperson using the W-NOMINATE method from Poole and Rosenthal (1997). This basic scaling method locates each politician in a two-dimensional policy space based on their roll-call votes in Congress. Figure 5.5 and figure 5.6 map foreign policy ideal-point estimates of the president and all of the legislators in the political

---

34. Lee 2009.
35. Poole and Rosenthal 1997, 2011.
36. Lewis et al. 2019.
37. These roll-call votes are categorized based on a set of issue codes from Clausen (1973).
38. To focus on substantive foreign policy votes, I include only competitive votes, defined as votes with an agreement threshold of 85 percent or lower.

TABLE 5.3. Competitive foreign policy roll-call votes by presidential administration

Administration	Congressional sessions	Foreign policy votes
Obama	111th to 114th	635
Bush II	107th to 110th	1,015
Clinton	103rd to 106th	828
Bush I	101st to 102nd	407
Reagan	97th to 100th	1,117
Carter	95th to 96th	623
Ford	93rd to 94th	533
Nixon	91st to 92nd	413

opposition (the opposite party of the president) for each administration.[39] The president (in black) is labeled with their last name, whereas legislators from the opposition party (in gray) are labeled by their state abbreviations. The black dot on each plot represents the median legislator in the political opposition. The black line on the plot represents the policy "distance" between the president and the median opposition legislator in foreign affairs. The further apart politicians are in two-dimensional space, the more dissimilar their foreign policy positions.

The distribution of ideal-point estimates across time yields a clear pattern. Most noticeably, the distribution of legislators in two-dimensional policy space is far more diffuse between the 91st and the 100th Congresses (figure 5.5) than it is in more recent Congresses (figure 5.6). By George W. Bush's administration (2001–2009), Democrats have largely cohered on the opposite side of the policy space, with the exception of a handful of legislators. And, by Barack Obama's administration (2009–2017), all congressional Republicans are a minimum distance of 0.5 units away from the president in the policy space.

What is striking about the temporal trend is not only the increasing distance between the president and legislators from the political opposition, but also the increasing cohesion demonstrated within the opposition party against the president. For example, there are relatively large policy distances between congressional Republicans and both President Jimmy Carter (95th–96th Congresses) and President Barack Obama (111th–114th Congresses).

39. These plots were constructed with the `wnominate` and the `Rvoteview` packages in R (see Lewis et al. 2019).

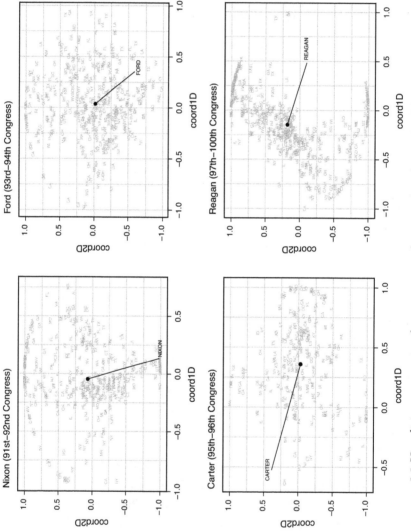

FIGURE 5.5. Visualizing congressional opposition on foreign policy using roll-call votes (91st to 100th Congresses)

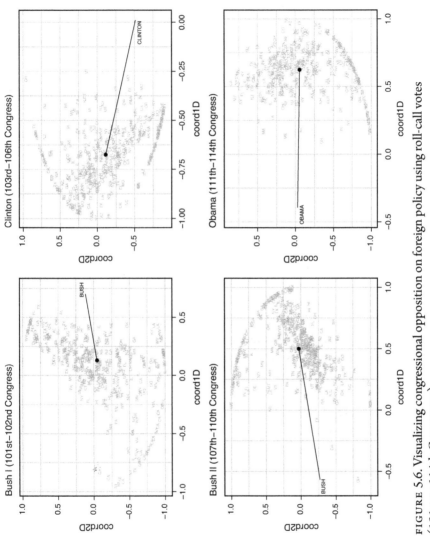

FIGURE 5.6. Visualizing congressional opposition on foreign policy using roll-call votes (101st to 114th Congresses)

This accords with the conventional understanding of Carter and Obama as "dovish" presidents who are less inclined to use military force. However, congressional Republicans in the Carter years are much more dispersed on the policy space relative to those in the Obama years. By the Obama administration, there is a remarkable degree of cohesion among Republican legislators in opposition to the Democratic president in foreign affairs.

These figures provide some evidence that the political opposition has more uniformly opposed the president in foreign affairs over the past eight presidential administrations. However, looking only at congressional roll-call votes may not provide a full picture of polarization in foreign policy. There are limits to this method. Since the two-dimensional policy space is constructed for each congressional session, the scale of the policy space is not directly comparable across plots.[40] In foreign affairs, it is also not straightforward to infer what the different dimensions of the figures represent. Moreover, some political scientists argue that to measure partisanship over U.S. foreign policy, we should distinguish between major and minor roll-call votes.[41] In *Bipartisanship and US Foreign Policy*, for instance, Jordan Tama shows that, while bipartisanship has declined over the past few decades, a sizeable percentage of important congressional votes on foreign affairs are still passed with support from both parties.[42]

An additional concern is that roll-call votes related to foreign policy are relatively infrequent. Inferring polarization from congressional votes on foreign affairs can be misleading because polarization shapes the scope or content of legislation. Legislators may pass an expressive resolution condemning an adversary for human rights violations because there was strong partisan disagreement over taking more concrete foreign policy actions. If this expressive resolution is adopted unanimously, we would mistakenly infer that there was no polarization around the issue. Because of these challenges with measuring foreign policy polarization from congressional roll-call votes, it is useful to consider other means of investigating how partisan the response is to certain events.

---

40. Measures of foreign policy positions that use a one-dimensional hawk–dove policy space similarly show an increase in polarization in foreign affairs based on congressional roll-call votes (Jeong and Quirk 2019).

41. Chaudoin, Milner, and Tingley 2010; Bryan and Tama 2022; Tama 2023.

42. Tama 2023.

5.2.2 Politicians and Partisan Responses to Crises

In a famous speech in January 1945, Republican Senator Arthur Vandenberg stated, "Here in the Senate we do not have perpetual agreement between the two sides of the aisle, but we have never failed to have basic unity when crisis calls."[43] In liberal democracies, the political opposition serves as a check on executive power. Relative disagreement or agreement of the political opposition with the leader should be informative both to the public and to foreign adversaries. During international crises, when national security is involved, the "stakes of the game" are heightened. Policymakers should in theory set aside partisan differences to resolve a pressing problem. In practice, this often means that legislators from the opposing party respond to a crisis by supporting the executive.[44]

In chapter 2, however, I argued that, in extremely polarized times, the opposition party may be far more reluctant to support the executive during crises. This could be because the opposition genuinely distrusts the leader's decision-making or disagrees with their policies. But, it could also be because the opposition seeks to vocally obstruct the leader for partisan gain. As a consequence, leaders may not be able to leverage domestic agreement to signal resolve to foreign adversaries during a crisis.

Credibility Hypothesis 2B: *As polarization becomes more extreme, politicians are less likely to defer to a leader from an opposing party in times of crisis.*

An implication of this hypothesis is that, as polarization becomes more extreme, debates between political officials about international crises will become more partisan. To demonstrate this, I look at changes in the partisan nature of responses to international crises involving the United States. The International Crisis Behavior project maintains data on security crises between countries.[45] Using this dataset, I identify the set of security crises involving the United States that were initiated by another country. Measuring polarization in response to an international crisis is challenging. Analyzing roll-call votes in this context is difficult because not all crises involve votes. As an alternative, I look at polarization of congressional rhetoric around security crises. The intuition is that if Republicans and Democrats are using

---

43. Vandenberg 1945.
44. Brody 1991.
45. Brecher et al. 2017; Beardsley et al. 2020.

systematically different language to describe the crisis, they likely have different perspectives on how to approach the crisis response.[46]

To measure polarization of congressional rhetoric around crises, I identify the foreign adversary that triggered the crisis and the congressional session in which that crisis occurred. I then extract all speeches from the *Congressional Record*[47] in which any variant of the country name appears during the relevant session. To measure polarization of congressional rhetoric, I follow a method developed by Andrew Peterson and Arthur Spirling, who use supervised machine learning based on texts from British parliamentary debates to measure polarization between Labour and Conservative members of parliament.[48] The application here is to use machine learning methods to predict whether a randomly drawn speech about a given country is from a Republican or a Democratic legislator. A higher predictive accuracy means that it is easier to predict the party of a legislator based on their speech, indicating higher levels of polarization.[49]

The intuition behind this method is to run a number of different classifiers and select the one that best predicts legislators' parties based on their speech in order to proxy polarization. In theory, the predictive accuracy of the classifier ranges from 0.5 to 1. At 0.5, the classifier is effectively randomly guessing with a fifty-fifty chance of accurately predicting the party of the speaker based on their speech. This means we are in an environment of low polarization in which there is no real distinction between Republican and Democratic speech. At 1, the classifier correctly predicts the party of the speaker 100 percent of the time, indicating an environment of high polarization in which it is easy to perfectly distinguish between a Republican and Democratic speaker.[50]

---

46. See Goet (2019) for a detailed overview of how supervised machine learning methods to measure partisanship of legislative speech can be considered valid measures of party polarization.

47. The *Congressional Record* contains: "House and Senate floor proceedings, substantially verbatim transcripts of floor debate and remarks, notice of all bills introduced, full text of all conference committee reports, notices of committee and Presidential actions and communications, and statements or documents submitted by members of Congress for publication." I use the digitized version of the *Congressional Record* from Gentzkow, Shapiro, and Taddy (2018).

48. Peterson and Spirling 2018.

49. See Peterson and Spirling (2018) for a technical description of this method.

50. Myrick (2021) contains data on the polarization of congressional rhetoric about U.S. foreign adversaries across all congressional sessions. See appendix for more details.

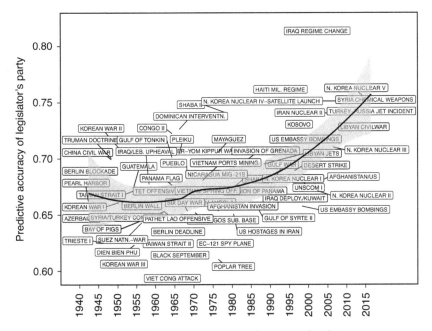

FIGURE 5.7. Relationship between international crises and polarization of congressional rhetoric

Figure 5.7 shows that the polarization of rhetoric around international crises mirrors trends in overall polarization, which remains low in the first few decades of the Cold War and steadily increases starting in the 1970s.[51] The figure is suggestive of the pattern described in chapter 4: over time, partisan polarization driven by domestic politics has likely spilled into foreign policy. This figure also supports the idea that, as polarization has increased, the opposition party is less likely to simply defer to the executive in times of crisis. This can undermine the credibility advantage because a lack of bipartisan agreement makes it more challenging for polarized democracies to signal resolve to foreign adversaries.

5.3 Application: The Case of the Iran Nuclear Deal

This chapter provided some evidence that, as polarization becomes more extreme, it could erode vertical and horizontal constraints on executive power.

51. Barber and McCarty 2015.

But, how might these dynamics ultimately affect the credibility advantage democracies have in foreign affairs? To answer this question, first recall why domestic constraints matter. In democracies, leaders can leverage domestic constraints to enhance their credibility in multiple ways. For one, democratic leaders can leverage agreement between domestic actors to credibly signal information to adversaries in an international crisis. Political scientist Kenneth Schultz explains that, if the opposition and the government pose a united front, this is a credible signal of resolve precisely because the opposition has no incentive to pretend to support the executive.[52]

In addition, leaders can leverage moderate forms of disagreement among domestic actors when they negotiate with foreign adversaries. In the framework outlined by political scientist Robert Putnam, international negotiations are thought of as a two-level game.[53] At the first level, delegations of countries negotiate with one another. At the second level, the negotiated agreement is ratified or otherwise approved by domestic actors. Because democratic leaders can credibly point out that their hands are tied by domestic constraints, they have greater leverage in the negotiation process and may ultimately be able to extract a deal with more favorable terms. In short, the domestic constraints democracies have improve the credibility of the signals they send, giving them more leverage when negotiating international agreements.[54]

As polarization becomes more extreme, however, it can undercut the credibility advantage. In international crises, it becomes increasingly unlikely that domestic actors will rally behind a leader in highly polarized environments. Driven by either principled or partisan disagreement, both the public and the political opposition are much less likely to support a leader from an opposing party, reducing the possibility of the signaling advantage that Schultz identifies.

In international negotiations, as polarization increases, the political opposition has more incentives to cohere against the leader or to obstruct them in making foreign policy. Although a moderate amount of disagreement can improve the leader's negotiating position, as the distance between the executive and the political opposition increases, it becomes likely that there is no agreement that will be acceptable to both domestic and international

---

52. Schultz 2001a.
53. Putnam 1988.
54. Schelling 1960; Putnam 1988.

stakeholders.[55] Anticipating these partisan dynamics, democratic leaders may be deterred from even starting complex negotiations in the first place. For negotiations that are ongoing, heightened polarization could influence how leaders approach both the negotiation and the ratification of international agreements. And, in the most extreme environments, negotiations with foreign adversaries are likely to be derailed by domestic politics.

> Credibility Hypothesis 3: *As polarization becomes more extreme, democracies are less likely to send credible signals to adversaries in international negotiations and crisis bargaining.*

I illustrate one way in which extreme polarization could affect the credibility advantage with application to an international negotiation with an adversarial country. I examine how polarization in the United States shaped the initiation, negotiation, and ultimate U.S. withdrawal from the JCPOA, also known as the Iran nuclear deal. I investigate this case by drawing on in-depth interviews with senior government officials that I conducted in July and August 2018 in Washington, D.C.[56] These interviews feature officials directly involved in either the negotiation process of the JCPOA or the passage of congressional legislation pertaining to it.

Heightened affective polarization and the timing of the negotiation—which preceded the 2016 Republican presidential primary—created incentives for congressional Republicans to be particularly hostile toward the JCPOA. Theories of two-level games would predict that credible signals of dissent from Republican opponents of the deal could be leveraged to extract concessions from Iranian negotiators. However, this was ultimately not what happened. Instead, high levels of polarization created an environment of mutual distrust that hampered information flow between negotiators and Congress. As the negotiation became increasingly politicized, the White House struggled to distinguish between principled and partisan disagreement. It became unclear which Republican legislators were pure spoilers—members of the domestic opposition that would not accept a deal with Iran, irrespective of its terms—and which legislators might consider a deal under more favorable terms. The Obama administration believed that the safest

---

55. For more on how domestic politics can hamper international negotiations see, e.g., Friedrichs 2022; Iida 1993; Milner 1997.

56. This research was reviewed by the Stanford University Institutional Review Board (Protocol No. IRB-45416). See appendix for more details about the interview process.

option was to largely box Congress out of the negotiation process, insulating the JCPOA from domestic partisan politics. As a result, the United States entered the JCPOA without substantive bipartisan buy-in, making the agreement less durable.

5.3.1 Background on the JCPOA Negotiation

The United States and Iran had a fraught, adversarial relationship for decades prior to the negotiation of the JCPOA. In 1953, U.S. intelligence agencies assisted in a coup that ousted Mohammed Mossadeq, Iran's democratically elected prime minister. His successor, Shah Mohammad Reza Pahlavi was supported by the United States but highly unpopular among the Iranian population. In the 1979 Iranian revolution, the shah was overthrown and his regime was replaced by an Islamic theocracy led by Grand Ayatollah Ruhollah Khomeini. During the revolution, Iranians stormed the U.S. embassy in Tehran, holding fifty-two Americans hostage for well over a year until their negotiated release in 1981. The Iran hostage crisis soured U.S–Iranian relations for decades to come.

Distracted by domestic unrest, Iran became an appealing target for Saddam Hussein, the dictatorial president of neighboring Iraq. In 1980, Iraq invaded Iran, and a protracted, bloody conflict ensued for eight years. Throughout the Iran-Iraq War, the United States provided assistance to Iraq, despite credible allegations that Hussein had used chemical weapons against Iranians. During this period, animosity between the United States and Iran increased as the Iranian regime sponsored a network of terrorist organizations in the Middle East—most notably the Hezbollah movement in Lebanon—that targeted Americans in militant attacks. In response to Iran's support for terrorism, the United States imposed waves of sanctions against Iran in the 1980s and 1990s.

By the outset of the twenty-first century, relations between the United States and Iran were highly strained. Washington became increasingly worried about Iran's nuclear ambitions. A nuclear-armed Iran would dramatically change the balance of power in the Middle East, threatening the United States and many of its allies, most notably Israel. To prevent Iran from acquiring nuclear capabilities, there were periodic, limited attempts at diplomatic engagement between the two countries. Shortly after the United States initiated the Iraq War in 2003, for example, Iranians developed a proposal for comprehensive negotiations over their nuclear program and transmitted it to U.S. officials via the Swiss ambassador to Tehran.[57] The proposal was ultimately shot down by hardliners in the Bush administration, chiefly Vice President Dick Cheney and Secretary of Defense Donald Rumsfeld.

During the 2008 presidential campaign, Democratic candidate Barack Obama struck a different tone by signaling a willingness to engage diplomatically with Iran. In March 2009, during his first year in office, President Obama released a video during Nowruz, the Iranian new year. In a short video with Farsi subtitles, the U.S. president appealed to the Iranian people for more "constructive ties" between the United States and Iran.[58] During the first year of the Obama administration, U.S. officials worked on a proposal to swap nuclear fuel with Iran via Russia. In October 2009, Iranian officials agreed in principle to the swap.[59] However, unrest over the June 2009 Iranian presidential elections—in which President Mahmoud Ahmadinejad's electoral victory was widely disputed—and pressure from Congress and the Israeli government led to a collapse in negotiations. By the end of 2009, Congress pushed for broad, nonnuclear (gasoline) sanctions, and tensions between Iran and the United States escalated.[60]

Over subsequent years, the United States and other members of the international community continued robust sanctions against Iran, citing the government's failure to suspend its uranium enrichment program. As sanctions pressure mounted, Iranian officials began meeting with the "P5+1," delegations from the permanent five members of the UN Security Council (United States, UK, France, China, and Russia) and Germany. In parallel to the official talks occurring between Iran and the P5+1 throughout 2012 and 2013, the United States established a secret back channel, via Oman, with Iranian officials.[61] During this period, the official position of the United States was that it would not allow Iran to enrich any uranium. This hard line had been Washington's position for many decades. But, through the back channel, however, U.S. officials secretly expressed to the Iranians that they would consent to very limited enrichment.[62]

57. Kessler 2006.
58. Black 2009.
59. Fitzpatrick 2010.
60. Parsi 2012.
61. Burns 2019.
62. Sherman 2018.

The election of Iranian President Hassan Rouhani, a more moderate, reformist candidate, in June 2013 signaled new opportunities for progress on nuclear issues. By the fall of 2013, the U.S. delegation revealed the existence of the back channel to the other P5+1 members and presented the proposal that U.S. and Iranian negotiators reached in secret. Iran would be allowed to enrich uranium in very limited quantities in exchange for thorough inspections of its facilities conducted by an independent monitor, the International Atomic Energy Agency (IAEA). In early 2014, an interim nuclear agreement, called the Joint Plan of Action (JPOA), went into effect. The JPOA proposed that, for a period of six months, Iran would freeze parts of its nuclear program in exchange for limited sanctions relief while a more permanent agreement could be negotiated.

As negotiations for a final agreement progressed, the Obama administration faced growing pressure from Congress. The White House anticipated opposition from congressional Republicans to a nuclear agreement. Therefore, the administration planned to avoid joining a final agreement by international treaty, which would have required ratification by a two-thirds majority vote in the Senate. However, there were still many ways in which Congress could effectively kill the deal. Legislators could pass new sanctions on Iran during the interim period, demand additional conditions for approval that Iran would not accept, or require congressional approval for the agreement to take effect.

While the American negotiating team continued to periodically meet with its counterparts in Europe, tensions in Washington between the White House and congressional Republicans increased. In March 2015, without consulting the White House, Republican Speaker of the House John Boehner invited Israeli Prime Minister Benjamin Netanyahu to address a joint meeting of Congress. In the speech, Prime Minister Netanyahu characterized the Iran nuclear deal as a "very bad deal" and passionately argued that the United States should not join it.[63] Shortly afterwards, in another act of defiance against the Obama administration, Republican Senator Tom Cotton of Arkansas wrote the open letter to Iranian leaders described at the outset of this chapter.

During this period, both Republican and Democratic legislators sought a way to exert some congressional oversight over the final agreement. They ultimately settled on legislation introduced by Republican Senator Bob Corker

63. Calamur 2015.

of Tennessee and Democratic Senator Ben Cardin of Maryland. The Corker–Cardin Bill—called the Iran Nuclear Agreement Review Act, or INARA—would give Congress a set time frame to review the final agreement and vote on a resolution of disapproval should they not find it acceptable.[64] The final agreement would stand if the disapproval resolution was not supported by a two-thirds vote in the Senate, the number of votes needed to override a presidential veto.

The P5+1 reached a final agreement with Iran, the JCPOA, in Vienna on July 14, 2015. In exchange for sanctions relief, the agreement would substantially restrict the ability of the Iranian government to develop nuclear weapons. Although Iran would be able to enrich a small amount of uranium for domestic energy consumption, its stockpile of enriched uranium would be greatly reduced, as would the number of centrifuges—machines used to enrich uranium—it maintained. Its facilities would be further subject to thorough inspections by the IAEA. If the UN were to find that Iran violated the agreement, it would be able to "snap back" sanctions on Iran.

For skeptics of the JCPOA in the United States, one controversial aspect of the agreement was that it contained "sunset clauses," periods of time after which the limits on Iran's nuclear materials would expire.[65] Another major objection was that it failed to address other actions of the Iranian regime, including its sponsorship of terrorism in the Middle East and its ballistic missile program.[66] Still other objectors were deeply suspicious of the Iranian regime regardless of other aspects of the agreement and saw little purpose in negotiating a nuclear deal until, and unless, the regime was overthrown.[67]

After the JCPOA was finalized, the Obama administration turned its efforts toward a fight on Capitol Hill to preserve the agreement. On September 17, 2015, the Senate voted on a resolution of disapproval. The resolution would have required sixty votes to pass in order to overcome a Democratic filibuster. The final vote was fifty-three in favor and forty-five against. Democrats had blocked efforts to reject the agreement, and the United States would remain party to the JCPOA.

---

64. Iran Nuclear Agreement Review Act, H.R. 1191, 114th Cong. (2015).

65. Davenport 2017.

66. See, e.g., concerns cited by Secretary of State Mike Pompeo in his speech at The Heritage Foundation on May 21, 2018, called "After the Deal: A New Iran Strategy" (Pompeo 2018).

67. See, e.g., Cotton 2017.

Although congressional Republicans failed to block the deal in September 2015, it remained highly polarized. Prior to the 2016 U.S. presidential election, Republican presidential candidates consistently campaigned against the JCPOA.[68] Then-candidate Donald Trump repeatedly labeled the agreement a bad deal for the United States. Once in office, President Trump decertified the deal in the fall of 2017, yet there was minimal de facto change in U.S. policy toward Iran. On May 8, 2018, President Trump announced that the United States would formally withdraw from the JCPOA.[69] The following year, the Iranian government declared it would break the terms of the JCPOA by developing centrifuges and increasing its stockpile of enriched uranium.[70] The IAEA documented Iran's blatant violations of the nuclear agreement, which accelerated in subsequent years.[71]

During the 2020 presidential campaign, the Democratic challenger, former Vice President Joe Biden, expressed a desire to rejoin the JCPOA if Iran were to comply with its terms. However, Iran's actions since President Trump withdrew the United States from the JCPOA complicated efforts to simply reenter the deal. By the first year of the Biden administration in 2021, the Iran nuclear deal was already a diplomatic "minefield."[72] It became evident that the Biden administration faced tremendous difficulties both working with Iranian counterparts abroad and navigating fierce opposition to the Iranian regime at home. A few years into the Biden administration, commentators proclaimed the nuclear deal "dead" and expressed deep concern about containing Iran's nuclear ambitions.[73]

5.3.2 Polarization and Credibility in the JCPOA Negotiation

To investigate how domestic partisan dynamics impacted the JCPOA negotiation, I supplemented primary and secondary sources about the Iran deal with semistructured interviews in Washington, D.C., from July to August 2018. These interviews were conducted on background to preserve anonymity and drew on the perspectives of three groups of senior government officials. The

68. Kelly 2015.
69. Trump 2018.
70. Wintour 2019.
71. Metzler and Rising 2020.
72. Wright 2021.
73. Sanger 2024.

first group was the set of international-facing officials in the Obama administration who were directly involved in the negotiation. These officials interacted primarily with Iran and the other P5+1 delegations, but also regularly briefed Congress. Therefore, they were best equipped to speak to how the domestic and international levels of the negotiation interacted. The second group was the set of domestic-facing officials in the Obama administration whose responsibilities were to interface with Congress around the Iran deal. These officials could provide insight into how the White House perceived opposition on the Hill during the negotiation. The third group was the set of congressional officials working on legislation related to the Iran deal in the Senate Foreign Relations Committee (SFRC), a committee of senators focused on foreign affairs. This group could offer the perspective of both Republican and Democratic legislators.[74]

Politicization of the Iran deal bred a sense of mutual distrust between the Obama administration and congressional Republicans. Anticipating congressional opposition, the White House felt it was necessary to keep initial negotiations with Iran secret given the highly sensitive nature of the negotiation process. In turn, congressional Republicans, who felt boxed out of the process, took more drastic actions to signal opposition to the JCPOA.

I argue that the polarized environment made it challenging for the negotiators to understand the credibility of signals coming from Republican legislators. It became difficult to distinguish between legislators who would never accept a plausible agreement with Iran, irrespective of its terms (what I refer to as pure spoilers), and those who would consider accepting some version of the agreement. The result was that the Obama administration effectively treated all congressional Republicans as spoilers and took steps to insulate the ongoing negotiations from domestic partisan politics.

Theories of two-level games would anticipate that costly signals of dissent from the domestic opposition—such as the Cotton letter described earlier in this chapter—would give U.S. officials more leverage in the international negotiation. However, I show that in reality these partisan antics had little impact on the substantive content of the deal. Instead, they only reinforced the Obama administration's distrust of the political opposition. This distrust

---

74. While a broader set of interviews were conducted for this study (see appendix), those featured in this chapter primarily draw on the perspectives of two senior officials within each group—a total of six officials—who participated in thirty- to sixty-minute one-on-one interviews.

shaped the Obama administration's decision to negotiate the JCPOA as an executive agreement. Without substantial congressional buy-in, however, the agreement was relatively easy to undo by the subsequent administration.

5.3.2.1 POLITICIZATION OF THE JCPOA NEGOTIATION

There were two factors that fueled politicization of the negotiation of the Iran nuclear deal in U.S. domestic politics. The first was the backdrop of congressional polarization and politicization of the U.S.–Iran relationship in the five to eight years prior to the JCPOA negotiation. The second was the timing of the negotiation process in conjunction with the start of the 2016 presidential primaries. These two forces contributed to a spiral of distrust, which had repercussions for how the White House approached the JCPOA negotiation and congressional approval process.

The first factor that contributed to the politicization of the JCPOA negotiation was simply that during the time the Iran deal was being negotiated, there was considerable polarization in Congress. The 114th Congress (2015–2017), during which Iran and the P5+1 finalized the JCPOA, was considered by many metrics to be the most polarized congressional session in roughly 100 years.[75] The government officials interviewed for this project—including both Republican and Democratic senior officials—all noted that congressional bipartisanship had eroded during their tenure in government. While most interviewees explained that SFRC tended to be less partisan than other major congressional committees, all expressed concern that polarization in SFRC had increased during this time and would likely continue to increase.

Despite this context, a cursory glance at congressional roll-call votes related to Iran in the years preceding the nuclear deal suggests that attitudes toward Iran were bipartisan. Republican and Democratic legislators continued to support tough economic sanctions on Iran prior to the start of the JCPOA negotiations. For example, the 2010 Comprehensive Iran Sanctions, Accountability, and Divestment Act, which targeted the petroleum sector in Iran, passed the House by a vote of 408–8 and the Senate by a vote of 99–0.[76] However, there was substantially more politicization around U.S.–Iran relations than roll-call votes would suggest. As one interviewee summarized: "The politics [around

---

75. Bump 2016.
76. Comprehensive Iran Sanctions, Accountability, and Divestment Act, H.R. 2194, 114th Cong. (2010).

the Iran deal] were pretty partisan from the start although some aspects look bipartisan."[77]

Congressional roll-call votes obscured a growing divergence between the Republican Party and the Democratic Party on U.S.–Iran relations. As the Obama administration began in 2009 to signal openness to a reevaluation of the U.S.–Iran relationship, Republicans vocalized their opposition to these overtures. The Republican establishment had established close ties with Israeli Prime Minister Benjamin Netanyahu, one of the staunchest critics of nuclear negotiations with Iran. The anti-Iran sentiment in the Republican Party likely reflected sincere animus toward the Iranian regime, but some also viewed it as politically advantageous to use U.S.–Iranian relations as a divisive "wedge issue."[78] A senior Democratic congressional staff member remarked: "Republicans have been trying to make Iran into a wedge issue. They have been trying for years to make the American Jewish community Republicans. They've been trying to say, 'Democrats are pro-Iran and Republicans are pro-Israel.' There is a lot of value in that for them. We see that attempt to sort of divide. . . . The Republican establishment was definitely trying to make it into a wedge issue to make it clear that Democrats are against Israel, because that's good for them politically."[79]

Analyses of congressional speeches also suggest that rhetoric around Iran had become increasingly polarized. This chapter emphasized that hyperpartisan environments give the opposition party incentives to grandstand and be critical of the president's foreign policy. These incentives are reflected in congressional speeches about Iran. Figure 5.8 shows the number of speeches about Iran in each congressional session by the party of the legislator between 1987 and 2017. Two periods with large partisan gaps in the number of speeches given by Republicans and Democrats are noticeable. The first is during the 100th session (1987–1989), after the Iran-Contra affair—a scandal in which the U.S. government illegally sold arms for Iran and used a portion of the funds to back Nicaraguan rebels—came to light. When Democrats were the primary opposition party, they were especially critical of the Reagan administration, and figure 5.8 shows that they mention Iran far more in

---

77. Author interview with former White House official (August 7, 2018).

78. See, e.g., Hillygus and Shields (2009) on the use of wedge issues in U.S. presidential elections.

79. Author interview with Democratic congressional senior staff member (August 22, 2018).

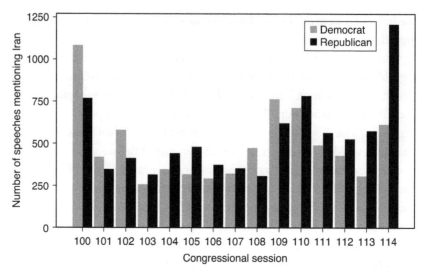

FIGURE 5.8. Speeches mentioning Iran in the *Congressional Record* (100th to 114th Congresses)

congressional speeches than their Republican counterparts. In the 113th (2013–2015) and 114th (2015–2017) congressional sessions, when Republicans were the primary opposition party, they were especially critical of the Obama administration during the JPOA and JCPOA negotiations.

The content of the congressional speeches paints a clearer picture of polarization around rhetoric about Iran. Using the method described earlier in this chapter,[80] I measure the partisanship of speeches from the digitized *Congressional Record*[81] that mention Iran. This measure represents the probability that a classifier correctly guesses the legislator's party based on the content of their speech. Higher predictive accuracy indicates that it is easier to distinguish between Republican and Democratic speech, and thus there is more polarization in congressional rhetoric. Figure 5.9 shows that congressional speech about Iran had increasingly polarized in the years prior to the JCPOA negotiation, and it reached an all-time high during the JCPOA negotiation in the 114th congressional session.

Against this broader backdrop of congressional polarization, the deal was further politicized given the timing of the negotiation. The JCPOA negotiators reached a framework for agreement in April 2015 and a final

80. Peterson and Spirling 2018.
81. Gentzkow, Shapiro, and Taddy 2018.

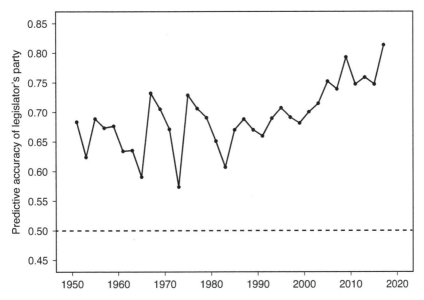

FIGURE 5.9. Partisanship of speech about Iran in the *Congressional Record* (1950–2016)

agreement in July 2015. This timing coincided with the start of the 2016 presidential primaries, which included a deep field of prominent Republican candidates, many of whom were engaged in foreign affairs or serving on SFRC. The first major candidate for the Republican presidential primary, Republican Senator Ted Cruz of Texas, announced in March 2015 that he was running for president. Additional candidates followed through the spring and summer of 2015, and the first Republican primary debate was held in August.

As the electoral cycle began, Republican presidential candidates positioned themselves as increasingly hawkish on Iran. One White House official working on legislative affairs pertaining to the Iran deal summarized: "This happened to be an electoral cycle where many aspiring Republican presidential candidates were on SRFC, so it made sense to be hawkish on Iran. ... During the Republican primary, you had to say what made sense politically. The first person would say 'I'm going to rip up the Iran deal,' and then the second would say, 'I'm going to rip up the Iran deal on the first day in office,' and the third would say, 'I'm going to burn it first and then rip it up.'"[82]

82. Author interview with senior White House official (August 13, 2018).

The rhetoric from presidential candidates became more extreme throughout 2015. When asked about the risks associated with the Iran deal, Senator Ted Cruz replied: "The greatest risk to this Iranian deal, it is that millions of Americans will be murdered by radical theocratic zealots."[83] Senator Marco Rubio of Florida, a vocal opponent of the Iran deal on SFRC, argued that the nuclear agreement would lead to a "cascade of nuclear proliferation in the Middle East" and a "broader unraveling of global order."[84] Former Wisconsin governor and presidential candidate Scott Walker asserted that military action against Iran would be an option on the table during the first day of his presidency.[85] During a Republican primary debate, then-candidate Donald Trump referred to the JCPOA as "horrible, disgusting, absolutely incompetent deal."[86]

Moderate Republicans vying for the presidential nomination who initially took a more conciliatory tone quickly sharpened their rhetoric. For example, former Florida Governor Jeb Bush noted that it was important to "check in with your allies first" before tearing up a nuclear agreement. After being criticized by other Republican presidential candidates for this statement, Bush corrected the record and advocated that the United States should be removed from a "terrible" deal "immediately."[87] By the time the primary debates began in August 2015, all fourteen candidates competing for the Republican presidential nomination had expressed strong opposition to the JCPOA.

5.3.2.2 INSULATING THE NEGOTIATION FROM DOMESTIC PARTISAN POLITICS

The polarized environment created a growing distrust between the White House and congressional Republicans. It shaped how the Obama administration approached the negotiations and assessed the role of Congress in the final agreement. Given the highly sensitive nature of the initial talks with Iran, the White House closely guarded early details about their progress. This decision was informed by the Obama administration's belief that Republican legislators would try to derail the negotiation from the outset. As the lead

---

83. Everett 2015.
84. Rubio 2015.
85. Sargent 2015.
86. *Washington Post* 2015.
87. Sargent 2015.

American negotiator for the JCPOA, Ambassador Wendy Sherman, writes in her memoir: "Not least, confidentiality allowed the two teams to explore new ideas without exposing them to criticism from partisans in our respective countries who would be looking to sabotage any deal, no matter its merits."[88]

American negotiators viewed secrecy around the initial talks as essential to the process and to their ability to build trust within the context of the negotiation.[89] On the Hill, however, this secrecy led to a great deal of resentment, souring legislators' attitudes toward the JCPOA. One Republican congressional staff member on SFRC explained: "There was no initial conversation [with Congress] about this. In fact, there was public disclosure in the newspaper that we were negotiating with Iran. To my knowledge, there was no classified conversation with Senate leadership. They [the Obama administration] kept the negotiations secret until they were no longer secret. The administration withheld from Congress that there had been secret negotiations in Iran."[90]

After the initial negotiations were disclosed, the White House was still concerned about keeping specifics of the deal confidential. While executive branch officials regularly briefed Congress, they were worried that Republican legislators would leak information in order to spoil the negotiations. When negotiators were asked about how information flowed between the White House and Congress during this period, they said: "We considered other things like having congressional observers in the negotiations, but that could have been to the detriment of confidentiality. We did what we thought was necessary."[91] "We were concerned about information leaking to the press. To their credit, for the most part, Congress didn't leak. We tried to be transparent but also very careful because the negotiations were ongoing."[92]

However, many White House officials still felt that Congress was informed of all of the substantive elements of the negotiation. As one interviewee remarked, "Every single piece of paper affiliated with this deal Congress got."[93] Senior congressional leadership on both sides of the aisle disagreed with this

88. Sherman 2018, 66.
89. Sherman 2018; Burns 2019.
90. Author interview with Republican congressional senior staff member (August 20, 2018).
91. Author interview with senior White House official (August 9, 2018).
92. Author interview with senior White House official (August 14, 2018).
93. Author interview with White House official (August 7, 2018).

sentiment, arguing that elements of the deal remained opaque throughout the process. A Democratic senior staff member on SFRC explained: "We were trying to understand the parameters of what the Obama administration was actually negotiating. To be honest, I found it quite difficult. Despite having personal contacts at State, there was a lock-down in terms of the detail of what they were doing. It was very close hold. That was just because there was so much mistrust. The Obama administration thought that if they told people what they were doing or were thinking, there would be this huge backlash."[94]

Based on how the White House approached the negotiation, legislators had already inferred that President Obama did not intend to submit the JCPOA as an international treaty for Senate confirmation. In doing so, congressional Republicans perceived the administration as trying to brush aside congressional leadership. A senior Republican congressional staff member commented: "The administration was clear in this point of view. They weren't going to work at all with Congress on this negotiation. They said: 'We're going to make this deal. Congress is not going to be involved. It's nice that you have some views about this, so what.'"[95]

Yet, officials in the Obama administration felt they had reason to distrust legislators' partisan motives. When asked for examples of how this distrust arose, interviewees noted the distinction between how Republican legislators approached classified briefings and public debate. With respect to classified briefings, one American negotiator said: "Behind the door, Congressmen tended to be very thoughtful and deliberate. In front of the door, things quickly became very partisan."[96]

This mutual distrust intensified as congressional Republicans took stronger actions to demonstrate their opposition to the ongoing negotiations in the spring of 2015. In March 2015, on the invitation of congressional Republican leadership, Prime Minister Benjamin Netanyahu spoke to Congress about his disapproval of the Iran nuclear deal. Days later, forty-six Republicans signed onto the open letter written by Senator Tom Cotton and directed at Iranian leaders. Both of these actions were perceived by the Obama administration as a major breach of informal norms in the foreign

---

94. Author interview with Democratic congressional senior staff member (August 22, 2018).

95. Author interview with Republican congressional senior staff member (August 20, 2018).

96. Author interview with senior White House official (August 14, 2018).

policymaking process. However, executive branch officials felt there was little that they could do in response to the partisan antics. From the perspective of the American delegation heading to another round of talks with Iran and the P5+1, these events were seen as blatant attempts to undermine the negotiation process. Interviewees noted:

> This was definitely not politics as usual . . . it indicated a very concentrated effort by Republicans to block the deal.[97]

> The Republicans never liked the JCPOA and were trying to kill it. Many of them expressed opposition [to the Deal] before they had even read it. I imagine a lot of Republicans never read it.[98]

> We couldn't do much here. We just had to kind of sit back and watch the crazy.[99]

As a result, negotiators took efforts to sidestep the "blatant partisan politics"[100] in order to keep Republican legislators from derailing the negotiation. The negotiating team was further encouraged by President Obama to focus on "the substantive concerns rather than the political concerns."[101] As one negotiator summarized: "During the substantive negotiations, we are really thinking more about the politics of the negotiation rather than the domestic politics."[102]

From the White House's perspective, the hawkish rhetoric of Republican legislators signaled that there was little point in trying to build bipartisan consensus around the agreement. The highly polarized environment made it difficult to distinguish between Republican legislators that were pure spoilers—those opposed to a deal with Iran irrespective of the terms—and legislators would that endorse a deal if they felt the terms were more favorable. In other words, the more costly signals Republican legislators sent to demonstrate opposition to the deal, the more the Obama administration moved to insulate the negotiation from domestic politics. The safer assumption in the polarized environment was to abandon hope of Republican support. Counterintuitively, this meant that more extreme forms of domestic opposition did not translate

---

97. Author interview with senior White House official (August 9, 2018).
98. Author interview with senior White House official (August 14, 2018).
99. Author interview with White House official (August 7, 2018).
100. Author interview with senior White House official (August 14, 2018).
101. Author interview with senior White House official (August 9, 2018).
102. Author interview with senior White House official (August 9, 2018).

into greater leverage in the JCPOA negotiation, but rather resulted in little substantive impact on its content.

Republicans were naturally critical of the approach taken by the Obama administration. As discussed in the introduction to this chapter, some legislators like Senator Rob Portman (R-OH) noted that they signed the Cotton letter specifically to give the United States more leverage in the international negotiation.[103] A congressional staff member on SFRC criticized the White House taking steps to insulate the negotiation: "When it came to US Congress, the administration would say to the Iranians, 'We got them boxed in. We'll handle them.' They could have much more easily, much more effectively used Congress. They could have said, 'We have to deal with these crazy Republicans in Congress—you need to give us a better deal'. . . But they didn't, so the deal got worse and worse with every negotiation."[104]

White House officials, by contrast, argued that there was no realistic alternative to their approach. There was no reason to pursue bipartisanship because they did not trust that more-moderate Republicans would set aside partisan politics, particularly as rhetoric about Iran became increasingly hawkish throughout the start of the Republican primary. Instead, the Obama administration focused on the substance of the negotiation first and would then try to sell it to Congress and the public later. In his memoir, Ben Rhodes, the deputy national security advisor for strategic communications, described that after the final agreement, the negotiating team "handed off a baton to me and my team, and we had sixty days to make sure Congress wouldn't undo their work."[105]

5.3.2.3 ENTERING AND EXITING THE JCPOA

A core reason why the Obama administration had more leeway to sidestep a polarized Congress was that they did not intend to submit the JCPOA as a treaty to the Senate for ratification by a two-thirds vote. This intention was clear to congressional leadership in the early stages of the process.[106] However, the exact form that any other sort of congressional approval process would take remained unclear. A senior White House official working on legislative

103. Dennis and Chacko 2015.
104. Author interview with Republican congressional senior staff member (August 20, 2018).
105. Rhodes 2018.
106. Author interview with Republican congressional senior staff member (August 20, 2018).

affairs during this period explained: "Increasingly, the administrations look for ways not to do treaties [because they're politically infeasible]. This was true with respect to the Iran deal ... Congress made it clear that they would want to be a part of the deal from the beginning. From the [Obama] administration's perspective, it was about figuring out how to do that while still ensuring flexibility."[107]

White House officials believed from the outset that a treaty was infeasible because of the high levels of congressional polarization. They pointed to the dramatic decline in international treaties as a consequence of increasing polarization, a subject this book discusses in greater depth in chapter 6. One negotiator said: "This is always an issue, but I think polarization has definitely increased. There have been no new major treaties—with the exception of New START,[108] which is a continuation of an existing one—in recent years. If you can't get the [UN treaty on disability rights] passed with Bob Dole on the floor in a wheelchair, I'm not sure what you can get passed."[109]

The mechanism that ultimately arose in the Iran Nuclear Agreement Review Act, passed in May 2015, gave Congress a vote of "disapproval" rather than approval. While this made it more likely that an agreement signed by the Obama administration would not be overturned by Congress, it also gave moderate Republicans no incentives to support the agreement. A senior White House official explained: "Originally, we thought for sure we would get Republican support for the deal. Simply because it was really good deal. We definitely thought it was sellable. We originally fought hard for moderate Republican support, support from 'Corker and co.' Practically, during the final voting process, there was no political upside for Republicans to support the deal. They could oppose the deal and it would still pass, which made more sense politically."[110]

Of course, entering a major international agreement without bipartisan support or a formal ratification process made it much more fragile. The Obama administration entered the deal as a nonbinding political commitment rather an international treaty. This meant that a subsequent president could easily unilaterally withdraw from the agreement. As previously noted,

107. Author interview with senior White House official (August 13, 2018).

108. As Kreps, Saunders, and Schultz (2018) point out, however, while New START should have easily won bipartisan support, the Obama administration still had to pay a high "ratification premium" in the form of commitments to modernize the U.S. nuclear arsenal in order to secure enough Republican votes for the treaty's ratification.

109. Author interview with senior White House official (August 14, 2018).

110. Author interview with senior White House official (August 13, 2018).

all sixteen Republican candidates in the 2016 presidential field campaigned against the JCPOA, vowing to overturn it immediately if elected. As Donald Trump emerged victorious from the Republican primary, his general-election campaign was animated by the promise of undoing major Obama-era policies and agreements like the JCPOA.[111] Positioning himself as a dealmaker, Trump asserted that he would undo the "horrible" Iran nuclear deal negotiated by the Obama administration and replace it with something more favorable to the United States.[112]

While many Republican candidates pledged to rip up the Iran deal in their first day in office, it took over a year for President Trump to officially withdraw the United States from the JCPOA in May 2018. The withdrawal was accompanied by a "maximum pressure" sanctions campaign against Iran, which differed substantially from Obama-era sanctions.[113] Interestingly, just before President Trump's announcement, public support of the Iran nuclear deal was at an all-time high. However, public attitudes were highly partisan. A poll conducted during this period found that only 10 percent of Democrats thought that President Trump should withdraw from the Iran deal, while slightly more than half of Republicans endorsed withdrawal.[114]

To understand the different arguments being made by each party prior to withdrawal, I collected social media data from Republican and Democratic legislators prior to President Trump's announcement of U.S. withdrawal from the Iran deal on May 8, 2018. I gathered the Twitter handles of the 100 senators and 435 house representatives, categorized them by party, and scraped the text of their tweets between January and May 8, 2018. After cleaning and processing the data, I identified 3,364 tweets from legislators that contained the words *iran* or *jcpoa*.[115] I calculated the relative frequency of words tweeted by Republicans and Democrats. The plots in figure 5.10 show which words about the Iran deal were tweeted more frequently by Republicans and which were tweeted more frequently by Democrats.

The coherence of partisan rhetoric about the Iran deal is somewhat striking. The most partisan word is "sanctions," which appears almost three times

---

111. Sokolsky and Miller 2019.
112. *Washington Post* 2015.
113. Jentleson 2022.
114. Sparks 2018.
115. Before conducting this analysis, I removed stop words and other commonly used words and phrases (such as *nuclear* and *iranian*), and then aggregated the text by party.

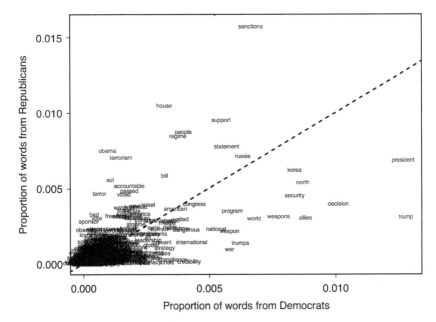

FIGURE 5.10. Partisan words in legislators' tweets about Iran (January to May 2018)

as frequently in Republican tweets than in Democratic tweets. Republicans were more likely to emphasize legislation (*bill, voted, passed, legislation, act*), ties with Israel (*israel*), and Iran's sponsorship of terror (*terrorist, terror, sponsor*). In contrast, rhetoric from Democratic legislators were consistent with principles of multilateralism and internationalism (*world, international, global, diplomacy, human rights, allies*). Democrats were also more likely to highlight issues of U.S. credibility (*credibility, compliance*) that were not mentioned by Republicans. Perhaps unsurprisingly, figure 5.10 also shows clear evidence of negative partisanship. Republicans were significantly more likely to emphasize President Obama (*obama*) made a "bad deal," while Democrats were critical of President Trump's (*trump*) actions to withdraw the United States from the JCPOA and undermine its credibility.

After President Trump withdrew the United States from the JCPOA, condemnation from the P5+1 and the Iranian leadership was swift. European allies expressed intent to continue abiding by the terms of the agreement, but, without the support of the United States, Iran was far less likely to hold up its end of the bargain. The Iranian interior minister, Abdolreza Rahmani Fazli, remarked: "The United States is not trustworthy.... How can we trust this country when it withdraws unilaterally from the nuclear deal?"[116] Some members of the U.S. foreign policy establishment echoed these concerns about credibility. In the concluding chapter of his memoir, Bill Burns, a diplomat who facilitated the secret back channel to Iran in advance of the JCPOA negotiations, wrote: "Trump's demolition of the Iran deal was a further blow to our own credibility, to international confidence that we could keep our end of a bargain.... With its echoes of the muscular unilateralism on the road to the Iraq War in 2003 and the seductive appeal of remaking regional order through American power, the decision to abandon the JCPOA signaled anew a dangerous dismissiveness toward diplomacy. It was exactly the kind of risky, cocky, ill-considered bet that had shredded our influence before, and could easily do so again."[117]

It is challenging to speculate about what may have happened during the JCPOA negotiations and implementation if domestic politics were less polarized in the United States. The JCPOA is universally acknowledged as a flawed agreement. Its supporters characterize it as imperfect while its detractors view it as disastrous. But, it is possible that less mutual distrust between the White House and congressional Republicans would have facilitated more congressional involvement from the outset of the negotiations in ways that could have benefited U.S. interests. Without concern for potential spoilers that would undermine the deal, the Obama administration may have not seen it as necessary to insulate the substance of the JCPOA negotiation from domestic politics. Interestingly, this may have made it easier for the administration to effectively leverage domestic dissent during the negotiation process. And, without pressure from the right flank, moderate Republicans may ultimately have supported the negotiation process, paving the way for greater congressional buy-in and a more durable international agreement.

The case of the JCPOA suggests that environments of extreme polarization may dissuade leaders from attempting complex negotiations with foreign adversaries. If polarization becomes even more extreme and extends into certain areas of foreign policy, we may be worried about scenarios in which the Republican and Democratic Parties have fundamentally different relationships with U.S. adversaries.

116. As quoted in Ritter (2018, 315).
117. Burns 2019, 387.

5.4 Conclusion

Democracies are thought to be more credible adversaries relative to non-democracies because accountability both to the public and to the political opposition prevents democratic leaders from issuing threats or promises that they are unable to keep. As a result, the signals that democracies send in international politics are more informative to their foreign adversaries. This chapter illustrated how the credibility advantage can be undermined in a highly polarized context where the opposition party is distrustful of the executive and has incentives to obstruct their foreign policymaking. The chapter used three empirical strategies, summarized in table 5.4, to demonstrate how this process unfolds.

This chapter first showed that, as the public becomes more ideologically and affectively polarized, partisans are less likely to trust the foreign policy decision-making of leaders from the opposite party. In a highly polarized environment, electoral accountability creates an atmosphere of zero-sum competition and provides incentives for the political opposition to score political "wins" by obstructing the executive. In a survey experiment of 4,330 adults fielded in advance of the 2024 U.S. presidential election, I presented hypothetical scenarios in which either the Republican (Donald Trump) or Democratic (Kamala Harris) candidate won the presidency. Respondents then read and reacted to foreign policy actions that could be taken by these presidents in the future. Survey respondents primed to think about the candidate from the opposite party winning were far more distrustful of the president's actions in foreign policy, more skeptical of their policy responses, and more likely to advocate for obstruction of the president. An implication of these results is that as the electorate grows more polarized, it will be difficult for presidents to effectively leverage public constraints to their advantage when bargaining with adversaries abroad.

I next explained how these electoral incentives reinforce behavior of politicians from the opposition party. I argued that, in highly polarized times, politicians from the opposition have less incentive to defer to the executive during a security crisis and more incentive to undermine the executive in foreign affairs writ large. Patterns of congressional roll-call votes on foreign relations and defense policy revealed more uniform out-party opposition to the president's foreign policy agenda across recent administrations.[118] An analysis

---

118. Lewis et al. 2019.

TABLE 5.4. Summary of findings from the Credibility Hypotheses

	As polarization becomes more extreme…	Empirical strategy	Summary of findings
Vertical constraints	The public is less likely to trust the decision-making of leaders from an opposing party.	Conduct a survey experiment in advance of the 2024 presidential election that varies the partisanship of the president and examines how respondents evaluate decision-making in foreign policy scenarios that involve international crises and negotiations.	Holding fixed the foreign policy scenarios and policy responses, survey respondents were more likely to distrust presidential decision-making and object to their policies when the president was from the opposite party.
	The public is more likely to reward co-partisan politicians for obstructing leaders from an opposing party.	Conduct a survey experiment in advance of the 2024 presidential election that varies the partisanship of the president and examines whether respondents are more likely to approve of co-partisan politicians obstructing an out-party president in foreign affairs.	Holding fixed the foreign policy scenarios and policy responses, survey respondents were more likely to approve of co-partisan legislators obstructing a president from the opposite party.
Horizontal constraints	Politicians are more likely to consistently oppose or actively undermine leaders from an opposing party in foreign policy.	Use data on congressional roll-call votes to see whether, as polarization has increased, the political opposition has become more likely to cohere against the president in foreign affairs.	As polarization has increased, the political opposition has become more unified against the president on congressional votes about foreign affairs.
	Politicians are less likely to defer to a leader from an opposing party in times of crisis.	Use speech from the *Congressional Record* to look at how politicians historically responded to security crises triggered by U.S. adversaries.	As polarization has increased, congressional rhetoric about foreign adversaries during international crises has become more partisan.
Implication for democratic advantage	Democracies are less likely to send credible signals to adversaries in negotiation and crisis bargaining	Investigate how polarization around U.S.–Iran relations affected the negotiation of the 2015 Joint Comprehensive Plan of Action.	While lower levels of polarization might have provided the United States with more leverage during negotiations, more extreme polarization led the White House to box out the political opposition from the negotiations. As a result, the JCPOA was made without substantial bipartisan support.

of legislative speeches suggested that there has been increasing partisanship in congressional responses to security crises. This implies that, as polarization grows, politicians will be less likely to rally behind the leader of an opposing party when facing new security threats.

Finally, I argued that these dynamics could undermine the credibility advantage when democracies bargain with their adversaries. A discussion of the negotiation of the 2015 Iran nuclear deal explored how politicization of U.S.–Iranian relations affected the way that the Obama administration approached the negotiation process. In international negotiations, some amount of partisan disagreement between the executive and the political opposition provides democracies with more leverage.[119] However, as partisan disagreement becomes more extreme, the domestic political environment can damage the credibility of the negotiators and lead to less durable international agreements.

---

119. Schelling 1960; Putnam 1988.

6

Polarization and the Reliability Advantage

ON A WARM Sunday afternoon in late May 2017, hundreds of Bavarians gathered in a beer tent in Munich. The occasion was an election rally for German Chancellor Angela Merkel. Merkel, who had served as chancellor since 2005, was campaigning for her fourth term in advance of the September 2017 election. Over the low buzz of slurps from beer steins and chatter from the crowd, Merkel delivered what would be among her most memorable remarks as chancellor. Reflecting on Germany's relationship with the United States, the UK, and the rest of Europe, she announced, "The times in which we could completely depend on others are, to a certain extent, over. ... We Europeans truly have to take our fate into our own hands."[1]

When Merkel concluded, her surprisingly firm and fiery words were met with resounding applause from the tent. With a campaign for reelection underway, the timing of her speech was significant. Chancellor Merkel had just returned from the Group of Seven (G7) Summit in Taormina, Italy, an annual meeting between the leaders of major economic powers: Germany, France, Italy, Japan, the UK, the United States, and Canada. This year, the G7 Summit had a markedly different tone than in previous years. A few weeks before the summit, the 2017 French presidential election captured global interest as Marine Le Pen, leader of the far-right party National Front, advanced to the run-off election. It was the first time in fifteen years that a National Front candidate made it to the second round of the presidential election. Less than a year before the 2017 G7, the UK had voted on a referendum on whether to withdraw from the EU, and 52 percent of voters had supported

1. Henley 2017.

"Brexit."[2] And a few months after the Brexit vote, the United States elected Republican presidential candidate Donald Trump. President Trump routinely criticized European allies, at times deeming the North Atlantic Treaty Organization (NATO)—a military alliance between North American and European countries founded in the aftermath of World War II—"obsolete."[3]

The chancellor's speech at the election rally in Munich reflected doubts about the willingness of the United States to honor its commitments to Europe. But, what was surprising is that these new threats to the democratic alliance arose neither from emboldened foreign adversaries nor from crippling economic shocks like the 2008 global financial crisis. Instead, they were rooted in the domestic political problems of alliance partners. The United States and many other advanced democracies were experiencing high levels of polarization that were creeping into their foreign policy and undermining their ability to be reliable partners.

Debates about U.S. commitments in the face of changing leadership call into question the reliability advantage democracies have in foreign affairs. The reliability advantage suggests that democracies are more reliable allies because they make more durable international commitments and are generally more cooperative in international politics relative to nondemocracies.[4] This advantage is reinforced by systems of constraint on democratic leaders that make them accountable to the public (vertical constraints) and to other actors in government (horizontal constraints). Leaders who do not abide by democratic norms and procedures entering into international agreements or who incur reputational costs by reneging on existing commitments anticipate being criticized by the political opposition or punished electorally.[5] Moreover, because major foreign policy decisions often require bipartisan support, the commitments democracies make in international politics are likely to be more durable than similar commitments made by autocratic governments.[6]

I argue, however, that extreme polarization can undermine the reliability advantage by eroding vertical and horizontal constraints on executive power. To develop this argument, this chapter proceeds in three sections. It begins

---

2. Aisch, Pearce, and Russell 2016.
3. Gray 2017.
4. See, e.g., Broz 2002; Cowhey 1993; Gaubatz 1996; Mansfield, Milner, and Rosendorff 2002; Martin 2000.
5. See, e.g., Leeds 1999; McGillivray and Smith 2000; Tomz 2008.
6. See, e.g., Martin 2000.

by examining the relationship between polarization and vertical constraints, or accountability to the public. I argue that relative to a nonpolarized public, a polarized public is more likely to overlook violations of democratic norms and procedures in the foreign policymaking process to see their preferred policy enacted. A survey experiment conducted before the 2024 U.S. presidential election shows that Americans are highly critical of a president unilaterally entering or withdrawing from international agreements when the president does not share their partisan affiliation. However, they are more willing to overlook these same unilateral actions when they are taken by a co-partisan president. These findings tell us that accountability to a polarized electorate may be a less effective means of constraining democratic leaders in foreign affairs.

The chapter next assesses the relationship between polarization and horizontal constraints, or accountability to other actors within government. I argue that the combination of a polarized electorate and an obstinate political opposition increases the likelihood that leaders will seek to subvert intragovernmental constraints on executive power. I provide suggestive evidence for this dynamic in the United States by illustrating how polarization is associated with declines and delays in the ratification of international treaties. Partisan gridlock is also correlated with the rise of executive agreements and other political commitments made by the president, which are not subject to ratification by the U.S. Senate. These patterns imply that, in polarized environments, presidents may be more likely to substitute executive agreements and nonbinding political commitments in place of more durable international treaties.

The erosion of both vertical and horizontal constraints in a democracy can damage perceptions of its ability to be a reliable ally. To illustrate how polarization ultimately affects the reliability advantage, I focus on the bilateral relationship between the United States and a close ally, the UK. Survey experiments fielded to 2,000 adults in the UK and 150 UK parliamentarians find that priming respondents to think about U.S. polarization negatively impacts evaluations of the UK's current and future relationship with the United States. Perceptions of extreme polarization can make allies uncertain about the future direction of U.S. foreign policy, less willing to engage in future partnerships with the U.S., and more skeptical of its global leadership. While these effects are modest in the U.S.–UK context, the impacts of polarization are likely to be even more pronounced in countries that have more tenuous security relationships with the United States.

6.1 Vertical Constraints and Democratic Reliability

Systems of vertical constraint in democracies make leaders accountable to their public through regular elections. In chapter 2, I argued that vertical constraints reinforce the reliability advantage that democracies have in international politics in two ways: by dissuading leaders from entering into and exiting from international commitments unilaterally, and by discouraging them from reneging on existing commitments.

First, liberal publics are thought to internalize commitments to democratic rule of law. The public should prefer that their leaders follow the democratic procedures established by the government when they make international commitments. These procedures could include informal norms (like consulting with the political opposition) or formal institutions (like a public referendum or a treaty ratification process). The public should object when their leaders attempt to circumvent these norms and procedures. In the context of making international agreements, this means that the public should generally be averse to leaders acting unilaterally—that is, on their own, without appropriate consent of other stakeholders—in foreign affairs.[7]

Second, democratic publics reinforce international cooperation because they object when their leaders renege on commitments made to their allies and partners. Chapter 2 discussed multiple reasons for why democratic publics might dislike it when leaders violate international agreements. One reason is that liberal publics often have normative preferences for cooperation and rule of law that extends to the international sphere. Another reason is that publics may be concerned about the reputational costs their country might suffer if leaders renege on international commitments.[8] Survey research shows, for example, that democratic publics believe abandoning alliance commitments will tarnish their country's reputation.[9]

In highly polarized democracies, however, democratic publics may display both strong ideological commitments and high levels of affective polarization. Partisans who have strong ideological commitments are likely to care a great deal about seeing their preferred policy enacted. Partisans who exhibit high levels of affective polarization are likely to care about political "wins" for their in-party and "losses" for their out-party. As a consequence, a highly

---

7. Reeves and Rogowski 2018; Christenson and Kriner 2020.
8. Leeds 1999; McGillivray and Smith 2000, 2008.
9. Tomz and Weeks 2021.

partisan public will care comparatively less about the democratic processes involved in making international agreements or the reputational costs of withdrawing from them. As polarization becomes more extreme, it erodes the vertical accountability that democratic leaders face when they make and break international commitments.

> Reliability Hypothesis 1: *As polarization becomes more extreme, the public is less likely to punish co-partisan leaders who act unilaterally when making foreign policy or who renege on international commitments.*

To explore the relationship between polarization, vertical constraints, and democratic reliability in the United States, I start with a survey experiment that shows how partisanship shapes attitudes toward presidents acting unilaterally in foreign policy. Arguably, the best test of Reliability Hypothesis 1 requires either a time machine or a parallel universe in which contemporary American politics was less polarized. In theory, we would like to know if during nonpolarized times, the public would be more likely to reinforce democratic norms and procedures around entering into and exiting from international agreements. Because this type of design is not directly testable, I focus on observable implications of Reliability Hypothesis 1. The main implication is that partisans should be less likely to reinforce norms around entering into and exiting from international agreements when they share the party of the president. In addition, strong partisans should be less likely to reinforce these norms relative to weak partisans. This would suggest that, as polarization increases and the public becomes more partisan, the vertical constraints on democratic leaders that reinforce the reliability advantage will continue to weaken.

I investigate these implications in a survey experiment embedded on the same public opinion survey introduced in chapter 5. This survey was fielded to 4,330 American adults in August 2024, prior to the 2024 U.S. presidential election.[10] At the outset of the survey, respondents were randomly assigned to one of two conditions: a hypothetical scenario in which either Republican candidate and former President Donald Trump or Democratic candidate and incumbent Vice President Kamala Harris won the presidential election. This means that each respondent was assigned to an in-party or an out-party treatment condition depending on whether they self-identified as sharing the

---

10. The text of the survey questionnaire and more details about the sample are in the appendix. See chapter 5 for additional discussion of the survey design.

party of the candidate or not. Alongside a description of the hypothetical scenario was a photograph of the presidential candidate on the campaign trail. To increase realism and engagement with the scenario, survey respondents were first asked to reflect in an open-ended response on what they expect the candidate to do in foreign policy over the next few years were they to win the 2024 election.

For the unilateral action experiment, respondents then considered actions taken by the hypothetical president and expressed an opinion on whether or not the president should be able to take the action without the approval of Congress. Since this chapter focuses on the reliability advantage, I examine attitudes toward the president's ability to unilaterally make and break international commitments. The survey focuses on three types of international commitments made to allies and partners: entering into and exiting from major international agreements, joining and leaving military alliances, and joining and leaving international organizations. The text of the experiment read:

> There is a lot of discussion about what the president can do on their own and what they need approval from Congress for in order to do. In your opinion, if elected, which of the following actions should [T1: Donald Trump / T2: Kamala Harris] be able to take on their own, without the approval of Congress? Check all that apply.
>
> - Enter into a major international agreement
> - Withdraw from a major international agreement
> - Join a military alliance
> - Leave a military alliance
> - Join an international organization
> - Leave an international organization

Figure 6.1 displays the proportion of respondents who thought it was acceptable for the president to take each action unilaterally. The results distinguish between respondents who were randomly assigned to a president that shared their party (in dark gray) or did not share their party (in light gray). For example, Republicans (Democrats) who were assigned a treatment condition in which Harris (Trump) won the presidential election would be in the out-party treatment condition.

There were a few key findings from the experiment. First, consistent with results from other surveys,[11] democratic publics had an overarching aversion

---

11. See, e.g., Reeves and Rogowski 2018, 2022.

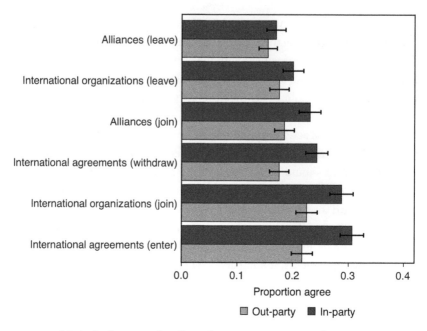

FIGURE 6.1. Attitudes toward unilateral action in entering and exiting international commitments among in-party and out-party survey respondents

to presidents acting unilaterally. Across all outcomes, the majority of respondents did not think the president should be able to take the action in foreign policy without the approval of Congress. Survey respondents were especially averse to unilateral actions that related to security commitments. For example, less than a quarter of respondents in the survey thought that the president should be able to leave military alliances without congressional approval.

The second finding, consistent with Reliability Hypothesis 1, is that, for every outcome, a larger percentage of respondents in the in-party condition (versus the out-party condition) thought that it was acceptable for the president to act unilaterally. For some of these outcomes, the gap between in-party and out-party approval was quite large. For example, 45 percent of survey respondents thought that their co-partisan president should be able to join an international organization on their own, while only 29 percent thought that a president from the opposite party should be able to do the same. The gap between in-party and out-party responses, however, was not statistically significant across all outcomes. For instance, given that a relatively small percentage of respondents thought that the president should be able to

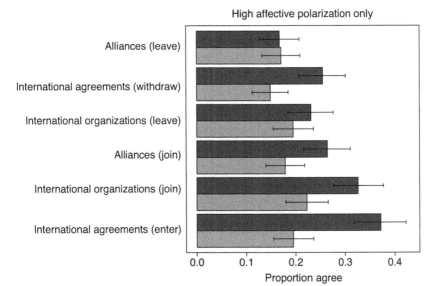

FIGURE 6.2. Attitudes toward unilateral action in entering and exiting international commitments among in-party and out-party survey respondents who display high levels of affective polarization

unilaterally leave a military alliance, there was not a significant difference in approval of this action across the different treatment conditions.

A third finding, also consistent with Reliability Hypothesis 1, is that respondents appeared to be particularly averse to executives unilaterally withdrawing from international commitments. If the public was concerned about the reputational consequences of reneging on commitments,[12] we would expect them to be more critical of unilateral withdrawal from (versus unilateral entry into) an agreement, alliance, or organization. Overall, respondents did seem to think that congressional approval should be more necessary for exiting or withdrawing from various international commitments. For example, 24 percent of respondents thought that presidents should be able to join international organizations on their own, but only 18 percent thought they should be able to leave them unilaterally. This finding is interesting given that entry into international commitments is a more institutionalized process than withdrawal.

12. See, e.g., McGillivray and Smith 2000.

An additional implication of Reliability Hypothesis 1 is that strong partisans should be even less likely to reinforce norms around entering into and exiting from international commitments. Figure 6.2 shows results from a subset of respondents who displayed high levels of affective polarization at the outset of the survey. Affective polarization is measured as the difference between a respondent's ratings of their in-party and their out-party on a 0–100 scale.[13] Respondents are coded as displaying high levels of affective polarization if they scored in the seventy-fifth percentile or above on this measure. As we see, the difference between average responses in the in-party versus out-party treatment conditions is larger among the most affectively polarized partisans. This pattern indicates that, as polarization increases, partisan identity will on average strengthen, and gaps in public attitudes toward unilateral action are likely to grow.

These survey results suggest that polarization could be problematic for the reliability advantage that democracies have in foreign affairs. Existing work suggests that democratic leaders who act unilaterally without appropriate authority, or who renege on international commitments, will be penalized electorally. One effect of these vertical constraints is that they make democracies more cooperative and reliable partners. However, this assumption may be less likely to hold in highly polarized contexts. While the survey results still show an overarching aversion to unilateral action, as polarization becomes more extreme, the public is likely to be more willing to tolerate unilateral action in foreign policy—including unilateral withdrawal from international agreements—if they share a partisan identity with the leader. In theory, this could weaken vertical constraints, providing democratic leaders with more incentives to subvert norms around entering into and exiting from international agreements.

6.2 Horizontal Constraints and the Reliability Advantage

The findings in this chapter so far indicate that, as the degree of polarization in a society increases, vertical constraints may do less to prevent leaders from

---

13. The wording of this question mirrors the wording of the affective polarization measure from the American National Election Studies (2020): "We'd also like to get your feelings about some groups in American society. Rate the following groups between 0 and 100. Ratings from 50–100 degrees mean that you feel favorably toward the group; ratings from 0–50 degrees mean that you don't feel favorably toward the group and that you don't care too much for that group: Democrats, Republicans."

acting unilaterally in foreign policy. The next step is to consider how growing polarization might affect horizontal constraints on executive power and the behavior of politicians. The primary intragovernmental constraint that reinforces the reliability advantage is that international commitments tend to be subject to a formal ratification process in democracies. This constraint makes it difficult to enter into and, in some cases, exit from international agreements, creating more durable agreements overall.[14] In practice, a formal ratification process often ensures some degree of support from the political opposition to make major commitments in foreign policy.

In chapter 2, I argued that extreme polarization provides incentives for the political opposition to actively oppose the leader's agenda. In anticipation of this opposition, democratic leaders have incentives to make international agreements unilaterally. As the previous section demonstrated, a polarized public is unlikely to effectively check unilateral action because co-partisans are willing to overlook violations of democratic norms and procedures to see their preferred policy enacted. In the context of American politics, this implies that growing polarization should make presidents more likely to make international commitments using executive agreements rather than treaties, which are subject to ratification by the U.S. Senate. Likewise, we expect alternatives to international treaties—like executive agreements and political commitments—to become increasingly expansive in nature.

Reliability Hypothesis 2: *As polarization becomes more extreme, politicians are more likely to bypass horizontal constraints in committing to international agreements, leading to less durable commitments.*

To explore Reliability Hypothesis 2, this chapter dives deeper into the expansion of executive authority in making international agreements in the United States. Scholars of international law conceptualize U.S. entry into international agreements as falling into one of three categories: international treaties ratified by Congress, congressional–executive agreements, and sole executive agreements.[15] *International treaties* are legally binding, formal agreements between two (bilateral) or more (multilateral) countries. In the United States, the executive has the ability to negotiate and sign international treaties on behalf of the country; they are then subject to domestic ratification. Article II of the U.S. Constitution asserts that the executive "shall have Power, by

14. Martin 2000.
15. Galbraith 2017.

and with the Advice and Consent of the Senate, to make Treaties, provided two-thirds of the Senators present concur."[16]

By contrast, executive agreements are not subject to Senate ratification. The most common form of executive agreement is a *congressional–executive agreement*. This occurs when the executive has ex ante congressional authorization to make an international agreement. In practice, the existence of congressional–executive agreements means that Congress consents to the content of an agreement prior to its negotiation by the executive branch. Another, less common form of executive agreement is a *sole executive agreement*, for which the president relies on their own constitutional authority. Legal experts note that the distinction between these two forms of executive agreements is easily muddied; some agreements do not fall cleanly into either category.[17] Both types of agreements, however, are retrospectively reviewed by Congress. In 1972, Congress passed the Case–Zablocki Act (often referred to as the Case Act), which stipulates that after any executive agreement is signed and entered into force, the White House is required to report it to Congress within sixty days.[18]

Executives may also pursue nonlegal agreements with other countries that are not binding under international law. These include *political commitments*, which are "nonlegally binding agreement[s] between two or more nation-states in which the parties intend to establish commitments of an exclusively political or moral nature."[19] Unlike treaties or executive agreements, there are no reporting requirements for political commitments. Presidents may enter into, and withdraw from, political commitments without congressional approval.

An implication of Reliability Hypothesis 2 is that growing polarization should affect patterns of U.S. entry into international treaties and executive agreements. As polarization increases, we should see more international commitments made using executive agreements and fewer made using international treaties. To investigate these patterns, I build on work and extensive data collection efforts from two sets of researchers. The data on international treaties extends data from a series of projects by political scientists Jeffrey

---

16. U.S. Const. art. II, §2, cl. 2
17. Bradley 2013; Bodansky and Spiro 2016.
18. Case–Zablocki Act, Pub. L. No. 92-403, 86 Stat. 619 (1972).
19. Hollis and Newcomer 2008, 51.

Peake, Glen Krutz, and their coauthors.[20] In their book *Treaty Politics and the Rise of Executive Agreements*, Peake and Krutz analyze trends in the use of treaties and executive agreements across different presidential administrations.[21] In this analysis, I update data from Peake on the timing, passage, and content of bilateral international treaties submitted to the Senate between 1949 and 2012.[22] I extend this dataset, collecting eight additional years of treaties through 2020.[23]

Finding reliable, current data on executive agreements is challenging because they are not maintained in a centralized repository. Inconsistencies in the reporting and publication of executive agreements also hinder data collection. For this chapter, I draw on a dataset of executive agreements from legal scholars Oona Hathaway, Curtis Bradley, and Jack Goldsmith, who used Freedom of Information Act requests to compile 5,000 cover memos that reported executive agreements to Congress.[24] The researchers code the timing, content, and legal authority under which each executive agreement was made. While this data is more complete than alternative datasets, it is limited in its time scale, ranging from 1989 to 2017.

Using these data sources, I highlight five stylized facts. First, heightened polarization is associated with a decline in the submission of international treaties. This decline has been especially pronounced since the start of Barack Obama's administration in 2009. Second, treaties signed in polarized times are more likely to experience delays in ratification. These delays are most likely to occur after the president has signed the treaty but before it has been submitted to the Senate for advice and consent. Third, the decline in treaties corresponds to a rise in executive agreements. Unlike treaties, executive agreements do not need to be ratified by the Senate. Fourth, according to legal experts, a considerable portion of executive agreements are based on questionable legal authority. Fifth, in recent presidential administrations, executive agreements and political commitments have arguably become more expansive in nature.

Collectively, these findings provide suggestive—but not definitive—evidence that presidents increasingly use alternatives to international treaties to avoid partisan gridlock, reducing transparency and legislative oversight of

---

20. Krutz and Peake 2006, 2009; Peake, Krutz, and Hughes 2012; Peake 2017, 2022.
21. Krutz and Peake 2009.
22. Peake 2017.
23. The appendix contains a list of the additional treaties coded for this analysis.
24. Hathaway, Bradley, and Goldsmith 2020.

international agreements. While allowing for more efficient policymaking, this could lessen the durability of agreements. This book does not take a position on whether or not leaders *should* use alternative tools to enact their preferred policies. In fact, many argue that because partisan gridlock makes it highly difficult to pass international treaties, it would be next to impossible for presidents to enter into important international agreements without acting unilaterally.[25] Instead, the book establishes the patterns that have led to executives seeking alternatives to international treaties and discusses what implications these trends have for foreign policymaking.

6.2.1 Declines and Delays in the Ratification of International Treaties

During his congressional testimony in July 2015, Secretary of State John Kerry lamented the fact that the contemporary era of congressional polarization prevented the U.S. Senate passing international treaties. When congressional Representative Reid Ribble, a Republican legislator from Wisconsin, asked Secretary Kerry why the Iran nuclear deal was not submitted to the Senate as a treaty for ratification, the Secretary quipped: "Well Congressman, I spent quite a few years trying to get a lot of treaties through the United States Senate, and it has become physically impossible. That's why. Because you can't pass a treaty anymore. It has become impossible to schedule, to pass, and I sat there leading the charge on the Disabilities Treaty which fell to basically ideology and politics. So I think that is the reason why."[26]

Kerry's sentiment reflects one way that polarization could impact foreign policy: by making it challenging—if not impossible—to secure the bipartisan support needed to make durable international commitments. Many researchers have noted this general pattern in the context of an increasingly polarized American political system.[27] Evidence for this claim is supported by two trends. For one, in the face of partisan gridlock, fewer treaties have been ratified by the Senate over time. Moreover, those that have advanced through the ratification process face longer delays than in less polarized times.

---

25. This intuition also follows other observations about the expansion of presidential unilateralism in the United States, which some researchers argue is in part indirectly related to growing polarization and weakening systems of constraint. See, e.g., Moe and Howell 1999; Howell 2003.

26. As quoted in Hains (2015).

27. Schultz 2018; Peake 2022.

The ratification of an international treaty can be a lengthy process that often lasts more than a year. The treaty process unfolds in four stages. After the president signs the agreement (signing stage), it is transmitted to the Senate for "advice and consent" (transmission stage). This process starts in the Senate Foreign Relations Committee (SFRC), a powerful congressional committee composed of senators who oversee foreign affairs. One responsibility of SFRC is to examine the text of treaties. In some instances, the committee may propose to alter the treaty's contents by adding "specified conditions, reservations, or understandings."[28] After committee deliberations, the chair of SFRC reports the treaty to the Senate (reporting stage). Once the Senate majority leader brings it to the floor, the Senate votes on whether or not to accept the treaty, with a two-thirds majority vote necessary for ratification (ratification stage).

While most treaties submitted to the Senate are ratified, there are notable cases of failure. Treaties also may hit stumbling blocks along the way that cause delays in ratification. One way a treaty fails is if the administration chooses not to submit it to the Senate in the first place. In 1998, the United States signed the Kyoto Protocol, a multilateral agreement designed to combat global warming by reducing greenhouse gas emissions. Anticipating Republican opposition from the Senate, Democratic President Bill Clinton never transmitted the Kyoto Protocol to the Senate for ratification. In other cases, a treaty may be transmitted to the Senate, but SFRC may choose not to report out the treaty to the rest of the Senate, or to do so with numerous conditions that alter its content. Other ways that the ratification process could be delayed are if the congressional session ends before a treaty is brought to the floor, or if the Senate leadership fails to call a floor vote on a treaty reported by SFRC.

Finally, a treaty could fail to be ratified if it is not supported by two-thirds of the Senate in the final vote. It is relatively rare for a treaty to fail in the floor vote. Agreements without adequate congressional support tend to fail earlier in the process. Nevertheless, there are cases of treaties narrowly failing ratification votes. For example, the Convention on the Rights of Persons with Disabilities (the treaty referenced by Senator Kerry) signed by President Barack Obama in 2009 took years to advance through the ratification process. In December 2012, when it reached the Senate floor, legislators voted 61–38 to ratify the convention, with thirty-eight Republicans opposed. Republican opponents stated that the primary reason for their position was that the convention

---

28. Congressional Research Service 2001, 1.

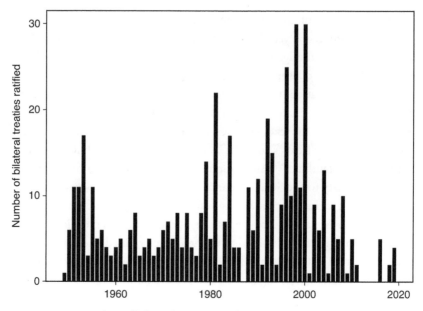

FIGURE 6.3. Number of bilateral treaties ratified by the U.S. Senate (1949–2020)

could infringe upon American sovereignty.[29] Since the vote failed to meet the two-thirds threshold, the convention was not ratified.

To illustrate how growing polarization is associated with treaty ratification, I extend data collected on international treaties by political scientist Jeffrey Peake.[30] Figure 6.3 shows the number of bilateral treaties ratified in the United States from 1949 through 2020. According to the dataset, between 2010 and 2020, only eighteen bilateral treaties were ratified, an average of 1.6 treaties per year. By contrast, in the preceding decade, ninety-six bilateral treaties were ratified by the Senate. As Peake and his coauthors point out, there was a substantial decline in treaty ratification beginning in Democratic President Barack Obama's administration (2009–2017), which is largely attributable to growing Senate polarization.[31] The researchers conclude, "Owing to an increasingly polarized policymaking process in the Senate, President Obama's opportunities to shape foreign policy through the treaty process

29. Steinhauer 2012.
30. Peake 2017.
31. Peake 2022; Peake, Krutz, and Hughes 2012.

was significantly constrained during his first three years in office."[32] This trend continued into the subsequent presidential administrations of Republican President Donald Trump (2017–2021) and Democratic President Joe Biden (2021–2025).

Another trend that parallels congressional polarization is delay in the treaty ratification process. Despite the fact that fewer treaties are submitted to, and ratified by, the Senate, the treaties that are submitted still take longer to advance to a floor vote. Delays could be a byproduct of a generalized atmosphere of partisan gridlock that stalls legislation in Congress or distracts the executive from advancing their foreign policy agenda. Alternatively, delays could be more strategic in nature as a response to a partisan environment. For example, the president may choose to delay transmission of the treaty to the Senate if they anticipate congressional opposition. Likewise, the SFRC chair may delay reporting on a treaty, or the Senate leadership may delay or prevent a floor vote.

Table 6.1 analyzes the association between ideological polarization in the Senate and delays in the ratification process, using the same sample of bilateral treaties that were ratified between 1949 and 2020. The dependent variable is the number of days elapsed between the president signing the treaty and the treaty being ratified in Congress. The main independent variable is Senate polarization, measured as the difference between the average Democratic senator's and the average Republican senator's ideal point on a liberal–conservative spectrum.[33] Senators' ideal points are estimated using the DW-NOMINATE procedure to scale Senate roll-call votes.[34] The models take into account two other sets of characteristics likely to influence the timing of treaty ratification: the substantive content of the treaty and the characteristics of the political environment at the time the treaty was transmitted to the Senate. The treaty is coded as containing legal, security, environmental and human rights, economic, or sovereignty (e.g., addressing border and boundary claims) content, based on Peake's classification scheme for international treaties.[35] Controls for the political environment are motivated by

---

32. Peake, Krutz, and Hughes 2012, 1312.

33. Poole and Rosenthal 1997; Lewis et al. 2019.

34. An alternative approach is to use the ideological distance between the president and the pivotal senator (in this case, the sixty-seventh senator) in the treaty ratification process rather than a measure of Senate polarization. This approach produces very similar results.

35. Economic treaties are the omitted reference category in table 6.1.

TABLE 6.1. Treaty ratification delay among ratified bilateral treaties

	Number of days from signature to ratification			
	(1)	(2)	(3)	(4)
Senate polarization	1.182***	1.399***	1.196***	1.378***
	(0.319)	(0.369)	(0.339)	(0.377)
Divided government		0.112		0.021
		(0.090)		(0.090)
Presidential approval		−3.499***		−3.167***
		(0.633)		(0.625)
Election year		0.103		0.038
		(0.096)		(0.095)
Republican Senate		−0.102		−0.109
		(0.090)		(0.090)
Legal treaty			0.211**	0.208**
			(0.094)	(0.094)
Environmental treaty			1.676***	1.484***
			(0.445)	(0.440)
Security treaty			0.156	0.034
			(0.221)	(0.218)
Sovereignty treaty			0.125	0.025
			(0.122)	(0.120)
Constant	5.737***	7.419***	5.605***	7.221***
	(0.193)	(0.411)	(0.206)	(0.411)
Observations	496	496	496	496
Log likelihood	−3,683.076	−3,666.599	−3,669.101	−3,656.238
θ	1.228*** (0.070)	1.296*** (0.074)	1.285*** (0.074)	1.341*** (0.077)
Akaike inf. crit.	7,370.152	7,345.198	7,350.201	7,332.477

Note: *p < 0.1; **p < 0.05; ***p < 0.01

existing literature. Presidents with high approval ratings are thought to be more likely to accomplish their agenda, as are those who govern under periods of unified government where the same party controls the White House and Congress.[36] In an election year, lame-duck presidents may have less ability to push international treaties through Congress and opt instead to use executive agreements.[37] Moreover, Republicans are usually less favorable toward international treaties relative to their Democratic counterparts, so a Republican-controlled Senate may be less likely to ratify treaties.[38] Therefore, the models in table 6.1 control for historical presidential approval ratings and indicators for divided government, election year, and a Republican-majority Senate.[39]

Since the dependent variable is the number of days in the ratification process, I use count models to model the relationship between treaty delay and polarization. Given that the data is overdispersed (the variance in the data is greater than the mean), the models are negative binomial regression models.[40] Model 1 in table 6.1 looks at the baseline association between Senate polarization and ratification delay. The remaining models add in different sets of control variables for characteristics of the political environment (model 2), of the treaty (model 3), or both (model 4). Across all models, the coefficient on Senate polarization is positive and statistically significant. This indicates that higher levels of polarization are associated with a greater number of days in the ratification process. To understand the substantive interpretation of the models, it is useful to distinguish between a hypothetical "low polarization" and "high polarization" Senate, using levels of Senate polarization at the twenty-fifth and seventy-fifth percentile, respectively. At such levels, model 1 suggests that a low polarization Senate would on average ratify a treaty in 579 days, while a high polarization Senate would ratify a treaty in 711 days.

An alternative, simple way to visualize the data is to use nonparametric survival analysis, which is used to model the time until an event occurs. In this application, the event of interest is the ratification of the treaty. Survival analysis is useful when some events are not observed before the end of the time

36. On presidential approval ratings, see Ostrom and Simon 1985; Rivers and Rose 1985. On unified versus divided government, see Edwards, Barrett, and Peake 1997; Lovett, Bevan, and Baumgartner 2015; Kernell 1991.
37. Potter 2016.
38. Martin 2005.
39. Gallup News 2020.
40. Duration models that include treaties that were never ratified produce similar takeaways about the relationship between polarization and treaty ratification delay.

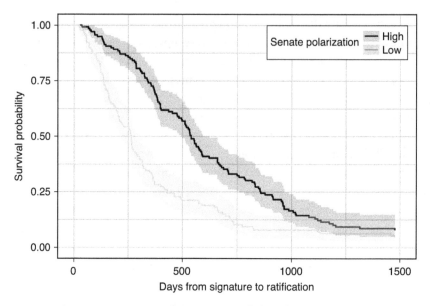

FIGURE 6.4. Time to treaty ratification among bilateral treaties transmitted during periods of low and high polarization

period. Figure 6.4 is a Kaplan–Meier plot that shows the time to ratification in the number of days elapsed since the president signed a treaty on the x-axis. The y-axis displays the survival probability, or the probability that the treaty is still not ratified after that number of days. I code low polarization Senates (in light gray) as those at the twenty-fifth percentile and below and high polarization Senates (in dark gray) as those at the seventy-fifth percentile and above. Comparing the two survival curves, the steeper curve for low polarization Senates indicates that Senates in less polarized times tend to ratify treaties at a faster rate relative to Senates in more polarized times.

The relationship between Senate polarization and ratification delay indicates that other political dynamics may be at play. One possibility is that the political opposition seeks to capitalize on heightened polarization to extract concessions from the president, making the ratification process more difficult. For example, political scientists Sarah Kreps, Elizabeth Saunders, and Kenneth Schultz argue that increasing Senate polarization has made it more difficult to ratify arms control agreements.[41] In an era of heightened polarization, Democratic presidents who are perceived as relatively dovish need

41. Kreps, Saunders, and Schultz 2018.

to make side payments to the political opposition to get the bipartisan support needed to pass arms control agreements. The researchers describe that the Obama White House anticipated an easy ratification process for the New START treaty, an arms control agreement with Russia signed in 2010. However, it became challenging for the White House to corral Republican support for New START. President Obama had to agree to larger investments in nuclear modernization in order to secure the necessary Republican votes in the Senate.

Ratification delay can also reflect the executive's hesitance in transmitting a treaty to a polarized Senate. Figure 6.5 breaks down the treaty ratification process into the four different stages: signature, transmission, reporting, and ratification. The figure shows how low polarization and high polarization Senates differ on average in the time elapsed between (a) the president's signature and the transmission of the treaty to SFRC, (b) the transmission and the reporting of the treaty by the chair of SFRC, and (c) the reporting and the ratification of the treaty by the full Senate. The figure suggests that the bulk of the delay comes in the first stage of the process: from signature to transmission. In a polarized environment, a president may wait for more favorable legislative conditions, delay to see the outcome of an election, or struggle with a gridlocked Congress to pass other legislation that takes precedence over treaties.

6.2.2 Trends in the Expansion of Executive Agreements

As the number of treaties transmitted to the Senate declines, the scope of executive agreements negotiated by the president—which do not require Senate ratification—has expanded. Executive agreements are not new tools, per se. Since 1937, the annual number of executive agreements has exceeded that of international treaties ratified by the U.S. Senate.[42] However, the increase in the use of executive agreements led political scientists to speculate as to whether they are symptoms of expanding executive power and the rise of an "imperial presidency."[43] Legal experts are especially critical of newer executive agreements that have "very thin forms of accountability for such a consequential form of presidential lawmaking."[44]

---

42. Fisher 2001.
43. Schlesinger 1973.
44. Hathaway, Bradley, and Goldsmith 2020, 634.

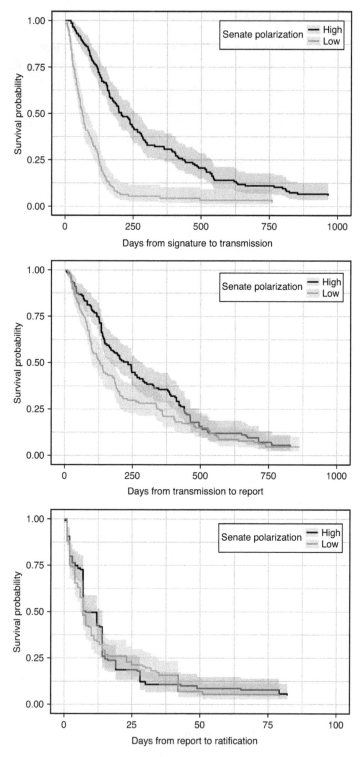

FIGURE 6.5. Time in different stages of the treaty ratification process among bilateral treaties transmitted during periods of low and high polarization

However, scholars disagree about whether executive agreements are increasingly substituting for international treaties or whether they serve a different function altogether. In an analysis of treaties ratified in the 1980s and 1990s, political scientist Lisa Martin finds no support for what she terms the evasion hypothesis: the idea that presidents use executive agreements instead of international treaties when they anticipate opposition from the legislature.[45] She points out that executive agreements do not seem to be any more likely during periods of divided government, where different parties control the White House and Congress. In one of the most comprehensive analyses of executive agreements and international treaties, Glen Krutz and Jeffrey Peake similarly conclude that executive agreements are not consciously being used to expand executive power. The researchers contend that an increase in the use of executive agreements relative to treaties is better explained by a need for efficiency.[46]

Yet, more recent scholarship links the decline of treaties and the expansion of executive agreements and nonbinding political commitments in contemporary American politics to polarization.[47] In *Dysfunctional Diplomacy*, Jeffrey Peake argues that polarization and legislative gridlock during the Obama administration (2009–2017) led to frustrations with the treaty process, prompting the White House to seek alternatives.[48] A prominent example is the Obama administration's unilateral entry into the Paris Climate Agreement, which angered congressional Republicans who viewed the president as "abusing his executive authority by pushing through major policies without congressional approval."[49]

A likely reason that this debate remains inconclusive is that thorough data on executive agreements is limited. Despite an obligation to report executive agreements to the Senate under the Case–Zablonski Act (1972), transparency around them is inconsistent. While publicly available, comprehensive databases of international treaties exist, there is no parallel collection of executive agreements. In fact, the analysis conducted by Krutz and Peake focuses only on a subset of roughly 500 international agreements concluded between 1949 and 1998. It is difficult to extrapolate these findings to executive agreements in the twenty-first century.

45. Martin 2005.
46. Krutz and Peake 2009.
47. Bodansky and Spiro 2016; Peake, Krutz, and Hughes 2012; Peake 2022; Schultz 2018.
48. Peake 2022.
49. Davenport 2014.

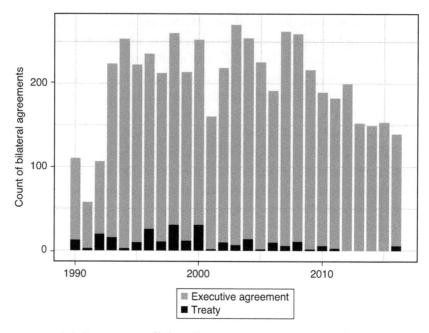

FIGURE 6.6. Comparison of bilateral executive agreements and bilateral ratified treaties (1990–2016)

To understand trends in the growth of executive agreements in the 2000s, I draw on a database compiled by legal scholars Oona Hathaway, Curtis Bradley, and Jack Goldsmith.[50] The researchers submitted a Freedom of Information Act request for cover memos of every executive agreement reported to Congress since 1989, resulting in a dataset of over 5,000 executive agreements. These cover memos are instructive because they cite the legal authority under which the executive made the agreement. Based on this information, Hathaway and co authors coded the strength of the legal basis for each agreement.

Since the time span of this data is limited to only a few congressional sessions, it is difficult to draw inferences about the relationship between congressional polarization and changes in executive agreements. Nevertheless, the data reveals a few interesting facts. For one, executive agreements are much more common than treaties and have become the primary way the American president makes agreements with other countries. Figure 6.6 compares the number of bilateral executive agreements with that of ratified treaties between 1990 and 2016. The figure shows that the number of executive agreements has

50. Hathaway, Bradley, and Goldsmith 2020.

TABLE 6.2. Legal authority of executive agreements by category

Category	Low	Medium	High	Constitution
Defense	0.12	0.25	0.50	0.13
Diplomacy and consular affairs	0.02	0.12	0.82	0.04
Educational exchanges and cultural cooperation	0.25	0.12	0.59	0.04
Environment, conservation and energy	0.07	0.31	0.58	0.03
Finance, trade, and investment	0.25	0.35	0.37	0.03
Humanitarian	0.03	0.13	0.83	0.01
Law enforcement	0.40	0.25	0.20	0.15
Maritime	0.12	0.20	0.57	0.11
Miscellaneous	0.07	0.28	0.60	0.02
Nonproliferation	0.04	0.72	0.20	0.04
Science, space, and technology	0.17	0.66	0.13	0.03
Taxation	0.40	0.29	0.29	0.02
Transportation and aviation	0.53	0.34	0.12	0.01

been persistently high since the early 1990s, but the ratio of executive agreements to treaties has increased over time as the number of treaties ratified continues to decline.

A second important finding is that a substantial portion of executive agreements were concluded with questionable legal authority. Hathaway and coauthors categorize each of the executive agreements in their dataset by the "quality of legal authority" cited in the cover memo submitted to Congress. The authors differentiate between agreements that rely on express legal authority ("high"), less explicit legal authority ("middle"), or no explicit legal authority ("low"), as well as those that only cite Article II of the Constitution ("Constitution"). Table 6.2 shows how the quality of legal authority differs by category of executive agreement.[51] The table emphasizes that a nontrivial percentage of executive agreements—including those related to defense and national security—are concluded with low to medium express executive authority.

Even among agreements categorized as having a "high" quality of legal authority that reference statues giving presidents authority to negotiate and enter into executive agreements, there is large variation in the applicability

51. This analysis includes both bilateral and multilateral executive agreements.

of a statute to a given agreement. One example is the frequent use of the Foreign Assistance Act of 1961 to justify the legal authority of presidents to enter into executive agreements. Hathaway and coauthors explain that "the entire Act is cited on cover memos on everything from providing radar data, to strengthening good governance in Afghanistan, to strengthening South Africa's reconstruction in Honduras after Hurricane Mitch."[52]

For many legal scholars, the most compelling evidence that presidents increasingly avoid Congress in an era of high polarization does not come from analyzing patterns of entry into treaties or executive agreements. Rather, it comes from discussions of major international commitments that the White House entered into without explicit congressional approval. Legal scholars Daniel Bodansky and Peter Spiro, for example, argue that four international agreements negotiated by the Obama administration—the Anti-Counterfeiting Trade Agreement, the Minamata Convention on Mercury, the Foreign Account Tax Compliance Act, and the Paris Climate Change Agreement—are better characterized as an entirely different class of executive agreements, which they term an *executive agreement+* or EA+.[53] EA+ agreements are "supported but not specifically authorized by congressional action" and will inevitably become more common "[i]n the face of political polarization and institutional gridlock."[54]

Executive agreements are also not the only form of international commitments likely to become more prominent during periods of congressional polarization. Despite the fact that nonbinding political commitments have been used by presidents for a century, their scope and content have also expanded. In 2007, for example, the George W. Bush administration sought to enter into the Strategic Framework Agreement between the United States and Iraq as a political commitment, which raised questions about the scope of presidential authority in making international commitments.[55] And, as discussed in chapter 5, the Obama administration pursued the Iran nuclear deal, signed in 2015, as a nonbinding political commitment.[56] This strategy deviated from norms around the negotiation of arms control and nonproliferation agreements, the vast majority of which are pursued as international

52. Hathaway, Bradley, and Goldsmith 2020, 680.
53. Bodansky and Spiro 2016.
54. Bodansky and Spiro 2016, 887–888.
55. Hollis and Newcomer 2008.
56. Weybrecht 2015.

treaties.[57] Critics of this approach pointed out it "was reflective of a larger trend of the [Obama] Administration eschewing treaties in favor of more Executive-friendly approaches."[58] Others argue that polarization makes it essential for the White House to develop new strategies to circumvent a gridlocked Congress in order to effectively govern.[59]

Trends in declines and delays in the treaty ratification process, entrance into executive agreements on the basis of questionable legal authority, and recent instances of expansive political commitments are all consistent with Reliability Hypothesis 2. The evidence, however, is not definitive. Instead, patterns suggest that executives in polarized times have more difficulty passing treaties and will be more likely to substitute treaties with executive agreements. This trend is likely to continue as polarization and congressional gridlock increase in American politics.

6.3 Application: Evidence from the U.S.–UK Bilateral Relationship

This chapter highlighted how extreme polarization undermines vertical and horizontal constraints on democratic leaders that contribute to the reliability advantage. Polarization erodes vertical constraints because a partisan public is less likely to reinforce democratic norms and procedures around entering into and exiting from international agreements. A polarized environment undermines horizontal constraints because it provides incentives for the leader to bypass intra-governmental constraints when making foreign policy, making less durable commitments in the process. The final step is to understand whether these effects are internalized by foreign allies. Because reliability is perceptual, we want to know how international observers interpret and respond to increasing polarization in the United States.[60]

Many scholars and commentators note that partisan politics could have damaging reputational impacts. Legal scholar Antonia Chayes points out, for instance, that U.S. treaty behavior in the post–Cold War era made observers view the United States as less reliable. Failing to ratify international treaties, delaying ratification processes, and reneging on existing commitments could

---

57. Jonas and Taxman 2018.
58. Jaffer 2019, 94.
59. Lowande and Milkis 2014.
60. Portions of this section are reprinted from Myrick (2022).

deter prospective U.S. allies from cooperation. She writes: "Negative reactions to US treaty behavior may well have undercut essential international cooperation. We cannot know for sure that the 'unsigning' of the ICC, walking away from Kyoto, rejecting the Land Mine Treaty, or any other form of American treaty behavior will lead to lack of future cooperation on issues that Americans value. But resentment runs deep."[61]

I argue that polarization has the potential to affect perceptions of the United States and its reliability as an international partner in a few ways. A first potential impact, and one that receives much attention in scholarship and policy writing, is that polarization may cause states to doubt existing commitments America has made to its allies. However, polarization also has two other long-term, or second-order, impacts on assessments of U.S. reliability that are less widely recognized. First, it can affect the willingness of allies to engage in future partnerships or agreements with the United States. Second, it can have downstream reputational consequences for the United States by affecting its perceived trustworthiness and global leadership. These second-order impacts arise from a generalized sense of uncertainty over the future of American foreign policy. Increasing divergence between the parties makes foreign policy more likely to change with presidential turnover and therefore less predictable.

Reliability Hypothesis 3: *As polarization becomes more extreme, democracies are more likely to renege on international commitments and less likely to be perceived as reliable allies.*

To explore how polarization in American politics affects perceptions of the country's reliability abroad, I rely on experimental public opinion research. I design and field survey experiments to 2,008 adults and 150 members of Parliament residing in the UK. These experiments prime respondents to think about polarization in the U.S. and subsequently evaluate U.S. foreign policy. Since the UK is one of America's closest allies, this setting provides a tough test for Reliability Hypothesis 3. Attitudes toward the United States are relatively entrenched in the UK, and the two countries have a robust history of security cooperation. If priming polarization negatively affects perceptions of the U.S.–UK bilateral relationship, we should anticipate stronger effects in countries whose alliances with the United States are more tenuous.

61. Chayes 2008, 74.

6.3.1 Short-Term Challenges: Existing Commitments

A short-term, first-order consequence of partisan polarization is that it may make the United States less likely to maintain its existing commitments. American commitments to foreign allies in Europe, the Middle East, and Asia are foundational elements of a liberal international order built upon "economic openness, multilateral institutions, security cooperation, and democratic solidarity."[62] Two sets of international commitments reflect bipartisan support for overarching principles of the liberal international order. The first set of commitments is to international institutions that promote cooperation among states. The second set of commitments is security guarantees to allies that the United States will come to their aid if their security is threatened.

Since the end of the Cold War, policymakers and scholars periodically issued warnings about the willingness of the United States to maintain existing commitments. Following the collapse of the Soviet Union, some predicted that U.S. departure from Europe would lead to the collapse of NATO, increasing the likelihood of a major international crisis.[63] After the U.S.-led invasion of Iraq, scholars argued that a unilateral approach pursued by the George W. Bush administration (2001–2009) would facilitate the "collapse of the Atlantic alliance"[64] and wondered if the U.S. would be able to renew its commitment to multilateralism.[65] During the Obama administration (2009–2017), fatigue from protracted wars in the Middle East increased advocacy for U.S. retrenchment,[66] which some warned would create power vacuums abroad.[67] The first Trump administration's (2017–2021) "America First" rhetoric and repeated attacks on longstanding alliances like NATO created worries about existing security commitments.[68] And major foreign policy disasters, such the Biden administration's (2021–2025) botched U.S. withdrawal from Afghanistan in August 2021, renewed debates about the reliability of U.S. commitments.[69]

---

62. Ikenberry 2018, 7.
63. Mearsheimer 1990.
64. Asmus 2003.
65. Jentleson 2007.
66. Gholz and Press 2010; Layne 2009; Peña 2006; Posen 2007; Preble 2009.
67. Dueck 2015.
68. Rapp-Hooper 2020; Wallcott 2020; Walt 2019.
69. Kertzer 2021.

Accompanying the actions of individual leaders is a larger, overarching worry that polarization within the United States could decrease support for liberal internationalism.[70] The argument is based on the idea that politicians in the center of the political spectrum have been responsible for sustaining commitments to foreign allies and engagement in international institutions. In a highly polarized era, however, accountability to the public pushes legislators further to the extremes. As a result, support for the principles of liberal internationalism and the international commitments that accompany them has waned. A natural question this argument raises is whether foreign allies share the perception that increasing polarization will erode the willingness or ability of the United States to maintain its existing commitments.

6.3.2 Long-Term Challenges: Future Partnerships and Reputational Impacts

Beyond concerns about existing commitments, there are two longer-term consequences that follow from how U.S. allies perceive its partisan politics. One possibility is that allies of the United States may not necessarily believe that polarization will cause the U.S. to renege on its existing international commitments, but they may fear long-run uncertainty in a hyperpartisan environment. This uncertainty could discourage prospective allies from pursuing future partnerships with the United States. This chapter discussed how existing research in international relations shows that democracies tend to be reliable allies and international partners. Yet, in highly polarized environments where parties have divergent foreign policy platforms, leadership turnover could result in significant changes in foreign policy. Perceptions of long-run uncertainty may diminish the willingness of allies to engage in future partnerships or major international agreements with the United States.

This uncertainty stems from multiple sources. One possibility is that allies may be skeptical that new international treaties will be ratified by the U.S. Congress in the first place, given the trends in treaty ratification highlighted in this chapter. In addition, allies may not believe that the start-up costs of a new agreement are worthwhile given that polarization increases the likelihood that executive turnover could result in the United States reneging on an agreement after its passage. As political scientist Keren Yarhi-Milo summarizes,

---

70. Bryan and Tama 2022; Kupchan and Trubowitz 2007, 2010.

"If other countries believe that American political commitments cannot survive a transition of power, they will be less likely to make significant or painful concessions."[71]

High levels of domestic polarization fuel a "general uncertainty, ambivalence, and volatility" in American foreign policy.[72] Chapter 4 explained that, in highly polarized environments, political officials are rewarded electorally by actively speaking against or even undoing policies of the political opposition. Uncertainty over U.S. foreign policy complicates future cooperation with the United States because it is significantly harder to create new agreements and institutions than to maintain existing ones.[73] If maintenance of existing agreements with a given country becomes challenging, potential partners will be skeptical about the ability of that country to enter into new, durable agreements. Actions short of withdrawal from existing agreements could also have destabilizing effects.[74] Simply inducing stress and uncertainty into current partnerships may make allies reticent to enter into new ones.

A second possible long-term consequence of polarization is that it may generate reputational costs by impacting assessments of America's trustworthiness or global leadership. Disentangling the effects of different forms of polarization in American politics—ideological polarization and affective polarization—can provide insight into why polarization might have negative reputational consequences abroad. If heightening foreign perceptions of affective polarization has strong negative repercussions on attitudes toward American foreign policy, allies may be concerned that domestic dysfunction will be destabilizing for the U.S. internationally. When the United States is unable to manage domestic dysfunction at home, its allies may perceive that it will be unable to maintain its global standing. Episodes in which partisan infighting directly or indirectly affected U.S. foreign policy highlight this dynamic. For instance, political scientist Yuen Foong Khong describes how partisan polarization indirectly complicated the bilateral relationship between the United States and China. The hyperpartisan atmosphere that led to a government shutdown in October 2013 in response to healthcare legislation had

71. Yarhi-Milo 2018.
72. Brands 2017.
73. Koremenos, Lipson, and Snidal 2001.
74. An annual U.S. threat report from the Office of the Director of National Intelligence highlights this strategic concern, noting that "US allies' and partners' uncertainty about the willingness and capability of the United States to maintain its international commitments may drive them to consider reorienting their policies." (Coats 2018, 4).

lasting negative repercussions for President Obama's strategic "pivot to Asia." As a result of the shutdown, Obama canceled his trip to the East Asia Summit, which "made it hard for the United States to twist some arms on the TPP or reassure its Asian partners about the TPP's clauses."[75] Subsequent government shutdowns in 2018 and 2019, as well as a narrowly averted shutdown in 2023, similarly troubled foreign allies.[76]

Concerns that affective polarization may lead to American decline parallel traditional ideas in international security about imperial overstretch.[77] Some are worried that identity-based political tribalism in the United States will erode America's capacity to project power internationally. As political scientist Joseph Nye summarizes, "Rome rotted from within, and some observers, noting the sourness of current US politics, project that the United States will lose its ability to influence world events because of domestic battles over culture, the collapse of its political institutions, and economic stagnation."[78] Concerns about foreign interference in U.S. presidential elections reveals how American adversaries believe that sowing affective polarization by amplifying identity-based cleavages can be destabilizing.[79] However, whether U.S. allies also perceive that affective polarization could precipitate a decline in American global leadership is unknown.

In contrast, if heightened perceptions of ideological polarization rather than affective polarization drive negative reputational consequences, a major concern for U.S. officials should be partisan divergence over foreign policy, which creates long-run uncertainty. As the Republican and Democratic Parties grow further apart in terms of their policy preferences, executive turnover will be increasingly likely to lead to changes in U.S. foreign policy. This inconsistency could lead U.S. allies to perceive the United States as less reliable. As a consequence, they may be less willing to initiate future partnerships with the United States and more skeptical of American global leadership overall.

75. Khong 2014, 174.
76. See, e.g., worries expressed by U.S. allies about a possible government shutdown related to foreign assistance to Ukraine and questions about U.S. border security in the fall of 2023 (Li 2023).
77. Snyder 1991.
78. Nye 2012, 37.
79. Friedersdorf 2018.

6.3.3 Survey Design

To investigate the effects of partisan polarization on perceptions of U.S. foreign policy, I embed an experiment in an omnibus public opinion survey fielded to 2,008 adults living in the UK. The survey, conducted by a survey firm called Respondi, recruited respondents from an online panel to match target demographic quotas for sex, age, and geographic region (England, Scotland, North Ireland, and Wales) in the UK. In addition to looking at the overall impacts of polarization on America's international reputation, the survey distinguished between the effects of ideological polarization (divergence in policy preferences between the Republican and Democratic Parties) and affective polarization (hatred or strong dislike of members of the opposite political party) on these assessments.

Why focus on the U.S.–UK bilateral relationship? Shared military alliances, economic ties, common memberships in international organizations, and agreements for intelligence sharing have reinforced a "special relationship" between the United States and the UK for more than a century.[80] While trying historic events have tested the enduring nature of this relationship, the perception that the United States and the UK remain the closest of allies is ingrained in both countries. Public opinion polls show that American adults consistently rank the UK among the United States' closest "friends" in international politics; similarly, adults in the UK continue to rank the United States as the UK's most important ally.[81] This means that the UK poses a tough test of the relationship between polarization and democratic reliability. If priming respondents in the UK to think about polarization lowers their assessment of U.S. foreign policy, we would anticipate larger negative effects in states where attitudes toward the United States are more malleable or existing alliances are more fragile.

Using survey experiments offers two advantages. First, public opinion research can identify potential second-order impacts of polarization that are not easily measurable. While we can observe whether the United States reneges on an existing international commitment, it is more challenging to observe negotiations that were never initiated in the first place. Similarly, concepts like reputation and perceptions of global leadership are difficult

---

80. Reynolds 1985.
81. Dinic 2015; YouGov Staff 2017.

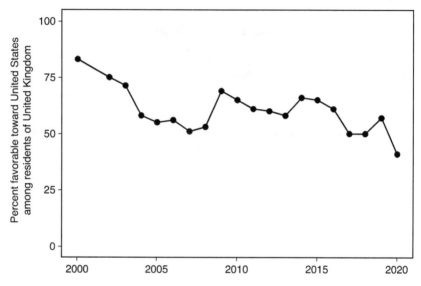

FIGURE 6.7. Favorability toward the US among residents of the UK (2000–2020)

to measure without drawing on public opinion polling. In addition, survey experiments allow us to disentangle perceptions of polarization in the United States from perceptions of other aspects of governance. For instance, with polling data from the Pew Research Center, figure 6.7 shows that residents of the UK have become less favorable toward the United States over time.[82] However, the extent to which these negative assessments are driven by perceptions of polarization cannot be inferred from observational data.

6.3.3.1 EXPERIMENTAL DESIGN

In the survey experiment, participants are randomly assigned to one of three groups. Those in the control group receive no information about polarization in the United States. Respondents in either of the treatment groups receive information about polarization both among American adults and political officials (i.e., polarization at both the "mass" and "elite" level). Those in the ideological group (T1) are primed to think about ideological polarization, while respondents in the affective group (T2) received information about affective

---

82. Wike, Fetterolf, and Mordecai 2020.

polarization. Survey respondents in the treatment groups first read information about American politics and polarization. The text, which differs based on the treatment, reads:

> We are now interested in understanding your attitudes toward the United States. We will first provide you with some information about American politics and then ask you for your opinions.
>
> The United States has two major political parties: the Republican Party and the Democratic Party.
>
> Studies show that the American public and its elected officials have become increasingly polarized along party lines.
>
> In other words, [T1: Republicans and Democrats increasingly disagree with one another on policy issues. OR T2: Americans increasingly dislike members of the other political party.].

On the next page, respondents in both treatment groups read information about polarization within the American public.

> Surveys from the United States show that, more than ever, Americans:
>
> - T1: Have different attitudes about social issues, such as abortion rights and gun laws. OR T2: Oppose the idea of their child marrying someone from the other political party.
> - T1: Have different preferences over economic policies, such as tax rates and welfare spending. OR T2: Have "just a few" or "no" close friends from the other political party.
> - T1: Think their political parties cannot agree on basic facts. OR T2: "Strongly dislike" or even "hate" members of the other political party.

Next, respondents in both treatment groups read information about polarization among American political officials.

> These differences are reflected in the US government. More than ever, Republican and Democratic politicians:
>
> - T1: Disagree on a wide range of basic policy issues. OR T2: Use extreme, negative language to taunt politicians of the other party.
> - T1: Vote the same way as members of their own political party. OR T2: Post angry or hateful posts on social media about members of the other party.

To ensure the delivery of the treatment, two attention checks within each treatment group ask respondents to identify information they previously read.[83] All respondents next evaluate a series of six statements on a seven-point Likert scale ranging from "Strongly disagree" to "Strongly agree." The statements are labeled from 1 to 6 to correspond to the regression tables in the next section, but they appear in random order to respondents. Two statements—one worded positively and one negatively—correspond to each of the three potential effects of polarization on foreign perceptions of the United States. As detailed previously, a potential short-term impact of polarization is that it can affect perceptions of existing commitments, such as military alliances and other security commitments. The corresponding statements read:

- Statement 1: The United States would come to the aid of my country in the event our security is threatened.
- Statement 2: The United States no longer maintains its commitments to foreign countries.

A second impact of polarization is that it can affect the willingness of U.S. allies to engage in future partnerships or international agreements because of concerns about its reliability. These statements read:

- Statement 3: My country should partner with the United States in future international agreements.
- Statement 4: The United States will not be a reliable future partner for my country.

A third potential impact of U.S. polarization is that it can affect America's reputation for leadership in international politics. These statements read:

- Statement 5: I trust the United States to do what is right in international politics.
- Statement 6: We should not look to the United States for global leadership.

6.3.4 Results

Before analyzing the impact of the polarization primes on respondent attitudes, I look at the data descriptively. For each of the six statements above,

---

83. See appendix for full survey questionnaire.

respondents express views using a seven-point Likert scale ranging from "Strongly disagree" to "Strongly agree." Figure 6.8 shows the distribution of the six dependent variables for the control group only (n = 843), which did not read the polarization prime. Negatively worded statements are inverse coded so that, in all figures, higher values indicate more favorable attitudes and greater perceived reliability.[84]

The most striking finding in figure 6.8 is that the baseline assessments of American foreign policy are fairly negative. Most respondents believe that the United States no longer maintains its commitments to foreign countries and is not a reliable future partner. In addition, most respondents think that the UK should not look to the U.S. for global leadership and do not trust the U.S. to do what is right in international politics. However, respondents expect that the United States would come to the aid of the UK were its security threatened. As I show in the following section, priming respondents to think about partisan polarization in the United States does not alter this confidence in U.S. security commitments.

Next, I consider how priming polarization shapes attitudes toward the United States. The dependent variables are responses to the six statements presented previously. Negatively worded statements remain inverse coded, meaning that the expected direction of all treatment effects is negative. I regress the six dependent variables on treatment indicators, using the control group as the omitted reference category. For simplicity, the main effects, displayed in table 6.3, are modeled using ordinary least-squares regression models and show the sample average treatment effects for both treatment conditions.[85]

These results show that priming respondents in the UK to think about partisan polarization in the United States negatively impacted their evaluations of U.S. foreign policy and the U.S.–UK relationship. However, in many cases, the strength of these effects was small and varied across both the outcomes and treatments. In general, priming ideological polarization exerted a stronger negative effect on respondents' attitudes. While priming affective polarization

---

84. For negatively worded statements (e.g., "The United States will *not* be a reliable future partner for my country"), "Strongly agree" is coded as "1." This means that higher values indicate more positive assessments of the United States.

85. The results are similar with and without demographic controls and when using other model specifications, like logistic regression models.

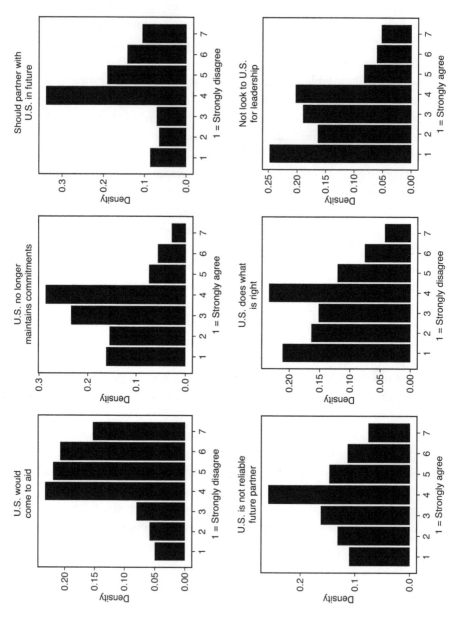

FIGURE 6.8. Attitudes toward U.S. foreign policy among UK survey respondents in the control group

TABLE 6.3. Effects of affective and ideological treatments on UK perceptions of United States

	Existing commitments		Future partnerships		Reputation for leadership	
	(1)	(2)	(3)	(4)	(5)	(6)
Affective treatment	−0.146 (0.090)	−0.030 (0.082)	−0.032 (0.089)	−0.077 (0.093)	−0.081 (0.093)	0.011 (0.094)
Ideological treatment	−0.131 (0.089)	−0.026 (0.082)	−0.178** (0.088)	−0.221** (0.093)	−0.203** (0.093)	−0.168* (0.094)
Constant	4.749*** (0.057)	3.241*** (0.052)	4.329*** (0.057)	3.846*** (0.059)	3.288*** (0.059)	3.100*** (0.060)
Observations	2,008	2,008	2,008	2,008	2,008	2,008

Note: *p < 0.1; **p < 0.05; ***p < 0.01

typically had a negative effect, these effects were not statistically significant at conventional levels.

We see the strongest negative effects, in terms of both magnitude and statistical significance, for the long-run impacts of polarization. Priming ideological polarization—that is, emphasizing increasing disagreement between the parties—decreases the likelihood that the respondent believes their country should partner with the United States in future international agreements and increases the likelihood that they will not perceive the United States as a reliable future partner. In addition, priming ideological polarization has important reputational effects: it causes respondents to be less likely to trust the United States to do what is right in international politics or view the United States as a global leader.

Despite the fact that many of these treatment effects attain statistical significance, their magnitude remains relatively small ($\approx$ 0.1 to 0.2 standard deviations). However, these results are still somewhat surprising for a simple priming experiment. The treatment is not especially strong because it primes respondents to think about polarization rather than delivering new information, per se. In addition, one would expect respondents in the UK to have strong prior beliefs about the United States that are not easily changed. Finally, as the descriptive data shows, baseline attitudes toward the United States are already fairly negative in the control condition. This makes it more difficult to find strong negative treatment effects.

There are a few concerns with this analysis that can be addressed by additional robustness checks. A common concern in survey experiments is that respondents did not closely read the treatment and were therefore not thoroughly primed to be thinking about polarization. I used two strategies to mitigate this concern. First, for the main results, I oversample ($n \approx 2,400$) respondents and drop "speeders," defined as the fastest 20 percent of respondents, from the analysis.[86] Second, in a robustness check, I analyze results within a subsample of respondents that passed two attention checks, which asked participants to identify information from the polarization treatment that they previously read (see the appendix). While we should exercise caution in directly interpreting these results, given that respondents who failed

---

86. "Speeding" here is measured before the treatment so that dropping respondents from the analysis does not bias the results.

TABLE 6.4. Perceptions of agreement between two major political parties

	Republican/Democratic (1)	Conservative/Labour (2)
Affective treatment	−0.120*** (0.041)	0.010 (0.042)
Ideological treatment	−0.130*** (0.041)	0.054 (0.042)
Constant	1.913*** (0.026)	1.989*** (0.027)
Observations	1,792	1,909

Note: *p < 0.1; **p < 0.05; ***p < 0.01

the attention check are dropped from the analysis posttreatment,[87] the effect sizes are larger in magnitude among this subset of respondents.

There are additional concerns, however, that arise in interpreting survey results. One critique of small or null effects in survey experiments is that the treatments do not sufficiently convey the core concepts. For example, perhaps respondents receiving polarization primes did not update their assessment of whether members of the Republican and Democratic Parties in the United States increasingly disagree. To demonstrate this was not the case, I added a series of questions about respondents' perceptions of polarization in the United States and in the UK at the end of the survey in order to test how effectively the polarization primes were working. One question asked: "The United States has two major political parties: the Republican Party and the Democratic Party. How often would you say these parties agree?" Respondents had the following answer options: "Almost always" / "Sometimes" / "Rarely" / "Almost never" / "I don't know". My expectation was that respondents receiving the treatment would be less likely to say that the two parties tend to agree. Model 1 in table 6.4 supports this intuition. The model is an ordinary least-squares regression model in which the dependent variable ranges from 1 ("Almost never") to 4 ("Almost always"), with "Don't know" removed. Respondents in *both* treatment groups were much more likely to perceive disagreement between the two parties (i.e., to say they "Almost never" agree) than were respondents in the control group.

87. Aronow, Baron, and Pinson 2019.

Another concern is that priming respondents to think about polarization leads to more general pessimism about politics rather than about the United States, per se. To ensure this is not the case, I consider whether the polarization primes affected respondents' perceptions of their politics at home in addition to their perceptions of American politics. Specifically, I asked: "The United Kingdom has two major political parties: the Conservative Party and the Labour Party. How often would you say these parties *agree*?" If priming polarization about the United States had no impact on attitudes toward UK politics, we should expect null effects. Model 2 of table 6.4 supports this finding; both treatments have no statistically significant impact on respondents' assessments of how often the Conservative Party and Labour Party in the UK tend to agree. This means it is likely that the polarization primes affect perceptions of the United States but do not result in a more general negative attitude toward politics overall.

While these robustness checks improve the internal validity of the study, the central limitation of this approach is that the results can only speak directly to one bilateral relationship: the U.S.–UK relationship. An important extension would be to explore whether the findings translate to other partners of the United States. It is possible that polarization primes would induce greater uncertainty into a relationship with the United States among allies and partners that face more direct security threats, such as Israel, South Korea, Taiwan, or Ukraine. Another possibility is that priming polarization—and affective polarization, in particular—may have stronger negative effects in contexts that are not experiencing similar partisan divides at home. The UK, for example, exhibited fairly high levels of affective polarization following the Brexit referendum,[88] so information about increased social distance and partisan tribalism in the United States may not have a large impact on attitudes.

6.3.5 *Extension to UK Elites*

To better illustrate the relationship between polarization and future uncertainty around policymaking, I conducted an additional simple survey experiment on a sample of UK members of Parliament in April 2019. This second survey was embedded on an omnibus survey fielded by the survey firm Savanta ComRes, which maintains a panel of 150 members of Parliament. The sample is representative of UK parliamentarians on characteristics like gender,

---

88. Hobolt, Leeper, and Tilley 2021.

political party, and region. Elite surveys are advantageous in studies related to international politics because politicians are the primary decision-makers in foreign policy. However, elite samples also have drawbacks. They tend to be much more difficult to access and are usually smaller in size than samples of the mass public, making it hard to detect statistically significant differences between treatment conditions in a survey experiment.[89]

The elite experiment contained a simplified extension of the UK public opinion experiment. UK members of Parliament were randomly assigned to one of two groups: a control group or a treatment group. Respondents in the control group were asked the following question about uncertainty around the future of U.S. foreign policy:

> We are interested in your views toward politics in the United States. Do you agree or disagree with the following: I am uncertain about what American foreign policy will look like in ten years.

Respondents in the treatment group were asked the same question but primed to think about growing polarization in the United States before evaluating the statement:

> Studies show that politics in the United States is more polarized than ever. The two main political parties, the Republican Party and the Democratic Party, increasingly disagree on policy issues. Considering this extreme polarization, do you agree or disagree with the following: I am uncertain about what American foreign policy will look like in ten years.

Like in the general public opinion survey, response options for this survey were on a seven-point Likert scale that ranged from "Strongly disagree" (1) to "Strongly agree" (7). In both groups, the majority of respondents expressed uncertainty about the future of U.S. foreign policy. However, respondents in the treatment group were more likely to agree that they were uncertain (70.7 percent) relative to respondents in the control group (60 percent). Given the small sample size (n = 150), this difference was not statistically significant at conventional levels. However, the results lend some support to the intuition that, in the eyes of foreign allies, polarization could generate negative reputational consequences by increasing uncertainty about the direction of the polarized country's foreign policy.

---

89. On the growth and use of elite experiments in political science, see Kertzer and Renshon (2022).

6.4 Conclusion

Democracies are thought to be more reliable allies relative to nondemocracies because they better commit to, and comply with, international agreements. In healthy liberal democracies, vertical and horizontal constraints prevent leaders from unilaterally reneging on their commitments to their allies and partners. This chapter used three empirical strategies outlined in table 6.5 to investigate how this reliability advantage can be eroded in a highly polarized setting.

First, as polarization becomes more extreme, democratic leaders are less likely to be held accountable by the public for unilaterally entering into, or exiting, international commitments. As the public grows more partisan, they are likely to care more about seeing their preferred policy enacted or their own side winning. As a result, they care comparatively less about upholding democratic norms and procedures in the creation and maintenance of international commitments. In a survey experiment fielded to 4,330 American adults before the 2024 U.S. presidential election, I randomize the hypothetical winner of the election and ask respondents to consider whether it is acceptable for the president to enter into, or withdraw from, different types of international commitments without congressional approval. While the results demonstrate an overarching aversion to unilateralism among the American public, there is also substantial partisan bias in their evaluations of presidential actions. Respondents who share the party of the president are more likely to consider unilateral actions acceptable relative to respondents who do not share the party of the president. These partisan biases are likely to grow as polarization continues to increase, weakening vertical constraints on democratic leaders.

Second, I argue that increased polarization gives democratic leaders incentives to bypass horizontal constraints in making international agreements. It also becomes structurally easier to do so. A polarized public and legislature will be unlikely to effectively prevent commitments from being made unilaterally. Extending data from Jeffrey Peake and coauthors, I show that polarization is correlated with declines and delays in treaty ratification given the challenges of amassing the bipartisan support necessary for to ratify treaties in the U.S. Senate. I provide suggestive—albeit not definitive—evidence that in more recent presidential administrations, executive agreements are systematically used to substitute for international treaties in the United States. Using data from Oona Hathaway and coauthors, I show that the number of executive

TABLE 6.5. Summary of findings from the Reliability Hypotheses

	As polarization becomes more extreme...	Empirical strategy	Summary of findings
Vertical constraints	The public is less likely to punish co-partisan leaders who act unilaterally when making foreign policy or who renege on international commitments.	Conduct a survey experiment in advance of the 2024 U.S. presidential election that varies the partisanship of the president and examines how respondents evaluate whether they should be able to act unilaterally in foreign affairs and renege on international commitments.	Survey respondents were more likely to object to unilateral action in entering into, and withdrawing from, international agreements when the president was from the opposite party.
Horizontal constraints	Politicians are more likely to bypass horizontal constraints in committing to international agreements, leading to less durable commitments.	Use data on treaties and executive agreements to examine whether increasing polarization in the U.S. is associated with less durable international commitments.	Growing polarization in the U.S. is associated with declines and delays in treaty ratification. There is suggestive evidence that presidents increasingly substitute executive agreements in place of more durable treaties.
Implication for democratic advantage	Democracies are more likely to renege on international commitments and less likely to be perceived as reliable allies.	Field a survey experiment in a country that is a close U.S. ally (the UK) that primes respondents to think about polarization in American politics and evaluates how they assess their current and future relationship with the United States.	Survey respondents in the UK who were primed to think about polarization in American politics were more uncertain about U.S. foreign policy, less willing to engage in future partnerships with the U.S., and more skeptical of U.S. global leadership.

agreements continues to dwarf the number of ratified international treaties. Moreover, a substantial amount of executive agreements are conducted on questionable legal authority.

Third, I argue that partisan polarization has reputational consequences abroad. It affects foreign perceptions of the United States and its ability to remain a reliable ally. Results from a public opinion survey fielded in the UK showed that perceptions of polarization did not seem to substantially affect respondents' assessment of the United States' ability to maintain its existing security commitments. However, priming polarization has larger effects on respondents' long-term evaluations of the U.S.–UK bilateral relationship. Heightened awareness of disagreements between the Republican and Democratic Parties in the United States led to more negative evaluations of America's reliability, trustworthiness as an ally, and role as a global leader. An extension of the survey to UK members of Parliament showed that this effect may be driven by the perception that diverging preferences between the Republican and Democratic Parties create uncertainty over the future of U.S. foreign policy. This uncertainty makes foreign allies perceive the United States as less of a trustworthy decision-maker or reliable partner in the long run.

7

Conclusion

ANNUALLY, A POLITICAL risk consultancy called Eurasia Group releases a forecast of the top ten global political risks for the year. The number one risk in the 2024 report may have surprised some readers.[1] The biggest threat identified by the consultancy was not Russian aggression in Eastern Europe, the growing conflagration in the Middle East between Israel and Hamas, or the simmering geopolitical rivalry between the United States and China. Rather, Eurasia Group listed the top risk as "The United States vs. itself." Over the last decade, research institutes, think tanks, and consultancies expressed similar concerns about how domestic divisions within the United States could jeopardize national security.[2] However, the precise nature and scope of the problem is challenging to characterize.

This book is part of a new body of work that takes seriously the consequences of polarization for American foreign policy and international relations theory.[3] A long line of scholarship in international relations theory posits that democracies are advantaged in various ways when making foreign policy. This book focused on three democratic advantages in particular: the ability to keep foreign policy relatively stable over time, to credibly signal information to adversaries, and to be reliable partners in international politics. It argued that extreme polarization undermines these advantages by eroding constraints on democratic leaders that keep them accountable to the public and the political opposition. As polarization becomes more extreme, the stakes of winning

1. Eurasia Group 2024.
2. See, e.g., Smeltz, Busby, and Tama 2018; Williams and McCulloch 2023.
3. Other examples in this vein include Borg 2024; Busby and Monten 2008; Chaudoin, Milner, and Tingley 2010; Friedrichs 2021; Friedrichs and Tama 2024; Kertzer, Brooks, and Brooks 2021; Kupchan and Trubowitz 2007, 2010; Milner and Tingley 2015; Musgrave 2019; Pillar 2023; Schultz 2018; Tama 2023; Trubowitz and Burgoon 2023.

political contests increase. Politicians have more incentives to disregard democratic norms, and partisan conflict becomes more likely to extend to new policy domains. As a consequence, we should expect democracies experiencing periods of high polarization to become less stable in their foreign policymaking, and to be both less credible adversaries and less reliable allies.

This chapter summarizes the key takeaways and contributions from this project to scholarship on international relations and U.S. foreign policy. It emphasizes that this book only scratches the surface of a much larger set of questions about the relationship between partisan polarization and international politics. The remainder of the chapter focuses on three questions central to future research about this subject. First, are there positive impacts of polarization on foreign policy that might outweigh the negative consequences? Second, what can be done to mitigate the negative effects of polarization on foreign policymaking or to reduce polarization more generally? Third, how might these findings extend beyond the American political context?

7.1 Overarching Takeaways and Contributions

This book undertook a systematic exercise to theorize about the impact that polarization could have on international relations. It drew on diverse sources of evidence—including cross-national analysis, public opinion data, data on the behavior of politicians, and case illustrations—to describe pathways through which polarization could impact democratic foreign policymaking. As emphasized in chapter 1, no one piece of evidence in this book was dispositive. Rather, the combination of theory and evidence emphasizes that the consequences of polarization for foreign policy in the United States and other advanced democracies are more likely to be negative than positive. This is especially true of contexts in which polarization is growing more extreme: where ideological and affective polarization coincide and reinforce one another.

The book makes three main contributions. The primary contribution is to integrate work across the fields of international relations, comparative politics, and American politics that links research on the effects of polarization on democratic institutions and political behavior to theories of international relations. Of course, polarization is not a new phenomenon. Many democracies experienced periods of high polarization at some point in their history. However, polarization has become an especially salient problem in the twenty-first century. In large part, this is because, since the turn of the century, scholars document troubling declines in the quality of democracy across many advanced democracies. Every year between 2005 and 2023, Freedom House's *Freedom in the World* project has reported that more countries have experienced democratic decline than improvement in the quality of their democracy.[4] Polarization is seen by many people as both a cause and a symptom of so-called processes of democratic decline, democratic backsliding, or democratic erosion.[5] Awareness of polarization among democratic publics is further heightened by dramatic changes in the technology and media landscape.

Political scientists have written extensively about the consequences of polarization for democracy and domestic politics. This book argued, however, that polarization also has direct and indirect consequences for international relations. Many of the most important domestic political trends in the twenty-first century—including polarization, populism, and democratic erosion—tend to be studied within individual countries. This book is part of a growing body of scholarship that argues that these domestic trends also have important international causes and consequences.[6] As polarization becomes an increasingly salient issue that advanced democracies grapple with, scholars, policymakers, and citizens alike should focus more on its international dimensions.

The second contribution of this book is to further a growing body of scholarship that critiques the democratic advantage tradition in international relations theory. As chapter 2 explained, scholars in this tradition argue that democracies are advantaged when making foreign policy relative to nondemocracies. Democracies are thought to be better able to issue credible threats and promises, and they make for more reliable allies and partners. The most prominent critics of the democratic advantage thesis tend to focus on the fact that domestic politics has minimal impact on foreign affairs. Scholars in the realist tradition of international relations theory, for example, emphasize that power and interests—rather than regime type—shape a country's foreign policy behavior.

4. Gorokhovskaia and Grothe 2024.
5. See, e.g., Graham and Svolik 2020; Kaufman and Haggard 2019; Riedl et al. 2024; Svolik 2019.
6. See, e.g., research about the international dimensions of other global political trends like democratic backsliding (Hafner-Burton and Schneider 2023; Hyde 2020; Gunitskiy 2017; Pevehouse and Glenn 2024; Samuels 2023) and populism (Copelovitch and Pevehouse 2019; Löfflmann 2022; Meyerrose 2020; Pevehouse 2020).

This book offered a different corrective to the democratic advantage tradition. It argues that not all democracies may be advantaged in foreign policy in part due to the nature of their domestic politics. By weakening institutional constraints on leaders, extreme polarization can make democratic foreign policy less stable, credible, and reliable. Chapter 3 provided some preliminary cross-national evidence to this effect, adding measures of extreme polarization to existing models of democratic advantages. In doing so, this book does not overturn the democratic advantage thesis but rather emphasizes that there is important variation in the foreign policy behavior of democracies that stems from domestic polarization.

The third contribution of this book was to characterize the trajectory of polarization in U.S. foreign policy. Periodically, researchers debate the extent to which U.S. foreign policy is polarizing. Some scholars raise alarm about increasing partisanship in foreign affairs, while others argue that foreign affairs remains insulated from partisan politics. Chapter 4 argued that, although domestic politics is more polarized than foreign policy, we observe partisan conflict extending to other domains of foreign policy. Much like partisan conflict gradually extended from economic issues to social issues during the latter half of the twentieth century, we should expect foreign policy issues to be pulled into the partisan divide if polarization continues to increase. Chapter 4 highlighted that not all areas of U.S. foreign policy are equally susceptible to politicization. Among the areas most vulnerable to conflict extension are foreign policy issues that involve aspects of social identity, relate to nontraditional security threats, or concern ideological debates about multilateralism.

As polarization persists—and potentially even increases—in American politics, this book anticipates that there are likely to be negative repercussions for U.S. foreign policy. Chapter 5 argued that polarization might undermine the credibility of signals sent by the United States to its foreign adversaries. The combination of affective and ideological polarization makes it hard for the executive and opposition to find common ground or present a unified front. As such, it will become harder to generate credible signals of resolve in international crises. Likewise, it will become more difficult for presidents to initiate and navigate complex or controversial international negotiations. Attempts to do so are likely to be derailed by the political opposition. Chapter 6 showed that, in the wake of increasing congressional polarization, presidents will seek to use executive agreements, nonbinding political commitments, and similar alternatives to conduct foreign policy. These agreements are less durable than treaties ratified by Congress, which makes it easier for future leaders to renege on commitments.

Much of the evidence presented in this book suggests that the effects of polarization on foreign policy have not been fully realized in the United States. Chapter 4, for example, discussed that, as polarization increases, we should expect the prevalence and intensity of episodes of politicization in national security institutions to increase. However, more blatant forms politicization characteristic of environments of extreme polarization remain rare. Likewise, chapters 5 and 6 showed that, while increased partisanship weakens electoral accountability, at present, Americans still largely hold politicians accountable for foreign policy decisions. For example, public opinion surveys in chapter 5 showed that the majority of partisans do not advocate for the congressional opposition to obstruct an out-party president in foreign affairs. Likewise, chapter 6 showed that the majority of partisans are still averse to the president unilaterally entering into and exiting from international agreements. Nevertheless, both these surveys also demonstrated clear partisan biases in evaluations of presidential actions. These biases were especially pronounced among strong partisans and individuals who exhibited high levels of affective polarization. As societal polarization grows, it is very likely that constraints on democratic leaders in foreign affairs will continue to weaken.

Early warning signs of heightened partisanship in foreign affairs should be worrisome. Similar to processes of democratic erosion, many of the negative impacts of polarization for foreign affairs may be incremental. Without identifying and describing the consequences of polarization for U.S. foreign policy, it will be difficult—if near impossible—to understand the scope of the problem and explore what can be done to remedy it.

7.2 What about the Positive Consequences of Polarization?

This book primarily emphasized the negative consequences that partisan polarization has for international politics. One objection to the book's argument is that not all polarization in foreign policy is *bad*, per se. Certainly, there is some truth to this claim. Organized political parties, fierce electoral competition, and open contestation of ideas are hallmarks of liberal democracies. The democratic advantage literature tells us that partisan disagreement is an important part of foreign policymaking. Democracies are characterized by public debate in a "marketplace of ideas" that can lead to better foreign policy outcomes.[7] As discussed throughout this book, moderate levels of

---

7. See, e.g., Reiter and Stam 1998, 2002; Van Evera 2003.

polarization reinforce the advantages that democracies have in foreign affairs. We know, for instance, that partisan disagreement between the executive and the political opposition allows democracies to extract more from international negotiations.[8] Democratic leaders can credibly say to their foreign counterparts in a negotiation that they will have difficulty ratifying an agreement that is not more favorable to a domestic audience. We also know that in polarized environments, when the political opposition rallies behind a democratic leader or endorses their policies, this is an especially credible signal of resolve to foreign adversaries.[9] And, because major international agreements often require buy-in from the political opposition, democratic commitments tend to be more durable.[10]

The important distinction, however, is that, while moderate levels of polarization confer democratic advantages, more extreme levels of polarization erode them. Environments of extreme polarization combine high levels of ideological polarization and affective polarization. In these settings, disagreement is not necessarily principled or reflective of substantive policy debates. Instead, politics becomes more about preventing the other side from winning. As the stakes of electoral competition heighten, the temptation to violate norms in the foreign policymaking process increases. Vertical and horizontal constraints operating in this environment are less effective at guarding against such violations.

Turning to the U.S. political context, is partisan disagreement in foreign affairs ever a good thing? In some instances, polarization can be beneficial. Partisan disagreement could reflect differences in beliefs about the future of U.S. foreign policy, including which national security threats to prioritize and how the U.S. should engage with major allies and adversaries. These are big, important questions that merit scrutiny and debate. Conversations during the 2020 Democratic presidential primary, for example, fueled an emerging debate about progressive foreign policy on the left.[11] Although some criticize the explicitly partisan nature of this debate,[12] others welcome attempts to broaden the spectrum of ideological viewpoints in mainstream commentary on foreign affairs. If the parties were to develop clear and ideologically coherent

---

8. Putnam 1988.
9. Schultz 2001a.
10. Martin 2000.
11. See, e.g., Jackson 2022, 2023; Rapp-Hooper and Lissner 2020; Wertheim 2022.
12. See, e.g., Ashford 2023.

foreign policy platforms, voters may have a better understanding of how the Republican and Democratic Parties differ on important values and issues related to national security.

Relatedly, *too much* bipartisanship could indicate pathologies in U.S. foreign policy. Historian Patrick Porter, for example, argues that an entrenched national security establishment in Washington has led to the persistence of a problematic framework for American grand strategy centered on military preponderance.[13] As discussed throughout this book, while polarization is increasing in some areas of foreign policy, the parties tend to be aligned on their support for defense and national security policy.[14] A downside of bipartisanship is that it can perpetuate status quo policies that may merit reexamination. For instance, many researchers and commentators describe the drawbacks of increasing militarization in U.S. foreign affairs throughout the twenty-first century.[15] One reason why foreign policy has become more militarized is that legislators from both sides of the aisle are reluctant to draw down defense spending.[16] In this sense, bipartisan consensus could indicate uncritical commitment to status quo policies. In fact, some researchers argue that congressional polarization could be a positive thing precisely because it could allow entrepreneurial politicians with anti establishment worldviews to advance alternative foreign policies.[17]

Another positive aspect of polarization is that, if foreign policy issues were to become more politically contested, it may suggest that American voters increasingly care about global affairs. Commentators typically lament the American public's apathy around global issues.[18] More polarized foreign policy debates could increase engagement in the same way that America's polarized politics has animated public engagement and mobilized voters.[19] Conversely, the absence of party conflict in foreign affairs could indicate disinterest in these topics, which is not necessarily a good thing. Chapter 5, for example, emphasized how the political opposition steadily cohered against the president across successive administrations. If the patterns in chapter 5 instead

13. Porter 2018, 2020.
14. Chaudoin, Milner, and Tingley 2010; Milner and Tingley 2015; Friedman 2023; Tama 2023.
15. See, e.g., Adams and Murray 2014; Brooks 2016; Kohn 2009; Toft and Kushi 2023.
16. Milner and Tingley 2015.
17. Homan and Lantis 2022.
18. See, e.g., Lindsay 2000.
19. Hetherington 2008.

revealed little to no contestation of the executive, it could be a worrying sign that legislators were disengaged on foreign policy issues.

In short, partisan disagreement about foreign policy is not itself a negative thing. Political contestation is a healthy feature of liberal democracies. However, a core argument advanced in this book is that, as polarization moves toward the extremes, it has troubling, second-order repercussions for foreign policy. This book explained that these consequences are most likely to be negative when polarization is an artifact of electoral incentives and partisan animus rather than principled disagreement on foreign policy ideas. Partisan conflict is not inherently bad, but the manner in which it is increasingly weaponized in foreign policy should alarm us.

7.3 How Can We Mitigate Negative Effects of Polarization?

If, as this book concludes, the consequences of more extreme forms of polarization for foreign policy are largely negative, what can be done to mitigate them? Although there is growing interest in this question, political scientists and policymakers unfortunately have reached few definitive conclusions. This chapter briefly reviews three sets of approaches. The first set is what I refer to as "strategies of insulation." These approaches seek to prevent partisan conflict in domestic policy from extending into foreign affairs. The second set is strategies to reduce congressional polarization. These approaches anticipate that tackling the roots of polarization among politicians will improve horizontal constraints in foreign policymaking. The third set of strategies aims to reduce affective polarization among the American public, with the expectation this will strengthen vertical constraints and electoral accountability in foreign affairs.

7.3.1 Strategies to Insulate Foreign Policy from Partisan Politics

Strategies of insulation take steps to prevent partisan conflict from extending into foreign affairs and national security issues. In practice, this is complex. At minimum, it requires careful coalition-building among legislators from opposing parties. At maximum, it requires major institutional reforms. Each approach comes with trade-offs.

One approach is to create and maintain legislative coalitions of "strange bedfellows" in foreign policy. The idea is that if legislators build common ground in certain policy areas, they can lay the foundation for bipartisan cooperation in other areas of foreign affairs. In his book *Bipartisanship and US Foreign Policy*, political scientist Jordan Tama explains that cross-partisan coalition-building is a staple of U.S. foreign policy that persists in our present partisan era.[20] Tama notes that policymakers reach across the aisle out of necessity. To accomplish their legislative agenda, legislators usually need support from the opposite party. And, it is easier to create and sustain bipartisan coalitions in foreign policy relative to domestic policy where the ideological divide is more central to policymaking. Tama cites many examples of entrepreneurial policymakers who built bipartisan coalitions in foreign affairs. For example, one of the most well known foreign policy partnerships between Republican Senator Richard Lugar of Indiana and Democratic Senator Sam Nunn of Georgia led to the Nunn–Lugar Cooperative Threat Reduction Program, which dismantled nuclear infrastructure after the collapse of the Soviet Union.[21]

There are difficulties with this strategy. The first is feasibility. As politics becomes more polarized, both ideological differences and electoral incentives make it more challenging to build and maintain bipartisan coalitions. A second challenge is that bipartisan coalition-building can sometimes lead to sub optimal foreign policy outcomes. If legislators prioritize bipartisanship above all else, they may adopt policies uncritically. Some observers express concern about emerging groupthink in Washington, D.C., regarding U.S.–China policy.[22] By the end of the Obama administration, there was widespread acknowledgement that the "responsible stakeholder"[23] strategy the United States had pursued toward Beijing had not led to the gains in cooperation anticipated by policymakers.[24] Rather, under Chinese President Xi Jinping, China became more authoritarian, nationalist, and hostile toward the United States. As a result of these shifts, American politicians and the public began to view the United States' relations with China as more adversarial.[25] By the 2020s, China policy was described as one of the rare areas of bipartisan consensus in U.S.

---

20. Tama 2023.
21. American Security Project 2012.
22. See, e.g., Greve and Gambino 2023; McKinley 2023; Weiss 2022.
23. The intuition behind this strategy, detailed by Deputy Secretary of State Robert Zoellick in 2005, was to continue to integrate China into the international community in anticipation that, over time, China would become more cooperative and more democratic (Zoellick 2005).
24. Brands and Cooper 2019; Campbell and Ratner 2018.
25. Kafura 2023.

foreign affairs.[26] But, one danger is that, over time, polarization will give politicians more incentives to weaponize the China threat. For example, an outbidding dynamic could emerge whereby the parties become increasingly hawkish on China, each accusing the other party of not being tough enough.[27] If parties become increasingly hard-line on the China threat, some commentators warn that a crisis between the United States and China could quickly escalate. Political scientist Jessica Weiss, for instance, expresses concerns that Washington's consensus around the threat of a Chinese invasion of Taiwan could create a sort of "self-fulfilling prophecy."[28]

A second, related strategy of insulation involves congressional leaders buying into a more general partisan truce on national security issues. Rather than building bipartisan coalitions around individual pieces of legislation, party leaders could agree to leave certain national security issues out of the more corrosive aspects of partisan politics. For example, recognizing the dangers of politicizing of the defense establishment, political scientist Peter Feaver proposes that both parties reach an agreement "to treat the military as noncombatants in the culture wars."[29] A sort of "arms control agreement" between Republican and Democratic legislators could also help to remedy declining public confidence in the U.S. military.[30]

A disadvantage of these tit-for-tat strategies is that they may be hard to maintain. In a contemporary era of congressional polarization, parties exercise less control over their more extreme wings. Legislators at the ideological extremes cultivate their identity around opposing the other party. Extreme partisans have more incentives to "go negative" on social media, to grandstand in Congress, or to otherwise vocally oppose the other party's foreign policies.[31] It is unclear how much congressional leaders will be able to induce legislators on the far right or the far left to recommit to a partisan truce in defense and security policy.

A third insulation strategy is to limit the public visibility of important foreign policy debates. Chapter 4 emphasized that, in a highly polarized context, spotlighting foreign policy issues increases the likelihood that they will

26. Nerkar 2021; Sarlin and Kapur 2021.
27. Myrick, Eng, and Weinberg 2022.
28. Weiss 2023.
29. Feaver 2023a.
30. Feaver 2023b, 2023a.
31. Yu, Wojcieszak, and Casas 2024.

be absorbed into the partisan divide. This idea is consistent with the work of American politics scholars who show that, as politics has become more polarized and zero sum, out-party legislators tend to oppose issues championed by the president.[32]

Presidents often campaign directly to the American people to pressure Congress to support their policies. This strategy, known as "going public," helps leaders rally support for their preferred policy."[33] However, in a polarized era, some researchers argue that democratic leaders may instead benefit by "staying private."[34] For example, political scientist George Edwards argues that, in contemporary politics, public appeals are more likely to induce backlash and increase polarization. Edwards explains that quiet negotiations—such as those conducted between the Clinton administration and Congress around the federal budget in 1990 and 1993—are more likely to lead to bipartisan compromise.

In foreign affairs, staying private could be advantageous during tenuous international negotiations. Many international agreements are conducted behind closed doors out of concern that domestic constituents might spoil a negotiation before an agreement is reached.[35] The benefits to staying private were emphasized in interviews with senior government officials described in chapter 5. Interviewees stressed that legislators approached problem-solving in a more thoughtful and bipartisan way when they were in classified hearings about the Iran nuclear deal rather than public hearings.[36] Similarly, individuals with higher public profiles find it more challenging to reach across the aisle. Congressional staffers, for example, are afforded much more opportunity for bipartisan cooperation than their respective legislators.[37] Conducting foreign policy debates behind closed doors could, in theory, reduce public attention and polarization. But, the obvious downside of staying private is that it is clearly in tension with democratic principles. Democratic publics tend to be averse to secret negotiations in international politics, especially if they are perceived to be conducted in private or in secret in order to avoid domestic criticism.[38] Keeping important government decisions out of public view could

32. Lee 2008, 2009.
33. Kernell 2006.
34. Edwards 2015.
35. Stastavage 2004.
36. Author interview with senior White House official (August 14, 2018).
37. Author interview with White House official (August 7, 2018).
38. Myrick 2024.

also undermine other aspects of liberal democracy related to transparency, accountability, and government oversight.

A fourth and final set of insulation strategies focus on reforming the foreign policy bureaucracy. The logic here is that, while congressional polarization may be too far gone to remedy, more could be done to bolster the nonpartisan character of foreign policy institutions and make them less vulnerable to politicization. Proposals in this vein vary widely. At the State Department, for example, proposed reforms focus on strengthening and empowering the foreign service as a means to retain the nonpartisan character of the institution. These include calls to increase the attractiveness of the foreign service as a career path and improve retention of Foreign Service Officers through enhanced job training and fellowship opportunities, increased flexibility, and better opportunities for spousal employment.[39] In the intelligence community, proposed reforms focus on improving processes of intelligence collection and analysis in order to "guard against politicization."[40] Given the conflicting incentives of politicians and intelligence analysts, politicization of the intelligence community has been a persistent concern since its establishment.[41] However, these political pressures are exacerbated in a highly polarized era. Concerns about politicization are also pervasive in the defense establishment. To maintain the integrity and nonpartisan character of the U.S. military, researchers call for greater public outreach and education about civil–military relations as well as improved integration of civilian perspectives into the military.[42] While such proposals may not address polarization as a whole, they could reduce the consequences of heightened partisanship in areas of the foreign policy bureaucracy.

7.3.2 Strategies to Address Polarization among Political Officials

Rather than trying to insulate foreign affairs from partisan politics, an alternative set of strategies would tackle the root causes of congressional polarization. Addressing congressional polarization could strengthen horizontal constraints on democratic leaders, more effectively checking executive power. Naturally, this is a tall order. While an exhaustive list of proposals for reducing congressional polarization is beyond the scope of this book, this chapter

39. Zeya and Finer 2020.
40. Gates 1992.
41. Jervis 2010a.
42. Lee and Margulies 2023; Schake and Mattis 2016.

summarizes key proposals made by political scientists and popular commentators. I first review five conventional proposals that emphasize institutional reform: overhauling the electoral system, reforming the primary system, introducing congressional term limits, changing how congressional districts are drawn, and reducing money in politics. All of these proposals could, in theory, improve the quality of democratic governance. However, evidence from political scientists suggests that none of them would be a silver bullet in reducing polarization. I then describe four less conventional solutions that emphasize bottom-up reforms: making political office more attractive, increasing voter engagement, strengthening political parties, and empowering entrepreneurial policymakers. Some of these strategies appear to be promising, but evidence on their efficacy is limited.

Beginning with the most dramatic institutional change, a common proposal to reduce congressional polarization is to overhaul the U.S. electoral system. Political scientist Lee Drutman argues, "Our system of single-member plurality-winner congressional districts has accelerated polarization, made most voters irrelevant, and ratcheted up negative partisanship."[43] Drutman, alongside many others, proposes to move to a proportional representation (PR) system in which legislative seats are allocated based on the number of votes each political party receives. The logic is that a PR system may make third parties more viable, reducing the zero-sum, two-party nature of congressional elections and—as a consequence—overall levels of congressional polarization. PR systems could also improve the quality of democratic representation by allowing individuals to vote for parties that more accurately reflect their political beliefs. Setting aside questions about the feasibility of moving to a PR system, it is not clear that this change would inherently moderate politics. As discussed later in this chapter (and evidenced by many multiparty democracies), PR systems are also subject to polarization. In some cases, they have enabled the creation of extremist parties on the far left and far right. Far-right parties that emerged in PR systems in Western Europe—which have risen and fallen in their popularity over time—are prominent examples.[44]

A second major set of proposals to reduce congressional polarization comes from reforms to the primary system. In the United States, voters select candidates from different parties to run for Congress in the general election.

---

43. Drutman 2017.
44. Golder 2016; Kitschelt 1997; Mudde 2007; Norris 2005.

States organize their primary elections in different ways, but an overarching concern is that voters in primary elections are more partisan and ideologically driven than voters in general elections.[45] As a consequence, the primary system could disadvantage moderate candidates relative to ideologically extreme candidates. Reforms to primary systems could address this problem. One proposal is to move to open primaries in which any voter can participate. Currently, some states hold closed primaries in which only voters registered to the relevant political party can participate. An alternative proposal, following states like California and Louisiana, is for states to hold "jungle primaries" in which those with the most votes advance to the general election irrespective of political party. If open primaries and jungle primaries increase voter participation, some research suggests more moderate legislators would be elected.[46]

Primary reforms are expected to reduce polarization in theory. But evidence that they would result in more moderate legislators is mixed.[47] On average, candidates selected in open primary systems do not appear to be more moderate than candidates selected in closed primary systems.[48] Moreover, reforms to the primary system, including the introduction of primary elections, are not associated with significant changes in congressional polarization.[49]

A third proposal to reduce congressional polarization is to impose term limits on legislators. The argument is that, if legislators' terms were limited, they would be more responsive to their constituents rather than to their political party.[50] Political scientists, however, point out that the opposite relationship might be true. Long-time incumbent politicians with widespread name recognition have more autonomy to deviate from the party line. Well-known legislators like Republican Senator Mitt Romney from Utah, Republican Senator John McCain from Arizona, and Democratic Senator Joe Manchin from West Virginia, who maintained high popularity with their respective constituencies, were better positioned to maneuver independently in Congress and criticize their own party. By contrast, junior legislators have incentives to adhere to the

45. Brady, Han, and Pope 2007; Jacobson 2004; Fenno 1978.
46. Grose 2020.
47. Drutman 2021.
48. McGhee et al. 2014.
49. Hirano et al. 2010; Hirano and Snyder 2019.
50. See, e.g., arguments made by supporters of term limits characterized by a report from the Congressional Research Service (2023).

party line. Evidence from state legislatures supports this pattern. Within states, the introduction of legislative term limits increased polarization and made parties more influential.[51] Extrapolating from these results suggests that introducing congressional term limits may not have the intended effect of curbing partisan politics.

A fourth proposal to reduce congressional polarization is to reform processes of drawing legislative districts. Redistricting processes are controlled by individual states. When the process is dominated by one political party, politicians might engage in gerrymandering, or changing the boundaries of districts to their own party's advantage. Gerrymandering could entrench some legislators in safe seats and reduce the competitiveness of congressional elections.[52] Incumbent legislators elected from solidly Republican or Democratic districts may be concerned about facing primary challengers who are more extreme members of their own party, giving them little incentive to reach across the aisle in Congress.

One proposed solution, following states like Virginia and Colorado, is to carry out redistricting processes using independent, nonpartisan commissions. There are many good reasons to make redistricting less partisan, but we should again be skeptical that such reforms alone would resolve congressional polarization. For one, the political geography in the United States is such that Democrats and Republicans are increasingly physically separated.[53] This means that nonpartisan redistricting processes still could result in many noncompetitive districts.[54] Researchers also show that a legislator's ideology is not strongly correlated with the electoral competitiveness of their district.[55] Most importantly, addressing the partisan nature of redistricting would solely affect outcomes in the House of Representatives. The Senate, however, has experienced similar increases in polarization.[56]

A final set of conventional proposals to reduce congressional polarization address money in American politics. A number of landmark Supreme Court decisions about campaign finance laws exacerbated concerns about donor

51. Olsen and Rogowski 2020.
52. McGann et al. 2016.
53. Bishop 2008; Rodden 2019.
54. Chen and Rodden 2013; Henderson, Hamel, and Goldzimer 2018; McCarty, Poole, and Rosenthal 2009.
55. Brunnell and Grofman 2008.
56. See, for example, standard measures of polarization in the US House and Senate constructed based on roll call voting (Lewis et al. 2019).

influence in electoral politics. Among these was the *Citizens United* decision in 2010,[57] which led to the proliferation of so-called super PACS: large, well-funded political action committees that are formally independent but informally champion a particular issue, candidate, or party. Super PACs are often funded by large donors, the identity of whom can remain concealed. Because many of these donors are perceived to have an ideological agenda, critics of the *Citizens United* decision argue that curbing the influence of super PACS will reduce polarization by preventing ideologues from shaping congressional elections.

Excessive donor influence in politics likely has negative impacts on democratic accountability. Studies show, for example, that super PAC spending increases perceptions of corruption and decreases public trust in government.[58] But, again, many political scientists are dubious of claims that campaign finance reforms would substantially impact congressional polarization. This is because, on average, larger donors are actually more ideologically moderate than smaller donors.[59] Reforms limiting the influence of large donors are unlikely to resolve polarization.

Beyond these institutional reforms, some political scientists propose more unconventional bottom-up solutions to the problem of congressional polarization. One set of strategies involves making political office more attractive to moderate candidates. Research suggests that American voters prefer more moderate candidates over extremist ones.[60] This implies that congressional polarization is a supply-side rather than a demand-side problem: the United States has a shortage of moderate aspiring politicians who want to run for office. In *Who Wants to Run?*, political scientist Andrew Hall argues that increasing congressional salaries and implementing other reforms to make holding political office more attractive could draw more professionalized, moderate candidates.[61]

In addition to making political office more attractive, others believe that making voting more attractive to the American electorate can moderate politics. In systems where voter engagement is high or voting is compulsory, politicians may be less focused on strategies that mobilize their political base

57. Citizens United v. Federal Election Commission, 558 U.S. 310 (2010).
58. Brennan Center for Justice 2012.
59. Bonica et al. 2013.
60. Hall and Thompson 2018.
61. Hall 2019.

to increase turnout and more focused on persuading members of the opposite party to support their candidacy. If voters are more engaged in politics overall, candidates may have incentives to tailor messaging to a median voter in the electorate. Once in office, legislators might also hear more from a more representative cross section of their constituency rather than only from a subset of extreme voices.[62]

A third unconventional proposal to reduce congressional polarization involves, perhaps counterintuitively, strengthening the political parties themselves. The argument is that a combination of strong partisanship and weak parties makes American politics vulnerable to capture by extreme politicians. Reforms to increase the influence of senior party leaders or the organizational structure of the party may moderate politics.[63] For example, political scientists Raymond La Raja and Brian Schaffner explain that if campaign finance contributions went directly to political parties rather than to individual candidates, this would reduce extremist voices.[64] The downside of such a strategy is that it could be difficult to sell to American voters. Further strengthening political parties in a polarized era may seem unappealing to those who are already frustrated by the two dominant political parties.

Finally, still others advocate for bottom-up solutions to congressional polarization that focus less on structural problems and more on the role of entrepreneurial policymakers. These strategies emphasize increasing the visibility of moderate legislators and building cross-partisan interpersonal relationships in Congress. One contributor to congressional polarization may be the fact that legislators today tend to only spend a few days per week in Washington, making it difficult to create and sustain friendships across the aisle. In an essay about reforming the U.S. House of Representatives, former Congressman Keith Rothfus of Pennsylvania wrote, "The frequency of these long weekends encourages members to spend time apart from one another, which makes it difficult for them to build the kinds of personal connections that grease the skids of the legislative process. This contributes to the trouble rank-and-file members have in building coalitions to pursue objectives that may not be consistent with what their party leadership is prioritizing."[65]

62. Neblo, Brennan, and Quesenbery 2022.
63. McCarty 2015.
64. La Raja and Schaffner 2015.
65. Rothfus 2021.

In interviews conducted for this book, government officials noted that political scientists tend to underestimate the importance of individual politicians in building bipartisan consensus. Staff members who worked on the Senate Foreign Relations Committee described how individual senators were responsible for creating norms of bipartisanship. For example, when I asked one interviewee what was driving the increasing polarization in foreign affairs that they observed in Congress, they responded: "My impression is that a lot of this stuff is driven by individuals. You can drive a lot as an entrepreneur [in Congress]... I think that my grandfather's generation had a very different view of America and cooperation based on their experiences of their lives. Their politicians from that generation embodied that perspective. I think we are further and further away from that generation. We're not all in it together. We don't have a sense of shared sacrifice. Over time, we've had a deterioration of these values. I think you're seeing that play out in politics."[66]

This discussion highlights a large and growing literature on ways to reduce ideological polarization in Congress, but a lack of consensus over which reforms are likely to be effective and feasible. Many ideas that are popular in public discourse—such as reforming the primary system or introducing legislative term limits—are unlikely to reduce partisan polarization. To be clear, these reforms may have other important benefits, but the evidence that they will decrease polarization in government is mixed at best. There may be promise in more unconventional solutions like making higher office more attractive or strengthening party control, but such proposals have yet to be directly tested.

7.3.3 Strategies to Address Polarization among the American Public

A final bucket of strategies to reduce polarization in foreign policy would tackle root causes of affective polarization among the American public. The logic is that, if the public was not so highly polarized, this might prevent the erosion of vertical constraints and give leaders fewer incentives to appeal to the extremes. Politicians who did not have to appease an affectively polarized public may anticipate greater rewards for pursuing bipartisan foreign policies. Much like reducing congressional polarization, addressing affective polarization among the American public is hard. Many solutions to affective polarization proposed by political scientists, psychologists, and sociologists

---

66. Author interview with Democratic congressional senior staff member (August 22, 2018).

rely on interpersonal interventions that expose partisans to other perspectives or correct misperceptions of the opposite party.[67]

Scholarship on intergroup contact theory explains how meaningful and prolonged engagement with members of an outgroup can reduce hostility between social groups.[68] Applications of contact theory to reducing political polarization imply that sustained contact between Republicans and Democrats decreases antipathy toward the opposite party. Subsequent studies focus on cultivating cross-party dialogue[69] or engaging in perspective-taking. The idea behind perspective-taking is to increase empathy and reduce hostility toward social outgroups by "walking in their shoes."[70] In an innovative field experiment conducted by political scientists Joshua Kalla and David Broockman, party activists engaged in "perspective-getting," taking part in in-depth conversations with prospective voters about salient political issues. Party activists who participated in the campaign reported lower levels of hostility toward members of the opposite party after hearing their perspectives.[71]

A related strategy is to correct misperceptions of the opposite party. Misperceptions, or false beliefs about politics, are pervasive in contemporary American politics.[72] One potential source of affective polarization is misunderstanding the attitudes and preferences of the opposite party. Partisans tend to see members of the opposite party as more ideologically extreme than they actually are. Correcting such misperceptions could, in theory, decrease animosity toward the out-party,[73] although evidence for the effectiveness of such corrections from public opinion surveys is mixed.[74]

To examine the promise of strategies for reducing partisan animosity, in 2022, the Polarization and Social Change Lab at Stanford University led an innovative coordinated test of twenty-five interventions embedded in public opinion surveys.[75] Many of the interventions were successful in reducing affective polarization. The two strategies that the researchers found to be

---

67. See, e.g., Hartman et al. 2022 for a review of interventions designed to reduce partisan hostility.
68. See, e.g., Allport 1954; Pettigrew 1998.
69. Levendusky and Stecula 2021; Levendusky 2023.
70. See, e.g., Adida, Lo, and Platas 2018; Broockman and Kalla 2016; Galinsky and Moskowitz 2000; Simonovits, Kezdi, and Kardos 2018.
71. Kalla and Broockman 2023.
72. Nyhan 2020.
73. Druckman et al. 2022.
74. Dias et al. 2024; Druckman 2023.
75. Voelkel et al. 2022.

the most effective in decreasing animosity toward the opposite party were "highlighting relatable, sympathetic individuals with different political beliefs" and "highlighting common cross-party identities."[76]

Although strategies that deal with interpersonal relationships are promising, they are difficult to scale. Other strategies for reducing affective polarization tackle issues related to contemporary media. Many scholars see a partisan fragmented media landscape as a major driver of polarization among the American public. Both partisan media programming and the growth of cable news, as well as the rise of digital media, facilitate a partisan sorting and the creation of so-called echo chambers that augment social polarization.[77] Proposed solutions often rely on encouraging media outlets, and social media platforms in particular, to play a more active role in reducing polarization. Social media companies could systematically expose users to alternative viewpoints, correct misperceptions of the opposite party, or facilitate better cross-partisan conversations.[78] The demonstrated efficacy of these strategies, however, is mixed.[79] In part, this is because many users are not blindly driven by social media algorithms to partisan content but rather actively select into more partisan media.[80] Other proposed solutions would involve developing entirely new social media platforms. In *Breaking the Social Media Prism*, sociologist Chris Bail discusses how to design alternative platforms that would generate higher quality political discussion from users.[81] Bail and other researchers at the Polarization Lab at Duke University developed a mobile chat platform that allowed users to engage in cross-partisan conversations about political issues anonymously, which ultimately decreased observed levels of political polarization.[82]

A final set of strategies to reduce affective polarization relies on heightening social identities other than partisan identity. In particular, increasing the salience of national identity relative to partisan identity could indirectly reduce affective polarization.[83] Following from this logic, a

---

76. Voelkel et al. 2022, 11.

77. Levendusky 2013; Lelkes, Sood, and Iyengar 2017; Sunstein 2009; Törnberg 2022. See, also, evidence for partisan "curation bubbles" on social media from Green et al. 2025.

78. Overgaard and Woolley 2022.

79. See, e.g., Guess et al. 2023b, 2023a, Nyhan et al. 2023.

80. See, e.g., Robertson et al. 2023; Tyler, Grimmer, and Iyengar 2022.

81. Bail 2021.

82. Combs et al. 2023.

83. Levendusky 2017.

common argument is that one way to generate partisan unity in the United States is to amplify a threat from a foreign adversary. When Americans conceptualize themselves as united against a common enemy—such as Nazi Germany during World War II or the Soviet Union during the Cold War—the expectation is that they will be less internally divided. Some commentators, for instance, speculate that the rise of China may pose an opportunity for reducing the partisan divide in American politics.[84]

Previous research, however, casts doubt on claims that external threats are inherently unifying. A study of security crises involving the United States that were initiated by foreign adversaries found that responses to crises tend to reflect the domestic political environment in which they arose.[85] New security threats introduced in partisan contexts were unlikely to be unifying and, in fact, could be more divisive when championed by polarizing figures. Naturally, there are exceptions. Very direct security threats to the American homeland—such as the terror attacks on September 11, 2001, that resulted in the deaths of close to 3,000 people—are likely to generate surges of national unity. However, it seems very unwise for Americans to wish for direct attacks on American soil or to seek to amplify foreign threats simply to resolve internal political problems.

An alternative approach would heighten national unity independent of foreign threat. One public opinion study, for example, found that national independence celebrations around the Fourth of July increase the public's sense of American identity and reduce affective polarization.[86] Following from this line of research, ambitious proposals seek other ways to heighten American identity at scale. For example, political scientist Lilliana Mason, an expert on affective polarization, endorses a compulsory national service requirement for graduating high school students that would deepen participants' sense of American identity.[87]

Clearly no one solution is a panacea for reducing polarization in foreign policy or more generally among politicians or the American public. Many conventional proposals that deal with overhauling institutions are both impractical and unlikely to reduce polarization. Some interpersonal interventions appear more promising, but they are difficult to scale and the

84. Brooks 2019.
85. Myrick 2021.
86. Levendusky 2017.
87. Mason 2019.

connections to foreign policy are somewhat tenuous. Overall, there is a need for more creative thinking and more compelling empirical evidence to identify workable solutions that would either prevent partisan conflict from extending into foreign affairs or tackle the roots of partisan polarization.

7.4 Extensions beyond the American Context

Most of the empirical evidence in this book focused on polarization and foreign policy in the American political context. As discussed in chapter 1, the primary reason for focusing on a single case was to better illustrate how polarization interacts with foreign policymaking processes, which vary widely across countries. However, the United States is unique in many ways, including its electoral system, media environment, political geography, and role in international politics. Extrapolating the results presented in this book to other contexts risks exacerbating a well-established American bias in the study of international relations theory.[88]

But, as chapter 3 emphasized, polarization is not a challenge unique to the United States. Many of the negative consequences of polarization for the democratic advantages identified in this book could hold in other highly polarized democracies. The salience of these negative consequences may be dampened or increased by other country-level characteristics. It is difficult to draw generalizable conclusions without careful study of the causes and consequences of polarization within a given a country, as well as consideration of the specific institutions and norms involved in the foreign policymaking process.

Following from this line of inquiry, perhaps the most natural extension of this project is to consider how the relationship between polarization and foreign policy outcomes is moderated by different systems of vertical and horizontal constraint. This section sketches out some preliminary intuitions about how basic institutional features of democracies may moderate the effects of polarization.

7.4.1 Variation in Electoral Systems

To explore variation in systems of vertical constraints, one starting point would be to consider how different electoral systems mitigate or exacerbate the negative impacts of polarization on foreign affairs. Electoral systems are the sets of rules that determine how elections are conducted and politicians are

---

88. See, e.g., Colgan 2019; Goh 2019; Levin and Trager 2019.

voted into office. While there are many types of electoral systems, the primary distinction is between majoritarian and PR systems. In majoritarian systems, candidates are elected with a plurality or majority of votes. In PR systems, seats in government are allocated based on the proportion of votes that parties receive in an election. Electoral rules can shape the type of party system that emerges within a country. French politician and political scientist Maurice Duverger famously observed that majoritarian systems with single-member districts tend to result in two-party systems.[89] PR systems, on the other hand, tend to result in multiparty systems.

It is not immediately clear how the impacts of polarization on foreign policy differ across majoritarian and PR systems. On the one hand, as discussed in chapter 2, much of the international relations literature on the democratic advantage hinges on a model of a majoritarian, two-party system competing over the median voter in the electorate. Regular electoral cycles in a two-party system are thought to facilitate foreign policy convergence by making political leaders accountable to the median voter.[90] In theory, this should moderate a party's policy positions. By contrast, a multiparty system includes parties with a wide array of political beliefs that represent specific constituencies. The heterogeneity of viewpoints across political parties could create large swings in foreign policy that arise from executive turnover. This logic would lead us to anticipate greater foreign policy volatility, on average, with party turnover in PR systems.

An initial wave of research about the relationship between electoral systems and party system polarization suggested that polarization is higher in countries with PR systems relative to countries with majoritarian systems.[91] However, other studies found mixed or no evidence for this relationship.[92] In large part, the findings in these studies are indeterminate because of the relatively small number of democracies that can be used to evaluate this claim.[93]

More recent research even suggests that majoritarian, two-party systems may be *more* prone to negative consequences that arise from polarization.

---

89. Duverger 1954.
90. Alesina 1988.
91. Dow 2011; Matakos, Troumpounis, and Xefteris 2016.
92. Ezrow 2008; Adams and Ezrow 2009.
93. See, e.g., characterization of the literature on electoral systems and polarization from Adams and Rexford (2018).

Political scientist Jonathan Rodden demonstrates that voters in multiparty, PR electoral systems perceive their out-parties as closer in ideological space than voters in two-party, majoritarian systems.[94] In majoritarian systems, new policy issues are quickly pulled into the partisan divide. Likewise, in *Citizenship in Hard Times*, Sara Wallace Goodman argues that threats to democracy that occur in majoritarian, two-party systems facilitate a zero-sum, "us versus them" dynamic that is less likely to materialize in a multiparty systems.[95] A possible implication of these findings is that the extension of partisan conflict into foreign affairs may be less likely to reinforce affective polarization in multiparty relative to two-party systems. As such, polarization in multiparty systems could have fewer damaging second-order consequences for foreign policy.

Overall, however, the existing literature is inconclusive about the broad relationship between electoral systems and polarization. In addition, these studies have overwhelmingly focused on right–left polarization. Even less is understood about how, if at all, electoral systems interact with polarization over foreign policy.

7.4.2 Variation in Systems of Government

A starting point to explore cross-national variation in systems of horizontal constraint is to consider how the relationship between polarization and foreign policy is moderated by the system of government. Specifically, whether a democratic government is a presidential system, a semi-presidential system, or a parliamentary system has implications for party discipline, executive autonomy, and the number of veto players involved in policymaking. Veto players are actors whose buy-in is necessary to make major policy changes.[96] On average, presidential systems tend to have more veto players than parliamentary systems.[97] In systems with more veto players, policymaking is more likely to be biased toward the status quo. With application to foreign policy, for instance, a higher number of veto players means that it may be harder to enter into international agreements.[98] This logic could imply that presidential systems

---

94. Rodden 2021.
95. Goodman 2022.
96. Tsebelis 2002.
97. Tsebelis 1995.
98. Oppermann and Brummer 2017.

are less susceptible to the foreign policy volatility that results from polarization and leader turnover.

However, this relationship is complicated by the fact that the number of veto players does not directly reflect the relative autonomy that executives have in foreign affairs. For example, while parliamentary systems have fewer veto players, leaders governing as part of a coalition may be constrained in foreign policy by a junior coalition partner.[99] And, while presidential systems tend to have more veto players, in some contexts presidents exert greater de facto control over foreign policy and can circumvent horizontal constraints on these issues.

The degree to which foreign policy is easy or difficult to change can also depend on institutional processes rather than the number of domestic veto players. As discussed in chapter 6, the treaty ratification process in the United States makes it hard to institutionalize international agreements without some degree of bipartisanship. Democratic governments with a less stringent treaty ratification process may not be as concerned about gridlock and the impact of polarization on their ability to make and keep international commitments.

Cross-national extensions of this book could generate testable hypotheses that explore variation in systems of vertical and horizontal constraint. Beyond systems of constraint, a great number of additional variables—such as the alignment of partisan cleavages with foreign policy preferences, the relative salience of foreign affairs in electoral politics, the role of coalition politics in foreign policymaking, the nature of national security institutions, and the country's threat environment—complicate the relationship between polarization and foreign policy. As the examples from this chapter illustrate, the predictions that arise from this exercise are not simple or straightforward. Extensions beyond American foreign policy could carefully consider how dynamics of polarization operate in other institutional contexts.

7.5 Conclusion

This book asked: How might partisan polarization affect international politics? It argued that extreme polarization has the potential to undermine different advantages that democracies have in foreign affairs relative to non-democracies. By eroding vertical and horizontal constraints on democratic leaders, polarization diminishes the advantages that democracies have in

99. Kaarbo 1996.

bargaining and negotiating international agreements. It can jeopardize the ability of democracies to make durable international commitments. And, it can make democratic foreign policy less stable and more unpredictable.

In the United States, while foreign affairs historically has been more insulated from partisan politics, partisan conflict steadily extends to certain areas of foreign policy. There are early indicators that polarization could, at minimum, hamper effective foreign policymaking and, at maximum, pose major national security challenges. Alongside growing domestic polarization, Americans have witnessed more instances of congressional gridlock, partisan obstruction of foreign policymaking, expansion of executive authority, and politicization of national security institutions. These trends could hinder the ability of the United States to negotiate effectively with adversaries and cooperate reliably with allies.

As this concluding chapter highlighted, many more questions arise from this book. Perhaps the most pressing next step is to extend this research beyond contemporary American politics to explore how polarization affects democratic advantages in other comparative contexts. One extension that follows directly from this project is to investigate how cross-national variation in vertical and horizontal constraints moderates the relationship between polarization and foreign policy. Other important sets of questions arise from probing the origins of polarization in American foreign policy and considering strategies to mitigate its negative effects. These extensions highlight exciting opportunities to integrate international relations theories with scholarship in the fields of comparative and American politics on partisan polarization, a phenomenon that both historically and presently poses critical challenges for democracies worldwide.

8

Appendix

THE ORIGINAL DATA and codebooks used to conduct the analyses in this book are available on the author's website: www.rachelmyrick.com

This appendix contains the following:

1. Description and coding notes for executive-term polarization dataset (chapter 3)
2. Description and coding notes for longitudinal data about U.S. public opinion on foreign affairs from the Chicago Council on Global Affairs (chapter 4)
3. Survey details and questionnaire for in-party/out-party survey (chapters 5 and 6)
4. Description and coding notes for data on partisanship of congressional rhetoric about international crises (chapter 5)
5. Details about Iran deal interviews with U.S. officials (chapter 5)
6. Description and coding notes for bilateral treaty data (chapter 6)
7. Survey details and questionnaire for UK survey on U.S. polarization (chapter 6)

8.1 Description and Coding Notes for Executive-Term Polarization Dataset (Chapter 3)

DESCRIPTION OF DATASET

The dataset created for chapter 3 identifies the political party of the executive and the main opposition party, as well as the popular vote for both parties.[1] The core dataset is based on a crosswalk of the Archigos version 4.1 data on

---

1. I thank Daniel Billings for research assistance in creating this dataset.

leaders[2] and data from the Manifesto Project (MARPOR)[3] which collects political party manifestos. This data first identifies the political party (and corresponding party platform) of the leader and the primary opposition party. To code the opposition party, the MARPOR dataset was cross-referenced with the Database of Political Institutions (DPI).[4] Vote totals primarily come from the MARPOR dataset as well as the IFES (International Foundation for Electoral Systems) ElectionGuide.[5] Additional sources are noted in the dataset. The unit of analysis for the data is the executive term. The sample is fifty-five democracies that appear in the MARPOR dataset from 1945 to 2020.

CODING PROCESS

- Begin with the Archigos dataset on political leaders. For each leader, create a separate dataset entry for each term they served in office, such that the unit of analysis is the "executive term." Retain leader codes from Archigos to match the dataset to leader-specific characteristics as needed.
- Use the DPI to determine the system of government (i.e., presidential, parliamentary) in each country.
- Identify the political party of the leader and match it to the corresponding party ID and election in the MARPOR dataset.
- Identify the main opposition party by cross-referencing the MARPOR dataset with the DPI. In presidential systems, the opposition party is the party of the runner-up in the final round of the presidential election. In parliamentary systems, the opposition party is the party with the most votes that is not part of the governing coalition. Match the opposition party to the corresponding party ID and election in the MARPOR datasets.
- Record vote totals for the executive and opposition parties. For most parliamentary elections, the primary resource consulted was the MARPOR datasets. For most presidential elections, the primary resource consulted was the IFES ElectionGuide. In presidential

2. Goemans, Gleditsch, and Chiozza 2009.
3. Lehmann et al. 2018.
4. Scartascini, Cruz, and Keefer 2021.
5. International Foundation for Electoral Systems 2022.

systems with run-off elections, the vote totals are from the second round/run-off election. Additional sources were consulted as needed.
- Use the party ID and corresponding election in the MARPOR dataset to match executive and opposition parties to policy positions in the MARPOR data.
- Construct right–left and hawk–dove scores for parties using the procedure described in chapter 3.
- Construct indicators for extreme right–left and hawk–dove polarization using scores at the ninetieth percentile or above as described in chapter 3.

This dataset differs in structure from the Archigos dataset in a few ways:

- New observations are added when the leader runs for reelection. In the Archigos data, U.S. President Barack Obama would have one entry since he served two consecutive presidential terms. In the executive-term dataset, there would be two entries for each of his two terms as president (USA-2009 and USA-2013).
- Entries for new executives that were not directly elected are matched with their party platform from the previous election.
- If a leader is appointed midway through a term because of resignation or death of the previous executive, but the executive party or coalition does not change, a new observation is not created until the next election.
- For executive elections occurring in January through May, the starting year of the executive term is coded as the election year. For executive elections occurring in June through December, the starting year of the executive term is coded as one year after the election.

REASONS FOR MANUALLY CODING DATA

- The MARPOR dataset codes political parties within legislatures, but executives may be elected separately.
- A change in leader/executive does not necessarily mean a change in executive party.
- The same leader from the same party can have a party platform that changes over time.
- The party of the executive is not always the party with the most votes.

- The MARPOR dataset does not directly code the opposition party, and the party of the opposition is not always the party with the second-most votes. For example, a coalition could be formed between parties with the first- and second-most votes. Therefore, it is necessary to consult other sources to determine the political party of the opposition. The primary resource consulted for this coding was the DPI.
- Some countries have rotating rather than elected executives (e.g., Bosnia, Switzerland). These have been coded two ways in the dataset: as the actual executive/leader ($alt\_coding = 1$) and as the party with the plurality in the legislature ($alt\_coding = 2$). The second coding—the political party with the plurality in the legislature—is the default used in analyses.
- The vote totals from the MARPOR dataset often reflect legislative rather than presidential elections.
- It is necessary to use the data from the MARPOR dataset because the DPI does not contain coding for foreign policy positions.

CAVEATS FOR DATA USAGE

- This dataset was designed for thinking about the executive and opposition party's foreign policy position. It may not be appropriate for application to different domestic policy issues. For example, in systems where there is both a president and prime minister, but the president is responsible for foreign affairs, the party of the executive is the party of the president.
- This dataset only codes the party of the executive, so we should be wary of interpreting the ideology of coalition governments. In many cases, however, the MARPOR data includes the platform for the coalition (when available) instead of the platform for party, such that the policy positions reflect the coalition as a whole.
- When executive is rotating (e.g., Bosnia), consider using alternative codings of "executive" and "opposition" for robustness.
- If executive elections are separate from legislative elections, party platforms may or may not be available for the same executive year (e.g., "year" does not always equal "cmp_year"). In this case, the party platform is the most recent platform available from the same party of the executive. The year corresponding to the party platform is preserved in the variable cmp_year.

- Different sources may disagree on the opposition party. For example, occasionally the DPI coding reports the opposition party as the party with the second-most votes. However, the coding rule used in this dataset is that the opposition party is the party with the second-most votes *not in the governing coalition*.
- Different sources may disagree on the vote totals. For example, in cases where there is a run-off election between the top two presidential candidates, sometimes these vote totals are not reported in the MARPOR data. The dataset contains case notes that describe the source of the vote totals. In general, researchers should exercise caution when using vote totals from this data.
- Much of this data was manually entered, and there may be errors based on human coding. Please report errors you find to the author, who can update the dataset. Thank you!

8.2 Description and Coding Notes for Longitudinal Data about U.S. Public Opinion on Foreign Affairs from the Chicago Council on Global Affairs (Chapter 4)

The longitudinal data on public opinion about U.S. foreign policy begins with the 2022 Chicago Council Survey questionnaire and matches variables from the 2022 survey to previous surveys from 1998 to 2021.[6] While the CCGA surveys were first run in 1974, the dataset compiled for this book begins in 1998, because it is the first year for which details about variables are documented in publicly available codebooks. It also is a useful starting point to characterize polarization over foreign policy within the twenty-first century. The years in which CCGA surveys were conducted in this period are: 1998, 2002, 2004, 2006, 2010, 2012, 2014, 2015, 2016, 2017, 2018, 2019, 2020, 2021, 2022. All data from the Chicago Council surveys is available through their website at www.globalaffairs.org.

The longitudinal dataset compiled for this study uses common variable names to standardize across the surveys. A codebook of variable names is available in the replication files for this book. Note that, across CCGA surveys, the language of some of the survey questions slightly changes. Below is a list of relevant discrepancies in question wording across the 1998–2022 surveys. All variables are recoded as described in the codebook.

---

6. I thank Xiaoxiao Li for research assistance in collecting this data.

1. 2022 (Q5/8a). In surveys from 1998 to 2006, questions used "global warming" rather than "climate change."
2. 2022 (Q5/21). In the 1998 and 2002 survey (q530a1), questions used "Military power of Russia" rather than "Russia's territorial ambitions."
3. 2022 (Q5/45). From 1998 to 2010, surveys asked about "The development of China as a world power" rather than "China's territorial ambitions."
4. 2022 (Q1005). Previous surveys in 1998, 2002, and 2006 included fewer categories than the 2022 ideology question.
5. 2022 (QPPA1648). Previous surveys offered fewer categories for religion and sometimes divided religious belief questions into multiple questions.
6. 2022 (Q30/1). In the 2021 survey, some respondents were presented with the term "attacked" rather than "invaded.
7. 2022 (Q30/2). In the 2021 survey, some respondents were presented with the term "attacked" rather than "invaded."
8. 2022 (Q30/13). In the 2021 survey, some respondents were presented with the term "attacks" rather than "invades."
9. 2022 (Q30/25). In the 2021 survey, the question wording was "counter terrorism in Africa" rather than "combat terrorist groups in Somalia".
10. 2022 (Q240/5). In the 2019 and 2015 surveys, this question mentioned the Iran nuclear deal.
11. 2022 (Q240/3). In the 2019 and 2015 surveys, this question mentioned the Iran nuclear deal.
12. 2022 (Q240A/6). In the 2019 and 2015 surveys, this question mentioned the Iran nuclear deal.
13. 2022 (Q240A/7). In the 2019 and 2015 surveys, this question mentioned the Iran nuclear deal.
14. 2022 (Q240A/8). In the 2019 and 2015 surveys, this question mentioned the Iran nuclear deal.
15. 2022 (Q8/3). In the 2014 and 2012 surveys, the questions added "that violate international law" after "placing sanctions on other countries."
16. 2022 (Q295). In the 2006 survey, the question asked about "global warming" instead of "climate change."
17. 2022 (Q1010). In the 1998 and 2004 surveys, "other" was not an option.

8.3 Survey Details and Questionnaire for In-Party/ Out-Party Survey (Chapters 5 and 6)

SURVEY DETAILS AND SAMPLE

The survey on partisanship and foreign policy attitudes described in chapter 5 and chapter 6 was fielded to 4,330 U.S. adults in August 2024, in anticipation of the 2024 presidential election between Democratic candidate Kamala Harris and Republican candidate Donald Trump. The survey was approved by the Duke University Institutional Review Board (protocol 2024-0536) and fielded online through Lucid Theorem. Lucid is a professional survey firm that maintains a marketplace used to recruit survey respondents. Lucid targets demographic quotas by age, sex, ethnicity, race, and region to match the population of adults living in the United States. The target and actual demographics of the sample drawn for this survey are displayed in Table 8.1.

TABLE 8.1. Targeted and actual demographic characteristics of pooled sample

Demographic	Target	Actual
Age (18–24)	0.13	0.14
Age (25–34)	0.20	0.18
Age (35–44)	0.20	0.18
Age (45–64)	0.33	0.34
Age (65+)	0.14	0.16
Male	0.49	0.48
Female	0.51	0.52
Hispanic	0.12	0.08
Black	0.12	0.12
White	0.68	0.70
Midwest	0.20	0.19
Northeast	0.20	0.20
South	0.34	0.37
West	0.26	0.24

SURVEY QUESTIONNAIRE

After reading a consent script and agreeing to participate in the survey, respondents first receive a basic screener question to decrease the likelihood of fraudulent responses. Incorrect responses are screened out before the questionnaire begins. Then, respondents are asked standard demographic questions, consistent with language from the American National Elections Studies.[7]

PART I: SCREENER AND DEMOGRAPHIC QUESTIONS

screener: *We are first confirming that you are a human who is reading these questions carefully. Do not click on your favorite sport. Instead, click on the third choice of the four options below in order to take this survey.*

- *Tennis*
- *Golf*
- *Soccer*
- *Football*

sex: *Are you male or female?*

- *Male*
- *Female*

age: *What is your age?*

race: *What racial or ethnic group best describes you?*

- *White*
- *Black or African American*
- *Hispanic or Latino*
- *Asian or Asian American*
- *Native American*
- *Middle Eastern*
- *Mixed Race*
- *Some other race* [Text Entry]

pid1: *Generally speaking, do you think of yourself as a . . .*

- *Republican*
- *Democrat*
- *Independent / Other*

pid2: [Display only if pid1=="Democrat" or "Republican"] *Would you call yourself a . . .*

---

7. American National Election Studies 2020.

- *Strong [Republican/Democrat]*
- *Not very strong [Republican/Democrat]*

pid2: [Display only if pid1=="Independent / Other"] *Do you think of yourself as closer to the . . .*

- *Republican Party*
- *Democratic Party*
- *Neither party*

ideo: *In general, do you think of yourself as . . .*

- *Extremely liberal*
- *Liberal*
- *Slightly liberal*
- *Moderate, middle of the road*
- *Slightly conservative*
- *Extremely conservative*

pres_approval: *Do you approve or disapprove of the way Joe Biden is handling his job as president?*

- *Disapprove Strongly*
- *Disapprove Somewhat*
- *Neither Approve nor Disapprove*
- *Approve Somewhat*
- *Approve Strongly*

vote_choice: *If you had to vote in the 2024 US presidential election tomorrow, which candidate would you vote for?*

- *Kamala Harris (Democrat)*
- *Donald Trump (Republican)*
- *Neither / I wouldn't vote*

affective: *We'd also like to get your feelings about some groups in American society. Rate the following groups between 0 and 100. Ratings from 50-100 degrees mean that you feel favorably toward the group; ratings from 0-50 degrees mean that you don't feel favorably toward the group and that you don't care too much for that group.*

- *Democrats*
- *Republicans*

PART II: CANDIDATE PRIME

Participants are asked to think through a hypothetical scenario in which one of the two presidential candidates wins the 2024 election. The presidential candidate is randomly assigned, and the same candidate appears throughout the rest of the survey.

prime_trump: *As you may know, the 2024 US presidential election is happening in November. Republican candidate and former president Donald Trump is running for president against Democratic candidate and current Vice President Kamala Harris. We want to understand what Americans expect will happen in foreign policy if Donald Trump wins the election. In a few sentences, tell us what kinds of things you would expect Donald Trump to do in foreign policy over the next few years if he wins the election.*

[OPEN TEXT]

OR

prime_harris: *As you may know, the 2024 US presidential election is happening in November. Democratic candidate and current Vice President Kamala Harris is running against Republican candidate and former president Donald Trump. We want to understand what Americans expect will happen in foreign policy if Kamala Harris wins the election. In a few sentences, tell us what kinds of things you would expect Kamala Harris to do in foreign policy over the next few years if she wins the election.*

[OPEN TEXT]

PART III: UNILATERAL ACTION EXPERIMENT

Respondents then consider different actions in foreign policy and select whether or not the president should need congressional approval to take each action. The analysis in chapter 6 focuses on this question.

unilateral_text: *There is a lot of discussion about what the president can do on their own and what they need approval from Congress for in order to do. In your opinion, if elected president, which of the following actions should [T1: Donald Trump / T2: Kamala Harris] be able to take without the approval of Congress?*

APPENDIX 291

unilateral_mil: Check all that apply.

- *Enter into a major international agreement*
- *Withdraw from a major international agreement*
- *Join a military alliance*
- *Leave a military alliance*
- *Join an international organization*
- *Leave an international organization*
- *None of these actions should require approval from Congress*

PART IV: CRISIS AND NEGOTIATION SCENARIOS

Participants next read and answer questions about two scenarios—one about a potential future crisis and one about a potential future negotiation—that involve foreign countries. The first scenario is about an international crisis. Respondents are randomly assigned to receive information about a crisis initiated either by Russia or China. The Russia crisis scenario reads:

Since Russia's invasion of Ukraine in 2022, the United States has been concerned that Russia may try to invade another country in Eastern Europe.

Consider the following hypothetical scenario: [T1: Donald Trump / T2: Kamala Harris] is elected President in 2024. During the administration, Russia launches a military attack on Estonia, a NATO member country in Eastern Europe.

crisis_russia_judge: *How likely or unlikely do you think it is that President [T1: Donald Trump / T2: Kamala Harris] would show good judgment in responding to this crisis?*

- *Very unlikely*
- *Somewhat unlikely*
- *Neither likely nor unlikely*
- *Somewhat likely*
- *Very likely*

[NEW SCREEN]

crisis_russia_policy: *Consider the following hypothetical scenario: [T1: Donald Trump / T2: Kamala Harris] is re-elected President in 2024. During the administration, Russia launches a military attack on Estonia, a NATO member country in Eastern Europe.*

In response, President [T1: Donald Trump / T2: Kamala Harris] decides to send more U.S. military troops to help Estonia.

In this scenario, would you approve or disapprove of President [T1: Donald Trump / T2: Kamala Harris] sending US military troops to Estonia?

- *Disapprove Strongly*
- *Disapprove Somewhat*
- *Neither Approve nor Disapprove*
- *Approve Somewhat*
- *Approve Strongly*

crisis_russia_opp: *Which of the following do you think [T1: Democrats / T2: Republicans] in Congress should do in response to [T1: Donald Trump's / T2: Kamala Harris's] actions?*

- *Express disapproval and also take actions to prevent the president from sending troops*
- *Express disapproval but not take any actions to prevent the president from sending troops*
- *Express approval but not take any actions to support the president in sending troops*
- *Express approval and also take actions to support the president in sending troops*
- *Do nothing*

The China crisis scenario reads:

crisis_china_judge: *Over the last several years, the United States has grown increasingly concerned that China may invade Taiwan.*

Consider the following hypothetical scenario: [T1: Donald Trump / T2: Kamala Harris] is re-elected President in 2024. During their administration, China launches a military attack against Taiwan in an attempt to reunify it with mainland China.

How likely or unlikely do you think it is that President [T1: Donald Trump / T2: Kamala Harris] would show good judgment in responding to this crisis?

- *Very unlikely*
- *Somewhat unlikely*

- *Neither likely nor unlikely*
- *Somewhat likely*
- *Very likely*

[NEW SCREEN]

crisis_china_policy: *Consider the following hypothetical scenario: [T1: Donald Trump / T2: Kamala Harris] is re-elected President in 2024. During their administration, China launches a military attack against Taiwan in an attempt to reunify it with mainland China.*

In response, President [T1: Donald Trump / T1: Kamala Harris] decides to send US military troops to help Taiwan.

In this scenario, would you approve or disapprove of President [T1: Donald Trump / T2: Kamala Harris] sending US military troops to Taiwan?

- *Disapprove Strongly*
- *Disapprove Somewhat*
- *Neither Approve nor Disapprove*
- *Approve Somewhat*
- *Approve Strongly*

crisis_china_opp: *Which of the following do you think [T1: Democrats / T2: Republicans] in Congress should do in response to [T1: Donald Trump's / T2: Kamala Harris's] actions?*

- *Express disapproval and also take actions to prevent the president from sending troops*
- *Express disapproval but not take any actions to prevent the president from sending troops*
- *Express approval but not take any actions to support the president in sending troops*
- *Express approval and also take actions to support the president in sending troops*
- *Do nothing*

Next, respondents will read and respond to a negotiation scenario. Only one of the two scenarios (about Iran or North Korea) is presented to each respondent. The Iran scenario reads:

nego_iran_judge: *Over the last several years, the United States government has considered negotiating with Iran over their nuclear weapons program. In 2015, the US signed a nuclear agreement with Iran but later withdrew from the agreement in 2018.*

Consider the following hypothetical scenario: [T1: Donald Trump / T2: Kamala Harris] is re-elected President in 2024. Their administration attempts to negotiate a new nuclear agreement with Iran.

How likely or unlikely do you think it is that President [T1: Donald Trump / T2: Kamala Harris] would negotiate an agreement with Iran that is good for the United States?

- *Very unlikely*
- *Somewhat unlikely*
- *Neither likely nor unlikely*
- *Somewhat likely*
- *Very likely*

nego_iran_policy: *In this scenario, would you approve or disapprove of President [T1: Donald Trump / T2: Kamala Harris] negotiating a new nuclear agreement with Iran?*

- *Disapprove Strongly*
- *Disapprove Somewhat*
- *Neither Approve nor Disapprove*
- *Approve Somewhat*
- *Approve Strongly*

nego_iran_opp: *Which of the following do you think [T1: Democrats / T2: Republicans] in Congress should do in response to [T1: Donald Trump's / T2: Kamala Harris's] actions?*

- *Express disapproval and also take actions to prevent the president from negotiating*
- *Express disapproval but not take any actions to prevent the president from negotiating*
- *Express approval but not take any actions to support the president in the negotiations*

- *Express approval and also take actions to support the president in the negotiations*
- *Do nothing*

The North Korea scenario reads:

nego_nk_judge: *Over the last several years, the United States government has considered negotiating with North Korea about their nuclear weapons program. The most recent round of negotiations between the US and North Korea occurred in 2019, but an agreement was not reached.*

Consider the following hypothetical scenario: [T1: Donald Trump / T2: Kamala Harris] is re-elected President in 2024. Their administration attempts to negotiate an agreement with North Korea about nuclear weapons.

How likely or unlikely do you think it is that President [T1: Donald Trump / T2: Kamala Harris] would negotiate an agreement with North Korea that is good for the United States?

- *Very unlikely*
- *Somewhat unlikely*
- *Neither likely nor unlikely*
- *Somewhat likely*
- *Very likely*

nego_nk_policy: *In this scenario, would you approve or disapprove of President [T1: Donald Trump / T2: Kamala Harris] restarting talks with North Korea about their nuclear weapons program?*

- *Disapprove Strongly*
- *Disapprove Somewhat*
- *Neither Approve nor Disapprove*
- *Approve Somewhat*
- *Approve Strongly*

nego_nk_opp: *Which of the following do you think [T1: Democrats / T2: Republicans] in Congress should do in response to [T1: Donald Trump's / T2: Kamala Harris's] actions?*

- *Express disapproval and also take actions to prevent the president from negotiating*

- *Express disapproval but not take any actions to prevent the president from negotiating*
- *Express approval but not take any actions to support the president in the negotiations*
- *Express approval and also take actions to support the president in the negotiations*
- *Do nothing*

[END OF SURVEY]

8.4 Description and Coding Notes for Data on Partisanship of Congressional Rhetoric about International Crises (Chapter 5)

This section of the appendix contains details about data collection for the partisanship of congressional speech data around international crises used in chapter 5.[8]

LIST OF INTERNATIONAL CRISES

To develop the dataset used in the analysis in chapter 5, I first identified a list of relevant crises involving the United States from the International Crisis Behavior dataset.[9] These crises are displayed in Table 8.2.

CLEANING SPEECHES

To measure polarization of congressional rhetoric around international crises, I closely adapt the method outlined by Andrew Peterson and Arthur Spirling,[10] who use the accuracy of machine learning classifiers as a proxy for polarization. In their application, Peterson and Spirling measure polarization of rhetoric between Labour and Conservative members of Parliament in British parliamentary debates.

The application in chapter 5 is to use machine learning algorithms to predict whether a randomly drawn speech about a given country is from a Republican or a Democratic legislator. Country-sessions in which there is higher predictive accuracy means it is easier to discern the party of a legislator from their speech, suggesting greater polarization. The measure of partisanship of

---

8. For additional information, please see Myrick 2021.
9. Brecher et al. 2017.
10. Peterson and Spirling 2018.

TABLE 8.2. List of international crises triggered by foreign countries involving the United States

Crisis no.	Crisis name	Triggering entity	Start date	Added
-1	USS MAINE EXPLOSION	Spain	1898-02-15	Yes
-2	BOXER REBELLION	China	1900-06-17	Yes
-3	UNRESTRICTED SUBMARINE	Germany	1917-01-31	Yes
59	PANAY INCIDENT	Japan	1937-12-12	No
88	PEARL HARBOR	Japan	1941-12-07	No
104	TRIESTE I	Yugoslavia	1945-05-02	No
108	AZERBAIJAN	Russia	1946-03-04	No
111	TURKISH STRAITS	Russia	1946-08-07	No
114	TRUMAN DOCTRINE	United Kingdom	1947-02-21	No
123	BERLIN BLOCKADE	Russia	1948-06-24	No
125	CHINA CIVIL WAR	China	1948-09-23	No
132	KOREAN WAR I	North Korea	1950-06-25	No
133	KOREAN WAR II	China	1950-10-31	No
140	KOREAN WAR III	North Korea	1953-04-16	No
144	GUATEMALA	Guatemala	1954-02-10	No
145	DIEN BIEN PHU	France	1954-03-20	No
146	TAIWAN STRAIT I	China	1954-09-03	No
152	SUEZ NATN.-WAR	Russia	1956-11-05	No
159	SYRIA/TURKEY CONFRNT.	Syria	1957-08-18	No
165	IRAQ/LEB. UPHEAVAL	Iraq	1958-07-14	No
166	TAIWAN STRAIT II	China	1958-08-23	No
168	BERLIN DEADLINE	Russia	1958-11-27	No
180	PATHET LAO OFFENSIVE	Thailand	1961-03-09	No
181	BAY OF PIGS	Cuba	1961-04-15	No
185	BERLIN WALL	Russia	1961-08-13	No
186	VIET CONG ATTACK	Vietnam	1961-09-18	No
193	NAM THA	Thailand	1962-05-06	No
196	CUBAN MISSILES	Russia	1962-10-16	No
206	PANAMA FLAG	Panama	1964-01-10	No
210	GULF OF TONKIN	Vietnam	1964-08-02	No
211	CONGO II	Congo—Kinshasa	1964-09-26	No
213	PLEIKU	Vietnam	1965-02-07	No
215	DOMINICAN INTERVENTN.	Dominican Republic	1965-04-24	No
222	SIX DAY WAR	Russia	1967-06-06	No
224	PUEBLO	North Korea	1968-01-22	No
225	TET OFFENSIVE	Vietnam	1968-02-27	No
230	VIETNAM SPRING OFF.	Vietnam	1969-02-22	No
233	EC-121 SPY PLANE	North Korea	1969-04-15	No
237	INVASION OF CAMBODIA	Vietnam	1970-04-21	No
238	BLACK SEPTEMBER	Jordan	1970-09-15	No
239	CIENFUEGOS SUB. BASE	Russia	1970-09-16	No
246	VIETNAM PORTS MINING	Vietnam	1972-03-30	No
249	CHRISTMAS BOMBING	Vietnam	1972-12-04	No

TABLE 8.2. (*continued*)

Crisis no.	Crisis name	Triggering entity	Start date	Added
255	OCTOBER-YOM KIPPUR WAR	Syria	1973-10-12	No
255	OCTOBER-YOM KIPPUR WAR	Egypt	1973-10-12	No
255	OCTOBER-YOM KIPPUR WAR	Israel	1973-10-12	No
259	MAYAGUEZ	Cambodia	1975-05-12	No
260	WAR IN ANGOLA	Angola	1975-09-01	No
274	POPLAR TREE	North Korea	1976-08-17	No
292	SHABA II	Angola	1978-05-14	No
292	SHABA II	Congo—Kinshasa	1978-05-14	No
303	AFGHANISTAN INVASION	Russia	1979-12-24	No
309	US HOSTAGES IN IRAN	Iran	1979-11-04	No
343	INVASION OF GRENADA	Grenada	1983-10-19	No
354	NICARAGUA MIG-21S	Russia	1984-11-06	No
363	GULF OF SYRTE II	Libya	1986-04-05	No
386	LIBYAN JETS	Libya	1988-12-21	No
391	INVASION OF PANAMA	Panama	1989-12-15	No
393	GULF WAR	Iraq	1990-10-30	No
408	N. KOREA NUCLEAR I	North Korea	1993-03-12	No
411	HAITI MIL. REGIME	Haiti	1994-07-17	No
412	IRAQ DEPLOY./KUWAIT	Iraq	1994-10-07	No
419	DESERT STRIKE	Iraq	1996-08-31	No
422	UNSCOM I	Iraq	1997-11-13	No
427	US EMBASSY BOMBINGS	Sudan	1998-08-07	No
427	US EMBASSY BOMBINGS	Afghanistan	1998-08-07	No
429	UNSCOM II	Iraq	1998-10-31	No
430	KOSOVO	Yugoslavia	1999-02-20	No
434	AFGHANISTAN/US	Afghanistan	2001-09-11	No
440	IRAQ REGIME CHANGE	Iraq	2003-01-13	No
441	N. KOREA NUCLEAR II	North Korea	2002-10-04	No
448	IRAN NUCLEAR II	Iran	2006-01-10	No
450	N. KOREA NUCLEAR III	North Korea	2006-05-05	No
459	N. KOREA NUCLEAR IV	North Korea	2009-03-11	No
464	LIBYAN CIVIL WAR	Libya	2011-02-22	No
469	N. KOREA NUCLEAR V	North Korea	2013-02-12	No
470	SYRIA CHEMICAL WEAPONS	Syria	2013-08-21	No
476	TURKEY–RUSSIA JET INCIDENT	Turkey	2015-11-24	No

speech around a given international crisis reflects the polarization of rhetoric about the country that initiated the crisis in that congressional session.

To implement this method, I use the digitized version of the *Congressional Record*.[11] I create a SQL database of congressional speeches in which any of the

---

11. Gentzkow, Shapiro, and Taddy 2018.

thirty countries that initiated international crises involving the U.S. are mentioned. I merge demographic and political information about each speaker into this database. I then take the following steps to clean the speeches:

1. Remove punctuation
2. Remove nonalphanumeric characters and numbers
3. Change to lowercase
4. Strip white space
5. Remove English stop words.[12] These are common words like "the," "she," and "is."
6. Remove procedural stop words for congressional speech.[13] These are words that appear frequently in congressional speeches like "chairman," "senator," and "adjourn."
7. Drop speeches that: (1) do not have an identifiable speaker from congressional speaker map, (2) are not from a Republican or Democrat, (3) are less than forty characters.
8. Drop country-sessions that do not have a minimum of fifty Republican and fifty Democratic speeches.

Following standard practice in computational text analysis, each speech is then treated as a "bag of words." This means that word order is discarded; each speech can be represented by a vector of terms and the number of time each term appears in the speech, normalized by how frequently the term appears across all speeches.[14] Vocabulary is fixed across all the speeches; words used infrequently (i.e., that do not appear in at least 200 unique speeches) are removed from the data.[15]

MEASURING POLARIZATION OF SPEECH

I segment the data by country-session (i.e., How polarized is speech about Iran in the 114th Congress?). Within each country-session from the 43rd Congress through the 114th Congress, I use a supervised machine learning method from Peterson and Spirling to predict the likelihood that a speech was given by a Republican or a Democrat. I run four different machine learning algorithms ("classifiers") and average over a stratified ten-fold cross-validation

12. Feinerer, Hornik, and Meyer 2008.
13. Gentzkow, Shapiro, and Taddy 2017
14. Jurafsky and Martin 2009; Grimmer and Stewart 2013.
15. Gentzkow, Shapiro, and Taddy 2017; Peterson and Spirling 2018.

for each. In stratified ten-fold cross-validation, speeches are randomly divided into ten equal subsamples or "folds." Within each fold, there are roughly the same number of Republican and Democratic speeches. Nine folds "train" the classifier and one fold "tests" how well the classifier predicts the party of the speaker. This process is repeated ten times, such that each fold serves as a test set once. The performance of each classifier is averaged over these ten test sets. For each session, speeches are inversely weighted by party, such that there are roughly equal numbers of Republican and Democratic speeches. The level of polarization within each session is proxied by the average predictive accuracy of the best performing algorithm. The machine learning algorithms are implemented using the Scikit-learn library in Python.[16]

The result is a country-session dataset that has a dependent variable: a measure of the predictive accuracy of the best performing classifier, which captures the level of polarization of rhetoric. Predictive accuracy theoretically ranges between 0.5 and 1, such that 0.5 indicates no distinction between Republican and Democratic speech (i.e., a 50–50 chance of accurately predicting the party of the speaker based on their speech), and 1 indicates perfect distinction. Country-sessions in which the average predictive accuracy of the classifier is closer to 1 are more rhetorically polarized relative to other country-sessions. The plot generated in chapter 5 only displays country-sessions in which an international crisis occurred. The predictive accuracy of the classifier for a given crisis reflects congressional speech about the country that triggered the crisis in the congressional session when the crisis occurred.

COMPARISON TO OTHER METHODS

There are many methods for measuring the partisanship of speech.[17] I use the methods from Peterson and Spirling for two reasons. First, in measuring the partisanship of speech, a supervised machine learning approach has greater construct validity than an unsupervised approach. As Goet summarizes, "In contrast to their unsupervised siblings, such supervised models attempt to identify which speakers use a vocabulary that is similar to speakers from one versus another party, ensuring that variation in word use is related to a stable construct."[18] Second, in contrast to parametric approaches like the approach used by Gentzkow, Shapiro, and Taddy, nonparametric approaches like the

16. Pedregosa et al. 2011.
17. See, e.g., Goet 2019
18. Goet 2019.

one employed by Peterson and Spirling are more easily interpretable and much less computationally intensive.

8.5 Details about Iran Deal Interviews with U.S. Officials (Chapter 5)

BACKGROUND

For the case illustration of the negotiation of the Iran nuclear deal in chapter 5, I conducted semistructured interviews with academic researchers, journalists, and policymakers that were involved in the negotiation of the deal or legislation related to its passage. The quotations in chapter 5 draw primarily on six interviews with senior government officials that were conducted on background to maintain anonymity and qualify for exempted review of this research from the Stanford University Institutional Review Board (protocol 45416). The interviews took place in Washington, D.C., in July and August 2018. Four of the six interviews were conducted in person, and two were conducted by telephone. Interviews lasted roughly thirty to sixty minutes.

To construct the sample, I began with five informal interviews with former officials who worked on subjects related to the JCPOA. These conversations helped me identify three sets of senior officials whose perspective I wanted to capture in subsequent in-person interviews in Washington, D.C. I interviewed two officials from each set for a total of six interviews. The first set were international-facing officials who were senior officials directly involved in the negotiation that interacted primarily with Iran and the other P5+1, but also regularly briefed or testified before Congress. The second set were domestic-facing officials who were senior members of the Obama administration and directly interacted with Capitol Hill on legislation related to the JCPOA. The third set were senior staff in the Senate Foreign Relations Committee—one senior Republican and one senior Democrat—that were outside the administration but worked on legislation related to the JCPOA.

INTERVIEW STRUCTURE

Each interview consisted of four parts:

1. *Background and context.* Questions about the nature of the role that the interviewee played in government during the JCPOA negotiation.
2. *Perceptions and information.* Questions about how the interviewee perceived other JCPOA stakeholders (e.g., how negotiators perceived

foreign counterparts and domestic opposition, how congressional staff perceived negotiators and Obama administration), and how they felt information flowed in the negotiation.
3. *Reactions to major events.* Questions about how the interviewee recollected and responded to a series of chronological events that occurred during the negotiation.
4. *Reflections on politicization of foreign policy.* Questions about the extent to which the interviewee felt U.S.–Iranian relations were partisan and/or the JCPOA negotiation was politicized. I also asked about their thoughts on the origins and effects of increasing polarization in U.S. foreign policy.

SAMPLE INTERVIEW SCRIPT (INTERVIEW WITH JCPOA NEGOTIATOR)

- Background and context
  - *I'm working on a project related to partisan polarization and international negotiation. One of the cases I'm focusing on specifically is the negotiation of the JCPOA. I'm particularly interested in the interplay between US domestic politics and ongoing international negotiations, so I wanted to ask you both some general questions about how these processes work and some more specific questions about your own experiences from mid-2014 through September 2015.*
  - *Can you walk me through your role in government during this time period, and what aspects of the negotiation you were working on?*
    * Follow up: *How did you get this role in government?*

- Perceptions and information
  - *In a major, multilateral negotiations like this one, to what extent are US negotiators actively thinking about what's happening simultaneously in domestic politics in response to the negotiation, or is that something that you sort of ignore or compartmentalize once you're at the negotiation table?*
  - *To what extent are your foreign counterparts paying attention to what's going on in US domestic politics in response to the negotiations? Are they watching that closely? Is that something that is brought up at the negotiating table or is that just sort of "politics as usual" in the US?*

- ◦ *Were there points at which your Iranian counterparts expressed doubts about that Congress would prevent the JCPOA from being implemented in the first place, or was that less of a concern?*
  - * Follow up: *Were there particular domestic events that fueled those doubts? Were those doubts legitimate?*
  - * Follow up: *How did you respond to those doubts?*
- ◦ *Can you walk me through how in practice this vertical integration works between domestic stakeholders in Congress all the way up to the negotiators in Vienna throughout the negotiation process? To what extent is Congress informed about the substance of the negotiations? How does this flow of information actually happen in practice?*
  - * Follow up: *What was similar or different from how information is transmitted to Congress in other international negotiations?*

- Reactions to major events
  - ◦ *I wanted to walk through some specific domestic events and get your perspective on the extent to which they were salient for your negotiating team and, if so, how they shaped your thinking and how you responded to them.*
  - ◦ **2014 Midterms**: *In the fall of 2014, Republicans made major gains in Congress, and in particular, took control of the Senate (and SFRC). To what extent did this shape any thinking about the ongoing negotiations, either within the US team or for your counterparts? Does this come up at all?*
  - ◦ **Netanyahu Speech**: *In early March, at the invitation of Speaker Boehner and Senator McConnell, Prime Minister Netanyahu comes to address Congress and heavily criticizes the negotiations. How do you and your counterparts in the negotiation respond to this?*
    - * Follow up: *What are the concerns and how, as negotiators, do you assuage them, if at all?*
  - ◦ **Cotton Letter**: *On March 9, 2015, Senator Cotton and 46 other Republicans send their open letter to the Iranian leaders. How do you and your counterparts in the negotiation respond to this?*
    - * Follow up: *What are the concerns and how, as negotiators, do you assuage them, if at all?*
  - ◦ **INARA**: *On May 7th, Congress passes INARA which requires the president to issue a certification about Iran's behavior to Congress every 90*

days. Does this legislation or the more general domestic conversations that are going about creating this legislation impact the negotiators at all?
  - **Republican primaries**: *In Fall 2015, after negotiations conclude but before implementation day, all 16 Republican presidential candidates come out in opposition to the deal. How do you and your counterparts respond to the primary announcements during the negotiation?*
  - **Any other events**: *Are there other events that happened in the US that you recall being important in the negotiations?*

- Reflections on politicization of foreign policy
  - *In some sense, particularly thinking about some of those events I just mentioned, much of the domestic politics around the Iran deal seemed highly partisan. On the other hand, there were significant pro-Israel contingents within both parties, and both sanctions legislation and INARA passed with wide-reaching bipartisan support. In this mid-2014 to late-2015 period, to what extent was there partisan polarization over the deal and US-Iranian relations more generally, and did the levels of this polarization fluctuate during the course of the negotiations?*
    * Follow up: *If you could point to particular moments, when would you say attitudes polarized in a partisan way?*
  - *Stepping away from the Iran deal in particular, I'm wondering when you think having a more polarized public provides the US more leverage in an international negotiations and when it can undermines or has an otherwise negative impact on our bargaining position?*

8.6 Description and Coding Notes for Bilateral Treaty Data (Chapter 6)

This section of the appendix lists additional international treaties that were coded by the author to add to a treaty list compiled by Jeffrey Peake.[19] The treaty data was used in the analyses of treaty ratification in chapter 6.

The additional treaties are:

19. Peake 2017.

TABLE 8.3. List of additional bilateral treaties involving the United States

	Treaty name	Treaty doc.
513	Investment Treaty with Rwanda	110-23
517	Mutual Legal Assistance Treaty with Bermuda	111-6
519	Protocol Amending Tax Convention with Luxembourg	111-8
520	Protocol Amending Tax Convention with Swiss Confederation	112-1
524	Protocol Amending the Tax Convention with Spain	113-4
526	Extradition Treaty with the Republic of Chile	113-6
527	Protocol Amending the Tax Convention with Japan	114-1
528	Treaty with Algeria on Mutual Legal Assistance in Criminal Matters	114-3
529	Treaty with Jordan on Mutual Legal Assistance in Criminal Matters	114-4
530	Extradition Treaty with the Dominican Republic	114-10
531	Treaty with Kazakhstan on Mutual Legal Assistance in Criminal Matters	114-11
533	Extradition Treaty with the Republic of Serbia	115-1
534	Extradition Treaty with the Republic of Kosovo	115-2

8.7 Survey Details and Questionnaire for UK Survey on U.S. Polarization

SURVEY DETAILS AND SAMPLE

This survey was fielded as part of an omnibus survey in October 2018 by a European-based survey firm called Respondi. The survey targeted a nationally representative sample based on sex, age, and region of approximately 2,000 adults living in the UK. Data collected from the survey is analyzed in chapter 6. More information about the sample and survey results (including additional analyses and robustness checks) is available in a previously published article.[20]

PART I: TREATMENT CONDITIONS

In the survey, respondents were randomly assigned to one of three groups: (1) control, (2) affective, or (3) ideological. The control group received no additional text, while the affective and ideological groups received specific primes

20. Myrick 2022

about polarization. These primes contained two attention checks to make sure the respondent was reading carefully. Respondents were then asked a series of questions about their opinion of the United States.

The text of the affective treatment condition read:

We are now interested in understanding **your attitudes toward the United States**. *We will first provide you with some information about American politics and then ask you for your opinions.*

Please read this information carefully

[PAGE BREAK]

The United States has two major political parties: the Republican Party and the Democratic Party.

Studies show that the American public and its elected officials have become **increasingly polarized along party lines.**

In other words, **Americans increasingly dislike members of the other political party.**

[PAGE BREAK]

Surveys from the United States show that, more than ever, Americans:

- *Oppose the idea of their child marrying someone from the other political party.*
- *Have "just a few" or "no" close friends from the other political party.*
- *"Strongly dislike" or even "hate" members of the other political party.*

Based on what you read, which of the following is correct?

- *Americans "strongly dislike" or even "hate" members of the other political party.*
- *Americans oppose the idea of their child marrying someone from the other political party.*

- *Neither of these statements is correct.*
- *Both of these statements are correct.*

[PAGE BREAK]

These differences are reflected in the US government. More than ever, Republican and Democratic politicians:

- *Use extreme, negative language to taunt politicians of the other party.*
- *Post angry or hateful posts on social media about members of the other party.*

Based on what you read, which of the following is correct?

- *US politicians use extreme, negative language to taunt politicians of the other party.*
- *US politicians post angry or hateful posts on social media about members of the other party.*
- *Neither of these statements is correct.*
- *Both of these statements are correct.*

[PAGE BREAK]

The text of the ideological treatment condition read:

We are now interested in understanding **your attitudes toward the United States**. We will first provide you with some information about American politics and then ask you for your opinions.

Please read this information carefully

[PAGE BREAK]

The United States has two major political parties: the Republican Party and the Democratic Party.

Studies show that the American public and its elected officials have become **increasingly polarized along party lines.**

In other words, **Republicans and Democrats increasingly disagree with one another on policy issues.**

[PAGE BREAK]

Surveys from the United States show that, more than ever, Americans:

- Have different attitudes about social issues, such as abortion rights and gun laws.
- Have different preferences over economic policies, such as tax rates and welfare spending.
- Think their political parties cannot agree on basic facts.

Based on what you read, which of the following is correct?

- Americans think their political parties cannot agree on basic facts.
- Americans have different attitudes about social issues, such as abortion rights and gun laws.
- Neither of these statements is correct.
- Both of these statements are correct.

[PAGE BREAK]

These differences are reflected in the US government. More than ever, Republican and Democratic politicians:

- Disagree on a wide range of basic policy issues.
- Vote the same way as members of their own political party.

Based on what you read, which of the following is correct?

- US politicians disagree on a wide range of basic policy issues.
- US politicians vote the same way as members of their own political party.
- Neither of these statements is correct.
- Both of these statements are correct.

[PAGE BREAK]

PART II: OUTCOMES

We would like to hear **your opinion on the United States and its relationship with your country.** *On the next page, carefully read the statements and indicate whether you agree or disagree.*

[PAGE BREAK]

The order in which the statements below appear is randomized. All response options were on a seven-point Likert scale ranging from "Disagree strongly" to "Agree strongly."

The United States would come to the aid of my country in the event our security is threatened.

The United States no longer maintains its commitments to foreign countries.

My country should partner with the United States in future international agreements.

The United States will <u>not</u> be a reliable future partner for my country.

I trust the United States to do what is right in international politics.

We should <u>not</u> look to the United States for global leadership.

[PAGE BREAK]

PART III: POLARIZATION QUESTIONS

The United States has two major political parties: the Republican Party and the Democratic Party.

How often would you say these parties <u>agree</u>?

- *Almost Always*
- *Sometimes*
- *Rarely*

- *Almost Never*
- *I don't know*

[PAGE BREAK]

The United Kingdom has two major political parties: the Conservative Party and the Labour Party.

How often would you say these parties *agree*?

- *Almost Always*
- *Sometimes*
- *Rarely*
- *Almost Never*
- *I don't know*

[PAGE BREAK]

Political polarization happens when major parties in a country increasingly *disagree* with one another.

In your opinion, is there more political polarization in the United States or in the United Kingdom?

- *There is more political polarization in the United States.*
- *There is more political polarization in the United Kingdom.*
- *Political polarization is the same in both countries.*
- *I don't know.*

PART IV: DEMOGRAPHICS

trump: *How favourable or unfavourable do you feel toward the current President of the United States, Donald Trump?*

[PAGE BREAK]

age: *What is your age?*

sex: *Are you male or female?*

- *Male*
- *Female*

[PAGE BREAK]

education_level: *What is the highest educational or work-related qualification you have?*

[PAGE BREAK]

birthplace: *What is your place of birth?*

- *England*
- *Wales*
- *Scotland*
- *Northern Ireland*
- *Outside the UK*

current_location: *Where do you currently live?*

- *England*
- *Wales*
- *Scotland*
- *Northern Ireland*
- *Outside the UK*

PAGE BREAK

The following question is asked only if the respondent selected "England" for **current_location**.

region_england: In which of the following regions in England do you currently live?

- *East Anglia*
- *East Midlands*
- *Greater London*
- *North*
- *North West*
- *South East*
- *South West*
- *West Midlands*
- *Yorkshire & Humberside*

[PAGE BREAK]

party_id: *Generally speaking, do you usually think of yourself as Conservative, Labour, Liberal Democrat, Scottish National Party (SNP) or Plaid Cymru, or don't you usually think of yourself as any of these things?*

[PAGE BREAK]

vote_2017: *Talking to people about the General Election in 2017, we found that a lot of people didn't manage to vote. How about you – did you manage to vote in the General Election?*

- *No, I did not vote.*
- *Yes, I voted.*
- *I don't know.*

[PAGE BREAK]

The following question is only displayed if the respondent selected "Yes, I voted" for **vote_2017**:

vote_choice_2017: *Which party did you vote for in the 2017 UK general election?*

- *Conservative*
- *Labour*
- *Liberal Democrat*
- *Scottish National Party*
- *Plaid Cymru*
- *UK Independent Party*
- *Green*
- *Don't know*

[PAGE BREAK]

voice_choice: *If there were a general election tomorrow, which party would you vote for?*

- *Conservative*
- *Labour*
- *Liberal Democrat*

- *Scottish National Party*
- *Plaid Cymru*
- *UK Independent Party*
- *Green*
- *Some other party*
- *Would not vote*
- *Don't know*

[PAGE BREAK]

left_right: *In politics people sometimes talk of left and right. Where would you place yourself on a scale from 0 to 10 where 0 means the 'left' and 10 means the 'right'?*

vote_euref: *In the Referendum on whether Britain should remain in or leave the European Union, which way did you vote, or did you not vote?*

- *I voted to Remain in the EU*
- *I voted to Leave the EU*
- *I did not vote*
- *I can't remember*

[PAGE BREAK]

pol_interest: *How much interest do you have about what is going on in politics?*

- *A great deal*
- *Quite a lot*
- *Some*
- *Not very much*
- *None at all*

[PAGE BREAK]

Thank you for your time. Do you have any comments about this survey?

[OPEN RESPONSE]

BIBLIOGRAPHY

Abbey, Michael H. and Nicholas Bromfield. 1994. "A Practitioner's Guide to the Maastricht Treaty." *Michigan Journal of International Law* 15(4):1329–1357.

Abramowitz, Alan. 2010. *The Disappearing Center: Engaged Citizens, Polarization, and American Democracy*. Yale University Press.

Abramowitz, Alan I. and Kyle L. Saunders. 2008. "Is Polarization a Myth?" *Journal of Politics* 70(2):542–555.

Abramowitz, Alan I. and Steven Webster. 2016. "The Rise of Negative Partisanship and the Nationalization of U.S. Elections in the 21st Century." *Electoral Studies* 41:12–22.

Adams, Gordon and Shoon Murray. 2014. *Mission Creep: The Militarization of US Foreign Policy?* Georgetown University Press.

Adams, James and Lawrence Ezrow. 2009. "Who Do European Parties Represent? How Western European Parties Represent the Policy Preferences of Opinion Leaders." *British Journal of Political Science* 71(1):206–223.

Adams, James F. and Nathan J. Rexford. 2018. "Electoral Systems and Issue Polarization." In *The Oxford Handbook of Electoral Systems*, ed. Erik S. Herron, Robert J. Pekkanen, and Matthew S. Shugart. Oxford University Press, pp. 247–261.

Adida, Claire L., Adeline Lo, and Melina Platas. 2018. "Perspective Taking Can Promote Short-Term Inclusionary Behavior toward Syrian Refugees." *Proceedings of the National Academy of Sciences* 115(38):9521–9526.

Adler, Emanuel and Michael Barnett. 1998. *Security Communities*. Cambridge University Press.

Agiesta, Jennifer. 2023. "CNN Poll: Majority of Americans Oppose More US Aid for Ukraine in War with Russia." *CNN*, August 4.

Aisch, Gregor, Adam Pearce, and Karl Russell. 2016. "How Britain Voted in the E.U. Referendum." *New York Times*, June 24.

Albertson, Bethany and Shana Kushner Gadarian. 2015. *Anxious Politics: Democratic Citizenship in a Threatening World*. Cambridge University Press.

Aldrich, John H. 1977. "Electoral Choice in 1972: A Test of Some Theorems of the Spatial Model of Electoral Competition." *Journal of Mathematical Sociology* 5(2):215–237.

Aldrich, John H. 2011. *Why Parties? A Second Look*. Chicago University Press.

Aldrich, John H., Christopher Gelpi, Peter D. Feaver, Jason Reifler, and Kristin Thompson Sharp. 2006. "Foreign Policy and the Electoral Connection." *Annual Review of Political Science* 9:477–502.

Aldrich, John H., John L. Sullivan, and Eugene Borgida. 1989. "Foreign Affairs and Issue Voting: Do Presidential Candidates 'Waltz Before a Blind Audience?.'" *American Political Science Review* 83(1):123–141.

Alesina, Alberto. 1987. "Macroeconomic Policy in a Two-Party System as a Repeated Game." *Quarterly Journal of Economics* 102:651–678.

Alesina, Alberto. 1988. "Credibility and Policy Convergence in a Two-Party System with Rational Voters." *American Economic Review* 78(4):796–805.
Algara, Carlos and Roi Zur. 2023. "The Downsian Roots of Affective Polarization." *Electoral Studies* 82(102581).
Allport, Gordon. 1954. *The Nature of Prejudice*. Addison-Wesley.
Almond, Gabriel. 1950. *The American People and Foreign Policy*. Harcourt Press.
Almond, Gabriel. 1956. "Public Opinion and National Security." *Public Opinion Quarterly* 20:371–378.
American Academy of Diplomacy. 2015. "Diplomacy at Risk." Washington, DC, April.
American National Election Studies. 2020. "ANES 2020 Time Series Study Full Release." Accessed from: www.electionstudies.org.
American Security Project. 2012. "The Nunn–Lugar Cooperative Threat Reduction Program: Securing and Safeguarding Weapons of Mass Destruction." Washington, DC, July 25.
Ansolabehere, Stephen and Shanto Iyengar. 1996. *Going Negative: How Political Ads Shrink and Polarize the Electorate*. Free Press.
Applebaum, Anne. 2020. "History Will Judge the Complicit." *The Atlantic*, July 2020.
Applebaum, Anne. 2023. "Netanyahu's Attack on Democracy Left Israel Unprepared." *The Atlantic*, October 21.
Arbatli, Ekim and Dina Rosenberg. 2021. "United We Stand, Divided We Rule: How Political Polarzation Erodes Democracy." *Democratization* 28(2):285–307.
Aronow, Peter M., Jonathan Baron, and Lauren Pinson. 2019. "A Note on Dropping Experimental Subjects Who Fail a Manipulation Check." *Political Analysis* 27(4):572–589.
Ashford, Emma. 2023. "Stuck on the Left with You: The Limits of Partisanship in US Foreign Policy." *Security Studies* 32(2):382–388.
Asmus, Ronald D. 2003. "Rebuilding the Atlantic Alliances." *Foreign Affairs* 82(5):20–31.
Atlantic Council. 2024. "Beijing's Least Favorite Candidate Wins Taiwan's Presidential Election." Washington, DC, January 13.
Autor, David, David Dorn, and Gordon H. Hanson. 2021. "On the Persistence of the China Shock." NBER Working Paper 29401, Washington, DC, October.
Autor, David, David Dorn, Gordon Hanson, and Kaveh Majlesi. 2016. "Importing Political Polarization? The Electoral Consequences of Rising Trade Exposure." NBER Working Paper 22637, Cambridge, MA, September.
Aydin-Düzgit, Senem. 2019. "The Islamist–Secularist Divide and Turkey's Descent into Severe Polarization." In *Democracies Divided: The Global Challenge of Political Polarization*, ed. Thomas Carothers and Andrew O'Donohue. Brookings Institution Press, pp. 17–37.
Bafumi, Joseph and Joseph M. Parent. 2012. "International Polarity and America's Polarization." *International Politics* 49(1):1–35.
Bail, Chris. 2021. *Breaking the Social Media Prism: How to Make Our Platforms Less Polarizing*. Princeton University Press.
Bailey, Michael A., Anton Strezhnev, and Erik Voeten. 2017. "Estimating Dynamic State Preferences from United Nations Voting Data." *Journal of Conflict Resolution* 61(2):430–456.
Bailey, Michael A., Daniel J. Hopkins, and Todd Rodgers. 2016. "Unresponsive and Unpersuaded: The Unintended Consequences of a Voter Persuasion Effort." *Political Behavior* 38:713–746.
Baker, Peter. 2017. "In Rejecting Popular Paris Accord, Trump Bets on His Base." *New York Times*, June 1.
Bakker, Ryan, Liesbet Hooghe, Seth Jolly, Gary Marks, Jonathan Polk, Jan Rovny, Marco Steenbergen, and Milada Anna Vachudova. 2020. "1999–2019 Chapel Hill Expert Survey Trend File." Chapel Hill Expert Survey.

Banda, Kevin K. and John Cluverius. 2018. "Elite Polarization, Party Extremity, and Affective Polarization." *Electoral Studies* 56:90–101.

Banerjee, Vasabjit and Sean Webeck. 2024. "Civil–Military Relations: Through a Perilous Lens." *Armed Forces & Society* 50(1):3–24.

Banks, William C. and Jeffrey D. Straussman. 1999. "A New Imperial Presidency? Insights from U.S. Involvement in Bosnia." *Political Science Quarterly* 114(2):195–217.

Barber, Michael and Nolan McCarty. 2015. "The Causes and Consequences of Polarization." In *Solutions to Polarization in America*, ed. Nathaniel Persily. Cambridge University Press, pp. 15–58.

Barnes, Julian E., Charlie Savage, and Adam Goldman. 2021. "Trump Administration Politicized Some Intelligence on Foreign Election Influence, Report Finds." *New York Times*, January 8.

Battig, Michele B. and Thomas Bernauer. 2009. "National Institutions and Global Public Goods: Are Democracies More Cooperative in Climate Change Policy?" *International Organization* 63:281–308.

Baum, Matthew A. 2002. "The Constituent Foundations of the Rally-Round-the-Flag Phenomenon." *International Studies Quarterly* 46(2):263–298.

Baum, Matthew A. 2004. "Going Private: Public Opinion, Presidential Rhetoric, and the Domestic Politics of Audience Costs in U.S. Foreign Policy Crises." *Journal of Conflict Resolution* 48(5):603–631.

Baum, Matthew A. and Philip B. K. Potter. 2015. *War and Democratic Constraint: How the Public Influences Foreign Policy*. Princeton University Press.

Baum, Matthew A. and Tim Groeling. 2009a. "Shot by the Messenger: Partisan Cues and Public Opinion Regarding National Security and War." *Political Behavior* 31:157–186.

Baum, Matthew A. and Tim Groeling. 2009b. *War Stories: The Causes and Consequences of Public Views of War*. Princeton University Press.

BBC News. 2016. "Trump Accuses China of 'Raping' US with Unfair Trade Policy." *BBC News*, May 2.

Bearak, Max and Carol Morello. 2018. "How a Change in U.S. Abortion Policy Reverberated around the Globe." *Washington Post*, October 8.

Beardsley, Kyle, Patrick James, Jonathan Wilkenfeld, and Michael Brecher. 2020. "The International Crisis Behavior Project." In *Oxford Research Encyclopedia*, ed. Thomas Preston. Oxford University Press. Accessed from: https://oxfordre.com/politics/view/10.1093/acrefore/9780190228637.001.0001/acrefore-9780190228637-e-1638.

Beaulieu, Emily, Gary W. Cox, and Sebastian Saiegh. 2012. "Sovereign Debt and Regime Type: Reconsidering the Democratic Advantage." *International Organization* 66(4):709–738.

Beehner, Lionel, Risa Brooks, and Daniel Maurer. 2020. *Reconsidering American Civil–Military Relations: The Military, Society, Politics, and Modern War*. Oxford University Press.

Beinart, Peter. 2008. "When Politics No Longer Stops at the Water's Edge: Partisan Polarization and Foreign Policy." In *Red and Blue Nation? Consequences and Correction of America's Polarized Politics*, ed. Pietro Nivola and David Brady. Brookings Institution Press, pp. 151–167.

Beliakova, Polina. 2021. "Erosion by Deference: Civilian Control and the Military in Policymaking." *Texas National Security Review* 4(3):55–75.

Benen, Steve. 2019. "White House Blasts Trump-Appointed 'Radical Unelected Bureaucrats'." *MSNBC*, October 23.

Berelson, Bernard R., Paul F. Lazarsfeld, and William N. McPhee. 1954. *Voting: A Study of Opinion Formation in a Presidential Campaign*. University of Chicago Press.

Berinsky, Adam J. 2007. "Assuming the Costs of War: Events, Elites, and American Public Support for Military Conflict." *Journal of Politics* 69(4):975–997.

Berinsky, Adam J. 2009. *In Time of War: Understanding American Public Opinion from World War II to Iraq*. University of Chicago Press.

Bermeo, Nancy. 2016. "On Democratic Backsliding." *Journal of Democracy* 27(1):5–19.

Bértoa, Fernando Casal and José Rama. 2021. "Polarization: What Do We Know and What Can We Do about It?" *Frontiers in Political Science* 3:1–11.

Binder, Sarah. 2014. "Polarized We Govern?" Brookings Institution, Washington, DC, May 27.

Bishop, Bill. 2008. *The Big Sort: Why the Clustering of Like-Minded America Is Tearing Us Apart*. Houghton Mifflin Harcourt.

Black, Duncan. 1948. "On the Rationale of Group Decision-making." *Journal of Political Economy* 56(1):23–34.

Black, Ian. 2009. "Barack Obama Offers Iran 'New Beginning' with Video Message." *The Guardian*, March 20.

Bobick, Talya and Alastair Smith. 2013. "The Impact of Leader Turnover on the Onset and the Resolution of WTO Disputes." *Review of International Organizations* 8:423–445.

Bodansky, Daniel and Peter Spiro. 2016. "Executive Agreements." *Vanderbilt Journal of Transnational Law* 49(4):885–929.

Boese, Vanessa A. 2019. "How (Not) to Measure Democracy." *International Area Studies Review* 22(2):95–127.

Bollen, Kenneth A. and Pamela Paxton. 2000. "Subjective Measures of Liberal Democracy." *Comparative Political Studies* 33(1):58–86.

Bond, Jon R. and Richard Fleisher, eds. 2000. *Polarized Politics: Congress and the President in a Partisan Era*. CQ Press.

Bonica, Adam. 2013. "Mapping the Ideological Marketplace." *American Journal of Political Science* 58(2):367–386.

Bonica, Adam, Nolan McCarty, Keith T. Poole, and Howard Rosenthal. 2013. "Why Hasn't Democracy Slowed Rising Inequality?" *Journal of Economic Perspectives* 27(3):103–124.

Borg, Stefan. 2024. "'A Battle for the Soul of This Nation': How Domestic Polarization Affects US Foreign Policy in Post-Trump America." *International Journal* 79(1):22–39.

Box-Steffensmeier, Janet M., Suzanna De Boef, and Tse-Min Lin. 2004. "The Dynamics of the Partisan Gender Gap." *American Political Science Review* 98(3):515–528.

Bradley, Curtis A. 2013. *International Law in the US Legal System*. Oxford University Press.

Brady, David W., Hahrie Han, and Jeremy C. Pope. 2007. "Primary Elections and Candidate Ideology: Out of Step with the Primary Electorate?" *Legislative Studies Quarterly* 32(1):79–105.

Brands, Hal. 2017. "The Unexceptional Superpower: American Grand Strategy in the Age of Trump." *Survival* 59(6):7–40.

Brands, Hal and Zack Cooper. 2019. "After the Responsible Stakeholder, What? Debating America's China Strategy." *Texas National Security Review* 2(2):68–81.

Brecher, Michael. 1979. "State Behavior in International Crisis: A Model." *Journal of Conflict Resolution* 23(3):446–480.

Brecher, Michael, Jonathan Wilkenfeld, Kyle Beardsley, Patrick James, and David Quinn. 2017. "International Crisis Behavior Data, Version 12." International Crisis Behavior Project, August 23.

Brenan, Megan. 2020. "Majority in U.S. Still Say United Nations Doing a Poor Job." *Gallup News*, March 13.

Brennan Center for Justice. 2012. "National Survey: Super PACs, Corruption, and Democracy." April 24.

Brennan, James P. 2018. *Argentina's Missing Bones: Revisiting the History of the Dirty War*. University of California Press.

Brock, Roby. 2015. "Poll: Hutchinson, Cotton Break 50% with Early Job Approval Ratings." *Talk Business & Politics*, February 8.

Brody, Richard A. 1991. *Assessing the President: The Media, Elite Opinion, and Public Support*. Stanford University Press.

Brody, Richard A. and Catherine R. Shapiro. 1989. "Policy Failure and Public Support: The Iran-Contra Affair and Public Assessment of President Reagan." *Political Behavior* 11(4):353–369.

Broockman, David and Joshua Kalla. 2016. "Durably Reducing Transphobia: A Field Experiment on Door-to-Door Canvassing." *Science* 352(6282):220–224.

Brooks, David. 2019. "How China Brings Us Together: An Existential Threat for the 21st Century." *New York Times*, February 14.

Brooks, Risa. 2020. "Paradoxes of Professionalism: Rethinking Civil–Military Relations in the United States." *International Security* 44(1):7–44.

Brooks, Risa, Jim Golby, and Heidi Urben. 2021. "Crisis of Command: America's Broken Civil–Military Relationship Imperils National Security." *Foreign Affairs*, May/June.

Brooks, Rosa. 2013. "Obama vs. the Generals." *Politico*, November.

Brooks, Rosa. 2016. *How Everything Became War and the Military Became Everything: Tables from the Pentagon*. Simon and Schuster.

Brooks, Stephen G. and William C. Wohlforth. 2016. *America Abroad: The United States' Global Role in the 21st Century*. Oxford University Press.

Brown, Roger. 1982. "Party and Bureaucracy: From Kennedy to Reagan." *Political Science Quarterly* 97(2):279–294.

Broz, J. Lawrence. 2002. "Political System Transparency and Monetary Commitment Regimes." *International Organization* 56(4):861–887.

Brunnell, Thomas and Bernard Grofman. 2008. "Evaluating the Impact of Redistricting on District Homogeneity, Political Competition, and Political Extremism in the U.S. House of Representatives, 1962–2006." In *Designing Democratic Government: Making Institutions Work*, ed. Margaret Levi, James Johnson, Jack Knight, and Susan Stokes. Russell Sage Foundation, pp. 117–140.

Bryan, James D. and Jordan Tama. 2022. "The Prevalence of Bipartisanship in U.S. Foreign Policy: An Analysis of Important Congressional Votes." *International Politics* 59(5):874–897.

Buarque, Daniel. 2022. "Upside-Down Diplomacy: Foreign Perceptions about Bolsonaro's Intentions and Initial Transformations of Brazil's Foreign Policy and Status." *Third World Quarterly* 43(10):2450–2466.

Bueno de Mesquita, Bruce, Alastair Smith, Randolph M. Siverson, and James D. Morrow. 2002. *The Logic of Political Survival*. MIT Press.

Bueno de Mesquita, Bruce and David Lalman. 1992. *War and Reason: Domestic and International Imperatives*. Yale University Press.

Bump, Philip. 2016. "Farewell to the Most Polarized Congress in More Than 100 Years!" *Washington Post*, December 21.

Burbach, David. 2019. "Partisan Dimensions of Confidence in the U.S. Military, 1973–2016." *Armed Forces & Society* 45(2):211–233.

Burns, William J. 2019. *The Back Channel: A Memoir of American Diplomacy and the Case for Its Renewal*. Random House.

Busby, Josh. 2021. "Gone Missing from Grand Strategy: Climate Change." *Duck of Minerva*, February 2.

Busby, Joshua and Jonathan Monten. 2018. "Has Liberal Internationalism Been Trumped?" In *Chaos in the Liberal Order: The Trump Presidency and International Politics in the Twenty-First Century*, ed. Robert Jervis, Francis J. Gavin, Joshua Rovner, and Diane N. Labrosse. Columbia University Press, pp. 49–60.

Busby, Joshua W. and Jonathan Monten. 2008. "Without Heirs? Assessing the Decline of Establishment Internationalism in U.S. Foreign Policy." *Perspectives on Politics* 6(3): 451–472.

Bush, George W. 2002. "Remarks by the President on Iraq." Cincinnati Museum Center, Cincinnati, OH, October 7. Accessed from: https://georgewbush-whitehouse.archives.gov/news/releases/2002/10/20021007-8.html.

Bush, George W. 2005. "Address to the United Nations General Assembly." Accessed from: https://2009-2017.state.gov/p/io/potusunga/207566.htm.

Bush, Richard C. 2021. "Taiwan's Democracy and the China Challenge." Brookings Institution, Washington, DC, January 22.

Calamur, Krishnadev. 2015. "In Speech to Congress, Netanyahu Blasts 'A Very Bad Deal' with Iran." *NPR*, March 3.

Cameron, Chris. 2022. "These Are the People Who Died in Connection with the Capitol Riot." *New York Times*, January 5.

Campbell, Angus, Philip E. Converse, Warren E. Miller, and Donald E. Stokes. 1960. *American Voter*. Wiley.

Campbell, David E., John C. Green, and Geoffrey C. Layman. 2011. "The Party Faithful: Partisan Images, Candidate Religion, and the Electoral Impact of Party Identification." *American Journal of Political Science* 55(1):42–58.

Campbell, James. 2016. *Polarized: Making Sense of a Divided America*. Princeton University Press.

Campbell, Kurt M. and Ely Ratner. 2018. "The China Reckoning: How Beijing Defied American Expectations." *Foreign Affairs*, March/April 2018.

Canes-Wrone, Brandice, William G. Howell, and David E. Lewis. 2008. "Toward a Broader Understanding of Presidential Power: A Reevaluation of the Two Presidencies Thesis." *Journal of Politics* 70(1):1–16.

Capehart, Jonathan. 2015. "Tom Cotton Picked Apart by Army General over 'Mutinous' Iran Letter." *Washington Post*, March 13.

Carothers, Thomas and Andrew O'Donohue, eds. 2019. *Democracies Divided: The Global Challenge of Political Polarization*. Brookings Institution Press.

Carter, David B. and Curtis Signorino. 2010. "Back to the Future: Modeling Time Dependence in Binary Data." *Political Analysis* 18:271–292.

CBPP. 2023. "Policy Basics: Where Do Our Federal Tax Dollars Go?" Center on Budget and Policy Priorities, Washington, DC, September 28.

Chafets, Zev. 2022. "Some Israelis Are More Scared of Netanyahu Than Iran." *Bloomberg*, September 6.

Chalberg, John C. 1989. "Realist as Moralist by George Kennan." *Reviews in American History* 17(3):482–500.

Charnock, Emily. 2018. "More Than a Score: Interest Group Ratings and Polarized Politics." *Studies in American Political Development* 32(1):49–78.

Chaudoin, Stephen. 2014. "Promises or Policies? An Experimental Analysis of International Agreements and Audience Reactions." *International Organization* 68(1): 235–256.

Chaudoin, Stephen, Helen V. Milner, and Dustin H. Tingley. 2010. "The Center Still Holds: Liberal Internationalism Survives." *International Security* 35(1):75–94.

Chaudoin, Stephen, Helen V. Milner, and Dustin Tingley. 2017. "A Liberal Internationalist American Foreign Policy? Maybe Down but Not Out." *H-Diplo/ISSF Policy Roundtable* 1(6).

Chaudoin, Stephen, Helen V. Milner, and Dustin Tingley. 2018. "Down but Not Out: A Liberal International American Foreign Policy." In *Chaos in the Liberal Order: The Trump Presidency and International Politics in the Twenty-First Century*, ed. Robert Jervis, Francis J. Gavin, Joshua Rovner, and Diane N. Labrosse. Columbia University Press, pp. 61–97.

Chavez, Leo R. 2001. *Covering Immigration: Population Images and the Politics of the Nation*. University of California Press.

Chayes, Antonia. 2008. "How American Treaty Behavior Threatens National Security." *International Security* 33(1):45–81.

Chen, Jowei and Jonathan Rodden. 2013. "Unintentional Gerrymandering: Political Geography and Electoral Bias in Legislatures." *Quarterly Journal of Political Science* 8:239–269.

Chiozza, Giacomo and H. E. Goemans. 2011. *Leaders and International Conflict*. Cambridge University Press.

Christenson, Dino P. and Douglas L. Kriner. 2020. *The Myth of the Imperial Presidency: How Public Opinion Checks the Unilateral Executive*. University of Chicago Press.

Chu, Jonathan A. and Stefano Recchia. 2022. "Does Public Opinion Affect the Preferences of Foreign Policy Leaders? Experimental Evidence from the UK Parliament." *Journal of Politics* 84(3):1844–1877.

Clark, Cal and Alexander C. Tan. 2012. "Political Polarization in Taiwan: A Growing Challenge to Catch-All Parties?" *Journal of Current Chinese Affairs* 41(3):7–31.

Clausen, Aage. 1973. *How Congressmen Decide: A Policy Focus*. St. Martin's Press.

Clayton, Katherine, Nicholas T. Davis, Brendan Nyhan, Ethan Porter, Timothy J. Ryan, and Thomas J. Wood. 2021. "Elite Rhetoric Can Undermine Democratic Norms." *PNAS* 118(23):1–6.

Clement, Scott, Dan Balz, and Emily Guskin. 2023. "Most Favor Military Aid to Ukraine, but Partisan Split Grows, Poll Finds." *Washington Post*, October 4.

Clinton, Joshua D. and David E. Lewis. 2008. "Expert Opinion, Agency Characteristics, and Agency Preferences." *Political Analysis* 16(1):3–20.

Clinton, William J. 1993. "Remarks to the 48th Session of the United Nations General Assembly." Accessed from: https://2009-2017.state.gov/p/io/potusunga/207375.htm.

Coats, Daniel R. 2018. "Worldwide Threat Assessment of the US Intelligence Community." Office of the Director of National Intelligence, Washington, DC.

Colaresi, Michael. 2007. "The Benefit of the Doubt: Testing an Informational Theory of the Rally Effect." *International Organization* 61(1):99–143.

Colaresi, Michael. 2012. "A Boom with Review: How Retrospective Oversight Increases the Foreign Policy Ability of Democracies." *American Journal of Political Science* 56(3):671–689.

Colaresi, Michael P. 2014. *Democracy Declassified: The Secrecy Dilemma in National Security*. Oxford University Press.

Coletta, Giovanni. 2018. "Politicising Intelligence: What Went Wrong with the UK and US Assessments on Iraqi WMD in 2002." *Journal of Intelligence History* 17(1):65–78.

Colgan, Jeff D. 2019. "American Perspectives and Blind Spots on World Politics." *Journal of Global Security Studies* 4(3):300–309.

Colgan, Jeff D. 2021. "Climate Change, Grand Strategy, and International Order." Wilson Center, Washington, DC, July 23.

Combs, Aidan, Graham Tierney, Brian Guay, Friedolin Merhout, Christopher A. Bail, D. Sunshine Hillygus, and Alexander Volfovsky. 2023. "Reducing Political Polarization in the United States with a Mobile Chat Platform." *Nature Human Behavior* 7:1454–1461.

Congressional Research Service. 2001. "Treaties and Other International Agreements: The Role of the United States." Washington, DC, January.

Congressional Research Service. 2023. "Term Limits for Members of Congress: Policy and Legal Overview." Washington, DC, May 10.

Converse, Philip E. 1964. "The Nature of Belief Systems in Mass Publics." *Critical Review* 18(1-3):1–74.

Copelovitch, Mark and Jon C. W. Pevehouse. 2019. "International Organizations in a New Era of Populist Nationalism." *Review of International Organizations* 14(2):169–186.
Cotton, Tom. 2015. "An Open Letter to the Leaders of the Islamic Republic of Iran." Letter, March 9.
Cotton, Tom. 2017. "A Conversation on the Iran Nuclear Deal with Senator Tom Cotton." Council on Foreign Relations, New York, October 3.
Cowhey, Peter F. 1993. "Domestic Institutions and the Credibility of International Commitments: Japan and the United States." *International Organization* 47(2):299–326.
Cox, Gary W. and Matthew D. McCubbins. 1993. *Legislative Leviathan: Party Government in the House*. Cambridge University Press.
Cox, Gary W. and Matthew D. McCubbins. 2005. *Setting the Agenda: Responsible Party Government in the U.S. House of Representatives*. Cambridge University Press.
Crescenzi, Mark. 2018. *Of Friends and Foes: Reputation and Learning in International Politics*. Oxford University Press.
Crespin, Michael H., David W. Rohde, and Ryan J. Vander Wielen. 2011. "Measuring Variations in Party Unity Voting: An Assessment of Agenda Effects." *Party Politics* 19(3):432–457.
Daugherty, William J. 2006. *Executive Secrets: Covert Action and the Presidency*. University Press of Kentucky.
Davenport, Coral. 2014. "Obama Pursuing Climate Accord in Lieu of Treaty." *New York Times*, August 27.
Davenport, Kelsey. 2017. "Iran Nuclear Deal 'Sunset' Gets Scrutiny." Arms Control Association, Washington, DC, October.
Davern, Michael, Rene Bautista, Jeremy Freese, Pamela Herd, and Stephen L. Morgan. 2024. "General Social Survey 1972–2024." Accessed from: https://gssdataexplorer.norc.org/.
Davis, Christina L. and Sarah Blodgett Bermeo. 2009. "Who Files? Developing Country Participation in GATT/WTO Adjudication." *Journal of Politics* 71(3):1033–1049.
Demirjian, Karoun. 2023. "Opposition to Ukraine Aid Becomes a Litmus Test for the Right." *New York Times*, October 5.
Democratic Staff. 2020. "Diplomacy in Crisis: The Trump Administration's Decimation of the State Department." Report prepared for the use of the Committee on Foreign Relations United States Senate, July 28.
Dennis, Steven T. and Sarah Chacko. 2015. "Portman: Tom Cotton Letter Should Yield Better Iran Deal." *Roll Call*, March 12.
Desch, Michael C. 1998. "War and Strong States, Peace and Weak States?" *International Organization* 50(2):237–268.
Desch, Michael C. 2002. "Democracy and Victory: Why Regime Type Hardly Matters." *International Security* 27(2):5–47.
Destler, I. M. and Ivo H. Daalder. 2000. "A New NSC for a New Administration." Brookings Policy Brief Series, Washington, DC, November 15.
Dias, Nicholas C., Laurits F. Aarslew, Kristian Vrede Skaaning Frederiksen, Yphtach Lelkes, Lea Pradella, and Sean J. Westwood. 2024. "Correcting Misperceptions of Partisan Opponents Is Not Effective at Treating Democratic Ills." *PNAS Nexus* 3(8).
Dias, Nicholas and Yphtach Lelkes. 2022. "The Nature of Affective Polarization: Disentangling Policy Disagreement from Partisan Identity." *American Journal of Political Science* 66(3):775–790.
Dinic, Milan. 2015. "Who Do the British Regard as Allies?" *YouGov Daily*, October 14.
DisGuiseppe, Matthew and Patrick E. Shea. 2015. "Sovereign Credit and the Fate of Leaders: Reassessing the 'Democratic Advantage.'" *International Studies Quarterly* 59(3):557–570.
Dow, Jay K. 2011. "Party-System Extremism in Majoritarian and Proportional Electoral Systems." *British Journal of Political Science* 41(2):341–361.

Downes, Alexander B. and Todd S. Sechser. 2012. "The Illusion of Democratic Credibility." *International Organization* 66(3):457–498.
Downs, Anthony. 1957. "An Economic Theory of Political Action in Democracy." *Journal of Political Economy* 65(2):135–150.
Doyle, Michael W. 1983. "Kant, Liberal Legacies, and Foreign Affairs." *Philosophy and Public Affairs* 12(3):205–235.
Drezner, Daniel. 2020. "Immature Leadership: Donald Trump and the American Presidency." *International Affairs* 96(2):383–400.
Drezner, Daniel W. 2021. "Grand Strategy in a Fractured Marketplace of Ideas." In *The Oxford Handbook of Grand Strategy*, ed. Thierry Balzacq and Ronald R. Krebs. Oxford University Press, pp. 657–672.
Druckman, James N. 2023. "Correcting Misperceptions of the Other Political Party Does Not Robustly Reduce Support for Undemocratic Practices or Partisan Violence." *PNAS* 120(37).
Druckman, James and Matthew Levendusky. 2018. "What Do We Measure When We Measure Affective Partisanship?" Northwestern Institute for Policy Research Working Paper Series, Evanston, IL.
Druckman, James N., Samara Klar, Yanna Krupnikov, Matthew Levendusky, and John Barry Ryan. 2022. "(Mis)estimating Affective Polarization." *Journal of Politics* 84(2):1106–1117.
Drutman, Lee. 2017. "This Voting Reform Solves 2 of America's Biggest Political Problems." *Vox News*, July 26.
Drutman, Lee. 2021. "What We Know about Congressional Primaries and Congressional Primary Reform." *New America*, July 2021.
Dudley, Rebecca. 2023. "The Use of U.S. Diplomatic Foreign Policy for Conflict Resolution." PhD Dissertation, Duke University.
Dueck, Colin. 2015. *The Obama Doctrine: American Grand Strategy Today*. Oxford University Press.
Dunlap, Riley E., Aaron M. McCright, and Jerrod H. Yarosh. 2016. "The Political Divide on Climate Change: Partisan Polarization Widens in the U.S." *Environment: Science and Policy for Sustainable Development* 58(5):4–23.
Duverger, Maurice. 1954. *Political Parties: Their Organization and Activity in the Modern State*. University Paperbacks.
Edwards, George C. 2015. "Staying Private." In *Solutions to Political Polarization in America*, ed. Nathaniel Persily. Cambridge University Press, pp. 275–284.
Edwards, George C., Andrew Barrett, and Jeffrey Peake. 1997. "The Legislative Impact of Divided Government." *American Journal of Political Science* 41(2):545–563.
Eurasia Group. 2024. *Top Risks 2024*, January 8. Accessed from: https://www.eurasiagroup.net/issues/top-risks-2024.
Everett, Burgess. 2015. "Cruz's Iran Doomsday: 'Murder' of Millions of Israelis, Americans." *Politico*, June 21.
Ezrow, Lawrence. 2008. "Parties' Policy Programmes and the Dog That Didn't Bark: No Evidence That Proportional Systems Promote Extreme Party Positioning." *British Journal of Political Science* 38(3):479–497.
Fearon, James D. 1994. "Domestic Political Audiences and the Escalation of International Disputes." *American Political Science Review* 88(3):577–592.
Fearon, James D. 1995. "Rationalist Explanations for War." *International Organization* 49:379–414.
Fearon, James D., Macartan Humphreys, and Jeremy M. Weinstein. 2009. "Can Development Aid Contribute to Social Cohesion after Civil War? Evidence from a Field Experiment in Post-Conflict Liberia." *American Economic Review* 99(2):287–291.

Feaver, Peter. 2003. *Armed Servants: Agency, Oversight, and Civil–Military Relations.* Harvard University Press.

Feaver, Peter. 2023a. "We Should Not Be Cavalier about Declining Public Confidence in the Military." *Townhall*, July 21.

Feaver, Peter D. 2023b. *Thanks for Your Service: The Causes and Consequences of Public Confidence in the US Military.* Oxford University Press.

Feaver, Peter D. and Richard H. Kohn. 2021. "Civil–Military Relations in the United States: What Senior Leaders Need to Know (and Usually Don't)." *Strategic Studies Quarterly* 2(15):12–37.

Feinerer, Ingo, Kurt Hornik, and David Meyer. 2008. "Text Mining Infrastructure in R." *Journal of Statistical Software* 25(5):1–54.

Feinstein, Brian and Daniel Hemel. 2020. "Outside Advisers Inside Agencies." *Georgetown Law Journal* 108(5):1139–1211.

Fennelly, Katherine and Christopher Federico. 2008. "Rural Residence as a Determinant of Attitudes toward U.S. Immigration Policy." *International Migration* 46(1):151–190.

Fenno, Richard F. 1978. *Home Style.* Little, Brown.

Field, Elizabeth A. and Suzanne M. Perkins. 2023. "Defense Workforce: Opportunities for More Effective Management and Efficiencies." US Government Accountability Office Testimony Before the Subcommittee on Personnel, Committee on Armed Services, U.S. Senate, July 26.

Filkins, Dexter. 2020. "Trump's Public-Relations Army." *New Yorker*, June 5.

Fiorina, Morris P. and Samuel J. Abrams. 2008. "Political Polarization in the American Public." *Annual Review of Political Science* 11:563–588.

Fiorina, Morris P., Samuel J. Abrams, and Jeremy C. Pope. 2004. *Culture War? The Myth of a Polarized America.* Pearson.

Fisher, Louis. 2001. "Historical Background and Growth in International Agreements." In *Treaties and Other International Agreements: The Role of the United States*, ed. Congressional Research Service. Library of Congress, pp. 27–42.

Fisher, Max. 2015. "The Uproar over Sen. Tom Cotton's Letter to Iran, Explained." *Vox*, March 10.

Fitzpatrick, Mark. 2010. "Iran: The Fragile Promise of the Fuel-Swap Plan." *Survival* 52(3):67–94.

Flynn, Michael. 2014. "The International and Domestic Sources of Bipartisanship in U.S. Foreign Policy." *Political Research Quarterly* 67(2):398–412.

Fordham, Benjamin. 2010. *Building the Cold War Consensus: The Political Economy of U.S. National Security Policy, 1949–51.* University of Michigan Press.

Fordham, Benjamin O. and Michael Flynn. 2023. "Everything Old Is New Again: The Persistence of Republican Opposition to Multilateralism in American Foreign Policy." *Studies in American Political Development* 37(2):56–73.

Fossati, Dieog, Burhanuddin Muhtadi, and Eve Warburton. 2022. "Why Democrats Abandon Democracy: Evidence from Four Survey Experiments." *Party Politics* 28(3):554–566.

Fravel, M. Taylor. 2010. "The Limits of Diversion: Rethinking Internal and External Conflict." *Security Studies* 19(2):307–341.

Freedman, Lawrence. 2008. "The CIA and the Soviet Threat: The Politicization of Estimates, 1966–1977." *Intelligence and National Security* 12(1):122–142.

Freedom House. 2018. "Country Report: Turkey." Accessed from: https://freedomhouse.org/country/turkey.

Freedom House. 2023. "Freedom in the World 2023: Marking 50 Years in the Struggle for Democracy." Accessed from: https://freedomhouse.org/report/freedom-world/2023/marking-50-years.

Friedersdorf, Conor. 2018. "Trump and Russia Both Seek to Exacerbate the Same Political Divisions." *The Atlantic*, January 23.

Friedman, Jeffrey A. 2022. "Is U.S. Grand Strategy Dead? The Political Foundations of Deep Engagement after Donald Trump." *International Affairs* 98(4):1289–1305.

Friedman, Jeffrey A. 2023. *The Commander-in-Chief Test: Public Opinion and the Politics of Image-Making in US Foreign Policy*. Cornell University Press.

Friedman, Jeffrey A. 2024. "The Myth of a Bipartisan Golden Age for U.S. Foreign Policy: The Truman-Eisenhower Consensus Remains." *International Security* 49(2): 97–134.

Friedrichs, Gordon. 2021. *U.S. Global Leadership Role and Domestic Polarization: A Role Theory Approach*. Routledge.

Friedrichs, Gordon. 2022. "Conceptualizing the Effects of Polarization for US Foreign Policy Behavior in International Negotiations: Revisiting the Two-Level Game." *International Studies Review* 24(1): 1–29.

Friedrichs, Gordon M. and Jordan Tama. 2022. "Polarization and US Foreign Policy: Key Debates and New Findings." *International Politics* 59(5):767–785.

Friedrichs, Gordon M. and Jordan Tama. 2024. *Polarization and US Foreign Policy: When Politics Crosses the Water's Edge*. Palgrave Macmillan.

Fukuyama, Francis. 1992. *The End of History and the Last Man*. Free Press.

Gadarian, Shana Kushner, Sara Wallace Goodman, and Thomas B. Pepinsky. 2022. *Pandemic Politics: The Deadly Toll of Partisanship in the Age of COVID*. Princeton University Press.

Gaines, Brian J., James H. Kuklinski, Paul J. Quirk, Buddy Peyton, and Jay Verkuilen. 2007. "Same Facts, Different Interpretations: Partisan Motivation and Opinion on Iraq." *Journal of Politics* 69(4):957–974.

Galbraith, Jean. 2017. "From Treaties to International Commitments: The Changing Landscape of Foreign Relations Law." *University of Chicago Law Review* 84(4):1675–1745.

Galinsky, A. D. and G. B. Moskowitz. 2000. "Perspective-Taking: Decreasing Stereotype Expression, Stereotype Accessibility, and In-Group Favoritism." *Journal of Personality and Social Psychology* 78(4):708–724.

Gallup News. 2020. "Presidential Approval Ratings: Gallup Historical Statistics and Trends." Accessed from: https://news.gallup.com/poll/116677/presidential-approval-ratings-gallup-historical-statistics-trends.aspx.

Gartzke, Erik. 2007. "The Capitalist Peace." *American Journal of Political Science* 51(1): 166–191.

Gartzke, Erik and Kristian Skrede Gleditsch. 2004. "Why Democracies May Actually Be Less Reliable Allies." *American Journal of Political Science* 48(4):775–795.

Gates, Robert M. 1992. "Guarding against Politicization." Remarks by the Director of Central Intelligence, March 16. Accessed from: https://www.cia.gov/resources/csi/studies-in-intelligence/1992-2/guarding-against-politicization/.

Gaubatz, Kurt Taylor. 1996. "Democratic States and Commitment in International Relations." *International Organization* 50(1):109–139.

Geer, John G. 2006. *In Defense of Negativity: Attack Ads in Presidential Campaigns*. University of Chicago Press.

Gelpi, Christopher, Jason Reifler, and Peter Feaver. 2007. "Iraq the Vote: Retrospective and Prospective Foreign Policy Judgments on Candidate Choice and Casualty Tolerance." *Political Behavior* 29:151–174.

Gentry, John. 2019. "'Truth' as a Tool of the Politicization of Intelligence." *International Journal of Intelligence and CounterIntelligence* 32(2):217–247.

Gentzkow, Matthew, Jesse M. Shapiro, and Matt Taddy. 2017. "Measuring Polarization in High-Dimensional Data: Method and Application to Congressional Speech." NBER Working Paper 22423, Cambridge, MA, May.

Gentzkow, Matthew, Jesse M. Shapiro, and Matt Taddy. 2018. "Congressional Record for the 43rd–114th Congresses: Parsed Speeches and Phrase Counts." Stanford Libraries, Palo Alto, CA.

Gerber, Alan S., Donald P. Green and Christopher W. Larimer. 2008. "Social Pressure and Voter Turnout: Evidence from a Large-Scale Field Experiment." *American Political Science Review* 102(1):33–48.

Gholz, Eugene and Daryl Press. 2010. "Footprints in the Sand." *American Interest* 5(4):59–67.

Gidron, Noam, James Adams, and Will Horne. 2020. *American Affective Polarization in Comparative Perspective*. Cambridge University Press.

Giebler, Heiko, Saskia P. Ruth, and Dag Tanneberg. 2018. "Why Choice Matters: Revisiting and Comparing Measures of Democracy." *Politics and Governance* 6(1):1–10.

Gillion, Daniel Q., Jonathan M. Ladd, and Marc Meredith. 2020. "Party Polarization, Ideological Sorting, and the Emergence of the US Partisan Gender Gap." *British Journal of Political Science* 50(4):1217–1243.

Ginsburg, Tom, Aziz Huq, and David Landau. 2021. "The Comparative Constitutional Law of Presidential Impeachment." *University of Chicago Law Review* 88:81–164.

Glasser, Susan B. and Peter Baker. 2022. "Inside the War between Trump and His Generals." *New Yorker*, August 8.

Goemans, Hein E. 2000. *War and Punishment: The Causes of War Termination and the First World War*. Princeton University Press.

Goemans, Henk E., Kristian Skrede Gleditsch, and Giacomo Chiozza. 2009. "Introducing Archigos: A Dataset of Political Leaders." *Journal of Peace Research* 46(2):269–283.

Goet, Niels D. 2019. "Measuring Polarization with Text Analysis: Evidence from the UK House of Commons, 1811–2015." *Political Analysis* 27(4):518–539.

Goh, Evelyn. 2019. "US Dominance and American Bias in International Relations Scholarship: A View from the Outside." *Journal of Global Security Studies* 4(3):402–410.

Golby, Jim. 2021. "Uncivil–Military Relations: Politicization of the Military in the Trump Era." *Strategic Studies Quarterly* 15(2):149–174.

Gold, Michael and Maggie Astor. 2024. "Trump, Using Harsh Language, Urges Democrats to Tone Down Theirs." *New York Times*, September 16.

Golder, Matt. 2016. "Far Right Parties in Europe." *Annual Review of Political Science* 19:477–497.

Goodman, Sara Wallace. 2022. *Citizenship in Hard Times: How Ordinary People Respond to Democratic Threat*. Cambridge University Press.

Gorokhovskaia, Yana and Cathryn Grothe. 2024. "Freedom in the World 2024: The Mounting Damage of Flawed Elections and Armed Conflict." Report published by Freedom House.

Gowa, Joanne. 1998. "Politics at the Water's Edge: Parties, Voters, and the Use of Force Abroad." *International Organization* 52(2):307–324.

Gowa, Joanne. 1999. *Ballots and Bullets: The Elusive Democratic Peace*. Princeton University Press.

Graham, Matthew H. and Milan W. Svolik. 2020. "Democracy in America? Partisanship, Polarization, and the Robustness of Support for Democracy in the United States." *American Political Science Review* 114(2):392–409.

Gray, Rosie. 2017. "Trump Declines to Affirm NATO's Article 5." *The Atlantic*, May 25.

Green, Donald, Bradley Palmquist, and Eric Schickler. 2002. *Partisan Hearts and Minds: Political Parties and the Social Identities of Voters*. Yale University Press.

Green, Jon, Stefan McCabe, Sarah Shugars, Hanyu Chwe, Luke Horgan, Shuyang Cao, and David Lazer. 2025. "Curation Bubbles." Forthcoming at American Political Science Review.

Greve, Joan E. and Lauren Gambino. 2023. "Capitol Hill Finds Rare Bipartisan Cause in China: But It Could Pose Problems." *The Guardian*, February 26.

Grose, Christian R. 2020. "Reducing Legislative Polarization: Top-Two and Open Primaries Are Associated with More Moderate Legislators." *Journal of Political Institutions and Political Economy* 1(2):267–287.

Grossman, Derek. 2023. "Upcoming Presidential Election Will Clarify Taiwan's China Policy." *RAND Corporation*, May 19.

Grossman, Matt and David A. Hopkins. 2016. *Asymmetric Politics: Ideological Republicans and Group Interest Democrats*. Oxford University Press.

Guay, Brian and Christopher D. Johnston. 2022. "Ideological Asymmetries and the Determinants of Politically Motivated Reasoning." *American Journal of Political Science* 66(2): 285–301.

Guess, Andrew M., Neil Malhotra, Jennifer Pan, Pablo Barberá, Hunt Allcott, Taylor Brown, Adriana Crespo-Tenorio, Drew Dimmery, Deen Freelon, Matthew Gentzkow, Sandra González-Bailón, Edward Kennedy, Young Mie Kim, David Lazer, Devra Moehler, Brendan Nyhan, Carlos Velasco Rivera, Jaime Settle, Daniel Robert Thomas, Emily Thorson, Rebekah Tromble, Arjun Wilkins, Magdalena Wojcieszak, Beixian Xiong, Chad Kiewiet de Jonge, Annie Franco, Winter Mason, Natalie Jomini Stroud, and Joshua A. Tucker. 2023a. "How Do Social Media Feed Algorithms Affect Attitudes and Behavior in an Election Campaign?" *Science* 381(6656):398–404.

Guess, Andrew M., Neil Malhotra, Jennifer Pan, Pablo Barberá, Hunt Allcott, Taylor Brown, Adriana Crespo-Tenorio, Drew Dimmery, Deen Freelon, Matthew Gentzkow, Sandra González-Bailón, Edward Kennedy, Young Mie Kim, David Lazer, Devra Moehler, Brendan Nyhan, Carlos Velasco Rivera, Jaime Settle, Daniel Robert Thomas, Emily Thorson, Rebekah Tromble, Arjun Wilkins, Magdalena Wojcieszak, Beixian Xiong, Chad Kiewiet de Jonge, Annie Franco, Winter Mason, Natalie Jomini Stroud, and Joshua A. Tucker. 2023b. "Reshares on Social Media Amplify Political News but Do Not Detectably Affect Beliefs or Opinions." *Science* 381(6656):404–408.

Guisinger, Alexandra and Elizabeth N. Saunders. 2017. "Mapping the Boundaries of Elite Cues: How Elites Shape Mass Opinion across International Issues." *International Studies Quarterly* 61(2):425–441.

Gunitskiy, Seva. 2017. *Aftershocks: Great Powers and Domestic Reforms in the Twentieth Century*. Princeton University Press.

Haas, Benjamin. 2017. "The President and the Peril of Politicizing Our Military." *Just Security*, February 17.

Haas, Benjamin and Kori Schake. 2020. "The Military Isn't at War with the Public: Trump Seems to Want to Change That." *Washington Post*, June 8.

Hacker, Jacob S. and Paul Pierson. 2015. "Confronting Asymmetric Polarization." In *Solutions to Political Polarization in America*, ed. Nathaniel Persily. Cambridge University Press, pp. 59–70.

Hafner-Burton, Emilie M. and Christina J. Schneider. 2023. "The International Liberal Foundations of Democratic Backsliding." IGCC Working Paper, Washington, DC, July 12.

Hafner-Burton, Emilie M. and Kiyo Tsutsui. 2005. "Human Rights Practices in a Globalizing World: The Paradox of Empty Promises." *American Journal of Sociology* 110(5): 285–298.

Haglund, Evan. 2015. "Striped Pants versus Fat Cats: Ambassadorial Performance of Career Diplomats and Political Appointees." *Presidential Studies Quarterly* 45(4):653–678.

Hains, Tim. 2015. "John Kerry Explains Why Iran Deal Is Not Legally a Treaty: 'You Can't Pass a Treaty Anymore.'" *Real Clear Politics*, July 29.

Hall, Andrew. 2019. *Who Wants to Run? How the Devaluing of Political Office Drives Polarization*. University of Chicago Press.

Hall, Andrew B. and Daniel M. Thompson. 2018. "Who Punishes Extremist Nominees? Candidate Ideology and Turning Out the Base in US Elections." *American Political Science Review* 112(3):509–524.

Halperin, Morton H. and Priscilla Clapp. 2007. *Bureaucratic Politics and Foreign Policy*. Brookings Institution Press.

Han, Seungwoo. 2022. "Elite Polarization in South Korea: Evidence from a Natural Language Processing Model." *Journal of East Asian Studies* 22(1):45–75.

Hartman, Rachel, Will Blakey, Jake Womick, Chris Bail, Eli J. Finkel, Hahrie Han, John Sarrouf, Juliana Schroeder, Paschal Sheeran, Jay J. Van Bavel, Robb Willer, and Kurt Gray. 2022. "Interventions to Reduce Partisan Animosity." *Nature Human Behavior* 6:1194–1205.

Hathaway, Oona A. 2007. "Why Do Countries Commit to Human Rights Treaties?" *Journal of Conflict Resolution* 51(4):588–621.

Hathaway, Oona A., Curtis A. Bradley, and Jack L. Goldsmith. 2020. "The Failed Transparency Regime for Executive Agreements: An Empirical and Normative Analysis." *Harvard Law Review* 134(2):629–725.

Heffington, Colton, Brandon Beomseob Park, and Laron K. Williams. 2019. "The 'Most Important Problem' Dataset (MIPD)." *Conflict Management and Peace Science* 36(3):312–335.

Helco, Hugh. 1977. *A Government of Strangers: Executive Politics in Washington*. Brookings Institution Press.

Henderson, John A., Brian T. Hamel, and Aaron M. Goldzimer. 2018. "Gerrymandering Incumbency: Does Nonpartisan Redistricting Increase Electoral Competition?" *Journal of Politics* 80(3):1011–1016.

Hendrickson, Ryan C. 2015. *Obama at War: Congress and the Imperial Presidency*. University Press of Kentucky.

Henley, John. 2017. "Angela Merkel: EU Cannot Completely Rely on Us and Britain Any More." *The Guardian*, May 28.

Hetherington, Marc J. 2001. "Resurgent Mass Partisanship: The Role of Elite Polarization." *American Political Science Review* 95(3):619–631.

Hetherington, Marc J. 2008. "Turned Off or Turned On? How Polarization Affects Political Engagement." In *Red and Blue Nation? Consequences and Correction of America's Polarized Politics*, ed. Pietro S. Nivola and David W. Brady. Brookings Institution Press, pp. 1–54.

Hickey, C. K. and Maya Gandhi. 2019. "11 Charts That Track the Weight of Foreign Policy in U.S. Primary Debates." *Foreign Policy*, June 26.

Hillygus, D. Sunshine and Todd G. Shields. 2009. *The Persuadable Voter: Wedge Issues in Presidential Campaigns*. Princeton University Press.

Hirano, Shigeo and James M. Snyder. 2019. *Primary Elections in the United States*. Cambridge University Press.

Hirano, Shigeo, James M. Snyder Jr., Stephen Daniel Ansolabehere, and John Mark Hansen. 2010. "Primary Elections and Partisan Polarization in the U.S. Congress." *Quarterly Journal of Political Science* 5(2):169–191.

Hobolt, Sara B., Thomas J. Leeper, and James Tilley. 2021. "Divided by the Vote: Affective Polarization in the Wake of the Brexit Referendum." *British Journal of Political Science* 51(4):1476–1493.

Hoffman, Stanley. 1995. "The Crisis of Liberal Internationalism." *Foreign Policy* 98:159–177.

Hollis, Duncan B. and Joshua J. Newcomer. 2008. "Political Commitments and the Constitution." *Virginia Journal of International Law* 49(3):507–584.

Holsti, Ole R. 1992. "Public Opinion and Foreign Policy: Challenges to the Almond–Lippmann Consensus." *International Studies Quarterly* 36:439–466.

Holsti, Ole R. 1996. *Public Opinion and American Foreign Policy*. University of Michigan Press.

Homan, Patrick and Jeffrey S. Lantis. 2022. "Foreign Policy Free Agents: How Lawmakers and Coalitions on the Political Margins Help Set Boundaries for US Foreign Policy." *International Politics* 59(5):851–872.

Hooghe, Liesbet, Gary Marks, and Carole J. Wilson. 2002. "Does Left/Right Structure Party Positions on European Integration?" *Comparative Political Studies* 35(8):965–989.

Hooghe, Liesbet, Gary Marks, and Jonne Kamphorst. 2025. "Field of Education and Political Behavior: Predicting GAL-TAN Voting." Forthcoming at American Political Science Review.

Horowitz, Michael C., Allan C. Stam, and Cali M. Ellis. 2015. *Why Leaders Fight*. Cambridge University Press.

Hotelling, Harold. 1929. "Stability in Competition." *Economic Journal* 39(153):41–57.

Howell, William G. 2003. *Power without Persuasion: The Politics of Direct Presidential Action*. Princeton University Press.

Howell, William G. and Douglas L. Kriner. 2007. "Bending So as Not to Break: What the Bush Presidency Reveals about Unilateral Action." In *The Polarized Presidency of George W. Bush*, ed. George Edwards and Desmond King. Oxford University Press, pp. 96–144.

Howell, William G. and Jon C. Pevehouse. 2005. "Presidents, Congress, and the Use of Force." *International Organization* 59(1):209–232.

Howell, William G. and Jon C. Pevehouse. 2007. *While Dangers Gather: Congressional Checks on Presidential War Powers*. Princeton University Press.

Hoyer, Steny. 2023. "Hoyer Statement on House Republicans' Political NDAA Legislation." Press Release from the Office of Congressman Steny H. Hoyer (MD-05). Accessed from: https://hoyer.house.gov/media/press-releases/hoyer-statement-house-republicans-political-ndaa-legislation.

Hrushetskyi, Anton. 2023. "Dynamics of Trust in Social Institutions in 2021–2023." Press Release from the Kyiv International Institute of Sociology. Accessed from: https://kiis.com.ua/?cat=reports&id=1335&lang=eng&page=1.

Hunter, Kelly. 2023. "The Political Economy of Gender in Global Health: How International Actors Shape Women's Outcomes." PhD Dissertation, Duke University.

Huntington, Samuel. 1957. *The Soldier and the State: The Theory and Politics of Civil–Military Relations*. Harvard University Press.

Huntington, Samuel P. 1991. *The Third Wave: Democratization in the Late 20th Century*. University of Oklahoma Press.

Hurst, Steven and Andrew Wroe. 2016. "Partisan Polarization and US Foreign Policy: Is the Centre Dead or Holding?" *International Politics* 53:666–682.

Hurwitz, Jon and Mark Peffley. 1987. "How Are Foreign Policy Attitudes Structured? A Hierarchical Model." *American Political Science Review* 81(4):1099–1120.

Hyde, Susan D. 2020. "Democracy's Backsliding in the International Environment." *Science* 369(6508):1192–1196.

Hyde, Susan D. and Elizabeth N. Saunders. 2020. "Recapturing Regime Type in International Relations: Leaders, Institutions, and Agency Space." *International Organization* 74(2): 363–395.

Iida, Keisuke. 1993. "When and How Do Domestic Constraints Matter? Two-Level Games with Uncertainty." *Journal of Conflict Resolution* 37(3):403–426.

Ikenberry, G. John. 2009. "Liberal Internationalism 3.0: America and the Dilemma of Liberal World Order." *Perspectives on Politics* 7(1):71–87.

Ikenberry, G. John. 2011. "The Future of the Liberal World Order." *Foreign Affairs* 90(3): 56–68.

Ikenberry, G. John. 2018. "The End of Liberal International Order?" *International Affairs* 94(1):7–23.

Inglehart, R., C. Haerpfer, A. Moreno, C. Welzel, K. Kizilova, J. Diez-Medrano, M. Lagos, P. Norris, E. Ponarin, and B. Puranen. 2014. "World Values Survey: All Rounds, Country-Pooled Datafile Version." World Values Survey. Accessed from: https://www.worldvaluessurvey.org/WVSDocumentationWV6.jsp.

Inhofe, Jim. 2016. "Inhofe Statement on the Future of U.S. Commitments to the Paris Agreement." *States News Service*, November 9. Accessed from: https://go.gale.com/ps/i.do?id=GALE%7CA469595647&sid=sitemap&v=2.1&it=r&p=EAIM&sw=w.

International Foundation for Electoral Systems (IFES). 2022. *ElectionGuide*. Accessed from: https://www.electionguide.org/

Irvine, William D. 1996. "Domestic Politics and the Fall of France in 1940." *Historical Reflections* 22(1):77–90.

Iyengar, Shanto, Gaurav Sood, and Yphtach Lelkes. 2012. "Affect, Not Ideology: A Social Identity Perspective on Polarization." *Public Opinion Quarterly* 76(3):405–431.

Iyengar, Shanto, Yphtach Lelkes, Matthew Levendusky, Neil Malhotra, and Sean J. Westwood. 2019. "The Origins and Consequences of Affective Polarization in the United States." *Annual Review of Political Science* 22(7):129–146.

Jackson, Van. 2022. "Left of Liberal Internationalism: Grand Strategies within Progressive Foreign Policy Thought." *Security Studies* 31(4):553–592.

Jackson, Van. 2023. *Grand Strategies of the Left*. Cambridge University Press.

Jacobson, Gary C. 2004. *The Politics of Congressional Elections*, 6th ed. Pearson.

Jaffer, Jamil N. 2019. "Elements of Its Own Demise: Key Flaws in the Obama Administration's Domestic Approach to the Iran Nuclear Agreement." *Case Western Reserve Journal of International Law* 51:77–101.

James, Robert Rhodes. 1987. *Anthony Eden*. Pan Macmillan.

Jardina, Ashley E. 2019. *White Identity Politics*. Cambridge University Press.

Jee, Haemin, Hans Lueders, and Rachel Myrick. 2022. "Towards a Unified Approach to Research on Democratic Backsliding." *Democratization* 29(4):754–767.

Jeffreys-Jones, Rhodri. 2022. *A Question of Standing: The History of the CIA*. Oxford University Press.

Jensen, Nathan. 2008. "Political Risk, Democratic Institutions, and Foreign Direct Investment." *Journal of Politics* 70(4):1040–1052.

Jensen, Nathan M. 2003. "Democratic Governance and Multinational Corporations: Political Regimes and Inflows of Foreign Direct Investment." *International Organization* 57:587–616.

Jentleson, Bruce. 2007. "America's Global Role after Bush." *Survival* 49(3):179–200.

Jentleson, Bruce. 2022. *Sanctions: What Everyone Needs to Know*. Oxford University Press.

Jentleson, Bruce W. 1992. "The Pretty Prudent Public: Post Post-Vietnam American Opinion and the Use of Military Force." *International Studies Quarterly* 36:49–74.

Jentleson, Bruce W. 2020. "Refocusing US Grand Strategy on Pandemic and Environmental Mass Destruction." *Washington Quarterly* 43(3):7–29.

Jentleson, Bruce W. and Rebecca L. Britton. 1998. "Still Pretty Prudent: Post–Cold War American Public Opinion on the Use of Military Force." *Journal of Conflict Resolution* 42(4):395–417.

Jeong, Gyung-Ho and Paul J. Quirk. 2019. "Division at the Water's Edge: The Polarization of Foreign Policy." *American Politics Research* 47(1):58–87.

Jervis, Robert. 2010a. "Why Intelligence and Policymakers Clash." *Political Science Quarterly* 125(2):185–204.

Jervis, Robert. 2010b. *Why Intelligence Fails: Lessons from the Iranian Revolution and the Iraq War*. Cornell University Press.

Jervis, Robert, Francis J. Gavin, Joshua Rovner, and Diane N. Labrosse. 2018. *Chaos in the Liberal Order: The Trump Presidency and International Politics in the Twenty-First Century*. Columbia University Press.

Jeung, Russell. 2023. "U.S.–China Tensions Are Feeding a New Wave of Anti-Asian Hate." *Los Angeles Times*, April 17.
Johnson, David K. 2004. *The Lavender Scare: The Cold War Persecution of Gays and Lesbians in the Federal Government*. University of Chicago Press.
Johnson, Loch K. 1989. "Covert Action and Accountability: Decision-Making for America's Secret Foreign Policy." *International Studies Quarterly* 33:81–109.
Johnson, Susan R., Ronald E. Neumann, and Thomas R. Pickering. 2013. "Presidents Are Breaking the U.S. Foreign Service." *Washington Post*, April 11.
Jonas, David S. and Dyllan M. Taxman. 2018. "JCP-No-Way: A Critique of the Iran Nuclear Deal as a Non-Legally-Binding Political Commitment." *Journal of National Security Law and Policy* 9:589–630.
Jones, Jeffrey M. 2022. "Confidence in U.S. Institutions Down: Average at New Low." *Gallup News*, July 5.
Jost, Tyler. 2024. *Bureaucracies at War: The Institutional Origins of Miscalculation*. Cambridge University Press.
Kaarbo, Juliet. 1996. "Power and Influence in Foreign Policy Decision Making: The Role of Junior Coalition Partners in German and Israeli Foreign Policy." *International Studies Quarterly* 40(4):501–530.
Kafura, Craig. 2023. "Americans Feel More Threat from China Now Than in Past Three Decades." Chicago Council on Global Affairs, Chicago.
Kalla, Joshua and David Broockman. 2018. "The Minimal Persuasive Effects of Campaign Contact in General Elections: Evidence from 49 Field Experiments." *American Political Science Review* 112(1):148–166.
Kalla, Joshua L. and David E. Broockman. 2023. "Which Narrative Strategies Durably Reduce Prejudice? Evidence from Field and Survey Experiments Supporting the Efficacy of Perspective-Getting." *American Journal of Political Science* 67(1):185–204.
Kalmoe, Nathan. 2020. *With Ballots and Bullets: Partisanship and Violence in the American Civil War*. Cambridge University Press.
Kalmoe, Nathan P. and Lilliana Mason. 2022. *Radical American Partisanship*. University of Chicago Press.
Karol, David and Edward Miguel. 2007. "The Electoral Cost of War: Iraq Casualties and the 2004 U.S. Presidential Election." *Journal of Politics* 69(3):633–648.
Karp, Jeffrey A. 2012. "Electoral Systems, Party Mobilization, and Political Engagement." *Australian Journal of Political Science* 47(1):71–89.
Karp, Jeffrey A. and Susan A. Banducci. 2007. "Party Mobilization and Political Participation in New and Old Democracies." *Party Politics* 13(2):217–234.
Katzenstein, Peter. 1996. *The Culture of National Security*. Cornell University Press.
Kaufman, Robert R. and Stephan Haggard. 2019. "Democratic Decline in the United States: What Can We Learn from Middle-Income Backsliding?" *Perspectives on Politics* 17(2):417–432.
Keith, Bruce E., David B. Magleby, Candice J. Nelson, Elizabeth Orr, Mark C. Westlye, and Raymond E. Wolfinger. 1986. "The Partisan Affinities of Independent 'Leaners.'" *British Journal of Political Science* 16(2):155–185.
Kelly, Nora. 2015. "Where the 2016 Candidates Stand on the Iran Nuclear Deal." *The Atlantic*, September 1.
Kennedy, Scott and Ilaria Mazzocco. 2022. "The China Shock: Reevaluating the Debate." *Big Data China*, October 14.
Keohane, Robert. 1984. *After Hegemony: Cooperation and Discord in the World Political Economy*. Reprint, 2005 ed. Princeton University Press.

Kernell, Samuel. 1991. "Facing an Opposition Congress: The President's Strategic Circumstance." In *The Politics of Divided Government*, ed. Gary W. Cox and Samuel Kernell. Westview Press, pp. 87–112.
Kernell, Samuel. 2006. *Going Public: New Strategies of Presidential Leadership*. CQ Press.
Kertzer, Joshua. 2016. *Resolve in International Politics*. Princeton University Press.
Kertzer, Joshua D. 2021. "American Credibility after Afghanistan: What the Withdrawal Really Meant for Washington's Reputation." *Foreign Affairs*, September 2.
Kertzer, Joshua D. 2023. "Public Opinion and Foreign Policy." In *Oxford Handbook of Political Psychology*, ed. Leonie Huddy, David Sears, Jack Levy, and Jennifer Jerit. Oxford University Press, pp. 447–485.
Kertzer, Joshua D., Brian C. Rathbun, and Nina Srinivasan Rathbun. 2020. "The Price of Peace: Motivated Reasoning and Costly Signaling in International Relations." *International Organization* 74(1):95–118.
Kertzer, Joshua D., Deborah Jordan Brooks, and Stephen G. Brooks. 2021. "Do Partisan Types Stop at the Water's Edge?" *Journal of Politics* 83(4):1764–1782.
Kertzer, Joshua D. and Jonathan Renshon. 2022. "Experiments and Surveys on Political Elites." *Annual Review of Political Science* 25:529–550.
Kertzer, Joshua D., Kathleen E. Powers, Brian C. Rathbun, and Ravi Iyer. 2014. "Moral Support: How Moral Values Shape Foreign Policy Attitudes." *Journal of Politics* 63(3):825–840.
Kertzer, Joshua D. and Ryan Brutger. 2016. "Decomposing Audience Costs: Bringing the Audience Back into Audience Cost Theory." *American Journal of Political Science* 60(1):234–249.
Kertzer, Joshua D. and Thomas Zeitzoff. 2017. "A Bottom-Up Theory of Public Opinion about Foreign Policy." *American Journal of Political Science* 61(3):543–558.
Kessler, Glenn. 2006. "In 2003, U.S. Spurned Iran's Offer of Dialogue." *Washington Post*, June 17.
KFF. 2021. "The Mexico City Policy: An Explainer." KFF Global Health Policy, January 28.
Khan, Beethika, Carol Robbins, and Abigail Okrent. 2020. "The State of U.S. Science and Engineering 2020." National Science Foundation. Accessed from: https://ncses.nsf.gov/pubs/nsb20201.
Khong, Yuen Foong. 2014. "Primacy or World Order? The United States and China's Rise." *International Security* 38(3):153–175.
Kim, Daegyeong. 2022. "Anti-Asian Racism and the Racial Politics of US–China Great Power Rivalry." PhD Dissertation, University of California San Diego.
Kim, Moonhawk. 2008. "Costly Procedures: Divergent Effects of Legalization in the GATT/WTO Dispute Settlement Procedures." *International Studies Quarterly* 52:657–686.
Kingzette, Jon, James N. Druckman, Samara Klar, Yanna Krupnikov, Matthew Levendusky, and John Barry Ryan. 2021. "How Affective Polarization Undermines Support for Democratic Norms." *Public Opinion Quarterly* 85(2):663–677.
Kirişci, Kemal and Amanda Sloat. 2019. "The Rise and Fall of Liberal Democracy in Turkey: Implications for the West." Brookings Institution, Washington, DC, February.
Kitschelt, Herbert. 1997. *The Radical Right in Western Europe: A Comparative Analysis*. University of Michigan Press.
Klein, Ezra. 2020. *Why We're Polarized*. Simon and Schuster.
Kohn, Richard H. 2009. "The Danger of Militarization in an Endless 'War' on Terrorism." *Journal of Military History* 73(1):177–208.
Koremenos, Barbara, Charles Lipson, and Duncan Snidal. 2001. "The Rational Design of International Institutions." *International Organization* 55(4):761–799.

Kraft, Patrick W., Milton Lodge, and Charles S. Taber. 2015. "Why People 'Don't Trust the Evidence': Motivated Reasoning and Scientific Beliefs." *ANNALS of the American Academy of Political and Social Science* 658(1):121–133.

Krebs, Ronald R. 2015. "How Dominant Narratives Rise and Fall: Military Conflict, Politics, and the Cold War Consensus." *International Organization* 69(4):809–845.

Krebs, Ronald R., Robert Ralston, and Aaron Rapport. 2023. "No Right to Be Wrong: What Americans Think about Civil–Military Relations." *Perspectives on Politics* 21(2):606–624.

Kreps, Sarah E., Elizabeth N. Saunders, and Kenneth A. Schultz. 2018. "The Ratification Premium: Hawk, Doves, and Arms Control." *World Politics* 70(4):479–514.

Kriner, Douglas L. and Eric Shickler. 2016. *Investigating the President: Congressional Checks on Presidential Power*. Princeton University Press.

Kroenig, Matthew. 2020. *The Return of Great Power Rivalry*. Oxford University Press.

Krupnikov, Yanna and John Barry Ryan. 2022. *The Other Divide: Polarization and Disengagement in American Politics*. Cambridge University Press.

Krutz, Glen S. and Jeffrey S. Peake. 2006. "The Changing Nature of Presidential Policy Making on International Agreements." *Presidential Studies Quarterly* 36(3):391–409.

Krutz, Glen S. and Jeffrey S. Peake. 2009. *Treaty Politics and the Rise of Executive Agreements: International Commitments in a System of Shared Powers*. University of Michigan Press.

Kupchan, Charles A. 2020. *Isolationism: A History of America's Efforts to Shield Itself from the World*. Oxford University Press.

Kupchan, Charles A. and Peter L. Trubowitz. 2007. "Dead Center: The Demise of Liberal Internationalism in the United States." *International Security* 32(2):7–44.

Kupchan, Charles A. and Peter L. Trubowitz. 2010. "The Illusion of Liberal Internationalism's Revival." *International Security* 35(1):95–109.

Kurd, Dana El. 2019. *Polarized and Demobilized: Legacies of Authoritarianism in Palestine*. Oxford University Press.

Kurth, James. 1996. "America's Grand Strategy: A Pattern of History." *National Interest*, March 1.

Lake, David A. 1992. "Powerful Pacifists: Democratic States and War." *American Political Science Review* 86(1):24–37.

Lane, Suzie, Sonja Ayeb-Karlsson, and Arianne Shahvisi. 2021. "Impacts of the Global Gag Rule on Sexual and Reproductive Health and Rights in the Global South: A Scoping Review." *Global Public Health* 16(12):1804–1819.

La Raja, Raymond J. and Brian F. Schaffner. 2015. *Campaign Finance and Political Polarization: When Purists Prevail*. University of Michigan Press.

Lau, Richard R. and Ivy Brown Rovner. 2009. "Negative Campaigning." *Annual Review of Political Science* 12:285–306.

Laver, Michael and Ian Budge, eds. 1992. *Party Policy and Government Coalitions*. Macmillan.

Lavine, Howard G., Christopher D. Johnston, and Marco R. Steenbergen. 2012. *The Ambivalent Partisan: How Critical Loyalty Promotes Democracy*. Oxford University Press.

Layman, Geoffrey C. and Thomas M. Carsey. 2002. "Party Polarization and 'Conflict Extension' in the American Electorate." *American Journal of Political Science* 46(4):786–802.

Layman, Geoffrey C., Thomas M. Carsey, John C. Green, Richard Herrera, and Rosalyn Cooperman. 2010. "Activists and Conflict Extension in American Party Politics." *American Political Science Review* 104(2):324–346.

Layman, Geoffrey C., Thomas M. Carsey, and Juliana Menasce Horowitz. 2006. "Party Polarization in American Politics: Characteristics, Causes, and Consequences." *Annual Review of Political Science* 9:83–110.

Layne, Christopher. 2009. "America's Middle East Strategy after Iraq: The Moment for Offshore Balancing Has Arrived." *Review of International Studies* 35(1):5–25.

Lee, Carrie. 2022. "Polarization, Casualty Sensitivity, and Military Operations: Evidence from a Survey Experiment." *International Politics* 59:981–1003.

Lee, Carrie and Max Margulies. 2023. "Rethinking Civil–Military Relations for Modern Strategy." Modern War Institute, West Point, NY, August 14.

Lee, Frances E. 2008. "Agreeing to Disagree: Agenda Content and Senate Partisanship, 1981–2004." *Legislative Studies Quarterly* 33:199–222.

Lee, Frances E. 2009. *Beyond Ideology: Politics, Principles, and Partisanship in the US Senate*. University of Chicago Press.

Lee, Frances E. 2015. "How Party Polarization Affects Governance." *Annual Review of Political Science* 18:261–282.

Lee, Yimou. 2019. "Taiwan Leader Rejects China's 'One Country, Two Systems' Offer." *Reuters*, October 9.

Leeds, Brett Ashley. 1999. "Domestic Political Institutions, Credible Commitments, and International Cooperation." *American Journal of Political Science* 43(4):979–1002.

Leeds, Brett Ashley. 2003. "Alliance Reliability in Times of War: Explaining State Decisions to Violate Treaties." *International Organization* 57:801–827.

Leeds, Brett Ashley and Burcu Savun. 2007. "Terminating Alliances: Why Do States Abrogate Agreements?" *Journal of Politics* 69(4):1118–1132.

Leeds, Brett Ashley, Jeffrey M. Ritter, Sara McLaughlin Mitchell, and Andrew G. Long. 2002. "Alliance Treaty Obligations and Provisions, 1815–1944." *International Interactions* 28:237–260.

Leeds, Brett Ashley and Michaela Mattes. 2022. *Domestic Interests, Democracy, and Foreign Policy Change*. Cambridge Elements.

Leeds, Brett Ashley, Michaela Mattes, and Jeremy S. Vogel. 2009. "Interests, Institutions, and the Reliability of International Commitments." *American Journal of Political Science* 53(2):461–476.

Leeper, Thomas J. and Rune Slothuus. 2014. "Political Parties, Motivated Reasoning, and Public Opinion Formation." *Political Psychology* 35:129–156.

Lehman, Howard P. and Jennifer L. McCoy. 1992. "The Dynamics of Two-Level Bargaining Game: The 1988 Brazilian Debt Negotiation." *World Politics* 44(4):600–644.

Lehmann, Pola, Matthieß Theres, Nicolas Merz, Sven Regel, and Annika Werner. 2018. "Manifesto Corpus." WZB Berlin Social Science Center, Berlin.

Lelkes, Yphtach, Gaurav Sood, and Shanto Iyengar. 2017. "The Hostile Audience: The Effect of Access to Broadband Internet on Partisan Affect." *American Journal of Political Science* 61(1):5–20.

Leslie, Jonathan G. 2022. *Fear and Insecurity: Israel and the Iran Threat Narrative*. Hurst.

LeVeck, Brad L. and Neil Narang. 2017. "How International Reputation Matters: Revisiting Alliance Violations in Context." *International Interactions* 43(5):797–821.

Levendusky, Matthew. 2009. *The Partisan Sort*. University of Chicago Press.

Levendusky, Matthew S. 2013. "Why Do Partisan Media Polarize Viewers?" *American Journal of Political Science* 57(3):611–623.

Levendusky, Matthew S. 2017. "Americans, Not Partisans: Can Priming American National Identity Reduce Affective Polarization?" *Journal of Politics* 80(1):59–70.

Levendusky, Matthew S. 2023. *Our Common Bonds: Using What Americans Share to Help Bridge the Partisan Divide*. Cambridge University Press.

Levendusky, Matthew S. and Dominik A. Stecula. 2021. *We Need to Talk How Cross-Party Dialogue Reduces Affective Polarization*. Cambridge Elements.

Levendusky, Matthew S. and Michael C. Horowitz. 2012. "When Backing Down Is the Right Decision: Partisanship, New Information, and Audience Costs." *Journal of Politics* 74(2):323–338.

Levin, Dov H. and Robert F. Trager. 2019. "Things You Can See from There You Can't See from Here: Blind Spots in the American Perspective in IR and Their Effects." *Journal of Global Security Studies* 4(3):345–357.

Levitsky, Steven and Daniel Ziblatt. 2018. *How Democracies Die*. Crown.

Levitsky, Steven and Kenneth M. Roberts, eds. 2011. *The Resurgence of the Latin American Left*. Johns Hopkins University Press.

Levy, Jack S. 2008. "Case Studies: Types, Designs, and Logics of Inference." *Conflict Management and Peace Science* 25:1–18.

Levy, Jack S., Michael K. McKoy, Paul Poast, and Geoffrey P. R. Wallace. 2015. "Backing Out or Backing In? Commitment and Consistency in Audience Costs Theory." *American Journal of Political Science* 59(4):988–1001.

Lewis, David. 2009. "Where Do Presidents Politicize? Evidence from the George W. Bush Administration." Working Paper 02-2009, Center for the Study of Democratic Institutions, Vanderbilt University, Nashville, TN.

Lewis, Jeffrey B., Keith Poole, Howard Rosenthal, Aaron Rudkin, and Luke Sonnet. 2019. "Congressional Roll-Call Votes Database." Voteview. Accessed from: https://voteview.com/data.

Li, Nigel. 2023. "Washington's Averted Shutdown, Divided House, and Concerned Allies." *The Diplomat*, October 10.

Li, Quan. 2009. "Democracy, Autocracy, and Expropriation of Foreign Direct Investment." *Comparative Political Studies* 42(8):1098–1127.

Lindsay, James M. 2000. "The New Apathy: How an Uninterested Public Is Reshaping Foreign Policy." *Foreign Affairs* 79(5):2–8.

Lippman, Daniel, Nahal Toosi, and Quint Forgey. 2021. "Biden's Beefed-Up NSC." *Politico*, August 2.

Lippmann, Walter. 1922. *Public Opinion*. Macmillan.

Lippmann, Walter. 1955. *Essays in the Public Philosophy*. Little, Brown.

Lipson, Charles. 2003. *Reliable Partners: How Democracies Have Made a Separate Peace*. Princeton University Press.

Lissner, Rebecca and Mira Rapp-Hooper. 2020. *An Open World: How America Can Win the Contest for Twenty-First Century Order*. Yale University Press.

Lodge, Milton and Charles S. Taber. 2013. *The Rationalizing Voter*. Cambridge University Press.

Löfflmann, George. 2022. "Introduction to Special Issue: The Study of Populism in International Relations." *British Journal of Politics and International Relations* 24(3):403–415.

Lovett, John, Shaun Bevan, and Frank R. Baumgartner. 2015. "Popular Presidents Can Affect Congressional Attention, for a Little While." *Policy Studies Journal* 43(1):22–43.

Lowande, Kenneth S. and Sidney M. Milkis. 2014. "'We Can't Wait': Barack Obama, Partisan Polarization and the Administrative Presidency." *The Forum* 12(1):3–27.

Lueders, Hans and Ellen Lust. 2018. "Multiple Measurements, Elusive Agreement, and Unstable Outcomes in the Study of Regime Change." *Journal of Politics* 80(2):736–741.

Lührmann, Anna, Kyle L. Marquardt, and Valeriya Mechkova. 2020. "Constraining Governments: New Indices of Vertical, Horizontal, and Diagonal Accountability." *American Political Science Review* 114(3):811–820.

Lührmann, Anna, Nils Düpont, Masaaki Higashijima, Yaman Berker Kavasoglu, Kyle L. Marquardt, Michael Bernhard, Holger Döring, Allen Hicken, Melis Laebens, Staffan I. Lindberg, Juraj Medzihorsky, Anja Neundorf, Ora John Reuter, Saskia Ruth-Lovell, Keith R. Weghorst, Nina Wiesehomeier, Joseph Wright, Nazifa Alizada, Paul Bederke, Lisa Gastaldi, Sandra Grahn, Garry Hindle, Nina Ilchenko, Johannes von Römer, Daniel Pemstein, and Brigitte Seim. 2020. "Codebook Varieties of Party Identity and Organisation (V–Party) V1." Varieties of Democracy (V-Dem) Project. Accessed from: https://v-dem.net/.

Lyall, Jason, Yang-Yang Zhou, and Kosuke Imai. 2020. "Can Economic Assistance Shape Combatant Support in Wartime? Experimental Evidence from Afghanistan." *American Political Science Review* 114(1):126–143.

Malis, Matt. 2021. "Conflict, Cooperation, and Delegated Diplomacy." *International Organization* 75(4):1018–1057.

Mansfield, Edward D., Helen V. Milner, and B. Peter Rosendorff. 2002. "Why Democracies Cooperate More: Electoral Control and International Trade Agreements." *International Organization* 56(3):477–513.

Maoz, Zeev and Bruce Russett. 1993. "Normative and Structural Causes of Democratic Peace, 1946–1986." *American Political Science Review* 87(3):624–638.

Marlon, Jennifer, Eric Fine, and Anthony Leiserowitz. 2016. "Majorities of Americans in Every State Support Participation in the Paris Agreement." Yale Program on Climate Change Communication, Yale School of the Environment, New Haven, CT, May 7.

Marshall, Monty G. and Ted Robert Gurr. 2018. "Polity5: Political Regime Characteristics and Transitions, 1800–2018." Polity Project. Accessed from: https://www.systemicpeace.org/polityproject.html.

Martin, Lisa L. 2000. *Democratic Commitments: Legislatures and International Cooperation*. Princeton University Press.

Martin, Lisa L. 2005. "The President and International Commitments: Treaties as Signaling Devices." *Presidential Studies Quarterly* 35(3):440–465.

Martínez-Gallardo, Cecilia, Nicolás de la Cerda, Jonathan Hartlyn, Liesbet Hooghe, Gary Marks, and Ryan Bakker. 2023. "Revisiting Party System Structuration in Latin America and Europe: Economic and Socio-Cultural Dimensions." *Party Politics* 29(4):780–792.

Masih, Niha and Joanna Slater. 2019. "U.S-Style Polarization Has Arrived in India: Modi Is at the Heart of the Divide." *Washington Post*, May 20.

Mason, Lilliana. 2015. "'I Disrespectfully Agree': The Differential Effects of Partisan Sorting on Social and Issue Polarization." *American Journal of Political Science* 59(1):128–145.

Mason, Lilliana. 2018. *Uncivil Agreement: How Politics Became Our Identity*. University of Chicago Press.

Mason, Lilliana. 2019. "Mandatory National Service." *Politico*. Accessed from: https://www.politico.com/interactives/2019/how-to-fix-politics-in-america/polarization/mandatory-national-service/.

Matakos, Konstantinos, Orestis Troumpounis, and Dimitrios Xefteris. 2016. "Electoral Rule Disproportionality and Platform Polarization." *American Journal of Political Science* 60(4):1026–1043.

Mattes, Michaela. 2012. "Democratic Reliability, Precommitment of Successor Governments, and the Choice of Alliance Commitment." *International Organization* 66:153–172.

Mattes, Michaela, Brett Ashley Leeds, and Naoko Matsumura. 2016. "Measuring Change in the Source of Leader Support: The CHISOLS Dataset." *Journal of Peace Research* 53(2):259–267.

Mattes, Michaela, Brett Ashley Leeds, and Royce Carroll. 2015. "Leadership Turnover and Foreign Policy Change: Societal Interests, Domestic Institutions, and Voting in the United Nations." *International Studies Quarterly* 59:280–290.

Mattiacci, Eleonora. 2023. *Volatile States in International Politics*. Oxford University Press.

Mavodza, Constancia, Rebecca Goldman, and Bergen Cooper. 2019. "The Impacts of the Global Gag Rule on Global Health: A Scoping Review." *Global Health Research and Policy* 4:1–21.

Maxey, Sarah. 2021. "Limited Spin: When the Public Punishes Leaders Who Lie about Military Action." *Journal of Conflict Resolution* 65(2–3):283–312.

Mayer, Frederick. 1992. "Managing Domestic Differences in International Negotiations: The Strategic Use of Internal Side Payments." *International Organization* 46:793–818.

McAllister, Ian. 2006. "A War Too Far? Bush, Iraq, and the 2004 U.S. Presidential Election." *Presidential Studies Quarterly* 36(2):260–280.

McCarty, Nolan. 2015. "Reducing Polarization by Making Parties Stronger." In *Solutions to Political Polarization in America*, ed. Nathaniel Persily. Cambridge University Press, pp. 136–145.

McCarty, Nolan. 2019. *Polarization: What Everyone Needs to Know*. Oxford University Press.

McCarty, Nolan, Keith T. Poole, and Howard Rosenthal. 2009. "Does Gerrymandering Cause Polarization?" *American Journal of Political Science* 53(3):666–680.

McCoy, Jennifer and Murat Somer. 2019. "Democracy in America? Partisanship, Polarization, and the Robustness of Support for Democracy in the United States." *Toward a Theory of Pernicious Polarization and How It Harms Democracies: Comparative Evidence and Possible Remedies* 681(1):234–271.

McCoy, Jennifer, Tahmina Rahman, and Murat Somer. 2018. "Polarization and the Global Crisis of Democracy: Common Patterns, Dynamics, and Pernicious Consequences for Democratic Polities." *American Behavioral Scientist* 62(1):16–42.

McGann, Anthony J., Charles Anthony Smith, Michael Latner, and Alex Keena. 2016. *Gerrymandering in America: The House of Representatives, the Supreme Court, and the Future of Popular Sovereignty*. Cambridge University Press.

McGhee, Eric, Seth Masket, Boris Shor, Steven Rogers, and Nolan McCarty. 2014. "A Primary Cause of Partisanship? Nomination Systems and Legislator Ideology." *American Journal of Political Science* 58(2):337–351.

McGillivray, Fiona and Alastair Smith. 2000. "Trust and Cooperation through Agent-Specific Punishments." *International Organization* 54(4):809–824.

McGillivray, Fiona and Alastair Smith. 2008. *Punishing the Prince: A Theory of Interstate Relations, Political Institutions, and Leader Change*. Princeton University Press.

McKinley, Gibbs. 2023. "The Pyrrhic Victory of a China Consensus." Center for a New American Security, Washington, DC, March 9.

McKinney, Richard J. 2002. "An Overview of the Congressional Record and Its Predecessor Publications: A Research Guide." *Law Library Lights* 46(2):16–22.

McManus, Roseanne. 2017. *Statements of Resolve: Achieving Coercive Credibility in International Conflict*. Cambridge University Press.

Mearsheimer, John J. 1990. "Back to the Future: Instability in Europe After the Cold War." *International Security* 15(1):5–56.

Mechkova, Valeriya, Daniel Pemstein, Brigitte Seim, and Steven Wilson. 2024. "Digital Society Project Dataset v6." Digital Society Project. Accessed from: https://digitalsocietyproject.org/.

Messing, Solomon and Rachel Weisel. 2017. "Partisan Conflict and Congressional Outreach." Pew Research Center, Washington, DC.

Metzler, Kiyoko and David Rising. 2020. "UN Agency: Iran Violating All Restrictions of Nuclear Deal." *Associated Press*, June 5.

Meyerrose, Anna M. 2020. "The Unintended Consequences of Democracy Promotion: International Organizations and Democratic Backsliding." *Comparative Political Studies* 53(10–11):1547–1581.

Miller, Michael K. 2021. "A Republic, If You Can Keep It: Breakdown and Erosion in Modern Democracies." *Journal of Politics* 83(1):198–213.

Milner, Helen. 1997. *Interests, Institutions, and Information: Domestic Politics and International Relations*. Princeton University Press.

Milner, Helen and B. P. Rosendorff. 1996. "Trade Negotiations, Information, and Domestic Politics." *Economics and Politics* 8(2):145–189.

Milner, Helen and Dustin Tingley. 2015. *Sailing the Water's Edge: The Domestic Politics of American Foreign Policy*. Princeton University Press.

Milner, Helen V. 1999. "The Political Economy of International Trade." *Annual Review of Political Science* 2:91–114.

Milner, Helen V. and B. Peter Rosendorff. 1997. "Democratic Politics and International Trade Negotiations." *Journal of Conflict Resolution* 41(1):117–146.

Milner, Helen V. and Keiko Kubota. 2005. "Why the Move to Free Trade? Democracy and Trade Policy in the Developing Countries." *International Organization* 59(1): 107–143.

Mitchell, Ellen. 2023. "The Hot-Button Measures Added, Blocked from Defense Bill." *The Hill*, July 13.

Mo, Jongryn. 1995. "Domestic Institutions and International Bargaining: The Role of Agent Veto in Two-Level Games." *American Political Science Review* 89(4):914–924.

Moe, Terry M. 1985. "The Politicized Presidency." In *The New Direction in American Politics*, ed. John E. Chubb and Paul E. Peterson. Brookings Institution Press, pp. 235–272.

Moe, Terry and William Howell. 1999. "The Presidential Power of Unilateral Action." *Journal of Law, Economics, and Organization* 15(1):132–179.

Moncus, J. J. and Aidan Connaughton. 2020. "Americans' Views on World Health Organization Split along Partisan Lines as Trump Calls for U.S. to Withdraw." Pew Research Center, Washington, DC, June 11.

Mondal, Sudipto. 2019. "India's Modi Criticised for Politicising Pakistan Standoff." *Al Jazeera*, February 28.

Morell, Michael, Avril Haines, and David S. Cohen. 2020. "Trump's Politicization of U.S. Intelligence Agencies Could End in Disaster." *Foreign Policy*, April 28.

Mudde, Cas. 2007. *Populist Radical Right Parties in Europe*. Cambridge University Press.

Mudde, Cas. 2019. *The Far Right Today*. Polity.

Mueller, John E. 1970. "Presidential Popularity from Truman to Johnson." *American Political Science Review* 64(1):18–34.

Mueller, John E. 1973. *War, Presidents, and Public Opinion*. John Wiley and Sons.

Munck, Ronaldo. 1985. "The 'Modern' Military Dictatorship in Latin America: The Case of Argentina (1976–1982)." *Latin American Perspectives* 12(4):849–867.

Musgrave, Paul. 2019. "International Hegemony Meets Domestic Politics: Why Liberals Can Be Pessimists." *Security Studies* 28(3):451–478.

Mutz, Diana C. 2021. *Winners and Losers: The Psychology of Foreign Trade*. Princeton University Press.

Myrick, Rachel. 2020. "Why So Secretive? Unpacking Public Attitudes toward Secrecy and Success in US Foreign Policy." *Journal of Politics* 82(3): 828–843.

Myrick, Rachel. 2021. "Do External Threats Unite or Divide? Security Crises, Rivalries, and Polarization in American Foreign Policy." *International Organization* 4(75): 921–958.

Myrick, Rachel. 2022. "The Reputational Consequences of Polarization for American Foreign Policy." *International Politics* 59:1004–1027.

Myrick, Rachel. 2024. "Public Reactions to Secrecy in International Negotiations." *Journal of Conflict Resolution* 68(4):703–729.

Myrick, Rachel, Catherine Eng, and Zoe Weinberg. 2022. "Countering Partisanship and Threat Inflation in U.S.–China Policy." In *On the Rise: Perspectives on Foreign Policy*, ed. Aspen Strategy Group Staff. Aspen Strategy Group, pp. 12–17.

Nathan, Richard P. 1983. *The Administrative Presidency*. Wiley.

Neblo, Michael, Jason Brennan, and Whitney Quesenbery. 2022. "Will Increasing Turnout So Everyone Votes Reduce Polarization and Extreme Partisanship?" Accessed from: https://gisme.georgetown.edu/news/the-impact-of-voter-turnout-on-polarization/.

Nerkar, Santul. 2021. "When It Comes to China, Biden Sounds a Lot Like Trump." *FiveThirtyEight*, September 28.

Neumayer, Eric. 2002. "Do Democracies Exhibit Stronger International Environmental Commitment? A Cross-Country Analysis." *Journal of Peace Research* 39(2).

Neumayer, Eric. 2005. "Do International Human Rights Treaties Improve Respect for Human Rights?" *Journal of Conflict Resolution* 49(6):925–953.

Nincic, Miroslav. 1992. "A Sensible Public: New Perspectives on Popular Opinion and Foreign Policy." *Journal of Conflict Resolution* 36(4):772–789.

Norris, Pippa. 2005. *Radical Right: Voters and Parties in the Electoral Market*. Cambridge University Press.

Nye, Joseph S. 2012. "The Future of American Power: Dominance and Decline in Perspective." In *The Domestic Sources of American Foreign Policy: Insights and Evidence*, ed. James M. McCormick. 6th ed. Rowman and Littlefield, pp. 33–46.

Nyhan, Brendan. 2020. "Facts and Myths about Misperceptions." *Journal of Economic Perspectives* 34(3):220–236.

Nyhan, Brendan, Jaime Settle, Emily Thorson, Magdalena Wojcieszak, Pablo Barberá, Annie Y. Chen, Hunt Allcott, Taylor Brown, Adriana Crespo-Tenorio, Drew Dimmery, Deen Freelon, Matthew Gentzkow, Sandra González-Bailón, Andrew M. Guess, Edward Kennedy, Young Mie Kim, David Lazer, Neil Malhotra, Devra Moehler, Jennifer Pan, Daniel Robert Thomas, Rebekah Tromble, Carlos Velasco Rivera, Arjun Wilkins, Beixian Xiong, Chad Kiewiet de Jonge, Annie Franco, Winter Mason, Natalie Jomini Stroud, and Joshua A. Tucker. 2023. "Like-Minded Sources on Facebook Are Prevalent but Not Polarizing." *Nature* 620:137–144.

Oakes, Amy. 2012. *Diversionary War: Domestic Unrest and International Conflict*. Stanford University Press.

Obama, Barack. 2002. "Remarks by Barack Obama in Chicago on October 2, 2002." Transcript accessed from *NPR*. Accessed from: https://www.npr.org/2009/01/20/99591469/transcript-obamas-speech-against-the-iraq-war.

O'Connell, Anne. 2009. "Vacant Offices: Delays in Staffing Top Agency Positions." *Southern California Law Review* 82(5):913–1000.

O'Hanlon, Michael E. 2024. "U.S. Defense Spending in Historical and International Context." *Econofact*, May 14.

Olsen, Michael P. and Jon C. Rogowski. 2020. "Legislative Term Limits and Polarization." *Journal of Politics* 82(2):572–586.

Oneal, John R. and Anna Lillian Bryan. 1995. "The Rally 'Round the Flag Effect in U.S. Foreign Policy Crises, 1950–1985." *Political Behavior* 17(4):379–401.

Oppermann, Kai and Klaus Brummer. 2017. "Veto Player Approaches in Foreign Policy Analysis." In *Oxford Research Encyclopedia of Politics*, ed. Cameron G. Thies. Oxford University Press. Accessed from: https://www.oxfordreference.com/display/10.1093/acref/9780190463045.001.0001/acref-9780190463045-e-386.

Ordoñez, Franco. 2024. "What Trump's First 100 Days in Office Could Look Like." NPR, November 6. Accessed from: https://www.npr.org/2024/11/06/nx-s1-5181800/2024-election-trump-first-100-days-agenda.

Osorio, Carlos. 2021. "Argentina's Military Coup of 1976: What the U.S. Knew." National Security Archive, Washington, DC, Briefing Book 752.

Ostrom, Charles W. and Dennis M. Simon. 1985. "Promise and Performance: A Dynamic Model of Presidential Popularity." *American Political Science Review* 79(2):334–358.

Overgaard, Christian Staal Bruun and Samuel Woolley. 2022. "How Social Media Platforms Can Reduce Polarization." Brookings Institution, Washington, DC, December 21.

Page, Benjamin I. and Robert Y. Shapiro. 1992. *The Rational Public: Fifty Years of Trends in Americans' Policy Preferences*. University of Chicago Press.

Palmer, Glenn, Roseanne W. McManus, Vito D'Orazio, Michale R. Kenwick, Mikaela Karstens, Chase Bloch, Nick Dietrich, Kayla Kahn, Kellan Ritter, and Michael J. Soules. 2020. "The MID5 Dataset, 2011–2014: Procedures, Coding Rules, and Description." *Conflict Management and Peace Science* 39(4):470–482.

Pandya, Sonal S. 2014. "Democratization and Foreign Direct Investment Liberalization." *International Studies Quarterly* 58:475–488.

Park, Dong Joon. 2022. "A Polarized Audience in South Korea and Its Impact on North Korea Policy." *Journal of Indo-Pacific Affairs* 5(6):95–108.

Park, Ju Yeon. 2021. "When Do Politicians Grandstand? Measuring Message Politics in Committee Hearings." *Journal of Politics* 83(1):214–228.

Parsi, Trita. 2012. *A Single Roll of the Dice: Obama's Diplomacy with Iran*. Yale University Press.

Patrick, Stewart M. 2009. "Obama at the UN: The Burden of the Anti-Bush." Council on Foreign Relations, New York, September 18.

Payne, Rodger A. 1995. "Freedom and the Environment." *Journal of Democracy* 6(3):41–55.

Peake, Jeffrey S. 2017. "The Domestic Politics of US Treaty Ratification: Bilateral Treaties from 1949 to 2012." *Foreign Policy Analysis* 13:832–853.

Peake, Jeffrey S. 2022. *Dysfunctional Diplomacy: The Politics of International Agreements in an Era of Partisan Polarization*. Routledge.

Peake, Jeffrey S., Glen S. Krutz, and Tyler Hughes. 2012. "President Obama, the Senate, and the Polarized Politics of Treaty Making." *Social Science Quarterly* 93(5):1295–1315.

Pedregosa, Fabian, Gaël Varoquaux, Alexandre Gramfort, et al. 2011. "Scikit-learn: Machine Learning in Python." *Journal of Machine Learning Research* 12:2825–2830.

Peña, Charles V. 2006. "A Smaller Military to Fight the War on Terror." *Orbis* 50(2):289–306.

Perera, Fabiana Sofia. 2019. "How Chávez Broke Venezuela's Military." *Americas Quarterly*, December 15.

Persily, Nathaniel. 2015. *Solutions to Political Polarization in America*. Cambridge University Press.

Peterson, Andrew and Arthur Spirling. 2018. "Classification Accuracy as a Substantive Quantity of Interest: Measuring Polarization in Westminster Systems." *Political Analysis* 26: 120–128.

Pettigrew, Thomas F. 1998. "Intergroup Contact Theory." *Annual Review of Psychology* 49: 65–85.

Pevehouse, Jon C. W. 2020. "The COVID-19 Pandemic, International Cooperation, and Populism." *International Organization* 74(S1):E191–E212.

Pevehouse, Jon C. W. and Caileigh Glenn. 2024. "International Dimensions of Democratization." *World Politics* 75(5):1–14.

Pfiffner, James P. and Mark Phythian. 2008. *Intelligence and National Security Policymaking on Iraq: British and American Perspectives*. Texas A&M University Press.

Pierce, Sarah, Jessica Bolter, and Andrew Selee. 2018. "U.S. Immigration Policy under Trump: Deep Changes and Lasting Impacts." Migration Policy Institute, Washington, DC.

Pierson, Michael D. 1995. "'All Southern Society Is Assailed by the Foulest Charges': Charles Sumner's 'The Crime Against Kansas' and the Escalation of Anti-Slavery Rhetoric." *New England Quarterly* 68(4):531–557.

Pilar, María, García-Guadilla and Ana Mallen. 2019. "Polarization, Participatory Democracy, and Democratic Erosion in Venezuela's Twenty-First Century Socialism." *Annals of the American Academy of Political and Social Science* 68(1):62–77.

Pillar, Paul. 2006. "Intelligence, Policy, and the War in Iraq." *Foreign Affairs* 85(2):15–27.
Pillar, Paul R. 2023. *Beyond the Water's Edge. How Partisanship Corrupts U.S. Foreign Policy.* Columbia University Press.
Piper, Christopher. 2022. "Presidential Strategy amidst the 'Broken' Appointments Process." *Presidential Studies Quarterly* 52(4):843–874.
Pirro, Andrea L. P. 2015. *The Populist Radical Right in Central and Eastern Europe: Ideology, Impact, and Electoral Performance.* Routledge.
Polyakova, Alina. 2015. *The Dark Side of European Integration: Social Foundations and Cultural Determinants of the Rise of Radical Right Movements in Contemporary Europe.* Columbia University Press.
Pompeo, Michael R. 2018. "After the Deal: A New Iran Strategy." The Heritage Foundation, Washington, D.C., May 21. Accessed from: https://2017-2021.state.gov/after-the-deal-a-new-iran-strategy/.
Poole, Keith T. and Howard Rosenthal. 1985. "A Spatial Model of Legislative Roll Call Analysis." *American Journal of Political Science* 29(2):357–384.
Poole, Keith T. and Howard Rosenthal. 1991. "Patterns of Congressional Voting." *American Journal of Political Science* 35(1):228–278.
Poole, Keith T. and Howard Rosenthal. 1997. *Congress: A Political-Economic History of Roll Call Voting.* Oxford University Press.
Poole, Keith T. and Howard L. Rosenthal. 2011. *Ideology and Congress.* Transaction.
Porter, Patrick. 2018. "Why America's Grand Strategy Has Not Changed: Power, Habit, and the U.S. Foreign Policy Establishment." *International Security* 42(4):9–46.
Porter, Patrick. 2020. *The False Promise of Liberal Order: Nostalgia, Delusion and the Rise of Trump.* Polity.
Posen, Barry R. 2007. "The Case for Restraint." *American Interest* 3(1):7–17.
Potter, Philip B. K. 2016. "Lame-Duck Foreign Policy." *Presidential Studies Quarterly* 46(4):849–867.
Preble, Christopher A. 2009. *Power Problem: How American Military Dominance Makes Us Less Safe, Less Prosperous, and Less Free.* Cornell University Press.
Przeworski, Adam. 2019. *Crises of Democracy.* Cambridge University Press.
Putnam, Robert D. 1988. "Diplomacy and Domestic Politics: The Logic of Two-Level Games." *International Organization* 42(3):427–460.
Quinn, Thomas, Nicholas Allen, and John Bartle. 2024. "Why Was There a Hard Brexit? The British Legislative Party System, Divided Majorities and the Incentives for Factionalism." *Political Studies* 72(1):227–248.
Rapp-Hooper, Mira. 2020. "Saving America's Alliances: The United States Still Needs the System That Put It on Top." *Foreign Affairs*, February 10.
Rapp-Hooper, Mira and Rebecca Friedman Lissner. 2020. *An Open World: How America Can Win the Contest for Twenty-First-Century Order.* Yale University Press.
Rathbun, Brian. 2018. "Does Trump Structure All? A Test of Agency in World Politics". In *Chaos in the Liberal Order: The Trump Presidency and International Politics in the Twenty-First Century*, ed. Robert Jervis, Francis J. Gavin, Joshua Rovner, and Diane N. Labrosse. Columbia University Press, pp. 98–103.
Rathje, Steve, Jay J. Van Bavel, and Sander van der Linden. 2021. "Out-Group Animosity Drives Engagement on Social Media." *PNAS* 118(26):1–9.
Ravid, Barak and Hans Nichols. 2022. "Biden in Newly Surfaced Video: Iran Nuclear Deal Is "Dead"." *Axios*, December 20.
Reed, William. 1997. "Alliance Duration and Democracy: An Extension and Cross-Validation of 'Democratic States and Commitment in International Relations'." *American Journal of Political Science* 41(3):1072–1078.

Reeves, Andrew and Jon C. Rogowski. 2018. "The Public Cost of Unilateral Action." *American Journal of Political Science* 62(2):424–440.

Reeves, Andrew and Jon C. Rogowski. 2022. *No Blank Check: The Origins and Consequences of Public Antipathy towards Presidential Power*. Cambridge University Press.

Reeves, Philip. 2024. "European Nations Bordering Russia Worry They Could Be Targeted after Ukraine." *NPR*, May 8.

Reiljan, Andres. 2020. "'Fear and Loathing Across Party Lines' (Also) in Europe: Affective Polarisation in European Party Systems." *European Journal of Political Research* 59(2): 376–396.

Reiljan, Andres, Diego Garzi, Frederico Ferreira Da Silva, and Alexander H. Treschsel. 2023. "Patterns of Affective Polarization toward Parties and Leaders across the Democratic World." *American Political Science Review* 118(2):654–670.

Reiter, Dan and Allan C. Stam. 1998. "Democracy, War Initiation, and Victory." *American Political Science Review* 92(2):377–389.

Reiter, Dan and Allan C. Stam. 2002. *Democracies at War*. Princeton University Press.

Republican Convention. 1920. "The Republican Convention." *Current History* 12(4).

Reynolds, David. 1985. "A 'Special Relationship'? America, Britain, and the International Order Since the Second World War." *International Affairs* 62(1):1–20.

Rhodes, Ben. 2018. *The World as It Is: A Memoir of the Obama White House*. Random House.

Rice, Susan E. 2020. "A Divided America Is a National Security Threat." *New York Times*, September 22.

Richards, Michael. 2006. "The Popular Front." In *A Companion to Europe 1900–1945*, ed. Gordon Martel. Blackwell, pp. 375–390.

Riedl, Rachel Beatty, Paul Friesen, Jennifer McCoy, and Kenneth Roberts. 2024. "Democratic Backsliding, Resilience, and Resistance." *World Politics* 75(5):1–28.

Riker, William H. 1982. "The Two-Party System and Duverger's Law: An Essay on the History of Political Science." *American Political Science Review* 76(4):753–766.

Risse-Kappen, Thomas. 1997. *Cooperation among Democracies: The European Influence on U.S. Foreign Policy*. Princeton University Press.

Ritter, Scott. 2018. *Dealbreaker: Donald Trump and the Unmaking of the Iran Nuclear Deal*. Clarity Press.

Rivers, Douglas and Nancy L. Rose. 1985. "Passing the President's Program: Public Opinion and Presidential Influence in Congress." *American Journal of Political Science* 29(2):183–196.

Roberts, Jason M. and Steven S. Smith. 2003. "Procedural Contexts, Party Strategy, and Conditional Party Voting in the U.S. House of Representatives, 1971–2000." *American Journal of Political Science* 47(2):305–317.

Robertson, Ronald E., Jon Green, Damian J. Ruck, Katherine Ognyanova, Christo Wilson, and David Lazer. 2023. "Users Choose to Engage with More Partisan News Than They Are Exposed to on Google Search." *Nature* 618:342–348.

Robinson, Michael A. 2022. *Dangerous Instrument: Political Polarization and US Civil–Military Relations*. Oxford University Press.

Rodden, Jonathan. 2010. "The Geographic Distribution of Political Preferences." *Annual Review of Political Science* 13:321–340.

Rodden, Jonathan. 2019. *Why Cities Lose: The Deep Roots of the Urban–Rural Political Divide*. Basic Books.

Rodden, Jonathan. 2021. "Keeping Your Enemies Close: Electoral Rules and Partisan Polarization." In *Who Gets What? The New Politics of Insecurity*, ed. Frances Rosenbluth and Margaret Weir. Cambridge University Press, pp. 129–160.

Rogowski, Jon C. and Joseph L. Sutherland. 2016. "How Ideology Fuels Affective Polarization." *Political Behavior* 38:485–508.

Rohde, David W. 1991. *Parties and Leaders in the Postreform House*. University of Chicago Press.
Rosato, Sebastian. 2003. "The Flawed Logic of Democratic Peace Theory." *American Political Science Review* 97(4):585–602.
Rose, Kenneth D. 2021. *American Isolation between the World Wars: The Search for a Nation's Identity*. Routledge.
Rothfus, Keith. 2021. "How to Fix the House of Representatives." *National Affairs*, Summer 2021.
Rothkopf, David. 2015. "Between Bibi Invite and Cotton Letter, GOP Are Blazing New Trails in Politicization of Foreign Policy—and Debasement of Their Institutions." Twitter, March 9.
Rovner, Joshua. 2011. *Fixing the Facts: National Security and the Politics of Intelligence*. Cornell University Press.
Rovner, Joshua. 2013. "Is Politicization Ever a Good Thing?" *Intelligence and National Security* 28(1):55–67.
Rubio, Marco. 2015. "Marco Rubio's Foreign Policy Vision." Interview with the Council on Foreign Relations, New York, May 13.
Rudalevige, Andrew. 2005. *The New Imperial Presidency: Renewing Presidential Power After Watergate*. University of Michigan Press.
Russett, Bruce. 1993. *Grasping the Democratic Peace: Principles for a Post–Cold War World*. Princeton University Press.
Sahoo, Niranjan. 2020. "Mounting Majoritarianism and Political Polarization in India." In *Political Polarization in South and Southeast Asia: Old Divisions, New Dangers*, ed. Thomas Carothers and Andrew O'Donohue. Carnegie Endowment for International Peace, pp. 9–23.
Samuels, David J. 2023. "The International Context of Democratic Backsliding: Rethinking the Role of Third Wave 'Prodemocracy' Global Actors." *Perspectives on Politics* 21(3): 1001–1012.
Sanger, David E. 2024. "With Nuclear Deal Dead, Containing Iran Grows More Fraught." *New York Times*, April 15.
Sanger, David E., Lara Jakes, and Farnaz Fassihi. 2021. "Biden Promised to Restore the Iran Nuclear Deal: Now It Risks Derailment." *New York Times*, July 31.
Sargent, Greg. 2015. "Scott Walker: We Might Have to Take Military Action against Iran on Day One." *Washington Post*, July 20.
Sarlin, Benjy and Sahil Kapur. 2021. "Why China May Be the Last Bipartisan Issue Left in Washington." *NBC News*, March 21.
Saunders, Elizabeth N. 2022. "Elites in the Making and Breaking of Foreign Policy." *Annual Review of Political Science* 25:219–240.
Saunders, Elizabeth N. 2014. *Leaders at War: How Presidents Shape Military Interventions*. Cornell University Press.
Saunders, Elizabeth N. 2015. "War and the Inner Circle: Democratic Elites and the Politics of Using Force." *Security Studies* 24(3):466–501.
Saunders, Elizabeth N. 2024. *The Insiders' Game: How Elites Make War and Peace*. Princeton University Press.
Scahill, Jeremy. 2021. "1981: Biden and Reagan's CIA Director, William Casey." *The Intercept*, April 27.
Scartascini, Carlos, Cesi Cruz, and Philip Keefer. 2021. "The Database of Political Institutions 2020 (DPI2020)." Accessed from: http://dx.doi.org/10.18235/0003049.
Schake, Kori and Jim Mattis. 2016. *Warriors and Citizens: American Views on Our Military*. Hoover Institution Press.
Schelling, Thomas. 1960. *The Strategy of Conflict*. Harvard University Press.
Schlesinger, Arthur M. 1973. *The Imperial Presidency*. Houghton Mifflin.

Schultz, Kenneth A. 1995. "Hawks and Doves: Estimating Military Policy Positions from Election Platforms." Working Paper, Stanford University, Stanford, CA.

Schultz, Kenneth A. 1998. "Domestic Opposition and Signaling in International Crises." *American Political Science Review* 92(4):829–844.

Schultz, Kenneth A. 1999. "Do Democratic Institutions Constrain or Inform?" *International Organization* 53(2):233–266.

Schultz, Kenneth A. 2001a. *Democracy and Coercive Diplomacy*. Cambridge University Press.

Schultz, Kenneth A. 2001b. "Looking for Audience Costs." *Journal of Conflict Resolution* 45(1):32–60.

Schultz, Kenneth A. 2018. "Perils of Polarization for U.S. Foreign Policy." *Washington Quarterly* 40(4):7–28.

Schultz, Kenneth A. and Barry R. Weingast. 2003. "The Democratic Advantage: Institutional Foundations of Financial Power in International Competition." *International Organization* 57:3–42.

Scoville, Ryan. 2019. "Unqualified Ambassadors." *Duke Law Journal* 69(1):71–196.

Sechser, Todd S. and Matthew Fuhrmann. 2017. *Nuclear Weapons and Coercive Diplomacy*. Cambridge University Press.

Shahla, Arsalan. 2024. "Iran Says Prospect for Talks over Nuclear Deal 'Still Exists.'" *Bloomberg*, January 1.

Shepherd, Christian and Alicia Chen. 2022. "Taiwan to Boost Defense Spending to Deter China's Military Threat." *Washington Post*, August 25.

Sherman, Wendy. 2018. *Not for the Faint of Heart: Lessons in Courage, Power, and Persistence*. PublicAffairs.

Sigelman, Lee and Emmet H. Buell. 2004. "Avoidance or Engagement? Issue Convergence in U.S. Presidential Campaigns, 1960–2000." *American Journal of Political Science* 48(4): 650–661.

Silver, Caleb. 2020. "The Top 20 Economies in the World." Investopedia. Accessed from: https://www.investopedia.com/insights/worlds-top-economies/.

Simmons, Beth A. 2000. "International Law and State Behavior: Commitment and Compliance in International Monetary Affairs." *American Political Science Review* 94(4):819–835.

Simonovits, Gabor, Gabor Kezdi, and Peter Kardos. 2018. "Seeing the World Through the Other's Eye: An Online Intervention Reducing Ethnic Prejudice." *American Political Science Review* 112(1):186–193.

Simonovits, Gabor, Jennifer McCoy, and Levente Littvay. 2022. "Democratic Hypocrisy and Out-Group Threat: Explaining Citizen Support for Democratic Erosion." *Journal of Politics* 84(3):1806–1811.

Sinclair, Barbara. 2014. *Party Wars: Polarization and the Politics of National Policy Making*. University of Oklahoma Press.

Slaughter, Anne Marie. 1995. "International Law in a World of Liberal States." *European Journal of International Law* 6(3):503–538.

Smeltz, Dina, Ivo Daalder, Karl Friedhoff, Craig Kafura, and Brendan Helm. 2020. "Divided We Stand: Democrats and Republicans Diverge on US Foreign Policy." Chicago Council on Global Affairs, Chicago.

Smeltz, Dina, Ivo H. Daalder, Karl Friedhoff, Craig Kafura, and Emily Sullivan. 2023. "2022 Survey of Public Opinion on US Foreign Policy." Chicago Council on Global Affairs, Chicago.

Smeltz, Dina, Joshua Busby, and Jordan Tama. 2018. "Political Polarization the Critical Threat to US, Foreign Policy Experts Say." *The Hill*, November 9.

Smith, Alastair. 1998. "International Crises and Domestic Politics." *American Political Science Review* 92(3):623–638.

Smith, Alastair. 2016. "Leader Turnover, Institutions, and Voting at the UN General Assembly." *Journal of Conflict Resolution* 60(1):143–163.
Smith, David. 2018. "The Anti-Obama: Trump's Drive to Destroy His Predecessor's Legacy." *The Guardian*, May 11.
Snyder, Jack. 1991. *Myths of Empire: Domestic Politics and International Ambition*. Cornell University Press.
Sokolsky, Richard and Aaron David Miller. 2019. "Trump Is Achieving His Goal of Being the Un-Obama, Except on Middle East Wars." *USA Today*, January 20.
Somer, Murat. 2019. "Turkey: The Slippery Slope from Reformist to Revolutionary Polarization and Democratic Breakdown." *ANNALS* 681:42–61.
Sparks, Grace. 2018. "Majority Say US Should Not Withdraw from Iran Nuclear Agreement." *CNN*, May 8.
Sparks, Grace, Lunna Lopes, Mellisha Stokes, Liz Hamel, and Mollyann Brodie. 2021. "KFF COVID-19 Vaccine Monitor: Views on the U.S. Role in Global Vaccine Distribution." KFF Polling, November 5.
Stastavage, David. 2004. "Open-Door or Closed-Door? Transparency in Domestic and International Bargaining." *International Organization* 58(4):667–703.
Staton, Jeffrey K. and Will H. Moore. 2011. "Judicial Power in Domestic and International Politics." *International Organization* 65(3):553–587.
Steinhauer, Jennifer. 2012. "Despite Bob Dole's Wish, Republicans Reject Disabilities Treaty." *New York Times*, December 5.
Stewart, Phil and Idrees Ali. 2024. "How the US Is Preparing for a Chinese Invasion of Taiwan." *Reuters*, January 31.
Summers, Juana. 2020. "Timeline: How Trump Has Downplayed the Coronavirus Pandemic." *NPR*, October 2.
Sunstein, Cass R. 2009. *Our Common Bonds: Using What Americans Share to Help Bridge the Partisan Divide*. Oxford University Press.
Svolik, Milan W. 2019. "Polarization versus Democracy." *Journal of Democracy* 30(3):20–32.
Svolik, Milan W. 2020. "When Polarization Trumps Civic Virtue: Partisan Conflict and the Subversion of Democracy by Incumbents." *Quarterly Journal of Political Science* 15(1):3–31.
Swasey, Benjamin. 2020. "Biden, Sanders Slam Trump Administration for Coronavirus Response." *NPR*, March 12.
Talmadge, Caitlin. 2015. *The Dictator's Army: Battlefield Effectiveness in Authoritarian Regimes*. Cornell University Press.
Tama, Jordan. 2023. *Bipartisanship and US Foreign Policy: Cooperation in a Polarized Age*. Oxford University Press.
Tankersley, Jim. 2021. "Biden Administration Officials Have Tried to Restart Talks with North Korea." *New York Times*, March 15.
Tarar, Ahmer. 2001. "International Bargaining with Two-Sided Domestic Constraints." *Journal of Conflict Resolution* 45(3):320–340.
Tarar, Ahmer and Bahar Leventoglu. 2009. "Public Commitment in Crisis Bargaining." *International Studies Quarterly* 53:817–839.
Theriault, Sean M. 2008. *Party Polarization in Congress*. Cambridge University Press.
Tocqueville, Alexis de. 1835. *Democracy in America*. Reprint, 1988 ed. Perennial Library.
Toft, Monica Duffy and Sidita Kushi. 2023. *Dying by the Sword: The Militarization of US Foreign Policy*. Oxford University Press.
Tomz, Michael. 2007. "Domestic Audience Costs in International Relations: An Experimental Approach." *International Organization* 61:821–840.
Tomz, Michael. 2008. "Reputation and the Effect of International Law on Preferences and Beliefs." Working Paper, Stanford University, Stanford, CA.

Tomz, Michael and Jessica L. P. Weeks. 2021. "Military Alliances and Public Support for War." *International Studies Quarterly* 65(3):811–824.

Tomz, Michael, Jessica L. P. Weeks, and Keren Yarhi-Milo. 2020. "Public Opinion and Decisions about Military Force in Democracies." *International Organization* 74:119–143.

Tomz, Michael R. and Jessica L. P. Weeks. 2013. "Public Opinion and the Democratic Peace." *American Political Science Review* 107(4):849–865.

Törnberg, Petter. 2022. "How Digital Media Drive Affective Polarization through Partisan Sorting." *Proceedings of the National Academy of Sciences* 119(42).

Trager, Robert F. and Lynn Vavreck. 2011. "The Political Costs of Crisis Bargaining: Presidential Rhetoric and the Role of Party." *American Journal of Political Science* 55(3):526–545.

Trinkunas, Harold. 2022. "Venezuela's Bolivarian Armed Force: Fear and Interest in the Face of Political Change." Wilson Center Latin America Program, Washington, DC.

Trubowitz, Peter and Brian Burgoon. 2023. *Geopolitics and Democracy: The Western Liberal Order from Foundation to Fracture.* Oxford University Press.

Trump, Donald. 2018. "Transcript of Trump's Speech on the Iran Nuclear Deal." *New York Times*, May 8.

Trump, Donald. 2019. "Remarks by President Trump in Roundtable on Immigration and Border Security." U.S. Border Patrol Calexico Station, April 5.

Tsebelis, George. 1995. "Decision Making in Political Systems: Veto Players in Presidentialism, Parliamentarism, Multicameralism, and Multipartyism." *British Journal of Political Science* 25(3):289–325.

Tseblis, George. 2002. *Veto Players: How Political Institutions Work.* Princeton University Press.

U.S. Code, Title 50, Chapter 44, Section 3093(e). Accessed from: https://www.law.cornell.edu/uscode/text/50/3093.

Tyler, Matthew, Justin Grimmer, and Shanto Iyengar. 2022. "Partisan Enclaves and Information Bazaars: Mapping Selective Exposure to Online News." *Journal of Politics* 84(2):1057–1073.

U.S. Department of State. 2024. "About the U.S. Department of State." Accessed from: https://www.state.gov/about/.

Van Evera, Stephen. 2003. "Why States Believe Foolish Ideas: Nonself-Evaluation by States and Societies." In *Perspectives on Structural Realism*, ed. Andrew K. Hanami. Palgrave Macmillan, 163–198.

Vandenberg, Arthur H. 1945. "American Foreign Policy." Accessed from: senate.gov. Accessed from: https://www.senate.gov/artandhistory/history/common/generic/Speeches_Vandenberg.htm.

Voelkel, Jan G., James Chu, Michael N. Stagnaro, Joseph S. Mernyk, Chrystal Redekopp, Sophia L. Pink, James N. Druckman, David G. Rand, and Robb Willer. 2022. "Megastudy Identifying Successful Interventions to Strengthen Americans' Democratic Attitudes." Working paper #22-38, Institute for Policy Research. Accessed from: https://www.ipr.northwestern.edu/documents/working-papers/2022/wp-22-38.pdf.

Voeten, Erik. 2021. *Ideology and International Institutions.* Princeton University Press.

Voeten, Erik, Anton Strezhnev, and Michael Bailey. 2009. "United Nations General Assembly Voting Data." Accessed from: hdl:1902.1/12379, Harvard Dataverse. Accessed from: https://dataverse.harvard.edu/dataset.xhtml?persistentId=doi:10.7910/DVN/LEJUQZ.

Von Stein, Jana. 2008. "The International Law and Politics of Climate Change: Ratification of the United Nations Framework Convention and the Kyoto Protocol." *Journal of Conflict Resolution* 52(2):243–268.

Wagner, Wolfgang, Dirk Peters, and Cosima Glahn. 2010. "Parliamentary War Powers around the World, 1989–2004: A New Dataset." Geneva Centre for the Democratic Control of Armed Forces, Geneva, Occasional Paper No. 22.

Waldner, David and Ellen Lust. 2018. "Unwelcome Change: Coming to Terms with Democratic Backsliding." *Annual Review of Political Science* 21:93–113.

Wallcott, John. 2020. "Unquiet on the Western Front: Why the 74-Year Alliance between Europe and America Is Falling Apart." *TIME*, June 17.
Walt, Stephen. 2019. "America Has a Commitment Problem." *Foreign Policy*, January 29.
Wamble, Julian J., Chryl N. Laird, Corrine M. McConnaughy, and Ismail K. White. 2022. "We Are One: The Social Maintenance of Black Democratic Party Loyalty." *Journal of Politics* 84(2):682–697.
Wang, Austin Horng-En. 2019. "The Myth of Polarization among Taiwanese Voters: The Missing Middle." *Journal of East Asian Studies* 19:275–287.
Ward, Nicole and Jeanne Batalova. 2023. "Refugees and Asylees in the United States." Migration Policy Institute, Washington, DC, June 15.
Washington Post. 2015. "5th Republican Debate: Who Said What and What It Meant". December 15.
Webster, Steven W. and Alan I. Abramowitz. 2017. "The Ideological Foundations of Affective Polarization in the U.S. Electorate." *American Politics Research* 45(4):621–647.
Weeks, Jessica L. 2008. "Autocratic Audience Costs: Regime Type and Signaling Resolve." *International Organization* 62(1):35–64.
Weeks, Jessica L. 2012. "Strongmen and Straw Men: Authoritarian Regimes and the Initiation of International Conflict." *American Political Science Review* 106(2):326–347.
Weeks, Jessica L. P. 2014. *Dictators at War*. Cornell University Press.
Weiss, Jessica Chen. 2013. "Authoritarian Signaling, Mass Audiences, and Nationalist Protest in China." *International Organization* 67(1):1–35.
Weiss, Jessica Chen. 2014. *Powerful Patriots: Nationalist Protest in China's Foreign Relations*. Oxford University Press.
Weiss, Jessica Chen. 2022. "The China Trap: U.S. Foreign Policy and the Perilous Logic of Zero-Sum Competition." *Foreign Affairs*, August 18.
Weiss, Jessica Chen. 2023. "Don't Panic about Taiwan: Alarm Over a Chinese Invasion Could Become a Self-Fulfilling Prophecy." *Foreign Affairs*, March 21.
Wertheim, Stephen. 2022. "The Crisis in Progressive Foreign Policy: How the Left Can Adapt to an Age of Great-Power Rivalry." *Foreign Affairs*, August 24.
Westwood, Sean J., Justin Grimmer, Matthew Tyler, and Clayton Nall. 2022. "Current Research Overstates American Support for Political Violence." *PNAS* 119(12):1–10.
Weybrecht, Matthew. 2015. "State Department Affirms That Iran Deal Is Only a Political Commitment." *Lawfare*, November 28.
Weyland, Kurt and Raúl L. Madrid, eds. 2019. *When Democracy Trumps Populism: European and Latin American Lessons for the United States*. Cambridge University Press.
White, Ismail K. and Chryl N. Laird. 2020. *Steadfast Democrats: How Social Forces Shape Black Political Behavior*. Princeton University Press.
Whiteley, Peter. 1996. *Lord North: The Prime Minister Who Lost America*. A&C Black.
White House Office of Policy Development. 1984. "US Policy Statement for the International Conference on Population." *Population and Development Review* 10(3):574–579.
White House Press Office. 2021a. "Fact Sheet: Prioritizing Climate in Foreign Policy and National Security." October 21.
White House Press Office. 2021b. "President-Elect Biden's Day One Executive Actions Deliver Relief for Families across America amid Converging Crises." January 20.
Wike, Richard, Janell Fetterfolf, and Maria Mordecai. 2020. "U.S. Image Plummets Internationally as Most Say Country Has Handled Coronavirus Badly." Pew Research Center, Washington, DC, September 15.
Wildavsky, Aaron. 1966. "The Two Presidencies." *Trans-Action* 4:7–14.
Williams, Heather J. and Caitlin McCulloch. 2023. "Truth Decay and National Security: Intersections, Insights, and Questions for Future Research." RAND Corporation, April 12.

Wintour, Patrick. 2019. "Iran Breaks Nuclear Deal and Puts Pressure on EU over Sanctions." *The Guardian*, July 1.
Wittkopf, Eugene R. 1990. *Faces of Internationalism: Public Opinion and American Foreign Policy*. Duke University Press.
Wittkopf, Eugene R. and James M. McCormick. 1990. "The Cold War Consensus: Did It Exist?" *Polity* 22(4):627–653.
Wolf, Julie. 1992. "Ministers Make EC Nuptials with Autographs and Champagne." *The Guardian*, February 8.
Wolfe, Jan. 2021. "Trump Wanted Troops to Protect His Supporters at Jan. 6 Rally." *Reuters*, May 12.
Woodward, Bob. 2005. *Veil: The Secret Wars of the CIA, 1981–1987*. Simon and Schuster.
Woolley, John T. and Gerhard Peters. 2021. "Biden in Action: The First 100 Days." American Presidency Project, Santa Barbara, CA, April 30.
Wootliff, Raoul. 2018. "Right–Left Rift Tops Ethnic Tensions as Biggest Source of Polarization in Israel." *Times of Israel*, December 3.
Wright, Robin. 2021. "Biden Faces a Minefield in New Diplomacy with Iran." *New Yorker*, January 4.
Wu, Yu-Shan. 2016. "Heading towards Troubled Waters? The Impact of Taiwan's 2016 Elections on Cross-Strait Relations." *American Journal of Chinese Studies* 23(1):59–75.
Yarhi-Milo, Keren. 2018. "After Credibility: American Foreign Policy in the Trump Era." *Foreign Affairs*, December 12.
Yarhi-Milo, Keren and David Ribar. 2023. "Who Punishes Leaders for Lying About the Use of Force? Evaluating the Microfoundations of Domestic Deception Costs." *Journal of Conflict Resolution* 67(4):559–586.
YouGov Staff. 2017. "America's Friends and Enemies." *YouGov*, February 2.
Younis, Mohamed. 2021. "Sharply Fewer in U.S. View Foreign Trade as Opportunity." *Gallup News*, March 31.
Yu, Xudong, Magdalena Wojcieszak, and Andreu Casas. 2024. "Partisanship on Social Media: In-Party Love among American Politicians, Greater Engagement with Out-Party Hate among Ordinary Users." *Political Behavior* 46(2):799–824.
Zaller, John. 1992. *The Nature and Origins of Mass Opinion*. Cambridge University Press.
Zeya, Uzra S. and Jon Finer. 2020. "Revitalizing the State Department and American Diplomacy." Council on Foreign Relations, New York.
Zhou, Li. 2021. "The Danger of Anti-China Rhetoric." *Vox News*, August 5.
Zoellick, Robert B. 2005. "Whither China: From Membership to Responsibility?" Remarks to National Committee on U.S.–China Relations, New York, September 21.
Zulauf, Barry A. 2021. Letter from Barry Zulauf to Senators Marco Rubio and Mark Warner, January 6. Accessed from: https://context-cdn.washingtonpost.com/notes/prod/default/documents/c3c41863-be9e-4246-9ed9-e43aedd013f9/note/4e677597-f403-4c9b-b838-f5613d79b341.page-1.pdf.

INDEX

abortion, 112–13, 151–53
Adams, James, 89
affective polarization, 2–3, 11, 64; in American public, 19–21; ideological polarization and, 13; measurement of, 85, 88–91
Afghanistan: refugees from, 122; U.S. withdrawal from, 237
Ahmadinejad, Mahmoud, 189
Albertson, Bethany, 128
Alesina, Alberto, 48
alliances, 71; violations of, 105–8
Alliance Treaty Obligations and Provisions (ATOP) project, 105
Almond, Gabriel, 39
al-Qaeda, 143
American identity, 275
American National Election Studies (ANES), 18–19
American Revolution, 43–44
Archigos dataset, 86, 92, 93, 281–83
Argentina, 45–46
al-Assad, Bashar, 147
assassinations and attempts, against Trump, 21
audience costs, 162
authoritarian governments, 41
autocracies: lack of vertical constraints in, 115; selectorate theory on, 47; UN votes and leader turnover in, 97–98

Bail, Chris, 274
bandwagoning, 134, 146, 147
Beliakova, Polina, 146
Berinsky, Adam, 164
Bharatiya Janata Party (BJP; India), 52

Biden, Joe, 142; in election of 2020, 20–21, 128, 150; in election of 2024, 165n22; immigration under, 78; on Joint Comprehensive Plan of Action, 66, 192; refugee policies under, 151; during Russian invasion of Ukraine, 148; U.S. returns to Paris Agreement under, 153
Biden administration: Afghanistan withdrawal by, 237; on climate change, 126; treaties ratified under, 225
Binder, Sarah, 75
bipartisanship, 263, 272; decline in, 182; downside of, 261
Blum, Léon, 1, 64, 163
Bodansky, Daniel, 234
Boehner, John, 190
Bolsonaro, Jair, 76
Bradley, Curtis, 221, 232
Brazil, 60–61, 76
Broockman, David, 273
Brooks, Preston, 14
Buarque, David, 76
Bueno de Mesquita, Bruce, 47
Bureau of Intelligence and Research (within State Department), 141
Burns, Bill, 206
Bush, George W., 92; in election of 2004, 117; United Nations speech of, 35–36
Bush, Jeb, 198
Bush, Richard, 82
Bush administration (G.W.B.), 137; Democratic opposition to, 179; foreign policies of, 237; Iran and, 189; Iraq War under, 143; Strategic Framework Agreement between the United States and Iraq under, 234; U.S. withdraws from Kyoto Protocol under, 153

campaign finance laws, 270
Cardin, Ben, 191
Carroll, Royce, 98–100, 110
Carsey, Thomas, 13, 113
Carter, Jimmy, 179, 182
Casey, William, 142
Case–Zablonski Act (1972), 231
Cecil, Robert (Lord Salisbury), 57
Central Intelligence Agency (CIA), 141–43; Iranian coup by, 188
Chapel Hill Expert Survey, 85
Chaudoin, Stephen, 73–74
Chávez, Hugo, 2, 54
Chavez, Leo, 121
Chayes, Antonia, 235–36
Cheney, Dick, 189
Chicago Council on Global Affairs (CCGA), 116; on attitudes toward foreign countries, 119; on attitudes toward refugees, 122; on multilateralism and internationalism, 130–31; on perceptions of security threats, 127–28
China: bilateral relationship between U.S. and, 239–40; Taiwan and, 81–82; trade with, 123–25; Trump on, 51; U.S. policies on, 263–64
Citizens United decision (2010), 270
climate change, 125–26; foreign policy and, 153; Kyoto Protocol on, 223; Paris Agreement on, 231
Clinton, Bill: Kyoto Protocol signed by, 73, 153, 223; Mexico City Policy repealed by, 112; United Nations speech of, 35, 36
Clinton administration, 137, 146
Comparative Study of Electoral Systems (CSES), 88–91
Comprehensive Iran Sanctions, Accountability, and Divestment Act (2010), 194–95
conflict extension, 13, 51–52, 113
Congress, U.S.: Joint Comprehensive Plan of Action negotiations and, 194, 199–204; reducing polarization in, 267; roll-call votes in, 178–82; speeches on Iran in, 195–96; term limits for, 269; Twitter tweets by members of, 204–5. *See also* Senate
congressional polarization, 15–16
Convention on the Rights of Persons with Disabilities, 223–24

Corker, Bob, 190–91
Correlates of War Project, 101
Cotton, Tom, letter on Iran nuclear deal by, 158–59, 162, 190, 193, 200
covert actions, 141–42
COVID-19 pandemic, 128
credibility advantage, 5, 32–33, 36, 57–61, 79; cross-national polarization and, 100–104; in Joint Comprehensive Plan of Action negotiations, 192–94; polarization and erosion of, 61–67, 160–62; reliability advantage and, 78; vertical constraints on, 162–85
crises. *See* international crises
Croatian Democratic Union, 94
cross-national polarization, 83–91; credibility advantage and, 100–104; measurement of, 91–93; reliability advantage and, 104–9; stability advantage and, 94–100
Cruz, Ted, 197, 198

Defense, U.S. Department of (DoD), 144–48
Defense Intelligence Agency, 141
democracies, 66; adherence to international law by, 71–72; advantages in foreign affairs of, 6–9; extreme polarization and, 11–14; reliability to military alliances of, 105; reneging on international commitments, 76; selectorate theory on, 47–48; separating civilian and military spheres in, 145; stable foreign policies in, 100; vertical and horizontal constraints in, 30
democratic advantages, 36–37; constraints on, 41–45; credibility advantage, 57–67, 100–104, 160–62, 207 (*See also* credibility advantage); history of and critics of, 38–41; interrelation of, 77–78; reliability advantage, 68–76, 211–12 (*See also* reliability advantage); stability advantage, 45–57, 96–100, 155–57 (*See also* stability advantage)
democratic erosion, extreme polarization and, 11–14
Democratic Party (South Korea), 65
Democratic Party (U.S.), 15, 21
democratic peace theory, 39–40
Democratic Progressive Party (DPP; Taiwan)., 81–82

Denmark, 44
Digital Society Project, 88
Dole, Bob, 203
domestic policy, extension into foreign affairs of, 115–17
Dong Joon Park, 65
Downs, Anthony, 46
Drezner, Dan, 140
Drutman, Lee, 267
Duverger, Maurice, 277
DW-NOMINATE (Dynamic Weighted Nominal Three-Step Estimation) scale, 16

Eden, Anthony, 42
Edwards, George, 265
Eisenhower, Dwight, 139
Eisenhower administration, 141–42
elections, 6; electoral cycles in, 117–19; international variations in systems for, 276–78; primary elections, 267–68; proportional representation in, 267; in United States, of 2016, 197–98, 204; in United States, of 2020, 20–21; in United States, of 2024, 125–26, 165–76; in United States, foreign policy as issue in, 117–18; as vertical constraints, 41–42; voting in, 270–71
elite polarization, 9, 15–18
Erdoğan, Recep Tayyip, 11–12
Eurasia Group (firm), 255
Europe, polarization in, 2
European Union (EU): Maastricht Treaty establishes, 68, 70; United Kingdom leaves, 74, 210–11
executive agreements: as alternative to treaties, 219, 221–22; expansion in use of, 229–35; not subject to Senate ratification, 220
executive orders, 150
extreme polarization, 3; decline in stability in foreign policymaking in, 57; democratic erosion and, 11–14; in erosion of democratic credibility, 61–67; in erosion of democratic reliability, 72–76; expanding from domestic to foreign affairs, 53–54; measurement of, 95–96; political opposition and, 177–82; politicization of foreign policy bureaucracy in, 55,
134–36; as threat to democratic advantage thesis, 41; volatility in foreign policies tied to, 149–55

Falklands War, 45
Fashoda crisis (Egypt), 57–59
Fazli, Abdolreza Rahmani, 205–6
Feaver, Peter, 54, 147–48, 264
Fiorina, Morris, 18
Flynn, Michael, 129
Ford, Gerald, 143
Fordham, Benjamin, 129
foreign affairs: extension of domestic policy issues into, 113, 115–17; obstruction in, 177–82
foreign aid, for abortion, 112–13
Foreign Assistance Act (1961), 234
foreign policy: Congressional roll-call votes on, 178–82; insulated from partisan politics, 262–66; as issue in U.S. presidential elections, 117–18; militarization of, 261; polarization and stability in, 113–14; volatility of, across presidential administrations, 148–55
foreign policy bureaucracy: politicization of, 55, 114, 134–36; State Department in, 136–41
Foreign Service Officers (FSOs), 136, 138, 266
France, 24; election of 1936 in, 64; election of 2017 in, 210; in Fashoda crisis, 57–59; Popular Front in, 1
Freedom House: *Freedom in the World* project of, 257; on Turkey, 12
Friedman, Jeffrey, 127
Friedrichs, Gordon, 129

Gadarian, Shana, 128
General Social Survey, 151
Germany, 210
Gidron, Noam, 89
Gingrich, Newt, 18
global health security, 128, 153
Goldsmith, Jack, 221, 232
Goodman, Sara Wallace, 278
government systems, variations in, 278–79
Gowa, Joanne, 48–49
Great Britain: American Revolution against, 43–44; in Fashoda crisis, 57–59. *See also* United Kingdom

Grossman, Matt, 17–18
Group of Seven (G7), 210

Hacker, Jacob, 18
Haglund, Evan, 140
Hall, Andrew, 270
Harris, Kamala, 165–76
Hathaway, Oona, 221, 232–34, 254
hawk–dove polarization, 93–95; credibility advantage and, 102–4
Hezbollah movement, 188
Hitler, Adolf, 1
Hooghe, Liesbet, 84
Hopkins, David, 17–18
horizontal constraints, 8, 30, 43–44, 113; avoiding in international agreements, 75; on credibility advantage, 63–64, 161, 177–85; on foreign policy stability, 97; on reliability advantage, 218–35; on stability advantage, 133–36, 155
Horne, Will, 89
Hoyer, Steny, 152
Hungary, 53
Huntington, Samuel, 145
Hussein, Saddam, 143, 188

ideological polarization, 2, 10; affective polarization and, 13; measurement of, 85; in U.S., 15
Ikenberry, John, 27
immigration, 78, 121, 151
Independents (nonaligned), in State Department, 137
India, 29, 52
Inhofe, Jim, 73
intelligence community, 49, 141–44, 266
international agreements, 73–74; avoiding U.S. Senate for, 75; negotiated in private, 265–66; survey on unilateral presidential actions on, 215–18; U.S. withdraws from, 154
International Atomic Energy Agency (IAEA), 190, 192
international crises, 160n10; opposition parties during, 64–65; partisan responses to, 183–85
International Crisis Behavior project, 183
internationalism, 129–33, 153–54
international law, 71–72

international negotiations, on Joint Comprehensive Plan of Action, 187–206
international order, 27–28
international trade, 122–25
international treaties. *See* treaties
Iran: Israeli policies toward, 62; Joint Comprehensive Plan of Action between U.S. and, 32–33, 66, 158–62, 187–206
Iran-Contra Affair, 44, 142, 195
Iran hostage crisis, 188
Iran-Iraq War (1980-1988), 188
Iran Nuclear Agreement Review Act (INARA; 2015), 191, 203
Iraq: Iran invaded by, 188; Strategic Framework Agreement between the United States and, 234
Iraq War (2003-2011): as issue in election of 2004, 117; as issue in election of 2008, 149; during Obama administration, 147; partisan differences over information on, 164; politicization of, 116; U.S. invasion of Iraq begins, 143
Israel, 2, 29–30; Iranian threat to, 188; policies toward Iran of, 62; public opinion in, 42–43

January 6, 2021 riots, 20–21, 147
Japan, 44
Jewish community, 195
Johnson, Boris, 74
Johnston, Christopher, 42
Joint Comprehensive Plan of Action (JCPOA; Iran nuclear agreement), 32–33; background of, 188–92; CIA involvement in, 143; Cotton letter and, 158–62; credibility in negotiations over, 192–202; entering and exiting, 66, 202–6; Kerry on, 222; not submitted for ratification, 200; Republican opposition to, 187–88
Justice and Development Party (AKP; Turkey), 11

Kalla, Joshua, 273
Kalmoe, Nathan, 14, 20
Kennan, George, 39
Kerry, John, 117, 222
Khomeini, Ruhollah, 188
Khong, Yuen Foong, 239–40
Kreps, Sarah, 228

Krupnikov, Yanna, 18
Krutz, Glen, 221, 231
Kuomintang (KMT; Taiwan), 81–82
Kyoto Protocol (1998), 73, 153, 223

Labour party (Norway), 94–95
Lai Ching-te, 82
La Raja, Raymond, 271
Lavine, Howard, 42
Layman, Geoffrey, 13, 113
Lee, Frances, 63–64
Leeds, Brett Ashley, 71, 97–100, 105–8, 110
left-right polarization, 93–95; credibility advantage and, 102–4
legislative bodies: as horizontal constraint, 44; international cooperation and, 70
Lehman, Howard, 60, 61
Le Pen, Marine, 210
Levitsky, Steven, 13
liberal democracies, 6
liberal internationalism, 238
liberal international order (LIO), 27–28
Lippmann, Walter, 39
Lodge, Henry Cabot (1850-1924), 129
Lugar, Richard, 263

Maastricht Treaty (1992), 68, 70
Maduro, Nicolás, 2, 54
majoritarian systems, 277–78
Malis, Matt, 140
Manchin, Joe, 268
Manifesto Project (MARPOR), 85–88, 91–96
Marks, Gary, 84
Martin, Lisa, 70, 231
Mason, Lilliana, 19, 20, 275
mass polarization, 9, 18–19
Mattes, Michaela, 71, 97–100, 105–8, 110
Mattiacci, Eleonora, 55–56, 154
May, Theresa, 74
McCain, John, 268
McConnell, Mitch, 152–53
McCoy, Jennifer, 60, 61
McGillivray, Fiona, 48
media, polarization in, 274
Merkel, Angela, 210
Mexico City Policy, 112–13, 151–52
militarized interstate disputes (MIDs), 101, 102

military agencies, 54; Defense Department, 144–48
military alliances, 71; Alliance Treaty Obligations and Provisions project studies of, 105; survey on unilateral presidential actions on, 215–18; U.S. in, 129–30
Milner, Helen, 125
Modi, Narendra, 52
monetary policy, 48
Morrow, James, 47
Mossadeq, Mohammed, 188
multilateralism, 129–33, 153
multiparty systems, 277, 278

Nassar, Gamal Abdel, 42
National Defense Authorization Acts, 152
National Security Council (NSC), 137–38
negative partisanship, 11n44
Netanyahu, Benjamin, 2, 62; on Iran nuclear negotiations, 190, 200; Republican ties to, 195
NewSTART Treaty (2011), 203, 203n108, 229
Nicaragua, 44
Nixon, Richard, 137
North, Frederick (Lord North), 44
North American Free Trade Agreement, 122–23
North Atlantic Treaty Organization (NATO), 130, 131, 211
North Korea, 65
Nunn, Sam, 263
Nunn–Lugar Cooperative Threat Reduction Program, 263

Obama, Barack: Convention on the Rights of Persons with Disabilities signed by, 223; in election of 2008, 149; Iran and, 189; on Joint Comprehensive Plan of Action, 158–62, 200, 201; treaties ratified under, 224–25; U.S. enters Paris Agreement under, 72–73, 153
Obama administration: China policy during, 263; drones used in Middle East under, 137; executive agreements under, 221, 234, 235; foreign policies of, 237; Iraq War (2009) under, 147; Joint Comprehensive Plan of Action negotiated by, 187–93, 195, 234; legislative gridlock

Obama administration (*continued*)
during, 231; NewSTART Treaty under, 229; Republican opposition to, 179, 182; special envoys undeer, 139; women serving in combat roles under, 146
Office of Intelligence and Analysis (within Homeland Security Department), 141
Office of the Director of National Intelligence, 141
open primary elections, 268
opposition parties: during crises, 64–65, 183; as horizontal constraint, 43–44, 177–82
Orbán, Viktor, 53

Pahlavi, Mohammad Reza, 188
Paris Agreement (on climate), 72–75, 153, 231
Park Geun-hye, 2
participatory democracy, in Venezuela, 10
partisan polarization, 2–3; benefits of, 260–61; definitions of, 9–11; insulating foreign policy from, 262–66; in U.S., 14–23
Peake, Jeffrey, 221, 224, 231, 252
People Power Party (South Korea), 65
pernicious polarization, 11n47
Perón, Isabel, 45–46
Peterson, Andrew, 184
Pierson, Paul, 18
plausibility probes, 84
Polarization and Social Change Lab (Stanford University), 273–74
Polarization Lab (Duke University), 274
political officials, polarization among, 266–72
political parties: campaign finance laws and, 270; opposition parties, 43–44; partisan polarization caused by, 260–61; proportional representation for, 267; in selectorate theory, 47; strengthening, 271; surveys of, 85–88
Poole, Keith T., 178
Popular Front (France), 1
Porter, Patrick, 261
Portman, Rob, 159–60, 202
preference polarization, 10
presidency: expansion in use of executive agreements by, 229–35; expansion of political power of, 137; survey on unilateral presidential actions on international agreements, 215–18; volatility of foreign policy across presidential administrations, 148–55
primary elections, 267–68
proportional representation (PR), 267, 277, 278
Protecting Life in Global Health Assistance policy, 113
Przeworski, Adam, 13
public opinion, 9; on abortion, 151; Almond and Lippmann on, 39; apathy about foreign policy in, 261; on foreign policy, in U.S. presidential elections, 117–18; on foreign policy making, 164–77; on military, 146; on multilateralism and internationalism, 130–33; strategies to address polarization in, 272–76; as vertical constraint, 42–43. *See also* vertical constraints
Putin, Vladimir, 42
Putnam, Robert, 60, 186

Reagan, Ronald, 44, 112, 142
Reagan administration, 142
realist perspective, 40
redistricting legislative districts, 269
refugees, 121–22, 151
regime types, 7n25
Reiljan, Andres, 89–91
Reiter, Dan, 40
reliability advantage, 5, 33–34, 36, 68–72, 79; credibility advantage and, 78; cross-national polarization and, 104–9; horizontal constraints on, 218–35; polarization and erosion of, 72–76, 211–12; vertical constraints on, 213–18
representative democracy, in Venezuela, 10
Republican Party (U.S.), 15; asymmetric political shift in, 17–18; in election of 2016, 197–98; internationalism opposed by, 129; Joint Comprehensive Plan of Action opposed by, 187, 190, 192, 193, 195, 198, 200–204; political realignment of, 16; public opinion on, 21
Rhodes, Ben, 202
Ribble, Reid, 222
right-left polarization. *See* left-right polarization
Robinson, Michael, 148

Rodden, Jonathan, 278
Romney, Mitt, 268
Rosenthal, Howard, 178
Rothfus, Keith, 271
Rothkopf, David, 159
Rouhani, Hassan, 190
Rovner, Joshua, 135
Rubio, Marco, 198
Rumsfeld, Donald, 189
Russia: interference in U.S. elections by, 144; NewSTART Treaty between U.S. and, 229; Ukraine invaded by, 30, 131, 148
Ryan, John Barry, 18

Sarney, José, 60–61
Saunders, Elizabeth, 228
Schaffner, Brian, 271
Schelling, Thomas, 59–60, 160
Schelling conjecture, 59–60, 160, 162
Schlesinger, Arthur, 137
Schultz, Kenneth: on Fashoda Crisis, 57–59; on opposition parties, 186; on right-left spectrum, 94; on Senate polarization, 228; on threats made by democracies, 101–4, 110
Scoville, Ryan, 140
selectorate theory, 47–48
Senate (U.S.): declines and delays in ratification of treaties by, 222–29; Foreign Relations Committee of (SFRC), 193, 194; polarization in, 63–64; ratification of treaties by, 75, 219–21
September eleventh terrorist attacks, 275
severe polarization, 11n47
Sherman, Wendy, 199
sidelining, 134–35; of military, 147; of State Department, 137, 139, 140
Siverson, Randolph, 47
slavery, polarization in U.S. over, 14, 26–27
Smith, Alastair, 47, 48, 97
social identities, 274–75
social media: reducing polarization through, 274; in U.S. elections, 118–19
soft politicization, 135, 142; in Iraqi War, 143
South Korea, 2, 65
special envoys, 139
Spirling, Arthur, 184

Spiro, Peter, 234
stability advantage, 5, 31–32, 36, 45–50, 79, 155–57; cross-national polarization and, 94–100; of democracies, 7; extreme polarization causing decline in, 57; horizontal constraints in, 48, 133–36; polarization and erosion of, 50–57; vertical constraints and, 114–17
Stam, Allan, 40
State, U.S. Department of, 136–41
Steenbergen, Marco, 42
Strategic Framework Agreement between the United States and Iraq, 234
Suez Canal, 42
Sumner, Charles, 14
super PACS, 270

Taiwan, 29, 81–82, 264
Tama, Jordan, 182, 263
term limits, 268–69
Tingley, Dustin, 125
Tocqueville, Alexis de, on foreign policies of democracies, 38–39
Tomz, Michael, 42–43
trade policies, 122–25
transformation process, in State Department, 135, 138, 140–41
treaties: declines and delays in ratification of, 222–29; executive agreements as alternative to, 219, 221–22; U.S. Constitution on, 219–20; U.S. reliability and, 235–36
Truman, Harry, 141
Truman administration, 145–46
Trump, Donald: assassination attempts against, 21; on COVID-19 pandemic, 128; in election of 2016, 51, 112–13, 146, 149; in election of 2020, 20–21; in election of 2024, 150, 165–76; on immigration, 121; immigration and refugee policies under, 78, 151; on Joint Comprehensive Plan of Action, 192, 198, 204, 206; leaves Paris Agreement, 74; military deployed by, 147; on NATO, 211; politicizing of State Department under, 139–40; U.S. withdraws from Paris Agreement under, 153; withdraws from Joint Comprehensive Plan of Action, 66, 204–6

Trump administration (first): America First policies of, 237; intelligence community under, 143–44; treaties ratified under, 225; U.S. withdraws from international agreements under, 154
Tsai Ing-wen, 81, 82
Turkey, 11–12
Twitter, 204–5
two-party systems, 277–78

Ukraine, Russian invasion of, 30, 42, 131, 148
United Kingdom (UK), 10, 212; bilateral relationship between U.S. and, 235–36; existing commitments between U.S. and, 237–38; in Falklands War, 45; impact of public opinion in, 43; leaves European Union, 70, 74, 210–11; during Suez Canal crisis, 42; survey of Parliament members in, 250–52; survey on bilateral relationship between U.S. and, 241–50
United Nations (UN), public opinion on, 132
United Nations General Assembly (UNGA): annual meetings of, 35–36; roll-call votes in, 85n10, 97, 98
United States: affective polarization in, 91; bilateral relationship between UK and, 235–36; bipartisan foreign policy of, 3; enters Paris Agreement, 72–73; existing commitments between UK and, 237–38; future partnerships with UK, 238–40; ideological polarization in, 86; impact of Russian invasion of Ukraine in, 30; Joint Comprehensive Plan of Action between Iran and, 187–206; leaves Joint Comprehensive Plan of Action, 192, 204; leaves Paris Agreement, 74; in military alliances and international organizations, 129–31; partisan polarization in, 14–23; polarization in, 2; polarization over slavery in, 26–27; politicization of the military and the defense in, 54; survey on bilateral relationship between UK and, 239–40
Uruguay, 44

Vandenberg, Arthur, 3, 183
Varieties of Democracy project, 85
Venezuela, 2, 9–10, 54
Versailles, Treaty of (1919), 129
vertical constraints, 8, 30, 41–43, 47, 113; on credibility advantage, 162–76; electoral cycles and, 117–19; on foreign policy stability, 50, 97; polarization and, 61–63; on reliability advantage, 213–18; on stability advantage, 114–17, 155
veto players, 278–79
Vogel, Jeremy, 71, 105–8, 110
voting, 270–71

Walker, Scott, 198
Weeks, Jessica, 43
Weiss, Jessica, 264
Wilson, Woodrow, 129
World Values Survey, 86–88

Xi Jinping, 81, 263

Yarhi-Milo, Keren, 43, 238–39
Yoon Suk Yeol, 65

Zelenskyy, Volodymyr, 42
Ziblatt, Daniel, 13
Zoellick, Robert, 263n23